Background Factors
of Juvenile Delinquency

American University Studies

Series XI
Anthropology and Sociology

Vol. 68

PETER LANG
New York • Washington, D.C./Baltimore
Bern • Frankfurt am Main • Berlin • Vienna • Paris

Huub Angenent
& Anton de Man

Background Factors
of Juvenile Delinquency

PETER LANG
New York • Washington, D.C./Baltimore
Bern • Frankfurt am Main • Berlin • Vienna • Paris

Library of Congress Cataloging-in-Publication Data

Angenent, Huub.
Background factors of juvenile delinquency/Huub Angenent, Anton de Man.
p. cm. — (American university studies. Series XI,
Anthropology and sociology; vol. 68)
Includes bibliographical references and index.
1. Juvenile delinquency—United States. 2. Deviant behavior—United States.
3. Juvenile delinquents—United States—Psychology. 4. Juvenile
delinquents—United States—Family Relationships. 5. Juvenile delinquents—
Education—United States. I. de Man, Anton Frans. II. Title. III. Series:
American university studies. Series XI, Anthropology/sociology; vol. 68.
HV9104.A82   364.3'6'0973—dc20   95-37310
ISBN 0-8204-2890-6
ISSN 0740-0489

Die Deutsche Bibliothek-CIP-Einheitsaufnahme

Angenent, Huub:
Background factors of juvenile delinquency/Huub Angenent; Anton de Man.–
New York; Washington, D.C./Baltimore; Bern; Frankfurt am Main;
Berlin; Vienna; Paris: Lang.
(American university studies: Ser. 11, Anthropology and sociology; Vol. 68)
ISBN 0-8204-2890-6
NE: de Man, Anton:; American university studies / 11

The paper in this book meets the guidelines for permanence and durability
of the Committee on Production Guidelines for Book Longevity
of the Council of Library Resources.

Printed in the United States of America.

ACKNOWLEDGEMENTS

The authors wish to thank Mrs. Paula de Man and Bishop's University for their generous assistance in preparing this publication.

TABLE OF CONTENTS

PREFACE

Juvenile delinquency almost never arises suddenly. There is usually a pattern of factors that make a youngster vulnerable to delinquency. In this book we concern ourselves with background factors that contribute to juvenile delinquency.

Point of departure is the question as to why youths behave in a criminal manner. Related to this are questions such as: why do some youngsters get involved in delinquency whereas others don't, and why do some youngsters commit crimes more often than others?

We describe juvenile delinquency as a form of deviant behaviour that takes on different forms depending on the age and sex of the perpetrators and the type of delinquents (Chapter 1). We note that the delinquency is an expression of the experiential world of youths and the stage of life in which they are (Chapter 2). We suggest that the background factors of juvenile delinquency further must be sought in the youths' personality (Chapter 3), family (Chapter 4), school (Chapter 5), friends and peers (Chapter 6), and social circumstances (Chapter 7).

Publications about juvenile delinquency usually answer the question concerning the background factors of this criminality by starting with youths who show delinquent behaviour and by subsequently comparing them with youngsters who behave in a more adjusted manner. In this book we work the other way around. We begin with "normal" (i.e., average) youths and then look at the extent to which delinquent youngsters resemble them and differ from them. Thus, taking the position that juvenile delinquents constitute a special group in the youth population, we first provide a general description of youths and then delineate the place of juvenile delinquents in this general framework. In doing so, we focus on factors which play a role in the behaviour of normal youngsters and illustrate that the extent to which juvenile delinquency becomes possible if not unavoidable, depends on the development of these factors.

1. JUVENILE DELINQUENCY

HOPE FOR THE FUTURE?

Complaints about the behaviour of the young are timeless! The oldest document about ethics, the maxims of Ptahhotep, already refers to such grievances. Ancient Egyptian and Hebrew sagas tell of juveniles who played fast and loose with the rules and regulations of society (Bengtson, 1970). Around 600 B.C. in Babylon, Nebukadnezar issued decrees against the defacing of temples (Wise, 1983). Graffiti avant la lettre! The Greeks also had problems with their youngsters. If youths are the hope for the future, the future does not look too promising, thus observed the Greek philosopher Hesiodos in the 8th century B.C. He went on to say that he was at a loss for words to describe the excesses of youths (Manning, 1983). Some 400 years later, Aristotle noted that adolescents are passionate, temperamental, and tend to be led by their impulses. He further mentioned their instability and inconsistency, their excesses and exaggerations (Conger, 1979). Socrates complained that youngsters did not listen and only did what they felt like doing.

It would not be too difficult to fill this book with similar complaints from earlier times and from all corners of the world. As long as history has been recorded, there have been complaints about the behaviour of juveniles!

A few examples of more recent date.

Reports from the Middle Ages tell us about youths who cut off noses of statues in church, sewed women's skirts together, and fought with knives.

In the 16th century, in 1538 to be exact, Luther and Melanchton discussed the excessive behaviour of juveniles, and how little control the law, religion, parents, and teachers had over them (Kranz and Vercruysse, 1959).

In the 17th century, Firmin complained about youths who quarrelled, threatened, swore, fought, and who made the streets unsafe (Schwendinger and Schwendinger, 1976). Pepys similarly noted in his diary the brutal behaviour and the coarse jokes of youngsters in the street (Kranz and Vercruysse, 1959).

From the 18th century we hear of complaints about juvenile disobedience, vandalism, and other forms of misbehaviour (Kranz and Vercruysse, 1959; Stoddard, 1717). In those days also, some held no high expectations for the future. Loring (1718), for instance, felt that youngsters were on the road to self-destruction (Manning, 1983).

In the 19th century —the story gets to be repetitious— there were similar complaints; quite a few books and brochures were published about juveniles' disobedience, unbridled behaviour, and other excesses. Burton (1863) complained that youngsters had usurped the parental powers in the family (Manning, 1983).

Little seems to have changed as far as such complaints are concerned; one only has to turn on the radio or television or read a newspaper to know this to be true.

YOUTH

Over the years, the term youth has been interpreted in many different ways. Even today, different authors have different ideas about this. These differences pertain to, among others, the age limits of the youth period. In this book, we have set the lower limit at twelve years (below this age we speak of children). It should be pointed out that —in part because of a progressively earlier onset of puberty— this limit has fallen over the past decennia. Furthermore, it should be noted that some children at a relatively young age already identify with the youth period and adopt the ideas, habits, language and so forth of their older peers. The lower age limit, therefore, is rather ambiguous. The upper limit is even more vague; some authors put it at eighteen years, whereas others place it at twenty-five or even higher. In this book the upper limit ranges from 18 to 25 years.

DEVIANT BEHAVIOUR

The topic under discussion is deviant behaviour of juveniles. Deviant behaviour is best described as activities which in terms of conventional norms and customs are regarded as undesirable or even unacceptable. The behaviour is experienced as bothersome and irritating by other people, and sometimes elicits feelings of annoyance and insecurity. It provokes responses from authorities, social agencies, and conventional institutions (e.g., family and school).

Less serious forms of deviant behaviour (e.g., smoking or having sex at an early age, knavery, insolence, and impertinence) are called *excessive behaviour*, whereas more serious deviant demeanour (e.g., running away, absenteeism from school, serious alcohol and drug use, gambling, and prostitution) is labelled *problem behaviour*. Juvenile delinquency is problem behaviour punishable by law. The boundaries between these concepts are not very clearly defined and occasionally the terms are used interchangeably (Angenent, 1988; Brusten and Hurrelmann, 1973; Elliott and Voss, 1974; Gibbs, 1981; Krohn and Massey, 1980; Lafaille, 1978).

DEVIANCY SYNDROME

Juveniles who show one particular type of deviant behaviour often exhibit other forms as well. In other words, different forms of deviant behaviour often go together, to the extent that one may speak of a stable, general pattern. This is referred to as the *deviancy syndrome* (Donovan and Jessor, 1985; Huba and Bentler, 1982; Jessor and Jessor, 1977; Osgood et al., 1988).

The relationship between various types of deviant behaviour may develop in one of two ways. First, it may be the result of direct causal associations among the various forms of deviancy, with one behaviour leading to another. Second, and more important, the relationship may result from the fact that several types of deviant behaviour share the same general background factors (common cause theory). These background factors are found in the juveniles' personalities, their milieu (e.g., family, school, friends), and their social circumstances (Elliott and Huizinga, 1984; Elliott et al., 1985; Gottfredson and Hirschi, 1986; Hirschi, 1969; Hirschi and Gottfredson, 1983; Jessor and Jessor, 1977; Sutherland and Cressey, 1978; West and Farrington, 1977).

This common background does not mean that the same specific factors are involved to the same degree in all forms of deviancy. So will a poor relationship with parents understandably play a greater role in running away behaviour than it will in school absenteeism, although parent-child interactions may contribute to either type of deviant behaviour. Furthermore, besides factors that are common to every form of deviant behaviour, there are also unique causes which play a role.

The development of deviant behaviour may be described as follows. Because of the influence of certain background factors, juveniles are to varying degrees susceptible to deviant behaviour. Which particular forms of deviant behaviour, if any, will materialize depends to a large extent on the role models the youngsters meet in everyday life. Once a particular deviant behaviour has been adopted, that behaviour in turn may lead to others and a chain of aberrant behaviour is established. Sometimes there is a *direct* relationship. For example, if youngsters are addicted to hard drugs, the next step could be criminal behaviour in order to support their addiction. Other times the relationship is more *circuitous*. By participating in certain deviant activities youngsters may end up in a subculture where deviant behaviour is more or less accepted as a fact of life. So may juveniles who use hard drugs end up in a subculture where the members have no qualms about committing crimes. Chances are that because of this environment, those involved are less hesitant to participate in criminal acts. Furthermore, there is the possibility that youngsters who display certain kinds of deviant behaviour will be labelled by others and considered abnormal. If they accept this evaluation and consider themselves to be abnormal, there may be a tendency to behave accordingly (self-fulfilling prophecy). Again our example: juveniles who use hard drugs are easily labelled as a-social; if they accept this image, they will likely display delinquent behaviour.

Despite the relationships which exist between various forms of deviant behaviour, the common background remains the most important cause of the assorted forms of deviancy. The collective background contributes to a significant extent to the fact that, to stay with our example, youngsters get into drugs *and* commit crimes (Donovan and Jessor, 1985; Elliott et al., 1985; Jessor and Jessor, 1977).

The presence of a common background can be easily demonstrated by comparing publications which discuss the causes of specific forms of deviant behaviour: such a comparison will reveal large similarities in background factors. Authors who focus on only one form of deviancy often are not aware of this coincidence. Consequently, there is little realization in the criminological literature that juvenile delinquents involved in one type of deviancy often have backgrounds that are similar to those of youngsters who show other forms of delinquency.

There is, however, a *communis opinio* that juvenile delinquents often do not limit themselves to one or even a few kinds of crimes, but in fact are involved in all sorts of delinquent behaviour. Youths who specialize in one form of criminal behaviour (e.g., breaking and entering, car theft, robbery) are actually only found among habitual delinquents, that is, youngsters who commit crimes repeatedly and whose offenses are more serious (Cernkovic, 1978b; Farrington, 1987; Farrington et al., 1988; Gold, 1970; Hindelang et al., 1981; Klein, 1984; Lab, 1984; Loeber and Walter, 1988; Lösel, 1975; Osgood et al., 1988; Rutter and Giller, 1983; West and Farrington, 1973, 1977; Wolfgang et al., 1972).

In this book we will regularly emphasize that different forms of deviant behaviour generally can be traced back to the same background factors. The existence of such a common background suggests *that the various forms of deviant behaviour to a large extent can be explained by the same model; this, of course, also applies to the various forms of delinquency*

(Hirschi and Gottfredson, 1983; Jessor and Jessor, 1977; Osgood et al., 1988). Thus, when we describe in this book the background of juvenile delinquency, this should be understood to mean the common background of deviant behaviour as applied to juvenile delinquency, supplemented at times by specific factors.

EARLY DEVIANT BEHAVIOUR

Some children already show maladaptive behaviours (e.g., hyper-activity, irritability, impulsiveness) shortly after they have been born. Others begin to display deviant behaviours during early childhood (e.g., lying, theft, aggression). This is referred to as *early deviant behaviour*, a phenomenon which generally is found more often in boys than in girls (Plomin and Rowe, 1979; Thomas et al., 1968).

Those who show deviant behaviour as a child, very probably will also do so later on in life (density theory). Of course, they do not necessarily have to display the same forms of deviancy (specification); in fact they often show other forms as well (generalization) (Elliott and Huizinga, 1983; Farrington, 1986; Lambert et al., 1987; Lefkowitz, 1977; Loeber, 1982; Loeber and Dishion, 1983; Mitchell and Rosa, 1981; Moore et al., 1979; Olweus, 1980a; Osborn and West, 1978; Reckless and Dinitz, 1972; Roff and Wirt, 1984, 1985; Rutter and Giller, 1983; Spivack and Cianci, 1987; Werner, 1987; West and Farrington, 1973).

The subsequent development of a child who early in life shows signs of deviancy depends, among others, on the way the family responds to the behaviour. Because the family plays such an important role in children's personal and social development, the reaction of the family to the deviant actions is of great importance. If the response is inadequate (e.g., impatient, cold, inconsistent, strict, permissive) the undesired behaviour may be strengthened and this may cause a snowball effect. The child will not adjust and will persist in the deviant behaviour (Bronson, 1966; Milliones, 1978; Olweus, 1980a).

Children who have not learned at home how to behave in a socially acceptable manner will act accordingly; not only in the family but also elsewhere. Because such behaviour normally is not accepted by society, they will encounter problems and as a result may enter a vicious circle. Early deviant behaviour has been found to be related to social adaptation problems at school, which leads to difficulties with teachers and other students. The result may be academic underachievement, absenteeism, and dropping out of school. Peers generally do not accept deviant age mates, and the latter are relegated to a peripheral status. They probably will join other deviant youngsters, which does not benefit their social adaptation. In the long run, they will find it difficult to adjust to society in general, and will find it hard to maintain themselves (Buikhuisen and Lachman, 1985; Göppinger, 1983; Patterson, 1986; West and Farrington, 1977).

Is deviant behaviour at an early age a forerunner of juvenile delinquency? In some cases the answer is indeed yes. Thus, early deviancy to a certain extent predicts subsequent delinquency. The greater the number of different deviant activities children display at an early age, the greater the probability that they will get involved in delinquency during their later years (Buikhuisen and Meys, 1983; Buikhuisen et al., 1984a; Burchard and Burchard, 1987; Janes et al., 1979; Loeber, 1982; Loeber and Dishion, 1983; Mitchell and Rosa, 1981; Olweus, 1979; Quay, 1987c; Wilson and Herrnstein, 1985). Youngsters who repeatedly cross the line (recidivists) and those who commit more serious offenses, often showed a deviant orientation when they were younger, particularly with respect to aggressiveness (Farrington, 1978, 1986; McCord, 1979; Roff and Wirt, 1984; West and Farrington, 1973).

The relationship between early deviant behaviour and subsequent delinquency is not an absolute one, but rather represents a trend. There are children who are deviant when young, but who are "cured" from such tendencies when they grow older, and there are those who show hardly any tendency toward deviancy during their early years, but who subsequently get involved in delinquency (Farrington, 1978; Snyder and Patterson, 1987).

DEVELOPMENT DURING YOUTH

Youth is a period during which children (particularly boys) in almost all cultures are given some breathing space and are allowed a certain degree of freedom to explore, to indulge themselves, and to "sow their wild oats" (Van Hessen, 1964). The first few years of the youth period coincide with puberty. Sexual development and experimentation are of primary importance. The youngsters possess a good deal of energy and have a great need for action. It is the age at which they congregate in noisy groups where bravura and attention seeking reign supreme. In later years, they calm down somewhat. They meet in smaller groups and the emphasis lies more on becoming independent, forming an identity, and adapting to conventional norms and customs (Bosma, 1986; Newman and Newman, 1976).

An increase in juvenile delinquency parallels this development (Greenberg, 1977; Hindelang, 1971a; Lab 1984; McKissack, 1973; West and Farrington, 1977; Wright, 1974). Children get involved in delinquent behaviour shortly before or during puberty. From the age of twelve on, the incidence of delinquency increases, particularly between the ages of 13 and 14 years. This trend persists until the age of 16 to 18 years, following which there is a decline which continues until the age of 25 when the curve gradually begins to taper off. Girls as compared to boys begin their delinquent career somewhat later and stop somewhat earlier. Thus, juvenile delinquency generally is transient in nature; most discontinue the behaviour when they reach maturity. Juvenile delinquency is a *developmental crimi-nality* one outgrows; it may be likened to an illness which cures itself spontaneously (Pinatel, 1971). However, some persist in the behaviour; many adult delinquents, particularly those who commit the more serious crimes, began their career when young (Roff and Wirt, 1984).

The above discussed age distribution is found in all industrialized societies. It does not only apply to delinquency but also to deviant behaviour in general and other problems one encounters during this period of life (Farrington, 1987; Greenberg, 1985; Hirschi and Gottfredson, 1983; Porteus, 1985; Trasler, 1979; Wilson and Herrnstein, 1985).

During the above described development there happens not only a quantitative change but also a qualitative one. Initially the emphasis lies on overt criminal behaviour, whereas later on more covert forms gain in importance. Vandalism reaches its peak quite early and seldom occurs after the age of 18. Crimes against property only begin to decline between the ages of 16 and 18 years, and personal violence and traffic offenses even later. Another development is that with increasing age the offenses become more serious in nature (Greenberg, 1977; Junger-Tas et al., 1983; Loeber, 1982).

The question as to why the age curve of juvenile delinquency is as it is, is in fact a question about background factors of juvenile delinquency. It concerns a network of causes, motives, and circumstances, some of which we will review here for illustrative purposes. The beginning of the delinquency curve coincides with the age at which youngsters develop characteristics and live under circumstances which have a delinquency-promoting effect. Physical characteristics (growth and increase in strength) enable youngsters to commit offenses which previously (in this case, before the age of 12 years) were beyond their physical abilities. The sexual maturation process and the associated delinquency-related behaviour (e.g., bravura, attention seeking) manifests itself shortly after the age of 12. It is interesting to note that the curve of the testosterone level in boys (often associated with juvenile delinquency) and the delinquency curve both have their peak during the youth period. Certain personality traits that are related to juvenile delinquency (e.g., impulsiveness, need for excitement) are characteristic of the young. Furthermore, age-related increases in experience and knowledge, and a particular attitude (e.g., looking for diversion, experimentation) may promote delinquent behaviour. The youngsters gradually outgrow the somewhat exclusive bond with their parents and the supervision exercised by the latter, and the influence of friends —who may have less principled attitudes than the parents— increases.

Near the end of the youth period many of the delinquency-promoting factors decrease in importance and factors which inhibit the behaviour begin to have an influence (Brown and Gable, 1979; Greenberg, 1977). The individual is faced with adult responsibilities, and opportunities to attain status in legitimate ways increase. Courtship, marriage, starting a family, and employment in particular keep the youngsters (now not so young any more) from going astray. In short, older youths participate more actively in society, accept responsibilities, and in fact have something to lose. Moreover, they have less energy left to devote to deviant activities. It seems that growing older is the best antidote for juvenile delinquency.

JUVENILE DELINQUENCY

Juvenile delinquency consists primarily of minor forms of criminal behaviour and seldom involves serious crimes, although there are exceptions. Serious criminal activities such as white-collar crime (e.g., tax evasion, investment fraud, computer fraud, crimes against the environment), organized crime (e.g., illegal trade in drugs, arms, cars, or art, and criminality related to gambling or prostitution), and hard-core criminal behaviour (e.g., homicide, manslaughter, robbery, rape) are more the domain of adults. Juvenile delinquency concerns a group of transgressions which may be referred to by the term *small criminality*: minor derelictions of many a different nature. However, they are committed so frequently as to cause great material and immaterial damage. A short survey follows (Angenent, 1988; Council of Europe, 1979).

Crimes against property primarily involve shoplifting, bicycle theft, theft from cars, breaking and entering, theft from vending machines, robbery (including purse snatching), and fare-dodging on public transportation.

Youths are responsible for a large number of thefts from stores. High school students in particular have a bad reputation in this respect. Shoplifting by students may take on epidemic proportions and in some cases may involve entire classes. School recess sometimes is feared by shopkeepers in the neighbourhood. Some prepare themselves by employing extra personnel during the recess periods or by closing some entrances to the store, thereby increasing the amount of control they exercise over the situation. Others do not permit students to enter their establishments or, in extreme cases, close the store completely, notwithstanding the financial losses they incur as a result. It is sometimes recommended that one does not set up business in close proximity to schools.

Youths are also responsible for a large number of bicycle thefts. They often take the bike for their own use, not seldom because their own bicycle has been stolen. In large cities in particular do many bicycles change hands this way at a rapid pace. Most youngsters who steal bikes are not necessarily interested in expensive models, but rather need immediate transportation. They often are satisfied with ramshackle vehicles, as long as they work. It frequently concerns bicycles which have not been locked by their owners or which have locks that can be easily forced. Sometimes, youngsters steal bikes to make only one trip because they have no money for public transportation or do not feel like walking. Or, after an evening on the town, they have missed the last bus and "borrow", sometimes under the influence of alcohol, a bicycle. The much smaller group of juveniles that steals bikes to sell them, is primarily interested in more expensive models. They do not even look at cheap bikes which could still give the average user several years of reliable service. The proceeds per bike are small, but turnover may be large. A relatively active thief is able to steal several hundred bikes annually.

Theft from cars primarily involves tape decks. But other car parts also enjoy the attention of young thieves, as do personal belongings that have been left in the vehicle. Juveniles who steal from cars are surprisingly often, but not exclusively, drug users.

Breaking and entering in many cases is a group activity. It generally takes place by day rather than by night. The perpetrators frequently commit burglaries in their own neighbourhoods, in buildings that are obviously deserted and generally are located in isolated areas. Basements, cafeterias, newsstands, sheds, and schools are popular targets. The youngsters often are familiar with the buildings in question. The profits of these break-ins are usually limited. In many cases nothing is taken because the would-be thieves could not find anything of value (they are usually after money or cheques) or they were interrupted in what they were doing. Besides theft, youngsters are also involved —albeit on a smaller scale— in fencing.

In some cases —and this is characteristic of theft by juveniles— the act is accompanied by vandalism. Often the damage caused by vandalism is greater than that resulting from the theft itself. If the emphasis is on vandalism, we speak of *wanton theft*. In those cases, the game is more important than the marbles. Sometimes, things are stolen that are of no value to the youngsters and are soon after discarded. The theft serves as entertainment or to impress friends. Wanton theft in particular often occurs in groups, sometimes under the influence of alcohol.

Theft and vandalism frequently go together in offenses involving automatic machines. Vending machines, telephones, parking meters, or slot-machines are damaged (sometimes more than necessary) in order to get to the money or the articles offered for sale. Using fake money with these machines is also popular.

Purse snatching is a crime to which especially older women fall victim. The spoils usually are rather meagre, and one might treat this type of crime as of little importance were it not that the psychological consequences for the victims often are quite serious. Purse snatching is not the only kind of street theft committed by juveniles; occasionally, they rob people in broad daylight whereby they threaten the victims (sometimes with weapons, often knives) and force them to hand over money and other valuables.

Fare-dodging on public transportation (bus, streetcar, subway, train) is, with shoplifting, the offense most often committed by youngsters. It frequently occurs in groups, with the slogan that one has to be crazy to pay. To save money is not always the main goal, even though it is viewed as a pleasant by-product. It is mainly regarded as an exciting activity with which one can impress one's friends.

Vandalism is almost without exception an act committed by youths, particularly by those under the age of 16. It usually takes place in groups. The most obvious form is street vandalism. This involves damaging public buildings, houses, streetlights, mailboxes, street signs, telephone booths, newsstands, cars, bicycles, and green spaces (trees, shrubs, parks). Besides street vandalism, there is also soccer hooliganism, school vandalism (within the school by the students), vandalism involving public transportation, and recreational vandalism (while going out on the town and during holidays). Vandalism may be behaviour such as scratching benches, smashing windows, knocking over flowerpots, bending street signs, and slashing seats of public vehicles.

A special type of vandalism is graffiti: scratching, chalking, or spray painting every possible surface available. This is a centuries-old phenomenon. For ages youngster have been writing their names and other words (sexual terms were popular before the sexual revolution) on benches, trees, fences, and so forth. Graffiti is not limited to single words; all sorts of slogans and drawings also appear. Although in some cases these have a certain artistic quality, it usually does not amount to much more than visual and environmental pollution which annoys many people.

Another form of vandalism is arson. It usually concerns little bonfires, although there are youngsters who prefer larger fires. Popular settings are abandoned sites, isolated buildings, containers, construction sheds, garbage cans, schools, and clubhouses.

Soccer hooliganism is a form of vandalism in which destruction and violence go hand in hand. Even though soccer hooligans repeatedly manage to grab the attention of the media, one should not forget that in reality it concerns only a very small group of individuals. We find soccer hooligans among the fans who get together on the day of the match and who then go down to the stadium in groups. They can be easily recognized by their club colours and club symbols, and by all sorts of paraphernalia they bring along, such as flags and whistles. There is a clear rivalry between them and the supporters of the opposite team. In fact, this rivalry is at the root of soccer hooliganism. Besides the match on the soccer field, there is also the battle in the stands between the fans of the two clubs. Each side tries to taunt, intimidate, and, if possible, provoke the other group by swearing, name calling, insulting, and by singing provocative songs. This sometimes leads to a fight which occasionally may be rather violent. Hooliganism is not restricted to the stadium. The more the violence inside the stadiums has been brought under control, the more it will move outside where the participants often leave a trail of destruction in trains, busses, and entrance routes to the stadium.

Soccer hooliganism is a group activity, usually involving transient groups characterized by a relatively rapid turnover in membership. On the average, youngsters belong to such groups for periods of less than four years; that is, four soccer seasons. Soccer hooligans tend to be somewhat older —they are on the average between the ages of 16 and 18— than juvenile vandals in general. Unlike these other vandals, they often, but not always, have a limited education, and many are school drop-outs.

Many soccer hooligans identify themselves with their club and derive from this an important part of their identity. They come from milieus that are rather tolerant of norm infringements and violence. They are part of a violent subculture and are besides soccer hooliganism guilty of all sorts of offenses. The need for action and excitement, the bravura, and peer pressure we find among youths in general is very pronounced among soccer hooligans.

Although most youngsters prefer to avoid *violence*, there is a lot of what might be called "minor violence" among them in the form of threats, arguments, fights, and less severe forms of physical abuse. Serious abuse is relatively rare. Minor violence is perceived by many youths as a part of life, and tends to be restricted to peers. Such cases usually involve fights between groups, whereby it is often difficult to determine who the aggressor is and who the victim. Because it is part of their world, the police are normally kept out of it, even by those who are at the receiving end.

If there is violence, it is usually committed by older youths. Many of these come from backgrounds which do not shun the behaviour and regard it as a way to assert themselves. The recreation sector in particular knows a lot of (alcohol related) violence. This violence breaks out during the evening and night in and around establishments such as bars and discos, particularly during the weekend.

Violence among youths is often the result of a situation that has spun out of control. One juvenile tries to outdo the other (bravura) until one goes too far. A particular remark made by someone or a joke which the other party does not understand or appreciate may lead to name-calling, followed by some pushing and shoving which may deteriorate into a fight. There are also youngsters who deliberately provoke a fight. Although these individuals are small in number, they tend to determine the overall picture. They often have received combat training at a sports academy and are not seldom armed. With such youngsters around, a minor irritation may easily result in an explosion of violence which at times may be rather bloody in nature. This kind of youths is found, among others, in the entertainment circuit; they sometimes feel that an evening out on the town is not complete unless there has been a good fight, often with a rival group.

Traffic offenses —understandably— are primarily committed by older youths. It may involve joy-riding, dangerous driving, driving under the influence, or a combination of these. It often consists of bravura behaviour in the sense that the youngsters want to show off their beautiful car and driving abilities, thereby endangering themselves as well as others.

Sexual offenses are rare at this age level. On the other hand, there is a great deal of sexually motivated excessive behaviour such as obscene language, songs and gestures, grabbing and groping, and unwanted sexual propositions. Sexuality is an important aspect of this stage of life. Especially when they go out for entertainment, there are many youths who are "on the make", either in more active sense (boys) or more passively (girls). When not successful, this may be experienced as frustrating and this is sometimes vented by abusing others. Jealousy toward peers who are more successful or who have stolen away a desired partner may play a role. It has been suggested that girls have an inhibiting effect on the criminal behaviour of boys. This may indeed be the case as far as serious delinquency is concerned (girls have a greater distaste for such behaviour than do boys), but it is questionable that this applies to less serious forms of misconduct. The latter are often shown by boys in order to impress the girls.

CONSEQUENCES OF JUVENILE DELINQUENCY

The victims of juvenile delinquency are surprisingly often other youngsters, especially students and those who are unemployed. This is very much the case with respect to (reciprocal) violence (recreation and alcohol related), but less with respect to theft and vandalism (Cohen and Felson, 1979).

Girls are relatively less often victims of violence (except for sex-related violence); with respect to property offenses, there is little difference between the sexes (Canter, 1982b; Feyerherm and Hindelang, 1974; Mawby, 1980).

The fact that youths are often the victim is a function of their life style which frequently places them in locations where they may be exposed to delinquency. This is related to their activity pattern and the manner in which they spend their leisure time. In that sense are organized activities (clubs, associations) safer than independent ones (entertainment life) (Riley, 1987; Smith, 1982).

Although juvenile delinquency normally consists of minor offenses, in exceptional cases it may involve rather serious crimes (Angenent, 1988). Examples are large-scale shoplifting, theft of expensive bicycles and cars, serious breaking and entering, robbery, and cases of significant vandalism, violence, and rape. Some youngsters are involved in these kind of activities, and in those cases one can not speak any more of minor misconduct.

Even though juvenile delinquency normally involves transgressions that are considered to be minor in nature, the consequences for the victims in *material* terms alone may be quite disconcerting. For example, it should not be too difficult for most people to get over the theft of one's bicycle. However, to someone with a limited income such a theft may mean a major setback. And what about the effects of breaking and entering? In many cases nothing is stolen. However, repairing the damage can be rather costly, because often so much is ruined. Shoplifting normally does not involve high-priced items, and it appears that it should not be too difficult for the store owners to absorb the costs. However, one should not forget that for each item stolen, some ten to thirty other ones must be sold to compensate for the loss. It sometimes happens that small store owners are forced out of business because of shoplifting.

Much more serious than the material damage are the *immaterial* consequences of juvenile delinquency. For instance, theft of a bicycle limits the mobility of the victim and may cause a great deal of inconvenience and aggravation. Burglaries, even minor ones, may cause the affected people to not feel safe any more in their own home. Some become anxious, need professional help, or even move to another residence. With respect to shoplifting, many owners and store personnel suffer from psychosomatic and neurotic problems as a result of these thefts. The non-material damage is even greater in cases of physical violence. The feelings of powerlessness and humiliation which result from such attacks may seriously affect the psychological well-being of the victims. They feel violated in their identity and self-esteem, and this may damage their sense of self-worth. Serious experiences of this nature may even cause changes in the victim's personality. Often, these people lose their spontaneity, they become suspicious, and feel insecure and tense in certain situations. Their trust in people has been damaged and they are quick to regard any person as a potential aggressor. Violence may cause psychological trauma which takes a long time to heal and in some cases may last a lifetime. The quality of life of these victims has been reduced, and some subsequently go through life with a cropped-up rage about what happened to them.

Juvenile delinquency, even in its minor forms, may produce feelings of resentment, irritation, and anxiety in people who personally have never been the victim of such crimes. The more they hear about delinquency in the media, the more insecure they feel. The elderly and women in particular change their perception of youths in a negative direction (e.g., children nowadays are disrespectful, norms disappear, the authorities and the police do not act enough), and anxiety feelings related to juvenile delinquency are strongest among these groups (and not among those who are most affected by it, namely, the young themselves).

Quite a number of people are to varying degrees preoccupied with the problem of delinquency. Many come up with all sorts of ideas about how to avoid becoming a crime victim. They turn their residences into fortresses, they buy weapons, behave inconspicuously when they are out in the street, always have a small amount of money ready to buy off muggers, and avoid, particularly after dark, deserted areas and places where crimes take place or where they think that they take place (Angenent, 1988; Brunt, 1989; Merry, 1981).

DELINQUENT AND NON-DELINQUENT YOUTHS

It is customary in the literature to differentiate between delinquent and non-delinquent youths. The use of these two words may give the impression that there is a clear dichotomy between youngsters who are and youths who are not guilty of delinquency. Nothing is further from the truth.

Almost every youngster at some point during his or her life does something that is forbidden by law (Farrington, 1973; Patterson, 1986; Schneider, 1987). Because so many youths take part in delinquency, there are some observers who regard it as an endemic phenomenon (Maxwell,

1966). Others go even further, and ask whether this is not a symptom that is characteristic of the young (Farrington, 1987; Robert, 1973). Most adults, particularly males, remember delinquent incidents from their youth, during which they were caught or not (Gold and Petronio, 1980; Mays, 1963). Prominent authors such as Augustinus, Cocteau, Sartre, and Genet were not ashamed to openly admit in their biographies their personal experiences in this respect.

It appears that it is not so much the question as to why some youngsters are guilty of delinquency, but more as to why some are more involved than others. Juvenile delinquency is a continuum ranging from less to more. Nevertheless, the literature contrasts delinquent and non-delinquent youths as if they were opposing ends of a scale. For the purpose of convenience, we will in this book adhere to this approach.

OPPORTUNITY

The expression "opportunity makes the thief" suggests that the cause of theft behaviour must be found not only in the person who commits the crime but also in the situation at the time, a situation which as it were invited the thief to strike. This saying expresses the age-old understanding that human behaviour is caused by an interaction between the person and the situation (Angenent, 1988; Cohen, 1981).

In 1935, Lewin summarized this notion in the formula $B = f(P,S)$, that is, behaviour (B) is a function of the person (P) and the situation (S). This formula has since enjoyed a certain degree of popularity and has often been selected as the point of departure for reflections on human behaviour (e.g., Cattell, 1965; Yinger, 1965), including criminology (e.g., Buikhuisen, 1985; Gibbons, 1971; Glaser, 1974).

Situation has been found to play an important role in juvenile delinquency (Angenent, 1988; Briar and Piliavin, 1965; Johnson, 1979). The question may be raised as to which particular factors in the concrete situation facilitates or even provokes delinquency. The circumstances at a particular time and place can be such that it has a promoting effect on criminality. For instance, if all the discos on the local entertainment strip close at the same time, the result will be the presence of a large number of youngsters in the street, and this may be the beginning of trouble.

Opportunity determines the *ease* with which delinquent acts can be committed. The more effort it takes, the more likely the youngsters will refrain from criminal behaviour. A simple example: a bicycle is less likely to be stolen when it is secured with a good quality lock. The "ease" factor is most noticeable in cases of vandalism. Vandals tend to focus on objects which more or less guarantee success. In that respect, metal articles have a longer life span than stone objects, which in turn last longer than wooden ones. The more secured the objects are, the less likely they are to be successfully vandalized. It is, for example, easier to upset a freestanding flower box than one that has been bolted to the ground. Finally, the more fire resistant an object is, the less often will it be set on fire.

Attainability is another factor. Objects that are out of reach (e.g., streetlights, business signs) are less often vandalised than are low hanging ones. Less is taken from a lot with a solid fence around it than from one that is virtually unprotected. Opportunity is given when a door is left open, when a door has a lock that can be easily forced, when a broken window has not been repaired. Shoplifting is made easier when the goods are displayed in a way that makes it easy to get at them.

Another factor is the *surveyability* of the situation. Situations that can be easily overseen are less susceptible to juvenile delinquency. This surveyability is determined by the extent to which the area has been built up (open spaces versus buildings; squares versus parks; etc.), and how well-lit it is during the night. The unsurveyable character of some public buildings, stores, railroad stations, and large apartment buildings increases the potential of delinquency.

Surveyability means *surveillance* (by neighbours, passers-by, the police) of the activities of youths. The effect is that delinquency can be easily noticed, which may inhibit aspiring delinquents. Supervision by persons with whom youngsters have a strong personal relationship, such as parents, is most effective. Unfortunately, these individuals are seldom present at the places where crimes are committed. In reality, supervision is exercised by people who have been hired specifically for this purpose (e.g., policemen, superintendents, doormen, wardens, and others).

Finally, the general public could keep an eye on the situation. Unfortunately, experience has taught that one can hardly count on one's fellow citizens who generally are not prepared to act —not even to phone the police— when they witness a crime. They prefer to look the other way and do not want to get involved (bystander apathy). Many of such cases have been described in the criminological literature. Perhaps the most classic case concerns Kitty Genovese, a young woman who was raped and murdered in a busy street in a residential area of New York. At least thirty-eight eyewitnesses observed the drama from the safety of their apartments without making an effort to come to the rescue of the woman, even though the whole episode lasted more than half an hour. Nobody even took the trouble to phone the police (Rosenthal, 1964; Wachs, 1988).

Although youths apparently have little to fear from the public, this does not mean that the latter have no inhibiting effect on juvenile delinquency.

There are indeed some delinquent youngsters who realize that they do not have to worry about the public and who act in an overt and daring manner, but others are inhibited by the presence of (potential) witnesses.

OCCASIONAL AND HABITUAL DELINQUENTS

Most youngsters who get involved in delinquency only do so in a limited way: they do not often commit crimes, and if they do, they restrict themselves to less serious offenses. We call these youths occasional or opportunity delinquents. Other youngsters are more often involved in unlawful behaviour, and frequently commit more serious crimes. These individuals are referred to as habitual or regular delinquents.

There is no categorical division between occasional and habitual delinquents. As was the case with the distinction between delinquent and non-delinquent youths, it concerns a sliding scale with the occasional delinquents and the habitual delinquents as opposing poles.

Opportunity plays a relatively important role in the criminal behaviour of *occasional delinquents*. These youngsters commit crimes only if an attractive opportunity presents itself; they won't get involved that readily if they have to rely on their own initiative. Occasional delinquents use simple methods and not much planning is involved. The crimes often are committed in groups, with the members looking for "some fun" and not necessarily something unlawful. Criminal behaviour plays only a marginal role in the life of occasional delinquents.

Habitual delinquents often start off as occasional delinquents. If their unlawful behaviour proves to be rewarding and if they are not caught or punished for it, they may repeat the behaviour. As habitual delinquents gain in experience, they become more proficient. Delinquent behaviour becomes routine and assumes a central role in their lives. Compared to occasional delinquents, habitual offenders prepare themselves better and use more complex methods. They are more likely to take the initiative and often go out of their way to commit crimes. These youngsters normally do not work in large groups, but prefer the company of a small group of people they know well. As far as crimes against property are concerned, they often cooperate with fences and sometimes steal to order. If necessary, they act daringly and sometimes do not shy away from violence.

Compared to occasional delinquents, the percentage of boys is higher among habitual delinquents. They usually are somewhat older, often live in the city, are more involved in delinquent subcultures, and more often come into contact with the police.

(Semi-)criminal youths constitute a subtype of habitual delinquents. They

are youngsters with a (semi-)criminal identity (Becker, 1963; Cloward and Ohlin, 1960; Cohen, 1955; Knight and West, 1975; Loeber and Schmaling, 1985a; Rojeck and Erickson, 1982). Criminality is an established part of their role behaviour. They have a (semi-)criminal lifestyle characterized by a disrespect for laws and regulations. They lack proper norms and internal inhibitions. They often come from a delinquent milieu where family members have had contact with the police. Among these (semi-)criminals we find potential professional delinquents.

Most youngsters (an estimated seventy-five to ninety percent) who are guilty of delinquency are occasional delinquents, the remainder is habitu-ally delinquent. This ratio, of course, varies depending on the offense. With shoplifting, for instance, the percentage of habitual delinquents is larger than is the case with vandalism (Elliott et al., 1987; Junger-Tas, 1983; Leeuw et al., 1987).

Even though habitual delinquents represent only a small percentage of delinquents, they are responsible for a large share (an estimated half) of juvenile criminality. As we previously discussed, habitual delinquents commit more serious crimes than do occasional delinquents. Of course, youngsters who commit serious crimes often also commit less serious ones (Elliott and Huizinga, 1983; Elliott et al., 1987; Farrington, 1986; Loeber, 1982; Schneider, 1987; Wolfgang et al., 1972). Habitual delinquents have a long criminal career which sometimes continues into adulthood (Cohen, 1966; Elliott et al., 1987; Hirschi, 1969; McCord, 1979; West and Farrington, 1973).

Furthermore, (semi-)criminal youths are distinguished by the fact that they were *early delinquents* who often showed criminal and other deviant behaviour (e.g., lying, stealing, vandalism, aggression, school absenteeism) at an early age and came into conflict with the police when they were still relatively young. The age at which juveniles have their first contact with the police appears to be a good predictor of delinquency later on in life (Farrington, 1986; Ganzer and Sarason, 1973; Hanson et al., 1984; McGurk et al., 1978; Rutter and Giller, 1983; West and Farrington, 1973); that is, the younger the age, the greater the probability. It has been suggested by some that measures against criminality should in the first place be directed at habitual delinquents (Farrington et al., 1986; Loeber, 1986; Wilson and Herrnstein, 1985).

The differences between occasional and habitual delinquents are based on approximately the same factors —which will be discussed in subsequent chapters— that form the basis for the differences between delinquents and non-delinquents, except that these factors are more distinct in habitual delinquents (Dunford and Elliott, 1984; Elliott et al., 1987; Fagan et al.,

1986; Gold, 1970; Hanson et al., 1984; Hirschi, 1969; Loeber and Schmaling, 1985a; Petersilia et al., 1978; Snyder and Patterson, 1987; West and Farrington, 1973).

The kinds of offenses committed vary with the type of delinquent. Occasional delinquents tend to commit offenses that are characterized by an expressive (entertainment value, bravura) rather than an instrumental (goal-directed) aspect. With habitual delinquents and particularly with (semi)-criminal youngsters this balance shifts toward the instrumental aspect.

In the case of *professional criminals* the balance has completely tipped toward the instrumental aspect. Professional criminals commit crimes with a specific goal in mind; the crime is the means to that end. This applies to all offenses, but most clearly to crimes against property where the perpetrator is not so much interested in the loot itself, but more in its saleability. Compared to the other types, professional criminals are more proficient and rational in their approach. For example, before they attempt a burglary, they first survey the premises. They do not only figure out how to enter the building but also how to get out of it quickly in case of an emergency. Moreover, they use professional methods and techniques.

Professional criminals are not often found among juveniles. Those youths who do participate in this activity, can hardly be considered juvenile delinquents in the traditional sense. Therefore, professional delinquents will be not discussed in this book.

RECORDED AND REPORTED CRIMINALITY

How does one determine whether or not a juvenile should be defined as delinquent or non-delinquent, as an occasional or a habitual delinquent? There are two important sources for this, namely, recorded criminality and delinquency reported by youths themselves in response to surveys. A third source of information, victim-surveys, will only be discussed in passing.

Recorded Criminality

The most common source of recorded criminality are police records. Besides police records, one can also use conviction records and records of sentencing. Whenever we refer in this book to recorded juvenile delin-quency, we normally mean police records.

Police records provide limited information because they reflect merely a small portion of the crimes that are committed. This is mainly because only a small percentage of these crimes are reported. Because of sheer volume and the fact that they can not be everywhere, the police by necessity have to rely on reports by citizens (victims, but also others). However, except for crimes that must be reported for insurance purposes, citizens are somewhat derelict in reporting incidences of criminal behaviour. There are several reasons for this:

1. Victims and eyewitnesses often do not realize that criminality is involved. In the case of theft it is not always clear whether something has been stolen or lost somehow (was the wallet stolen or lost?). With vandalism it is sometimes not apparent whether the damage was caused by misuse, abuse, or accident, or whether deliberate hooliganism was at play. Fraud is often so complicated that it is difficult to find out what exactly happened. When children are sexually abused, they often do not realize that a crime is being committed.

   Victims and witnesses often offer a non-criminal explanation for criminal behaviour. People have the tendency to interpret a certain behaviour as non-criminal. If someone is seen around a locked bike with heavy tools, one almost automatically assumes that this person lost his key. If someone climbs through a window, one quickly assumes that it is the owner who forgot his key. Shoplifting committed right in front of other customers is often perceived as a mistake and not as a theft in progress.

2. The less one identifies with the victim, the less one is inclined to report a crime. This is even more the case where it concerns large businesses (shoplifting) or society in general. Understandably, people who themselves are the victim are most prepared to report crimes.

3. The closer one is to a perpetrator, the less likely one is to report; particularly if one is personally involved with the culprit.

4. One feels sorry for the delinquent or one shows understanding in view of his personal situation (e.g., age) or the circumstances under which the offense took place (e.g., misconduct on New Year's Eve or on graduation day).

5. One is guilty oneself. For instance, in cases of violence among youngsters themselves, it is often not clear who the victim is and who the aggressor.

6. One is apprehensive about contacts with the police and the justice system. In some circles criminality is more or less a way of life, and the police are not particularly regarded as friends. But also in circles where one has a positive attitude toward the police, one is not always eager to inform the authorities.

7. The circumstances under which people live (e.g., the city as opposed to a rural area) can cause them to be exposed to criminality on a more

or less regular basis. If that is the case, habituation (crime absorption) may occur which is not conducive to a willingness to report crimes.

8. One personally takes care of the problem; for instance, in cases where the stolen goods are returned or the damage is repaired. Taking care of it may also mean that the victim takes revenge in one way or another.

9. One wishes to avoid publicity. Institutions (e.g., schools, companies) do not want to get their name involved; individual citizens want to protect their privacy. Sometimes, one is afraid to lose face. Reporting may give malicious pleasure to the perpetrator if one can not prove the charges. Others may feel ashamed (e.g., in the case of rape). In some cases, the victims do not want to hear about it any more and prefer to forget the case. Reluctance to wash one's dirty linen in public is an important motive, particularly in closely-knit groups.

10. One fears repercussions by the perpetrator.

11. One is discouraged by the inconveniences associated with reporting a crime.

12. One thinks that reporting is a useless activity because the police will not do much about it, and criminals do not get the punishment they deserve anyway.

13. Finally, sheer indifference and laziness also inhibit reporting.

Willingness to report may change as a result of a changing attitude toward certain infractions (Angenent, 1972). For instance, when prosperity increases, the population's sensitivity to even the less violent crimes also increases, and, correspondingly, one is more willing to report such offenses (McClintock, 1963; Wilson, 1968). The readiness to report also grows if the media report an alarming escalation in the occurrence of a particular offense (Council of Europe, 1973).

The hesitation of people to report offenses to the police has as result that the latter are only aware of a small fraction of the criminality that occurs. One is reminded of the proverbial tip of the iceberg. It should be noted, however, that even though there is little reporting of even serious crimes, the willingness to report does increase with the severity of the violations.

Besides these reporting problems, recorded criminality is also influenced by the criminal investigation policy of the authorities. The fact that the police are aware of a particular infraction does not necessarily mean that the identity of the perpetrator or perpetrators are known. For the latter to be the case, the crime needs to be solved; and the percentage of solved crimes is, unfortunately, rather small. Moreover, not all crimes that have been solved are entered in the official records. If the police were to do that, they (and the courts) would be flooded with paperwork. Similar to what happens with reporting, the percentage of solved crimes and the probability that official records are filed increases as the severity of the crime rises. Conclusion: the more serious the crime, the more complete the recording (Gottfredson and Hindelang, 1979; Sellin, 1968).

Because of these problems, police statistics do not adequately reflect the real extent of criminality. This is further illustrated by the fact that surveys of perpetrators (people are asked about crimes they have committed themselves) and victims (people are asked of which crimes they have been the victim) produce figures that are much higher than those found in police statistics.

Crime statistics should not be regarded as primary statistics (i.e., a direct measure of a phenomenon). They are secondary statistics that are indirectly related to criminality and that are also determined by several other factors. These factors are, as far as their influence is concerned, not the same for all crimes. The relationship between committed and recorded offenses varies greatly per crime. At least, this is what victim surveys —the best indicators of actual criminality— show. Moreover, the relationship between occurrence and recording of a particular crime is not constant over the years. It sometimes happens that victim surveys indicate that there is an increase in a specific form of criminal behaviour in a particular year, while at the same time there is a decrease in the number of recorded cases.

To draw conclusions about the actual extent of criminality on the basis of crime statistics may be compared to estimating the number of opera lovers on the basis of the total number of compact discs sold. One is somehow related to the other, but the exact relationship is not known. In fact, crime statistics are more an indication of *reactions* to criminality than of criminality itself. These reactions reflect the public's attitude toward crime and the (discretionary) actions taken by the police. Hence, these statistics above all provide information about the workload of the police and the courts (Hood and Sparks, 1972; Janswoude and De Mulder, 1980; Kommer, 1985; Salas and Surette, 1984).

The question, therefore, is whether crime statistics —as far as they concern factual criminality— obscure rather than clarify the facts; a question answered in the affirmative by many criminologists. Mannheim (1965), for instance, in his classic text concluded that crime statistics are of little value as a measure of criminality. Similarly, Wiegman et al. (1982) advised that statistical data of this nature should not be used as the basis for statements about the magnitude and development of actual criminality. Taft (1950) was of the opinion that crime statistics are notoriously unreliable. According to Sutherland and Cressey (1978), crime statistics are perhaps the most questionable type of statistics that exist; to draw conclusions about the level of criminality on the basis of these data is a useless exercise. And yet, this is what happens on a regular basis in the media, thereby misinforming the public (Savitz, 1967). Rutter and Giller (1983), therefore, concluded that it is rather irresponsible to interpret statistical data as a measure of actual criminality.

Thus, police statistics do not provide a realistic picture of the scope of juvenile delinquency. However, police records are useful in determining whether or not a youngster has been guilty of delinquent behaviour and if so, to what degree. Although few offenses are reported to the police and although in many of these cases the perpetrator remains unknown, it is true that youths who commit more serious crimes are more likely to end up with a police record. As we have seen, more serious crimes are more readily reported. Moreover, the police pays greater attention to them, so that in more cases a guilty party is found and an official report is drawn up. Also, youngsters who do not stop at one crime (recidivists) are more likely to be recorded by the police at one time or another. As a result, police data tend to be skewed in the sense that they mainly include youths who have committed many and more serious crimes: *habitual delinquents*.

Surveys

Surveys of who commits crimes ask respondents about the kind of offenses they have committed. The survey may ask about crimes committed at any time, or about crimes committed during a particular period (e.g., the past year). Results obtained on the basis of the first question are very similar to recorded criminality (Hindelang et al., 1981).

Surveys about criminality are mainly conducted among youngsters, which is fine within the framework of this book. Besides inquiries about criminality, these surveys often contain questions about characteristics assumed to be related to the behaviour. Almost invariably these surveys are anonymous, even though anonymity seems to have little effect on the results (Elliott and Ageton, 1980; Hindelang et al., 1981).

There are two kinds of surveys: the questionnaire (the respondent indicates which of the crimes listed he or she has committed, and how often) and the interview (an interviewer questions the youngster about his or her delinquent behaviour, if any). A common criticism of questionnaires is that less literate respondents are not as proficient in understanding the instructions and the descriptions of the various offenses and therefore report fewer crimes. It may be noted that delinquent youths generally have lower reading skills and consequently feel less comfortable with question- naires. For this reason it may be preferable to use interviews rather than questionnaires. Some people (e.g., Erickson and Empey, 1963; Gold, 1966) suggest that interviews provide better results than questionnaires, particularly because the interviewer can clarify matters if necessary; others maintain that the format in which the survey is conducted makes little or no difference (Elliott and Huizinga, 1988; Hindelang et al., 1981).

Surveys of juvenile delinquency almost exclusively deal with less serious forms of criminal behaviour. Questions about serious offenses are avoided in order to make the instrument less threatening to the respondents. Another reason is that the surveys are often conducted in schools. That means that school officials and parents must approve of the contents of the questionnaire. This occasionally leads to problems when questions pertaining to more serious matters are included (Elliott and Huizinga, 1988; Gold and Reimer, 1975; Huizinga and Elliott, 1986).

Besides the fact that juvenile delinquency surveys are restricted to questions dealing with less serious offenses, they have several other limitations. They rely on the memory and sincerity of the respondents, and not all are equal in that respect. It is conceivable that youths who steal, vandalize, and are violent, also lack in honesty. At any rate, most youngsters report fewer crimes than they actually have committed, even though some report crimes they have not committed at all. Moreover, youths who have had contact with the police and the courts usually are noncommittal and guarded in their responses. The willingness to respond decreases when the survey covers heavier crimes (Clark and Tifft, 1966; Elliott and Voss, 1974; Hindelang et al., 1979, 1981; Hirschi, 1969).

For these reasons one might expect an overreporting of minor offenses. On the other hand, there is a tendency to omit reporting such crimes. They are more easily forgotten, because of their triviality or because they are committed so frequently that the respondent overlooks a number of them when reviewing his or her career as delinquent. It is also possible that lighter crimes are not reported because youngsters regard them as normal behaviour (Gottfredson and Hindelang, 1979, Hennessy et al., 1978; Kraus and Bowmaker, 1982; Skogan, 1977). On the other hand, through follow-up interviews after surveys it has been determined that behaviours which youngsters themselves consider delinquent (and which therefore were reported) often do not deserve that qualification (Gold and Reimer, 1975; Elliott and Huizinga, 1988).

Because surveys are usually administered in schools, several groups of youngsters who with respect to delinquency differ in qualitative as well as quantitative terms from the average youth, are not reached. Hence, it is obvious that truants and drop-outs are underrepresented among survey respondents. Similarly, youngsters who are less well integrated in society and who run a greater risk of becoming involved in delinquent activities are only to a limited extent reached by such surveys. Examples include runaways, homeless youths, child-prostitutes, youngsters from the traditional lower level of society, nonconformists, and youths with high-risk habits (e.g., alcohol, drugs, gambling). All in all, juveniles who commit more serious crimes and who do so repeatedly are less likely to be included in surveys (Cernkovich et al., 1985; Hirschi, 1969; Johnson, 1980; Wolfgang, 1983).

We will not discuss the technical objections that may be raised with respect to delinquency surveys. They do not differ from the difficulties one normally encounters when conducting scientific research. In survey research one is, among others, faced with problems relating to the definition of juvenile delinquency to be used, the selection and description of crimes to be included in the survey, the size and representativeness of the sample, the percentage of youngsters who refuse to participate, and the fact that most surveys are conducted in cities (Cernkovich, 1978b; Elliott and Ageton, 1980; Elliott and Huizinga, 1988; Empey and Lubeck, 1971; Hindelang et al., 1981; Huizinga and Elliott, 1986; Nettler, 1978; Rutter and Giller, 1983).

Previously, we argued that police records do not provide adequate information to determine the extent to which juvenile delinquency actually exists. It is generally assumed that survey data are more suitable for this purpose, even though these are not an ideal source of information either. Considering the above reviewed objections, surveys do seem to furnish consistent information in spite of the different ways in which the data are collected and the different situations in which the surveys take place (reliability). This information offers a credible picture of juvenile delin-quency (validity) (Clark and Tifft, 1966; Dentler and Monroe, 1961; Elliott and Voss, 1974; Erickson, 1972; Erickson and Empey, 1963; Farrington, 1973; Gibbons et al., 1970; Gold, 1970; Gould, 1969b; Hardt and Peterson-Hardt, 1977; Hindelang et al., 1979, 1981; Hirschi, 1969; Kulik et al., 1968; Nye, 1958; Nye et al., 1958).

Moreover, survey data provide —and this is important within the framework of this book— a reasonable opportunity to find out which youngsters are involved in delinquency (and which ones are not), and to what extent.

However, one has to accept two limitations when using survey data. First, one is restricted to less severe forms of criminality; second, the results pertain to youths who are more or less integrated into society. In other words, the emphasis lies on *occasional delinquents* (Black and Reiss, 1970; Gold, 1966, 1970; Hindelang, 1971a; Hindelang et al., 1979, 1981; Hirschi, 1969; Rossi et al., 1974).

Survey Data and Recorded Data

There is a considerable relationship between survey data and recorded data. Even though many crimes are not recorded, the respective rankings of youngsters in terms of reported and recorded criminality show some similarity. Those who have been recorded often also report many offenses (Belson, 1975; Chilton and Spielberger, 1972; Elliott and Ageton, 1980; Farrington, 1973; Rutter and Giller, 1983; Thornberry and Farnworth, 1982).

In comparing reported and recorded criminality, four types of youths may be differentiated (Farrington, 1979; Rutter and Giller, 1983; West and Farrington, 1973). The first type are youngsters who report little criminality and who are also not often recorded. Usually, they are youths who are seldom involved in delinquency. The second category concerns youths who report many crimes and who are often recorded. These are simply youngsters who commit many offenses. The third type includes those who report many crimes, but who are only recorded for a few. This type falls between the previous two categories. They generally are youngsters who commit less serious crimes. A large percentage of these, however, will eventually end up with a record. Possibly, it concerns youths whose family backgrounds are somewhat more favourable, as a result of which contacts with the police (at least initially) are avoided. The fourth category comprises youths who, even though they report few crimes, in fact have many recorded crimes to their name. They resemble the second type, except that they refuse to report their crimes.

In summary, we conclude that survey data and recorded data both offer information that is useful in determining the involvement of youngsters in delinquency. The methods can be used separately as well as in combination. In surveys the emphasis is on occasional delinquents, whereas in recorded data the accent is on habitual delinquents.

CRIMINALITY OF BOYS AND GIRLS

There are quantitative as well as qualitative differences between the delinquent behaviours of boys and girls (Canter, 1982b; Elliott and Voss, 1974; Giallombardo, 1980; Gold, 1970; Gold and Reimer, 1975; Hagan et al., 1985; Hindelang, 1971; Hindelang et al., 1979, 1981; Mawby, 1980; Ouston, 1984; Rutenfrans, 1989; Rutter and Giller, 1983; Toby, 1957; Warner, 1982; Williams and Gold, 1972; Wilson and Hernnstein, 1985). Some authors declare gender to be an important, if not the most important, factor in explaining juvenile delinquency (Ellis, 1982; Hindelang, 1979a,b;

Sutherland and Cressey, 1978; Wootton, 1959).

As far as *quantitative* differences are concerned, boys commit more crimes than girls. This difference is less pronounced in cities than in rural areas. The larger part of recorded delinquency may be attributed to boys. Not only are more boys than girls recorded, but the boys who are recorded also are recorded more frequently, especially for more serious offenses. Similarly, in surveys, more boys than girls report violations and these boys on the average report a greater number of crimes, especially more serious ones.

The difference between boys and girls found in surveys is thus smaller than that found in recorded delinquency. This is caused, among others, by the fact that boys more often commit more serious offenses and as a result are more likely to have a record. Surveys tend to deal with relatively less serious crimes, and with such crimes the difference between boys and girls is less pronounced.

When examining the data for each individual type of crime one will find that in all cases boys are more often implicated than are girls. This gender difference varies from crime to crime, with as general guideline that the more serious the offense, the greater the difference (Canter, 1982b; Hauber et al., 1987a; Hindelang et al., 1979, 1981). Furthermore, when boys commit crimes, the outcomes tend to be more serious. For example, with theft, they steal larger amounts of money; with vandalism, they cause greater damage; with assault, they inflict more serious wounds (Hindelang et al., 1979).

As far as *qualitative* differences are concerned, it has been found that the respective patterns of crimes committed by boys and by girls do not differ much. That is to say, if we rank crimes from most to least often committed, then the list is about the same for the two sexes, except that for boys, crimes of a more serious nature such as breaking and entering appear relatively higher in the list, whereas for girls less serious crimes such as shoplifting occupy that position (Canter, 1982b; Elliott, 1988; Gold, 1970; Hindelang, 1971; Hindelang et al., 1981; Johnson, 1979).

But there are differences. The criminal behaviour of girls is more *instrumental* in nature, whereas that of boys is more *expressive*. Girls tend to have a certain goal in mind; for instance, they steal cosmetics in order to improve their looks. Among boys, delinquency is often less goal-oriented and more meant as a way of showing off and entertaining themselves. They may steal things for which they have little or no use (Fiselier, 1974; Normandeau, 1971).

With boys the emphasis lies more on *overt* offenses, especially crimes that entail violence and aggression, that require (physical) strength, and in which risk and sensation seeking play a role. Examples are break-ins, robbery with assault, car theft, joyriding, serious physical abuse (Cowie et al., 1968; Wadworth, 1979). With girls the accent lies more on *covert* crimes; violations that are not easily discovered, such as theft (at home, shoplifting), cheating, swindling, and fraud (fare dodging on public transit) (Adler, 1975; Angenent, 1976b, 1988; Bonger, 1916, Loeber and Dishion, 1983; Mannheim, 1965; Pollak, 1950). However, this difference in emphasis is relative, because in terms of sheer numbers boys commit more covert crimes than do girls (Scutt, 1978).

Because these qualitative differences decrease the likelihood that girls are recorded, they indirectly give rise to quantitative differences between the sexes. Another contributing factor is that girls are less likely to be the main perpetrator; they more often are accomplices or hangers-on who play a less important role. Moreover, in dealing with delinquent girls one tends to take a non-judicial approach more often than is the case with boys.

Because of the qualitative and quantitative differences it seems logical to search for different causes of criminality of boys and girls. Yet, studies of juvenile delinquency usually focus on boys. Even though the need for research on the behaviour of girls has been emphasized repeatedly, in reality very few studies of this nature are conducted. Nevertheless, it has been found that the respective factors related to delinquency in boys and girls differ very little and that the same explanatory models may be applied to either sex (Farrington, 1987; Johnson, 1979; Riley and Shaw, 1985; Rutter and Giller, 1983).

In this book we will primarily concern ourselves with the criminality of boys, which does not exclude the fact that we will regularly refer to the delinquency of girls.

The difference in criminal behaviour of boys and girls is based in part on biological characteristics. From birth on —actually from conception— there are differences between the sexes that go beyond merely having a penis or not (Kohnstamm, 1987). To begin with, girls tend to be more mature than boys of the same age and enjoy a physical and cognitive advantage (Tanner, 1962). For example, the bone structure of girls develops at a quicker rate than that of boys. To give a few other examples: boys are more vulnerable, active, and react more readily to stimuli; they respond more readily to visual stimulation, whereas girls react more to auditory stimulation; girls are more sensitive to touch and are orally more active (sucking, tongue movements) (Osofsky and O'Connell, 1977). Innate differences are involved here; possibly genetically determined, possibly the result of the fact that very early in prenatal development the brains of males and females respectively are subjected to different biochemical influences (Bontekoe, 1984; Caesar and Weber, 1979; Kohnstamm, 1987).

Block (1982, 1983) suggested that the degree to which a person conforms is a natural ability. That is, girls tend to adapt, whereas boys are more likely do what they want and are more inclined toward deviant behaviour. Indeed, shortly after birth already one may note differences in deviant behaviour (Maccoby and Jacklin, 1974, 1980; Wilson and Herrnstein, 1985). Taking aggression as an example, one will find that even before the age of two, boys are more aggressive than girls (McGuire, 1973). This can not be the result of physical development, because girls are bigger than boys at that age. This difference in aggression exists already before the tots become cognizant of the fact they are a girl or a boy (Rutter, 1971a), a realization which arises only around the ages of 2 and 3 (Money and Ehrhardt, 1972). There is also a qualitative difference. In boys there is greater emphasis on direct physical aggression (e.g., fighting, destroying), whereas in girls the emphasis lies more on verbal aggression (e.g., gossiping, name calling), a difference which persists for the rest of their lives (Archer et al., 1988; Maccoby and Jacklin, 1980; Sears et al., 1957).

The biological basis for the contrast in aggressiveness between boys and girls (and men and women) is illustrated by the fact that in virtually all societies, notwithstanding large cultural differences, males show more aggression than females. This difference has been attributed to, among others, the influence of sex hormones. Although the exact nature of the relationship is not clear, the male sex hormone testosterone seems to be associated with aggressive and other acting-out behaviour. The female sex hormone oestrogen appears to have a calming effect, which generally leads to a withdrawing into oneself. Perhaps, this relationship between testosterone and aggression is especially strong during the youth period when the production of this hormone reaches a peak (Bontekoe, 1984; Maccoby and Jacklin, 1974).

A simple biological explanation for gender differences in delinquency might be the dissimilarity in physical strength (Mannheim, 1965). However, one should be careful with such a linear explanation. Besides the fact that the physical strength of girls in reality may exceed one's expectations, any lack of it may be easily compensated for by certain instruments, tools, or weapons. An important factor appears to be that girls often are taught not to get involved in matters that require much physical strength ("girls do not lift heavy things"). This brings us to social explanations for gender-related differences in juvenile delinquency (Bellebaum, 1972; Keupp, 1982). These are based on the fact that boys and girls are treated differently. This is related to the social roles the sexes play in society and the associated role expectations. Boys and girls play different roles; roles which relate to the place they eventually will take in society as adults

(Neidhart, 1970). Moreover, the role expectations for boys are not the same as those for girls. Boys are expected to be rational, tough, active, and determined, whereas girls are supposed to be quiet, soft, vulnerable, sensitive, dependent, emotional, a-technical, and docile.

These role expectations are reflected in child rearing (Loeber and Dishion, 1983). Virtually from birth on, parents interact with their children in a gender-specific manner, whereby sons are treated in ways that differ from the treatment daughters receive. Moreover, parents assume that very early in life already they see different characteristics in their sons (strong, attentive) and daughters (weak, less alert) (Rubin et al., 1974). In subsequent years, the different approaches taken with boys and girls can be observed in the selection of toys, sports, clothing, and so forth.

In many areas of life boys are faced with different and more exacting demands than are girls, particularly where it concerns initiative, independence, and assertiveness. Boys are allowed to be more rough and aggressive, whereas girls are taught to be less assertive, to take a wait-and-see attitude, and to be accommodating. Boys are raised to be more independent and are given greater freedom. More than is the case with girls, the street is the place of action for boys. Girls are more controlled and supervised. They are shielded more, grow up under protective circumstances, and have stronger bonds with the family (Box, 1981; Gove and Crutchfield, 1982; Van Hezewijk and Bruinsma, 1979; Jessor et al., 1968; Kok, 1983; Leonard, 1982; Nye, 1958; Wilson and Herrnstein, 1985).

Because of the biological differences between boys and girls, the variation in role expectations, and the related child rearing practices, it is not surprising that boys and girls develop different personality characteristics (Angenent, 1976b; Block, 1983). Girls tend to be more passive-dependent. They are less assertive than boys; they prefer harmony, are more flexible, and adapt more easily. They are conforming, ready to cooperate, and give in more readily. Boys, on the other hand, show more dominance and a need to assert themselves. They want to perform and do not shy away from competition. Girls are less interested in status and do not aim to achieve such by delinquent behaviour. Girls are less tied to groups and as a result suffer less from group pressure. However, this does not mean that they are not influenced by groups and subcultures (Wright, 1974). Because they are more committed to people and conventional institutions such as the family and school, they internalize conventional norms to a greater extent than boys. They also adhere more to these norms. They suffer more from shame, possibly because they do not want to harm their reputation (Morris, 1965). Many matters that are related to delinquency are just not very "ladylike". In any case, girls are more motivated to make a good impression (Wright, 1971).

Because boys enjoy greater freedom, their range of action is greater. Consequently, they have more opportunity to behave in a delinquent way. Furthermore, they are more accepting of delinquency than girls are. They have no qualms about committing rather overt forms of criminal behaviour. Girls, on the other hand, tend to be inhibited with respect to delinquency. If they do get involved, they restrict themselves to offenses that are less noticeable, and they certainly do not draw attention to themselves. More than is the case with boys, criminal behaviour by girls may be related to frustrations in their own social milieu (in the first place, the family) and the personality of the girl in question (Bol, 1975; Cloninger and Guze, 1970; Cowie et al., 1968; Felice and Offord, 1971; Konopa, 1966; Nye, 1958; D'Orban, 1972; Rutenfrans, 1983; Toby, 1957; Vedder and Sommerville, 1970).

Consonant with these role patterns, delinquency by boys is perceived differently than delinquency by girls (Morris, 1965). Moreover, the reaction of their own environment as well as of official agencies (e.g., school administration, youth protection, police) to their behaviour is congruent with this perception. Society appears to expect and tolerate more deviant conduct from boys, to the extent that sometimes a certain amount of this behaviour is (secretly) admired. The latter is particularly the case if it concerns expressions of ambition and assertiveness. Delinquency, therefore, is an activity which (traditionally) has been associated with the male sex (Wright, 1974). Hence, there is little cultural and subcultural understanding for criminal behaviour committed by girls, a not insignificant reason why girls are less delinquent than boys (Morris, 1964). The attitude of disapproval toward criminal behaviour by girls also extends to other deviant behaviours such as alcohol and drug abuse, sexual promiscuity, and aggressive conduct.

Furthermore, society is usually more concerned when a girl commits crimes than when a boy is implicated. In such cases intervention takes place more readily, within the milieu itself as well as by agencies. As has been previously discussed, the intervention methods used with girls tend to rely more on non-judicial measures (e.g., youth protection).

Fewer girls than boys come into contact with the police; they are also less likely to be recorded. This underrepresentation of girls is even more pronounced where it concerns prosecutions and convictions. Sentencing is often lighter when it involves a girl. Boys more often receive unconditional jail sentences, whereas girls more often are fined. All this, of course, is related to the fact that boys commit more serious crimes and in many cases do so repeatedly (recidivism).

Although boys are more often involved in juvenile delinquency than girls, this distribution has become a little less skewed recently (Adler, 1975, 1977; Giordano, 1978; Gold and Reimer, 1975; Hindelang et al., 1981; Junger-Tas and Kruissink, 1987; Leonard, 1982; McClelland, 1982; Oakly, 1972; Rutter and Giller, 1983; Simon, 1975; Smith and Visher, 1980; Steffensmeier, 1980; Weiss, 1976). This applies to recorded criminality as well as to criminality reported in response to surveys. It seems, therefore, that girls —albeit at a slow rate— are catching up. This catching-up phenomenon is also found with other forms of deviant behaviour (e.g., early smoking, alcohol use, drug abuse).

It is sometimes thought that this catching-up process is related to the feministic ideas held by some girls (Adler, 1975). However, research shows that girls with feministic views are less involved in delinquency than other girls. Delinquent girls usually do not adhere to a feministic, but rather to a more traditional notion of their (gender related) role in society (Giordano and Cernkovich, 1979; James and Thornton, 1980; Leventhal, 1977).

The relative increase in participation by girls in juvenile delinquency may be explained by the fact that girls (and women) have assumed a different position in society as a result of more active social involvement. Girls increasingly are offered the same opportunities as boys, and are faced with the same demands. At the same time, the differences in role patterns between boys and girls are decreasing. The behaviour of girls more and more begins to resemble that of boys. As a result, the criminality of girls will increase and they will gradually gain on boys in this respect also. Against this background one would expect that this will happen relatively fast; research, however, suggests more modest developments.

2. THE YOUTH PERIOD

CROSSROADS OF TWO DEVELOPMENTS

Juvenile delinquency must be viewed in the context of the every-day environment as experienced by youths. This experiential world is the result of two developments: on the one hand youngsters live in a society that is the product of a long historical development, and on the other hand they are in the process of developing a personality as part of growing up. Thus, they simultaneously live in a phase of a changing society and a stage of personal development.

Societal changes over the ages have had as result that youths today occupy a special position in society with a culture of their own. This culture, which is hedonistic and impulsive in nature, does not view delinquency as critically as the dominant culture of society does. In terms of their personal development, youths are in a stage of life (the youth period) characterized by puberty and adolescence related phenomena which cause them to temporarily adhere less to conventional norms and customs. Consequently, one can not expect them to show adjusted behaviour all the time.

It is at the crossroads of these two developments where one finds the experiential world of youths, and thus juvenile delinquency.

THE SOCIAL POSITION OF YOUTH

Youth in Society

The place youths occupy in today's society can be best understood by reviewing the important changes which that position has undergone in recent history, and the corresponding increase in its significance. We will discuss some of the more salient points of this process as it slowly took place over the ages. We will see that the youth period only gradually gained recognition as a separate stage of life. In fact, early authors such as Plato, Aristotle, Hobbes, Locke, and Rousseau who wrote about the human life span, make no reference to this period in their works (Rodick and Henggeler, 1982). The youth period came into existence as an offshoot of adulthood, and only over time became an independent stage of life (Ariès, 1960; De Mause, 1976; Johanson, 1980; Shorter, 1976).

Until the Middle Ages, developmental stages were hardly recognized. This does not mean that people did not see differences between children and adults (adults traditionally are persons who have finished their education and who are socially independent because they have joined the workforce and are legally responsible). However, children and adolescents were regarded as adults in miniature. Young people were acknowledged as soon as they assumed responsibilities in the adult world, which normally happened at a rather young age. Education was simple and youths performed the same activities as adults and had the same rights and responsibilities. Medieval law considered individuals at the age of 11 or 12 to be adults, and from that age on —in some cases from the age of seven— held them legally responsible. The concept of juvenile delinquency did not yet exist at that time.

In the 16th century, as a result of new social conditions which emerged under the influence of the Renaissance, the social position of youths underwent an important change. At that time, a general expansion of awareness took place, and as part of this development greater attention was paid to the individual. People became more self-confident and increasingly began to rely on their own knowledge and abilities. Moreover, more possibilities opened up as a consequence of voyages of discovery and scientific inventions. The world became larger and more exploited, and more was demanded of people in terms of knowledge and abilities. Youngsters had to be prepared for this, so it took longer before they entered the world of adults. Hence, gradually a gap was created between youths and adults, and the youth period as a separate stage of life began to emerge.

Initially, this life-stage did not have significance in itself, but merely served to prepare children for adulthood. Children were viewed as individuals who were learning how to become adults. They were kept apart from the adult world and were expected to concentrate on acquiring useful knowledge. Yet, there was no youth period as we know it today. As late as the 17th century and even more recently, seven-year-old children left home to earn money; at the age of fourteen, they were completely independent; teenage marriages were the norm.

It was not until the 18th century —under the influence of the Enlightenment— that adults really began to pay attention to children and appreciate them for what they are. They were no longer viewed as miniature adults, but rather as independent persons with their own characteristic nature (Dasberg, 1975). Childhood as an independent stage of life had arrived. It was in those days that the first games, books, and clothing specifically made for children appeared.

In the meantime, preparation for adulthood required more and more time. Because one wanted to give children the opportunity to be children for a while, this preparation was postponed during the early years of life and concentrated during the later years: the youth period came into existence. Hence, there were now two stages before adulthood: childhood and the youth period. Youths are not children any more, but also not yet adults. On the one hand they want to establish their own independence by challenging the world of adults, on the other hand they want to be part of that world. This ambiguity has as consequence that these youngsters experience a problematic and sometimes crisis-like existence. Juvenile delinquency must be viewed against this background.

Notwithstanding these changes, interest in youths was still limited, even during the last century. It is interesting to note that in 1875, it was the Society for the Prevention of Cruelty to Animals which was the first organization to champion the cause of abused children.

Any attention given to youths centred around integrating them into the adult world. With this purpose in mind, many publications about child rearing appeared. These publications for the most part reflected a Victorian attitude and focused on the moral problems of youths, the dangers they might encounter in society, and the authority of parents. Compared to modern standards, child rearing at that time was domineering and strict in nature (Demos and Demos, 1969).

By the end of the last century fewer unskilled labourers (particularly younger ones) were needed because of the industrial revolution which affected not only industry but also rural life. Consequently, many youngsters became unemployed. A complicating factor was that, because of improved hygiene and medical care (lower death rate for children), there was already a large number of youths, particularly in the cities which had attracted more and more people. One solution was to lengthen the time children were to stay in school. Because one also needed better educated labourers, this solved two problems at once. However, the longer youngsters remained in school, the longer they were excluded from the adult world, and the longer they were treated as children. Therefore, one might say that the youth period had its true origin around the turn of this century (Ariès, 1960; Binder, 1987; Demos and Demos, 1969; Gilles, 1974).

This postponement (again) of adulthood had consequences comparable to the ones we observed in the 18th century. Once again, youth's own place in society was emphasized. There was a renewed interest in youngsters who came to be treated as a separate group of society. Besides education —the term youth became synonymous with student— one began to pay attention to the leisure activities of the young. It was the beginning of the coming of age of the youth movement (Brentjens, 1978). Scientific interest in the young also increased as evidenced by the large number of publications, such as the standard work "Adolescence" by Stanley Hall which appeared in 1904. Scientific advice regarding child rearing made its appearance in the popular press (ladies' journals).

The increased interest in juveniles had four important legal consequences. First, laws were created to regulate the *working conditions* of youth (and children). Second, laws were passed requiring youngsters to *remain in school* longer. Third, several legal measures were introduced to *protect and promote the well-being* of youngsters, and organized child protection had its beginnings. Fourth, the problem of *juvenile delinquency* was addressed: the introduction of child laws led to the creation of a legal network to deal with juvenile delinquency. Hence, the concept of juvenile delinquency acquired a significance it has maintained until today.

In the present century, the youth period (and thus the delay of adulthood) has grown even longer because of educational requirements which necessitate an increasing investment of time. As a result, youngsters enter the workforce at a much later age. The lengthening of the education process had two causes which we briefly touched upon before. First, there often were no jobs for youths, and thus it made sense to keep them in school longer. Second, the labour market increasingly required well-educated and specialized workers. In the past, many youngsters —frequently at a young age— joined the large army of unschooled and semi-skilled workers. However, it is exactly the jobs that require little or no schooling that have disappeared in our technological information society.

And thus we see that the development of the youth period —and as an extension to this, juvenile delinquency— has been related to social developments through the centuries (Greenberg, 1977).

Youth Culture

Because of the postponement of adulthood, youths begin participating in the adult world at a later age. Because of the inaccessibility of the adult world and the related uncertainty of their status, they seek the company of peers. Consequently, youths have become a separate group in society, and the youth period has developed into an independent stage of life with a culture of its own which differs from the dominant culture of the adult world (Brentjens, 1978; Coleman, 1961; Parsons, 1951) and which varies from generation to generation (Blücher, 1966; Schelsky, 1957).

Youths are distinguished by their appearance (clothing, hair-style), behaviour, language, music, norms, and ideals. Compared to the dominant culture —with its values such as conformity, achievement, hard work, competition, self restraint, long-range-perspective, and career advancement— the youth culture is hedonistic and impulsive in nature. It has interests which the dominant culture considers less important, and it is geared towards the needs and desires of the young. The youth culture is a culture which to a large extent is determined by the youngsters themselves. An important basis for and cohesive principle of this culture is the strong tendency to imitate each other (Csikszentmihalyi and Larson, 1978). Other interests that are central include the opposite sex, music, going out, dancing, fashion, and so forth. The youth culture is a culture in which leisure time plays an important role, and in which independence, rebellion against authority, and rejection of conformity are emphasized. This, in turn, leads to the development of deviant norms and evasion of supervision. Deviant behaviour in general and delinquency in particular are less taboo than is the case in the dominant culture (Brennan et al., 1978; Cernkovich, 1978a,b; Sebald, 1968; Sykes and Matza, 1961).

The fact that youngsters have created their own world with its own culture means that they can deviate from and even rebel against the adult world and its dominant culture, not only by rejecting the latter but also, and especially so, by opting for an environment to which only they and their peers have access.

An important factor in the development of this youth culture is the increase in material opportunities youngsters have as a result of the rise in prosperity society has experienced over the past decades. Consequently, they are now able to live their lives in material terms the way they want to, and create their own world. Often, youngsters have their own room —also made possible by small family size— where they can socialize with their friends. They have their own belongings and equipment (e.g., audio-visual) to entertain themselves in their leisure time. They also can afford quite a bit with respect to grooming and appearance (clothing, cosmetics), entertainment (movies, pop concerts, eating out), transportation (mopeds, cars), and so forth. They eagerly participate in the consumer society. They are first in line as customers of mass consumption and mass entertainment, and consequently form an economic force to be reckoned with. The consumption industry has taken advantage of this by producing all kinds of necessary and superfluous products especially for youngsters, and by convincing them to buy these (commercials!).

Participation in the youth culture takes place at the expense of participation in the dominant culture and conventional institutions such as family and school. Distance is taken from traditional norms and values, and the norms and values of the youth culture usurp a more important position. This does not take away from the fact that youngsters live in the dominant culture as well as in the youth culture. They stand, as it were, with one leg in the dominant culture and with the other in the youth culture. Youngsters differ from one another in the amount of weight they put on one or the other leg (Gipser, 1975; Van Hessen, 1964).

One may not assume, however, that the youth culture is completely different from the dominant culture. The youth culture is an infra-culture of the dominant culture from which it is derived, and there is an ongoing interaction and smooth transition between the two. It is not so much that youths follow completely different norms and customs, but more that the emphasis is different and that certain norms and customs relating to sensation seeking, play, and experimentation are considered more important. In reality, the youth culture is a subculture within the dominant culture, although in this book we prefer to reserve the term subculture to indicate subgroups within the youth culture (Eisenstadt, 1956).

Of course, dominant cultures and subcultures should not be viewed in too absolute terms. Descriptions of cultures reflect dominant trends at varying levels of abstraction (Bandura, 1964). When we speak of the dominant culture, we mean society as a whole, whereby society is perceived as a more or less homogenous entity. We thereby conveniently disregard the many groups and subgroups (subcultures) which exist within society. In any case, many of these groups share to a large extent the ideas of the dominant culture as these are defined by those in power (upper class, wage earners, men). The concept of youth culture similarly is an abstraction. Nevertheless, affinity for the youth culture characterizes the life of youngsters —for some more than for others— because they derive to some extent their identity from that culture (Sebald, 1968).

Youth subcultures usually are embedded in the framework of the overall youth culture: in most cases they may be viewed as special manifestations of this culture involving specific groups of youngsters. There are broad subcultures that come and go with changing social developments. In recent times these included punks, beatniks, provos, mods, rockers, skinheads, and hippies; movements that followed one another in a fadlike fashion. But there are also subcultures which function in a more local context, such as the criminal youth gang which will be discussed later on.

Thus, the concept of subculture is a very general notion. Subcultures may take on forms that fall anywhere between the (abstract) level of the general society and the (concrete) level of the specific group. It is therefore important to define what is meant by the concept whenever it is used.

In this book we will come across several youth subcultures. These subcultures offer role models which allow members to satisfy their needs to imitate and identify with peers. It is especially in these subcultures where youths find their identity, particularly in response to peer evaluations (Cohen, 1966; Harlan and McDowell, 1980). Furthermore, subcultures are attractive to youngsters because they correspond to their ideas and attitudes. Moreover, through the customs and especially through interpersonal contacts within the subcultures, frustrations are released (Brusten and Hurrelmann, 1973; Starr, 1981). If delinquency is an important part of a subculture, we refer to the latter as a delinquent subculture.

Sometimes, a subculture emerges as a reaction to the dominant culture in the sense that it consciously rebels against the latter. Conflict is an integral part of such subcultures. The subculture then becomes a counter-culture with norms which occasionally are the opposite of those of the dominant culture. Politically-based counter-cultures may be found at the left as well as the right side of the political spectrum. Counter-cultures are not very popular among youngsters (Empey and Lubeck, 1971; Parsons, 1951; Yinger, 1960).

As youngsters grow older the influence of the youth culture and sub-cultures dwindles and they increasingly begin to conform to the dominant culture. They enter a phase of life which is referred to as young adulthood (a phenomenon which developed following the Second World War). It is a period during which they are psychologically and socially mature (adults), but have not yet found their definite place in society.

CHARACTERISTICS OF THE YOUTH PERIOD

Identity Development

Probably the most characteristic aspect of the personal development of youths is that they are searching for an *identity* of their own (Erikson, 1974, 1980; De Levita, 1965; Konopka, 1973). In other words, they want to develop into unique individuals, different from others, with their own place in society, vision of the future, value system, and lifestyle. According to Erikson (1974), a well-developed identity means: self-confidence, a belief in one's own abilities as well as faith in other people, optimistic expectations for the future, autonomy, independence, will-power, and initiative and purpose in behaviour.

The manner in which youths experience their identity is important. This *self-image*, which is based on self-reflection and self-esteem, gives youngsters the feeling that they are independent individuals. It lends consistency and continuity to their inner experiences and to their relationship with others. Although one's self-image is primarily determined by the manner in which one perceives oneself, this perception is influenced by the reactions of others. These reactions serve as a mirror one faces daily and help shape one's self-image. Thus, in that sense one's self-image is a reflection of what others, especially persons within one's own milieu, think of one. Youngsters who frequently hear how intelligent they are, will —whether or not it is true— in the long run believe this to be the case. On the other hand, youths who always hear that they are stupid, generally will not consider themselves intellectually gifted. Youngsters who are regularly told that they are good for nothing and will come to nothing may easily develop a delinquent self-image.

The extent to which the self-image is experienced as positive or negative will be reflected by one's level of *self-esteem*. For youths to develop an acceptable self-image (i.e., positive self-esteem), it is crucial that they are taken seriously, not only by themselves but also by others. For this reason, youngsters try to prove themselves verbally as well as through concrete behaviour. They want to convince others that they are capable of achievements, and sometimes show an excessive need for assertiveness. The resulting bravura and showing-off behaviour may lead to extreme conduct. This may induce maladapted and unacceptable behaviour, including delinquency. We will discuss these matters in greater detail in Chapter 3.

In their search for identity, youths strive for *self-reliance* and independence. In order to achieve this, they must let go of childhood, the period of life during which they were part of a family and followed the prevailing conventional norms and customs (Neidhart, 1970). They begin to question the truths of childhood (which are in the first place those of the family), and begin to think about themselves and the world. A reorientation takes place in which they take a critical, often uncompromising stand vis-à-vis their own milieu and society in general. They relinquish the concrete attitudes of childhood and develop an interest in abstract problems (e.g., the environment, discrimination, war and peace).

Youths are aware of the fact that they are on the way to adulthood and normally strive toward this goal. On the other hand, they very much criticize this next stage of life and sometimes try to postpone the transition in order to participate as long as possible in the youth culture. This results in a somewhat ambivalent attitude towards adulthood. In any case, most youngsters do not feel very responsible for the adult world, a sentiment they can well afford because they have not (yet) invested a great deal into it and thus have little or nothing to lose. Sometimes, they strongly oppose the adult world; society in general as well as their own milieu, in particular their parents. This attitude is more common among boys; girls feel greater affinity with their own milieu and family.

Criticizing mistakes and identifying weaknesses in society and their own milieu often accompanies this rebellion, behaviour which leads to lower integration in society and to a less close relationship with parents. Youths establish contacts with people outside their family and shift their interests accordingly. They become aware of different norms and customs, and begin to view those held by the family in relative terms. This may lead to disagreements with the parents; usually about clothing, appearance, ways of spending money, leisure time, choice of friends, curfews, and so forth, and less often about norms and values.

Parents may experience this emancipation process, which is a normal part of development, as painful. It may come as a shock to them when they realize that their children are going their own ways (Rodick and Henggeler, 1982). They may not understand this need for independence; perhaps, because they have forgotten that once they were young themselves, or because they compare their children's youth period with their own, not realizing that in doing so they are applying old-fashioned standards.

Some publications, especially qualitative-sociological and clinical-psychological ones, attribute the disagreements between parents and children to a *generation conflict* (Bettelheim, 1966; Coleman, 1974, 1979; De Haas, 1975; Freud, 1958; Friedenberg, 1969; Sebald, 1968). The youth period is portrayed as a problematic phase during which children and parents often clash violently. These conflicts are considered to be a normal and necessary part of the process of becoming independent. Youngsters need to rebel in order to find their own direction; disagreements with parents are an essential part of growing up. According to this line of reasoning —as cynically observed by Velema (1983)— a good parent-child relationship would be suspect.

The generation conflict is a myth however (Mönks and Heusinkveld, 1973). Research has shown that youths generally get along well with their parents (Bandura, 1964; Bengtson, 1970; Blücher, 1966; Brennan et al., 1978; Conger, 1973; Cornelissen, 1970; De Wuffel and Mönks, 1983; Douvan and Adelson, 1966; Elliott and Voss, 1974; Kandel and Lesser, 1969; Van der Linden and Stoop, 1977; Velema, 1983). Serious conflicts with parents are an exception rather than the rule, and it hardly ever comes to a break in relationship. In spite of the greater independence youngsters demand for themselves and the greater distance this creates, parents and children generally do not reject one another. On the contrary, usually there is a solidarity and loyalty. Youths identify with their parents and imitate them. As a result, they tend to adopt the same norms and values as their parents. However, as will be discussed later, exceptions to all of the above include, among others, delinquent youths.

The massive *physical changes* which take place at the onset of puberty and which, among others, lead to sexual maturity, play an important role in the search for identity (Katchadourian, 1976). The most striking changes involve growth (height and weight) and the development of primary and secondary sex characteristics. These developments start in girls about two years earlier than in boys. This is not surprising, because from conception on girls are ahead in biological maturity. Changes happen rather suddenly and proceed so rapidly that some youths are overwhelmed by them or at least feel bewildered. From this time on, youths are usually very sensitive to the internal and external changes in their physique. They take a greater interest in their bodies, particularly their appearance. The identity and self-image of youngsters depend to a large extent on how they experience their appearance. This is related to the fact that physical appearance is an important factor in the relationship with peers: an attractive appearance increases popularity, an unattractive one decreases it (Cavior and Dokecki, 1973; Conger, 1973; Dodge, 1983; Eme et al., 1979; Kleck et al., 1974; Langlois and Stephan, 1977; Lerner and Lerner, 1977). Delinquent young-sters put, relatively speaking, a lot of emphasis on their appearance. In fact, for boys it is a way to express machismo (Glueck and Glueck, 1950).

At the same time that these physical developments take place, sexual feelings surface and youngsters begin to experiment with sexuality. This initially involves fantasy and masturbation, and only in the middle of the youth period or even later may move on to actual intercourse. Youngsters —particularly boys— frequently talk about sex, often in superlatives. In the overall context of identity formation, establishing an acceptable sexuality is an important factor in developing a gender-specific role. Much experi-mentation takes place, as is evidenced by the many heterosexual but also homosexual behaviours which surface intuitively.

As part of their search for a gender-specific role, youngsters increasing-ly orient themselves toward the opposite sex. The bravura behaviour that is so characteristic at this age level is often motivated by a desire to impress the opposite sex. Some youngsters seek contact with the opposite sex at a relatively young age, whereas others wait until they are somewhat older. Juvenile delinquents often start early in this respect. Youngsters who have relationships with multiple partners seem to be more involved in delinquency than are youngsters who prefer stable relationships (Hirschi, 1969; Junger-Tas and Kruissink, 1990).

About five percent of youths appear to have homosexual tendencies (Karlen, 1971). These youngsters find their identity by a different route than their heterosexual peers. They usually accept their homosexuality with some hesitation after vague premonitions which surfaced over the years were succeeded by concrete indications. It is often much later that they dare to admit to their homosexuality. This is related to society's attitude toward homosexuality: although tolerated by many, only a minority truly accepts it. Hence, homosexual youths have to cope with a lot of prejudice and discrimination.

Apart from this, homosexual youngsters do not have many opportunities to develop an identity of their own. The relationship with parents and other identification figures is often ambivalent. Their heterosexual peers offer little comfort because they lack understanding. The homosexual youths' reaction is the same as that of minorities and people who suffer discrimination: they look for soulmates. The homosexual subculture therefore plays an important role in the life of those who have accepted their homosexuality. But even if they admit their homosexuality, it is not as easy for them to meet others as it is for their heterosexual peers who only have to walk to the corner of the street, so to speak, to find sexually compatible friends.

Little research has been done on delinquency among homosexual youths. There is a feeling that it is not out of the ordinary. Specific deviant behaviour among homosexual youngsters of course reflects their sexual orientation (e.g., prostitution, blackmail).

Motives

The motives which influence youngsters' behaviour are (mixed) biological, cognitive, emotional, and social in nature (Agnew, 1985; Canter, 1982a; Hellmer, 1978; Kaiser, 1982; Kreuzer, 1983, 1985; Krohn and Massey, 1980). Some begin in childhood and are still present (sometimes strongly, sometimes weakly) in the youth period. Others only surface during the youth period (puberty and adolescence). They are activated at the beginning of this stage, reach their peak during the youth period, and decline again when the individual approaches adulthood.

Youngsters look for *novelty*. They want something new and different, even though they often do not exactly know what this might be. They are curious, like to know how the world works, and are ready to explore. Not in theory but in reality; in other words, they want to personally experience life. They are attracted to the unusual: extraordinary events, circumstances, and people. Due to their lack of experience, they may sometimes ignore rules and violate regulations in the process.

Driven by a need for action, youths *experiment* with new experiences, especially with social roles. This experimentation is a matter of trial and error. In their need to explore, they like to test the limits, find out what is permitted and what is not, what adults will allow and what not. This leads to a testing of parents, teachers, police officers, and so on. They particularly try to figure out to what extent rules can be broken without having to face too severe penalties. Their behaviour therefore is not always very congruent with the prevailing norms and customs (Merton and Nisbet, 1961).

Youngsters like to be *active*, even though they do not always give that impression to the outside world. Being active does not necessarily mean a great deal of excitement; it could be something that keeps only their mind occupied. So, a group of youths who appear to be hanging around in a rather listless way may be very busy socializing, something that is (very) important to them. Usually, however, the behaviour is more boisterous. Youths are looking for things to happen. It does not matter what happens, as long as something happens. In this context, "something happening" may mean delinquency (Downes and Rock, 1982).

Boredom has been found to be directly related to juvenile delinquency, a fact which youngsters themselves understand very well (Hirschi, 1969; Klinkmann, 1982; Kraus, 1977; Tobias, 1970). For many, being bored is about the worst thing that could happen. They will go to great lengths to avoid it. This is particularly true of juveniles who are not very good at entertaining themselves; they look for action, and delinquency may be a good way to get rid of boredom. On the surface such delinquency appears to be without motive, but in reality it serves a purpose.

A large part of what youngsters do is a *game* in the larger sense of the word. It is a matter of social practice, a participating in the adult world without having to fear the real consequences that follow certain behaviours in that world. This is how youngsters learn how to behave. The testing of limits, as discussed above, is part of this process. Adults who do not understand the game aspect of this behaviour may develop a mistaken impression. In many cases, delinquency is a "jeu de criminalité". This kind of criminality is almost always committed in groups and is primarily found among younger youths. Examples are vandalism and petty shoplifting.

Related to the game motive is the *sport* motive, which is more prevalent among older youngsters. Unlike the game motive, the sport motive is more geared towards achievement. One tries to outdo one another in initiative, capability and strength, and especially in courage and bravura. The further one dares to go, the more one impresses friends and peers. Delinquency offers many possibilities in that respect. Stealing, vandalism, participating in fights, can all lead to success.

Youngsters search for ways to *entertain* themselves. They look for diversions, and the amusement value of many forms of delinquency is high. Besides vandalism, there are other activities (e.g., theft, violence, driving under the influence of alcohol) that are appealing to some youths under certain circumstances. In those cases, it is usually the *excitement* and *sensation* which attract the youngsters. Sometimes, they actually go out of their way to look for the "kick of the moment" and in doing so may lose sight of rules and regulations. Some specifically look for *risks*, even if it were only the risk of getting caught. To them, delinquency is a challenge.

This risk-seeking behaviour, by the way, is a rather common phenomenon. We find it also in mountain climbers, racecar drivers, motorcycle riders, gamblers, and so forth. Youngsters with a strong risk-motive may actually be encouraged by rules and warnings; the stricter they are, the greater the desire to try the forbidden behaviour (Kraus, 1977).

Youths react spontaneously, reason why their behaviour is sometimes *impulsive* in nature. They quickly change goals, their moods shift easily, and their emotions may vary from elation to depression within a short period of time. Their thinking is more short-term in nature (better today than tomorrow) than that of adults. They do not always realize the consequences of their actions and often do things on the spur of the moment without worrying too much about the effects; there is a lack of self-control. Hence, youngsters' behaviour is rather situation-related. They live a concrete reality and are not yet able to generalize from specific situations to more general rules and vice versa (Bohnsack, 1973). They rely on impressions of the moment; as a result the immediate situation influences their actions to a greater extent than is the case with adults. Consequently, they are more open to temptation. As noted earlier, opportunity plays an important role in the causation of delinquency. It sometimes happens that youngsters look back on their criminal behaviour with surprise.

The partial loss of the protection provided by the family, the new things youngsters discover about themselves and the world, the conflicting emotions they experience, the ambivalent relationship with the adult world, and the uncertainty about what the future may bring, cause the youth period to be a slightly *unstable* time of life. This is more true for boys than for girls (Feldman, 1972). That does not mean that the youth period is characterized by tension and conflict (Erikson, 1974); in fact, most youngsters have quite a good time (Adelson, 1979; Coleman, 1980; Kuiper and Feij, 1983; Offer and Offer, 1978). A majority uses this period as a time of experimentation and eventually develops a stable identity. A minority accepts life as it is and from the beginning conforms to milieu and to society. Others, also a minority, experience the youth period as turbulent and full of conflict ("Sturm und Drang"; "storm and stress"). For them, this is a period characterized by identity-confusion and negative self-image. They doubt themselves and almost everything else. They suffer from mood changes, irritability, inactivity, and depression. Especially at home and at school they encounter problems. This kind of instability, however, still falls within the limits of normal behaviour, and should be distinguished from pathological depressions, fears, psychopathological disorders, and psychoses which also may occur in the youth period, but which are not characteristic of this stage of life (Rutter et al., 1976).

Utility Principle

The behaviour of juveniles is not only caused by expressive factors (e.g., the above described motives); there are also instrumental factors which result in a rational balancing process comparing costs and benefits. Like all people, youths are "utility maximizers". Following the utility principle, they do what is beneficial to them and avoid doing what is detrimental. Pragmatic thinking increases with age and is more prominently present in girls than in boys. The utility principle also plays a role in delinquency (Ajzen and Fishbein, 1980; Ghali, 1982; Kraus, 1977; Piliavin et al., 1969; Williamson, 1978; Wilson and Herrnstein, 1985).

Admittedly, juvenile delinquents are no accountants; a rational approach whereby expected profits and losses are compared is more the domain of hard-core criminals (e.g., white-collar crime, organized crime). Juvenile delinquents are usually less rational and plan even less (Cohen, 1971; Wiatrowski et al., 1981; Wilson and Herrnstein, 1985). However, that does not mean that they act mindlessly. Usually, they are aware that criminal behaviour has its disadvantages. If they foresee too many drawbacks they may refrain from criminal behaviour.

This decision process is very much influenced by the youngsters' own experiences and by the perceived advantages of crime (advantages weigh heavier than disadvantages). The latter is related to the fact that advantages are usually immediate as opposed to disadvantages which often only become apparent over time; and youths are short-term thinkers. The evaluation of the disadvantages is strongly influenced by what they have to lose, materially but also personally (e.g., appreciation, recognition, status). Youngsters who value good relations with their milieu (e.g., with their parents) will be reluctant to engage in delinquent behaviour because of the damage it could do. Others don't want to jeopardize their position in society. Youths who conform to society, who aspire to be successful and who already have made some efforts in this respect, will usually think twice before getting involved in delinquency. This is, for example, true for youngsters who have devoted a lot of time and energy to getting an education or a job. Also the fear of losing face should the crime become known (at school, in the neighbourhood, at work) may act as a deterrent.

Finally, some may get caught, with all the related legal consequences. However, punishment acts less as a deterrent than one might expect (this also applies to adult offenders), certainly less than the expected probability of getting caught (Bursik & Baba, 1986; Fraser & Norman, 1988; Leeuw et al., 1987; Paternoster, 1989; Piliavin et al., 1986; Van Tulder, 1985).

3. THE JUVENILE DELINQUENT

PERSONALITY AND PERSONALITY TRAITS

"That's just the way he is", "that is so typical of him", "I would never have thought she had it in her." Statements such as these suggest that we expect a certain individual to behave in a certain way in a particular situation. The behaviour the person shows is characteristic of him or her, it is different from the behaviour shown by others. Moreover, we notice that different people when faced with the same situation may respond in different ways. These variations in behaviour are the result of the fact that each individual has a unique *personality*.

A person's personality may be inferred from the characteristic behaviour pattern he or she shows in a wide variety of situations. In other words, personality is the consistent manner in which one adjusts to one's environment. It implies a certain predictability of behaviour in the sense that people with a particular personality structure will behave differently in certain situations than people who have a different character structure (Golding, 1975; Stagner, 1974; Van Heck et al., 1990).

One may think of personality as a dynamic organization of *traits* within the person. However, the extent to which these traits will be expressed in behaviour depends very much on the situation as perceived by the individual. Thus, personality traits should not be regarded as internal factors which operate independently of the situation. In fact, one can only speak of *personality traits in relation to the situation*. In other words, personality traits are general dispositions which together determine one's unique behaviour and thoughts in certain situations (Cattell, 1957, 1965).

Even in children who are still very young can one already detect consistent behaviour patterns which suggest the presence of personality traits. These traits will become more stable with age, and once fully developed will remain relatively constant throughout life (Plomin and Rowe, 1977; Rushton et al., 1985; Ryder, 1967; Schaie and Parham, 1976).

HEREDITY AND MILIEU

Personality traits are the product of an interaction between heredity and milieu. This interaction begins at conception (because even in the womb the child experiences all sorts of environmental influences and reacts to stimuli). This early in life already, the characteristic way in which a child reacts to the environment emerges on the basis of hereditary neurological and endocrinological factors (Buss and Plomin, 1975; Cattell, 1957; Ellis, 1982; Strelau, 1982).

After birth, the interaction between natural ability and milieu continues, a process in which the social environment plays an increasingly important role (Ellis, 1982; Kohnstamm, 1987; Scarr and McCartney, 1983). Particularly in young children, is it easy to see that the development of personality traits is a question of heredity and milieu, maturation and learning, disposition and experience. This is not to say that all hereditary influences manifest themselves immediately at birth. They may be "dormant" and may surface only later on in life (e.g., sexual drives which appear during puberty). The respective contributions of disposition and milieu varies from personality characteristic to personality characteristic. Some are more determined by heredity (maturation), whereas others are primarily the product of environmental influences (learning) (Eysenck, 1960; Plomin, 1983; Scarr and McCartney, 1983).

LEARNING AND IMITATION

Learning results from daily experiences, which can be positive or negative in nature. Positive experiences lead to a sense of elation, a feeling of well-being, whereas negative ones result in discomfort, a feeling of uneasiness. One tends to continue behaviours which produce positive feelings (reward learning), whereas those which have unpleasant consequences will not be learned or are even suppressed.

Personality development is greatly influenced by experiences one has during social interactions with others. We speak here of a social learning process (Bandura, 1965, 1973, 1977; Bandura and Walters, 1959). Central to this process is imitation; that is, the conscious or unconscious adoption of observed norms, ideas, habits, and behaviours, even if these are not accompanied by personal rewards (although rewards do encourage imitation).

Imitation particularly occurs in the context of relationships with important models in one's own milieu; one tends to imitate parents, relatives, friends, teachers, and so forth. However, one may also emulate people with whom one has a more abstract relationship, people one only knows from a distance (e.g., TV personalities, pop stars, movie stars, etc.). The influence of these individuals in some instances is just as great as that of persons in one's own milieu. Generally, however, the latter have a deeper and longer lasting influence on personality development.

Imitation is greater when contact with the model is more frequent, longer lasting, and particularly when it is more intense. Furthermore, the probability that imitation will occur increases when it involves matters that are relevant to the observers; things they understand and which they can use in their own life. Most important, however, are the power and prestige (at least in the eyes of the observer) of the model, and the quality of the contact. Imitation will be more likely when there is good contact; in that case, it may be based on partial or complete identification with the model. Any person with whom one has a good relationship may serve as an identification figure. We call these people significant others, meaningful persons, or key figures (Akers et al., 1979; Bandura, 1977).

Learning from relationships with others, one develops one's identity. We have already seen that one's self-image is one's own view of this identity. Experiences that are congruent with the self-image are easily assimilated (selective learning). Experiences that are not compatible generally are distorted to make them acceptable, or are disregarded or repressed. Thus, learning is subjective. In this way, everybody determines the personal character of one's own experiences and thus of one's own personality development.

BASIC TRAITS

Because the number of potential personality traits is large (Allport and Odbert, 1936; Cattell, 1957), it does not appear easy at first glance to get a good overview. However, traits are not independent; they are intercorrelated. People who have certain traits often have certain other ones too. Some sets of traits are more intercorrelated than others. Traits that are strongly correlated may be traced back to *one* underlying basic (source) trait; there is a hierarchical structure. For example: suppose that someone is good at mathematics, that his verbal ability is above average, that he quickly sizes up situations and can solve complicated problems easily. It would be simpler to say that this person is intelligent. All the traits mentioned are namely based on the source trait "intelligence". Another example: personality traits such as emotionally unstable, depressive, and worrisome on the one hand, and calm, stable, and stress resistant on the other, may be summarized under the basic trait "emotionality". Thus, a large number of personality traits may be traced back to a smaller number of source traits.

As a result of a long research tradition (Cattell, 1946; Eysenck, 1947; Guilford, 1934) we are able to differentiate within the personality the basic traits of *intellectual functioning*, *emotionality* (also referred to as emotional instability, neuroticism, anxiety, ego-weakness), *extraversion, toughness*, and *conscientiousness*. Because of the topic addressed in this book, we add the trait of *(im)maturity* to this list (Angenent, 1985; Buss and Plomin, 1975; Cattell, 1957; Eysenck, 1960; Feij, 1979; Groenier et al., 1973; Lawrence, 1985; McCrae and Costa, 1985, 1986; Mischel, 1976; Norman, 1963; Pawlik, 1968; Zuckerman et al., 1988).

Intellectual functioning, emotionality, and extraversion have been the subject of much research. Descriptions of these concepts already existed in the early years of personality theory, although not always under the same names (Roback, 1927; Kouwer, 1963). They assumed a central place in the theories of Jung (1922), Heymans (1927), Kretschmer (1955), Eysenck et al. (1969), Cattell (1957) and others.

Research into the relationship between these basic traits and juvenile delinquency began in the 1940's and 1950's, and progressed as the psychological understanding of these concepts increased (e.g., Ackerson, 1942; Cole, 1952; Comrey, 1958; Hewitt and Jenkins, 1946; Jenkins and Glickman, 1947; Lewis, 1954; Topping, 1941).

In the following sections we will provide descriptions of the basic traits, whereby we combine the results of various studies into one definition. The traits will be presented as dimensions and the (opposite) poles will be described. Next, we will discuss how the respective traits are related to juvenile delinquency.

INTELLECTUAL FUNCTIONING

Intellectual functioning is a broader concept than intelligence. By intellectual functioning we mean the manner in which intelligence operates in daily life, the way in which we use our intellect. It refers to thoughtfulness, resourcefulness, insight, and intellectual curiosity (or the lack thereof).

Of course, intellectual functioning and *intelligence* are highly related. What is exactly meant by intelligence, however, is open to discussion. Yet, everybody knows to some extent what it is. It involves the way in which one gathers knowledge and applies this knowledge. The essence of intelligence is the ability to distinguish between important matters and trivia, to discover principles, to generalize, and to detect relationships. Intelligence is especially apparent in problem solving and goal directed behaviour.

Intellectual level is to a large extent determined by heredity; however, this does not preclude the influence of environmental factors. To what extent heredity and environment respectively contribute to intelligence is still a topic of heated debate.

Intelligence is usually assessed by means of an *intelligence test*. Following the development of such a test in the beginning of this century, intelligence could be expressed in a number: the *intelligence quotient* (IQ). The average IQ is 100. So, if one scores above 100, one is above average in intelligence; if one scores below 100, one is intellectually below average. The average range falls approximately between 70 and 130. If one scores below 70, one is retarded; if one scores above 130, one is gifted. Of course, the IQ does not disclose everything about intelligence; it tells us as much about intelligence as blood pressure does about blood. Nevertheless, it seems that scores on intelligence tests are reasonably good predictors of intellectual achievements such as success in school, and that they are pretty stable over time for the same person.

When testing the intellectual level of delinquents, it was found that their IQ generally was below average (Goddard, 1921; Zeleny, 1933). It should be noted that this research usually involved (adult) delinquents who were in prison. Moreover, some authors from the beginning have suggested that there is no real difference in intelligence between delinquents and others. Sutherland (1931), for instance, believed that if tests were to improve, the difference would disappear. He did not turn out to be right in this respect. Delinquents today still score lower on intelligence tests, even though over the years the difference has decreased from 12 to 15 points to approximately 8 points. This difference is not that impressive if one realizes that the average difference between siblings is 12 points, and that "white collar" and "blue collar" professions differ by 15 points (Caplan, 1965; Hirschi and Hindelang, 1977; Prentice and Kelly, 1963; Quay, 1987b; Rowe and Plomin, 1981). A fair estimate would be that delinquents' IQs are usually between 60 and 100. People with very low IQs, below 60, are less often involved in criminality (Hirschi, 1969; Hirschi and Hindelang, 1977; Wilson and Herrnstein, 1985).

The relationship between (low) IQ and juvenile delinquency has been reported by many (Cattell and Cattell, 1975; Empey and Lubeck, 1971; Farrington, 1986; Hindelang et al., 1981; Hirschi and Hindelang, 1977; Lawrence, 1985; Moffit and Silva, 1988; Ouston, 1984; Pierson and Kelly, 1963; Werner, 1987; West, 1982; West and Farrington, 1977; Wilson and Herrnstein, 1985; Wolfgang et al., 1972), although other authors have not been able to confirm this (Cloward and Ohlin, 1960; Menard and Moore, 1984; Offord et al., 1978; Rutter et al., 1970; Woodward, 1955).

The relationship exists for survey-reported delinquency as well as (even stronger) for recorded delinquency. The association with recorded delinquency holds notwithstanding the fact that intelligent youngsters report their deviant behaviour somewhat better (Wiatrowski et al., 1981).

A problem is that tests used to measure intelligence too often reflect the dominant culture, so that people who are at the fringe (e.g., ethnic minorities) by definition are at a disadvantage. The fact that individuals from these groups obtain lower scores on these tests does not mean that they are less intelligent. Rather, it suggests that IQ depends in part on environmental factors. Nevertheless, within these groups it also applies that the lower a youngster's IQ, the greater the probability that he or she shows delinquent behaviour. The conclusion therefore remains that there is a negative relationship between intelligence and juvenile delinquency (Berzonsky, 1978b; Braithwaite, 1981; Hirschi, 1969; Hirschi and Hindelang, 1977; Reiss and Rhodes, 1961; Wolfgang et al., 1972).

The association between intelligence and delinquency is based, among others, on the fact that intelligent youths are better able to assess the disadvantages of delinquent behaviour and therefore are more inclined to reject it. Moreover, they are more successful in reaching conventional goals, are therefore better integrated in conventional structures, and consequently feel less need for delinquency (Hirschi, 1969).

As far as this relationship applies to recorded delinquents, it may be noted that intelligent persons are less likely to get caught (Hirschi, 1969; Lawrence, 1985; West and Farrington, 1977).

The correlation between low intelligence and juvenile delinquency may be explained in part by the fact that less intelligent youths do not do as well in school. They particularly have trouble with theoretical-abstract subject matters, and it is exactly this aspect of intelligence that is important in school (Berman and Siegal., 1976; Hargreaves, 1982). This results in alienation from school, which may encourage delinquency (see Chapter 5).

Juvenile delinquents primarily lack *verbal* intelligence. They encounter difficulties when confronted with verbally coded information. This goes for the perception (spatial perception, symbolic representation) as well as the processing of verbal information. The problem is apparent in their vocabulary, formulation, and verbal reasoning, and expresses itself among others in inadequate reading ability. The juvenile delinquents' retardation in verbal intelligence may be the result of limited reactivity of the nervous system as well as of insufficient cultural stimulation, especially within the family (Berman and Siegal, 1976; Caplan, 1965; Ganzer and Sarason, 1973; Hirschi, 1969; Jurkovic and Prentice, 1977; Offord et al., 1978; Quay, 1987b; Slavin, 1978; Walsh and Berger, 1989; West and Farrington, 1973; Wilson and Herrnstein, 1985).

The lower verbal intelligence goes hand in hand with a less adequate *mastery of language*. Mastery of language facilitates an evaluation of one's own behaviour in the past, present, and future, as well as an assessment of the consequences thereof. Someone who does not have adequate command of the language very likely understands less and in a way trails behind the facts. This may lead to feelings of insecurity and may contribute to the development of low self-esteem. Moreover, language is the key to social interaction. If one is not capable of expressing oneself properly and of communicating one's opinions, one will not be very proficient at defending one's rights and will not be taken seriously. In short, an insufficient mastery of the language is clearly a social handicap. This is, by the way, one of the reasons why girls —who from early childhood on are more verbally gifted than boys— are better able to adapt socially.

There are indications that youngsters with low intelligence are particularly involved in criminal behaviour committed in groups, in crimes against property, and in impulsive offenses which lead to immediate rewards (Randolph et al., 1961; Wilson and Herrnstein, 1985; Wright, 1971).

Even though juvenile delinquency generally is correlated with low intelligence, occasionally the opposite is true. In those cases it is the more intelligent youths who instigate and carry out criminal activities. These youngsters drag other youths along in their delinquent endeavours because of the influence they exercise over them. Sometimes, they even take the lead, for example in youth gangs. These same youngsters know better than others how to avoid undesirable consequences of their criminal behaviour (as we have seen earlier). For example, they disappear as soon as the police arrive and leave it to the others to deal with the situation.

EMOTIONALITY

The basic trait of "emotionality" differentiates between emotional and stable persons.

Emotional people make an unbalanced impression. Their moods vary and may fluctuate without apparent reason. They are inhibited (intellectually as well as socially), fragile, sensitive to criticism, and easily thrown of course. Emotional persons are sombre, worrisome and often fret about matters that are not really important. They usually are self-centred and do not have an optimistic view of themselves and the world. They may suffer from depression, feelings of shame, inferiority, guilt, and self-pity. They report many personal problems, not seldom psychosomatic in nature (e.g., concentration problems, insomnia, fatigue, heart palpitations, perspiration). To escape these problems, they often fantasize or daydream.

Stable people, on the other hand, are quiet, calm, and consistent in their moods. Any fluctuation in mood usually has a clear cause. They are resilient and not easily upset, they see things in perspective, do not worry about trivialities, generally do not take things personally, and do not have more problems than is necessary (Angenent, 1974, 1985; Eysenck, 1977; Feij, 1979; Royce, 1973; Vagg and Hammond, 1976).

Emotionality is to a large extent hereditary in nature. Its biological basis is the autonomic nervous system's ability to be stimulated. How emotionality is shaped in one's life depends on the environmental influences to which one is subjected. Emotional people are born with a weak and unstable autonomic nervous system. Because of this, general anxiety reactions are elicited, which under the influence of environmental factors may develop into specific fear responses, especially fear of certain situations (Buss and Plomin, 1975; Buss et al., 1973; Cattell, 1957, 1965; Dworkin et al., 1976; Feij, 1979; Floderus-Myrhed et al., 1980; Plomin and Rowe, 1977; Rushton et al., 1985; Scarr, 1966).

Relatively much research has been devoted to the question of the relationship between emotionality and criminality, usually with (adult) prisoners as subjects. In these investigations, delinquents were found to be more emotional than average (e.g., Burgess, 1972; Eysenck, 1977; Eysenck and Eysenck, 1970, 1971, 1977a,b). Denkers (1973) in a review study compared the findings of fourteen investigations, ten of which identified delinquents as more emotional, whereas four found no difference. Angenent (1974) compared sixteen investigations; fourteen of these found delinquents to be more emotional, in two studies there was no difference. Eysenck (1977) cited thirteen studies, in nine of which delinquents turned out to be more emotional.

Two comments should be made at this point. First, convicts do not constitute a true sample of delinquents and thus may differ from them in terms of personality characteristics. Second, results of research involving prisoners will be influenced by the prison situation.

What can be said about the emotionality of juvenile delinquents? Juvenile delinquents most often are young *and* male. Concerning age, it may be noted that young people usually are more emotional than older ones; in fact, emotionality decreases with age (Eysenck, 1956, 1958, 1959; S.B.G. Eysenck, 1960; Eysenck and Eysenck, 1964, 1969, 1970, 1977a; Eysenck and Wilson, 1975). On the other hand, men (boys) are less emotional than women (girls) (Bourduin et al., 1985; Buss and Plomin, 1975; Eysenck and Eysenck, 1964; Feij, 1979; Furnham, 1984; Hauber et al., 1986a; Kuiper and Feij, 1983; Stagner, 1974; Van Kampen, 1974; Zuckerman et al., 1988). Thus, on the basis of age one would expect higher emotionality, whereas on the basis of gender one would anticipate the opposite.

At issue here, as elsewhere in this book, is the comparison of juvenile delinquents with their peers. Well, juvenile delinquents generally do not appear to be more emotional than their peers. In other words, the percentage of emotional youngsters among juvenile delinquents is not very high. This is the case for recorded delinquency as well as for criminality reported in surveys. Emotionality appears to play a less important role in juvenile delinquency than it does in adult criminality (Arbuthnot et al., 1987; Farrington et al., 1982a; Forrest, 1977; Furnham, 1984; Hauber et al., 1986a; Lane, 1987; Rushton and Chrisjohn, 1981; Shapland et al., 1975).

The finding that emotional youngsters do not show much delinquent behaviour is surprising in light of the fact that (see the above provided description) their social adaptation is not optimal and that they also lead a problematic existence in other ways. Emotional youths, however, express their problems more readily through introverted deviant behaviour such as illness, use of medication, alcohol and drugs, suicide and so forth, than through extraverted behaviour such as delinquency. They certainly do not play a leading role in group delinquency, particularly because they are inclined to feel inferior to others and tend to play second fiddle when in a group. Moreover, they often display neurotic symptoms (e.g., daydreaming, crying easily), which do not make them too popular with other youngsters. Juvenile criminality more often leads to emotional problems than vice versa (Rutter and Giller, 1983).

This does not take away from the fact that within the population of juvenile delinquents there is a *type* labelled the "emotional delinquent". The delinquency of these youngsters is usually related to problematic personal functioning. Because of anxiety-proneness and fragility, these youngsters are inhibited in their self-expressions and social activities. They generally do not work through their frustrations or respond to them in some other active way. Instead, they keep their problems to themselves. Their criminality is sometimes an expression of resentment whereby they blame others for their own negative experiences.

The families from which these juvenile delinquents come are usually closed and not very harmonious, although there do not always have to be many conflicts. The parents are emotional and sometimes have neurotic tendencies. They have few social contacts. Their child rearing is dominant in nature and characterized by overprotection and intolerance. The child has little opportunity to become independent, and is offered too little chance to develop a normal social life (Hetherington et al., 1971; Jenkins, 1955, 1957; Jenkins and Lorr, 1953; Palmer, 1974; Quay, 1987c).

EXTRAVERSION

The basic trait of "extraversion" differentiates between extraverted and introverted persons.

Extraverted people are oriented toward the external world. They need company and fellowship. They have trouble entertaining themselves. They are active, lively, and talkative. They are happy and do not worry too easily. They like to have fun, liven up things, and love to go out and party. Extraverted persons are easily bored, they like activity, excitement, and sensation, and lean toward risky habits (smoking, drinking, gambling, drugs). They are impulsive and changeable (often change jobs, often move).

Introverted persons are the opposite. They are internally oriented, have little need to express themselves, and are independent and self sufficient in the sense that they are happy to be by themselves. They do not need a lot of people around them, except for a few good friends. Generally they stay in the background, especially when in the company of other people. They do not like to go out a lot and prefer to work by themselves (Angenent, 1974, 1985; Eysenck, 1977; Feij, 1979; Vagg and Hammond, 1976).

Extraversion is primarily genetically determined (Buss et al., 1973; Carey et al., 1978; Cattell, 1957, 1965; Floderus-Myrhed et al., 1980; Plomin and Rowe, 1977; Scarr, 1969). The biological basis for extraversion is the reactivity and the stimuli saturation level of the central and autonomic nervous systems; particularly the degree of activation of the frontal cortex and the activity of the reticular formation. How somebody ends up being extraverted depends on the environmental influences to which he or she is subjected. Introverts have a nervous system that is more sensitive to stimuli than that of extraverts. This means that they are more sensitive to very weak stimuli and that they dislike strong stimuli which they try to avoid. Extraverts, on the other hand, are hardly aware of weak stimuli. They do not avoid strong stimuli; on the contrary, they are attracted to them. Extraverts, therefore, need stronger stimulation than do introverts. Extraverts also get more easily accustomed to stimuli and therefore have a greater need for variation. In concrete terms this has as a result that extraverts are less sensitive to social influences, including child rearing practices. Because their need for stimulation is not sufficiently satisfied in daily life, they search for compensation, preferably in exciting activities, usually within the limits of what is acceptable. Some, however, exceed these limits. As an example of the latter, one may think of juvenile delinquents (Eysenck, 1977; Feij, 1979; Van der Kooij, 1987).

The extraversion of delinquents has been studied extensively, especially in (adult) prisoners. The results of these studies are not unanimous. In some investigations, delinquents appear more extraverted than average, whereas in others there is either no difference between delinquents and other people, or delinquents are found to be more introverted (Burgess, 1972; Eysenck and Eysenck, 1970, 1971, 1977a). Review studies confirm this picture. Denkers (1973) examined fourteen studies: delinquents turned out to be more extraverted in six studies, whereas in eight studies there was no difference. Angenent (1974) compared fifteen studies. Six of these showed delinquents to be more extraverted; eight found no differences between delinquents and others; in one study delinquents proved to be more introverted. Eysenck (1977), in reviewing thirteen studies, found that delinquents were clearly more extraverted in only four cases. Farrington et al. (1982a) compared fourteen studies. In five, delinquents were more extraverted, in another five there was no difference, and in the remaining four, they were more introverted. In short, there are no consistent results.

What is the situation with respect to juvenile delinquents? Where it concerns young delinquent boys, we might expect them to be rather extraverted. This expectation is based on two empirical facts: extraversion decreases with age, and males are more extraverted than females (Eysenck, 1977; S.B.G. Eysenck, 1960; Eysenck and Eysenck, 1964, 1969, 1970, 1977a; Eysenck and Wilson, 1975; Eysenck et al., 1969; Fitch, 1962; Van Kampen, 1974; Shaw and Hare, 1965).

What is more important, however, is the comparison between delinquent youths and their non-delinquent peers. Some studies have found that extraversion and delinquency are related. This applies to recorded as well as to survey-reported criminality (Alsopp and Feldman, 1976; Arbuthnot et al., 1987; Feldman, 1977; Forrest, 1977; Furnham, 1984; Glueck and Glueck, 1968, 1974; Hauber et al., 1986a; Lane, 1987; Rushton and Chrisjohn, 1981; Shapland et al., 1975). Other studies have not been able to confirm this (Farrington, et al., 1982a).

Extraversion is a very broad concept, a heterogenous notion comprising several sub-concepts (Angenent, 1985; Feij, 1979; Stewart, 1977). The fact that —as we have seen earlier— research results in this area are contradictory, could be because the respective studies focused on different sub-concepts. With respect to juvenile delinquency, the following three sub-concepts of extraversion are important: *sociability* (liking other people, looking for company), *impulsive behaviour* (restless, impatient, no self-control, thoughtless) and *need for excitement* (yearning for adventure, liking change and variety, not avoiding risks).

Because these concepts are sub-concepts of extraversion it is understandable that there is some overlap between them. That applies especially to impulsive behaviour and need for excitement. Zuckerman (1974, 1979) regarded impulsiveness as part of need for excitement. According to Buss and Plomin (1975) the reverse is true. Feij (1979) considered both concepts to be of the same order. Eysenck and Wilson (1975) looked upon impulsiveness as an extravert concept, and regarded need for excitement as a part of the basic characteristic of "toughness" (which will be examined later on). We won't pursue this discussion and will limit ourselves to an ideal-typical description of sociability, impulsiveness, and need for excitement, and their respective relationships with juvenile delinquency.

Sociability

Sociable people have a clear need to be with other people. They are socially responsive and prefer activities that involve contacts with others. They look for company, have many friends and acquaintances, and love parties. Besides this quantitative aspect (frequency of contacts), sociability also has a qualitative facet. Sociable people like contacts in which they are able to give and receive attention. In young children, sociability is mainly expressed by a need for interpersonal contact (for instance, with the mother). Later on in life, sociable people generally prefer social over non-social gratification (Buss and Plomin, 1975; Cattell, 1975; Eaves and Eysenck, 1975; Feij, 1979; Plomin and Rowe, 1977).

With respect to sociability, there is little difference between the sexes (Feij, 1979; Wilde, 1962). Sociability is to a large extent genetically determined (Carey et al., 1978; Dworkin et al., 1976; Floderus-Myrhed et al., 1980; Gottesman, 1963, 1966; Owen and Sines, 1970; Rushton et al., 1985; Scarr, 1965; 1969). Of course, the specific form of anyone's sociability depends on environmental influences (Buss and Plomin, 1975; Cattell, 1957; Eaves and Eysenck, 1975; Feij, 1979; Folker et al., 1980; Plomin and Rowe, 1977; Thomas and Chess, 1977).

Little research has been conducted on the relationship between sociability as such and juvenile delinquency. However, in studies of the relationship between extraversion and criminality, extraversion is often (more or less) defined as sociability (Angenent, 1974; Feij, 1979). Hence, some investigations of extraversion among juvenile delinquents actually deal with sociability. These studies indicate that juvenile delinquents are more sociable than other people. However, the last word concerning this question has not yet been said.

Furthermore, within the population of juvenile delinquents there is a *type* referred to as "sociable juvenile delinquent" (Hewitt and Jenkins, 1946; Loeber and Schmaling, 1985a; Peterson et al., 1959; Quay, 1964a,b, 1966, 1987c). Sociable juvenile delinquents have many friends, even though from a conventional point of view these friends usually are of the wrong kind. The influence of these friends and, in a wider context, of the subculture is considerable. Sociable juvenile delinquents maintain much contact with their friends and are very loyal to them (Akumatsu and

Farudi, 1978; Jenkins, 1955). These friends mean a lot to them and it is very important for them to be accepted and taken seriously by these comrades. In this context, bravura behaviour to impress friends is quite common. Contacts with friends to a certain extent replace those with family and school; the youngsters are not often home (come home late) and spend most of their time with friends. Sociable delinquents come from families where there is little consistency and where child rearing is permissive. There is a certain indifference toward each other within the family. Discipline is usually lax. The children are not adequately taught norms, supervision is slack (Hetherington et al., 1971). The children turn to the streets for amusement. In case of serious problems they run away from home. According to Quay (1987c) we find many truants among these youngsters.

Impulsiveness

There is not much agreement in the literature regarding the concept of impulsiveness. Gerbing et al. (1987) found at least twelve meanings of the concept (see also Eysenck and Eysenck, 1977b). Consequently, research results are rather divergent (Rotenberg and Nachshon, 1979).

In this book we will use a limited, narrowly defined meaning of impulsiveness; namely, an impaired ability to reflect on one's behaviour, as a result of which the possible consequences of a particular behaviour are only perceived in a restricted way. Impulsiveness is based on impaired impulse control because of a lack of inner inhibitions. There is less control exercised over need satisfaction, feelings, and decision taking (Buss and Plomin, 1975; Feij, 1979; Kipnis, 1971; Soppe, 1975). In impulsiveness we can distinguish sub-components such as, for example, high decision taking speed, lack of persistence, being bored easily, and dislike of monotony (Buss and Plomin, 1975).

Impulsive people act on the spur of the moment. They act in a determined manner. They are more doers than thinkers. This often causes them to regret their behaviour afterwards. But at the moment itself all that counts is the situation at hand. Previous experiences and subsequent consequences are pushed aside. All of a sudden an opportunity presents itself or a need arises and the impulsive person acts quickly without considering the pros and cons. All attention is absorbed by something for a short period of time.

Impulsive people do not stay with anything for very long and are easily distracted. One reason is that they have limited time perspective; for example, they do not like to make long-term plans, especially where it concerns abstract matters (Shapiro, 1965). An other reason is that they do not persevere; they are easily bored. All too soon things lose their interest; attention declines and is drawn toward something else. They are inclined to jump from one subject to the next. They are restless, can't sit still, and have trouble concentrating. They dislike monotony, need new and exciting experiences, have risky habits (smoking, drinking), and have trouble accepting conventional norms. Consequently, at a young age already they may run into problems (e.g., at school).

Buss and Plomin (1975) determined that about half of the studies they consulted made reference to a genetic component. Evidence for genetic factors has also been supplied by Buss et al. (1973), Eaves and Eysenck (1975), Folker et al. (1980), Owen and Sines (1970) and Zuckerman et al. (1988). Buss and Plomin (1975) assumed that impulsiveness develops mainly under the influence of environmental factors. In this context, Gordon et al. (1979) mentioned a cold and disciplinary child rearing regime. Zuckerman et al. (1980) pointed at the social influences that are related to the social role of the sexes (see Chapter 1). Feij (1979) doubted the existence of a hereditary component.

Although there generally is little difference between boys and girls in terms of impulsiveness (Buss and Plomin, 1975; Feij, 1979; Hauber et al., 1986a), boys seem to be somewhat more impulsive than girls (Saklofske and Eysenck, 1983; Zuckerman et al., 1978).

Many juvenile delinquents stand out because of their impulsiveness (Arbuthnot et al., 1987; Block and Block, 1980; Eysenck and McGurk, 1980; Feij, 1979; Hauber et al., 1986a; Saklofske and Eysenck, 1983; Wilson and Herrnstein, 1985). This impulsiveness causes them to easily engage in an activity without considering whether it exceed the limits of what is acceptable. The temptation of the moment causes them at times to succumb to matters that are really not permissible. Added to this is that they don't have much affinity with conventional norms. Moreover, the fact that impulsive youngsters pay little attention to the consequences of their behaviour implies that they have little understanding of the relationship between undesirable behaviour and the punishment that possibly follows. Because of this, they are not constrained in their criminal behaviour.

Time Perspective

A striking characteristic of impulsive people is their restricted time perspective, particularly their narrow perspective of the future. The latter perspective has a qualitative as well as a quantitative aspect. The qualitative aspect concerns the attitude one adopts toward the future (i.e., positive or negative). Juvenile delinquents often have a less positive outlook on the future. The quantitative aspect concerns how far the perspective stretches into the future. This is often related to the process of socialization (Stein et al., 1968) in which one adopts the future perspective that is common in one's own milieu because one has to function within that milieu.

Anticipating the future is essential for adequate behaviour. One can not live in the present only, because whatever one does today may have significant consequences tomorrow (or much later). Do youngsters look far into the future or only as far as their nose is long? Indeed, juveniles' perspective of the future is relatively short; it increases with age (Davids and Falkof, 1975; Tismer, 1987). More than is the case with adults, youngsters are inclined to immediately react to situations and not to worry too much about future consequences, particularly if these are far away in time. In this respect, delinquent youngsters are noted for their tendency to exaggerate matters. Their perspective of the future is more limited than that of their peers (Arbuthnot et al., 1987; Landau, 1976; Mischel, 1961; Mischel and Galligan, 1964; Stein et al., 1968; Wilson and Herrnstein, 1985).

Need for Excitement

The basis for the need for excitement is a craving for new, varied, and especially intense experiences (Zuckerman, 1974; Zuckerman and Link, 1968). Sub-components of the need for excitement include: sense of adventure, sensation-seeking, disinhibition, and being bored easily.

People who have a high need for excitement look for unexpected and stimulating experiences. They may find these in sports, especially in highly competitive and risky sports and all other kinds of activities involving speed and danger. They like change and are attracted to unusual events and experiences; they are not easily scared. They dislike monotony, routine, and the treadmill of everyday life. Furthermore, they detest dull people, that is to say, people *they* perceive as dull. In principle, they live rather independently of other people whom they mostly need for decor. They choose an unusual and, if necessary, unadapted lifestyle and enjoy extravagant experiences. They often change jobs, move often, like to let off steam by socially unrestrained behaviour (wild parties), and are sexually active (change sexual partners frequently). They have trouble accepting conventional norms and indulge in risky habits (smoking, drinking, gambling, drugs) (Ellis, 1987a; Feij, 1979).

The hereditary component of the need for excitement is discussed, among others, by Farley (1986), Folker et al. (1980), and Zuckerman et al. (1972, 1988).

As far as the relationship between need for excitement and juvenile delinquency is concerned, we notice in the first place that this need decreases with age (Ball et al., 1984; Zuckerman et al., 1978, 1980). In personality development, the need for excitement reaches its peak in the youth period (Farley, 1986; Hamilton, 1983). We have seen in Chapter 2 that youngsters are adventurous and inquisitive, whereas older people have a greater need for order and safety. According to Ball et al. (1984), this decrease with age is caused by biological factors.

Furthermore, men generally have a greater need for excitement than women, and boys a greater one than girls (Bontekoe, 1984; Farley, 1986; Feij, 1979; Saklofske and Eysenck, 1983). This difference may probably be explained by the dissimilarity in role patterns (Ball et al., 1984; Kuiper and Feij, 1983; Zuckerman, 1974; Zuckerman et al., 1978). Among juvenile delinquents there appear to be quite a few youngsters with a great need for excitement (Donelly, 1981; Farley, 1986; Farley and Farley, 1972; Feij, 1979; Hauber et al., 1986a; Laufer et al., 1981; Rotenberg and Nachshon, 1979; Wallbank, 1985; Whitehill et al., 1976; Wilson and Herrnstein, 1985; Zuckerman, 1974).

In school, youngsters with a need for excitement do stand out because they misbehave more often (out of boredom) (Wasson, 1980, 1981). Of course, youths may try to satisfy their need in a socially permissible way by looking for acceptable risky and adventurous experiences (e.g., car-, motor-, gocart-, and motorbike races). The need for excitement by definition renders youngsters with such needs more susceptible to deviant behaviour, which usually is more exhilarating and adventurous than adapted behaviour. Moreover, excitement seekers are less sensitive to socialization and as a result have adopted fewer conventional norms (Feij, 1979). Consequently, they are less susceptible to feelings of guilt and shame. This, in combination with an absence of anxiety, causes such youngsters to be attracted to delinquency and other forms of deviant behaviour.

TOUGHNESS

This basic trait (toughness versus mildness) contrasts an intellectual and practical attitude with an emotional and aesthetic orientation (Cattell, 1957, 1965, 1973; Eysenck, 1977; Eysenck and Wilson, 1975; Feij, 1979; Orlebeke, 1972; Vagg and Hammond, 1976). Control, realism, and alertness as opposed to sensitivity, dreaminess and warmheartedness.

Toughness consists of sub-characteristics such as: aggressiveness, self-consciousness, achievement orientation, tendency toward manipulation, dogmatism, and masculinity. In the literature toughness is sometimes referred to with terms like (dis)agreeableness and excitability.

Tough people are capable, creative, and decisive; they show initiative, and are able to assume responsibility. They rely more on intellect than on intuition, but especially on themselves. They dislike sentimentality. Their behaviour is cool and indifferent, reserved, dry, and impersonal; they show little emotion and are not easily thrown off balance. They have a practical, logical, not very idealistic attitude, are inflexible, rigid, and tenacious, and do not believe in compromise. They are self-sufficient individualists who take an independent and egocentric stance. Their self-interest usually comes first and they know how to fend for themselves. They are ambitious and greedy, out to improve their position, and aggressive in competition with others. They are domineering and bossy, like to prove themselves, and try to impose their wishes on other people. When frustrated, they easily resort to obstructive behaviour.

Mild people are the opposite of tough people. They are nice, friendly, cordial, attentive, open, and spontaneous. They are expressive and sensitive and have a good sense of humour, but little patience. Their intuition, aesthetic taste, fantasy, and imagination are well developed. They trust others and are sometimes somewhat gullible. They cooperate, accommodate, and tend to be dependent on other people. Mild people are more idealistic than materialistic.

Hereditary factors of toughness have been mentioned by Cattell (1957, 1965), Eysenck and Eysenck (1976) and Rushton et al. (1985).

There is a clear gender difference which shows men to be more tough and women to be more mild (Eysenck and Wilson, 1975; Feij, 1979; Miller, 1974; Zuckerman et al., 1988). Compared to their peers, juvenile delinquents are characterized by toughness (Allsop and Feldman, 1976; Furnham, 1984; Rushton and Chrisjohn, 1981).

Aggressiveness

The sub-trait of toughness which traditionally is most often related to juvenile delinquency, is aggressiveness (Campagna and Harter, 1975; Fodor, 1972, 1973; Jurkovic and Prentice, 1977; Quay, 1965a).

A distinction should be made between aggressiveness and aggression (Megargee and Hokanson, 1970; Steenstra and Bogaards, 1978). Aggressiveness is a personality characteristic, which encompasses more than merely showing aggressive behaviour at a higher than usual rate. Aggression is belligerent behaviour which may be the result of this personality characteristic, but which also may have different causes. Much aggression is displayed by people who qua personality are not very aggressive, for example, aggression related to professional criminality. The aggressive behaviour of youngsters is often the result of group influences and of a situation getting out of control (see Chapter 6).

Aggressive people are egocentric, do not stand for much, and show little consideration for other people. They are not very constructive, do not avoid confrontation, and do not think anything of exploiting others. They are maladapted in social intercourse, even when other people treat them in a friendly manner. Some behave rudely, use foul language, and show off. Aggressive people have little fear. Their ability to empathize is limited and they do not easily attach themselves to others. Because of their egoism and untrustworthiness they have few friends. They are often at odds with the people around them, particularly with their parents. They are not easy to raise. The word obedience is foreign to them. They particularly care little for authority figures. With respect to the latter, some are constantly on the attack and challenge and defy authority figures. Already in childhood (e.g., in school) do they run into problems because of this (Lane, 1987). Aggressive persons may be suspicious, jealous, and bitter. As children they sometimes out of spite commit petty theft within their own milieu (at home and at school).

Aggressive persons show much overt and covert aggressive behaviour which expresses itself in many different ways (e.g., sarcasm, gossiping, and swearing). They also commit violent acts against persons, animals, and objects, showing little compassion in the process. They quarrel frequently and are often involved in fights. Their moral development is not at a very high level. They are impervious to punishment, feelings of guilt, and remorse. They readily place the blame on others.

Aggressiveness decreases with age (Hyde, 1984). Boys are more aggressive than girls (Deluty et al., 1988). The cause for this is sought in biological differences (hypoactive nervous system, higher testosterone level in boys which makes them more excitable) as well as in environmental differences (social role, differences in child rearing, see Chapters 1 and 4). Girls are not as easily tempted to behave aggressively because their sense of self-worth is not that easily hurt. They are less status and achievement oriented than boys, which makes them less sensitive in this respect. It may be noted, however, that girls express their aggression more indirectly (compare what we said in Chapter 1 about the covert and indirect delinquency of girls). Because aggression to some extent is the result of environmental factors, it is to be expected that aggression in girls will increase with the emancipation of women (Hyde, 1984).

There has been much discussion concerning the possible hereditary nature of aggressiveness. For example, Rushton (1987) and Rushton and Erdle (1987) believe that the behaviour is hereditary, whereas Campbell et al. (1985, 1987) do not (see also: Eysenck and Eysenck, 1976; Owen and Sines, 1970; Rushton et al., 1985; and Scarr, 1966). These disagreements are undoubtedly related to the fact that the term aggressiveness is not understood by everyone to mean the same thing.

Aggressive youngsters have a greater chance of getting involved in delinquency (Eysenck and Wilson, 1975; Glueck and Glueck, 1950; Lorr and Jenkins, 1953; Mannheim, 1965; Olweus, 1978; Quay, 1987c; Rushton and Chrisjohn, 1981; West and Farrington, 1977). Instead of aggressive delinquents, the literature often uses the terms asocial delinquents, antisocial delinquents, psychopaths, or sociopaths.

Aggressiveness may already be noted during childhood, and it correlates with delinquency at a later age (Hanson et al., 1984; Hyde, 1984; Roff and Wirt, 1984). Aggressive delinquents frequently come from disharmonious families (Andry, 1960; Bandura and Walters, 1959; Fodor, 1972; Gordon et al., 1979; Hewitt and Jenkins, 1946; McCord and McCord, 1964; Roff and Wirt, 1984; Steenstra and Bogaards, 1978). Child rearing often is cold and inconsistent. The relationship between the parents is problematic. The latter are not very prepared for their task or refuse to accept their parental role. The youngsters usually have a bad relationship with their parents and experience their child rearing as cool and rejecting and sometimes even as openly hostile. Discipline is arbitrary. Really surprising is the permissive attitude of the parents toward aggressive behaviour, and their detached child rearing methods such as corporal punishments, threats, and emotional outbursts (DiLalla et al., 1988). We often see that aggressive children have aggressive parents (Hyde, 1984). Finally, aggressive delinquents frequently are recidivists and often come in contact with police and justice officials (Mack, 1969; Quay, 1987c; Quay et al., 1960).

CONSCIENTIOUSNESS

This basis trait is expressed in a sense of duty, punctuality, loyalty, and adherence to conventional norms and rules (Cattell, 1957, 1973; Cattell and Nichols, 1972; Eysenck, 1977; Feij, 1979; Orlebeke, 1972; Royce, 1973; Sells et al., 1970; Vagg and Hammond, 1976).

Conscientiousness refers more to general common decency than to a high-principled conscience. In the literature it is also referred to as superego-strength, meticulousness, conformity, and conventionality.

Conscientious people are decent, serious people who are honest and trustworthy and have an adequate sense of responsibility. They are usually disciplined and dedicated to their work. They show devotion and care in their dealings with others, take the feelings of others into account, and act with tact and attention. They are flexible, have no trouble adapting themselves, are cooperative, and look for harmony rather than conflict. As children they are obedient. They need order and neatness. In their work they are precise and accurate. This also applies to youngsters at school; they are interested in educational matters and try their best.

In contrast to conscientious people, there are *careless* people. Socially, the latter have an egocentric, self-serving attitude, and they do not care too much about other people. They neglect their social responsibilities, do not honour agreements and promises, have no feeling for "fair play", and have little in the way of scruples. They avoid their obligations. Rather, they are boastful and immune to social disapproval. They are unconventional or even eccentric in their behaviour. One can not rely on them. They often do things in a haphazard fashion. As children they are disobedient. They usually have little regard for norms and formal rules, which may easily lead to maladapted behaviour, including delinquency.

Carey et al. (1978) and Rushton et al. (1985) suggested that conscientiousness may have hereditary origins. Negative relationships have been found between the behaviour and impulsiveness and need for excitement, whereas there appear to be no relationships with sociability and gender (Feij, 1979; Zuckerman, 1974). Conscientiousness and intelligence are somewhat related. Conscientious behaviour is usually preceded by a moral judgment for which insight is a prerequisite (Jurkovic and Prentice, 1977; Selman, 1971; Tomlinson-Keasy and Keasy, 1974).

The relationship between conscientiousness and juvenile delinquency is a particularly interesting one. The aspect of conscientiousness that is specifically associated with juvenile delinquency is the question of whether or not one follows conventional norms. Norms (or their absence) generally play a central role in the development of juvenile delinquency. Therefore, we will discuss norms more extensively later on, after we have completed our discussion of personality traits.

IMMATURITY

Immaturity is a trait often mentioned in publications about juvenile delinquency (Dublineau, 1964; Frisk et al., 1966; Glueck and Glueck, 1968; Peterson et al., 1959; Quay, 1964a,b, 1966, 1987c; Quay et al., 1960).

Compared to their peers, immature youths often have an identity that is not yet very clear (Newman and Newman, 1976). They live their lives in the unrealistic manner of a child. They lack goal-directedness, drive, and decisiveness, and passively allow matters to take their course. They are not able to face the problems of everyday life, especially if their immaturity is coupled with a low intelligence. Immaturity is often accompanied by hyperactivity and learning disabilities, especially concentration problems. Immature youngsters usually realize that they are different. Of course, being different in the youth period can be detrimental in itself. Immature youngsters are treated as if they were younger than they actually are, and they have low social status among their friends and peers. The feeling of not being accepted easily causes them to feel isolated (Palmer, 1974). This may be accompanied by low self-esteem, feelings of inferiority, and neurotic symptoms. Immature youths tend to look up to others, accommodate themselves to others, and allow themselves to be led, especially by authority figures (Akamutsa and Farudi, 1978). They have a need for security and safety (Frisk et al., 1966), which they try to satisfy by seeking recognition from others (e.g., by showing off, by playing the clown).

Boys generally are more immature than girls. In girls, it is early maturity that is the greater problem, especially because they are on the average two years ahead of boys to begin with. Precocious girls associate with older boys and girls and as a result act as if they were older: they participate earlier in activities such as smoking, absenteeism, and so forth. Although there seems to be hardly any relationship between immaturity and delinquency in girls (Magnusson et al., 1985), the relationship is rather obvious in boys. Immature boys show little initiative and thus are dependent on others. Moreover, they are easily influenced, particularly by friends who may have a certain degree of power over them. If criminal acts are demanded of them, they do not often resist. Their need to prove themselves, if any, forms an extra motivation to participate in criminal behaviour.

PERSONALITY TRAITS AND JUVENILE DELINQUENCY

In popular language one sometimes refers to a "delinquent tendency", as if there were a specific personality trait or a coherent organization of personality traits which predisposes people —in our case, juveniles— to delinquent behaviour. Such "criminal" personality traits do not exist. The personality traits discussed in this chapter are present in everybody, albeit not to the same degree.

The relationships between the various personality traits and juvenile delinquency generally are not very strong. One may therefore conclude that the average influence of traits on delinquency is limited. Only if *extreme* personality traits are present is there an increased possibility that youngsters will get involved in delinquency. It should be noted, however, that extreme personality traits do not inevitably lead to deviant behaviour (besides the fact that in every kind of behaviour, including deviant behaviour, there are always many factors at play). Extremes may result in either positive or negative consequences (Zuckerman, 1974). "The hero and the psychopath are types from the same branch" (Lykken, 1981). Creative artists are often extremely emotional and impulsive (Eysenck and Wilson, 1975). A person's need for excitement may be expressed in flair and creativity (Feij, 1979). Science also profits from the need for excitement in people: volunteers who sign up to serve as subjects in a scientific experiment have been found to have a strikingly high need for excitement (Wallbank, 1985).

Yet, it may be said that extreme personality traits carry with them a lack of balance. Although most of the time this lack of balance is well compensated for, it sometimes creates problems, and thus generally requires attention (Buss and Plomin, 1975; Eysenck and Wilson, 1975). Eventual negative complications do not always have to be criminal in nature. The extreme types are not only found among juvenile delinquents, but also among youths with other forms of deviant behaviour (e.g., running away, alcohol abuse, drug addiction) (Hewitt and Jenkins, 1946; Quay, 1987c).

It should be noted, of course, that in reality it is not the separate traits, but the total personality which determines whether or not criminal acts will be committed. Therefore, attempts have been made —with varying degrees of success— to find the combination of personality traits, (personality profile) which possibly predisposes a youngster toward delinquency. Many of such combination found thus far may actually be traced back to the basic traits of our model (Gearing, 1979; Gough et al., 1965; Hathaway and Monachesi, 1963; Monachesi and Hathaway, 1969).

The relationship between personality traits and juvenile delinquency is in part *direct*. Less intelligent youngsters are less able to foresee the consequences of their behaviour. Impulsive youngsters do not reflect sufficiently before they start something. Youngsters with a need for excitement tend to weigh this need heavily in their deliberations of whether or not they will get involved in delinquency. Aggressive youngsters are not very concerned about the negative consequences their behaviour may have for others. Youths who are not very conscientious do not worry about conventional rules. Immature youngsters want to maintain themselves no matter what, and are prepared to go far for this, even if it involves delinquency.

There is also an *indirect* relationship between personality traits and juvenile delinquency. Personality traits may have as result that one functions less adequately in interpersonal relationships, which in turn has negative repercussions for one's acquisition of norms and identity formation.

The relationship between extreme personality traits and juvenile delinquency is more evident in two cases:

1. Extreme personality traits (e.g., extreme aggressiveness) may contribute to a failure in social adjustment at a very young age. In that case, children may already in the family behave in an antisocial manner (fighting, stealing, lying, temper tantrums, irritability). If the parents, possibly after having sought professional help, are not able to do anything about it, this *early-deviant behaviour* will also be shown elsewhere, for example at school and in contacts with peers. Because such behaviour will not be tolerated, such youngsters will be ostracized. They will turn into maladapted loners or will search for contacts with similarly afflicted individuals. As a result, they end up in a vicious circle from which it is difficult to escape. Especially when people behave criminally throughout their lives, or at least the greater part of their lives, this indicates the presence of extreme personality traits (Glueck, 1966; Loeber, 1982; Loeber and Dishion, 1983; Olweus, 1979, 1980a,b; Roff and Wirt, 1984, 1985; Spivack and Cianci, 1987; Werner, 1987).

2. In the youth period, during normal development, certain traits that are related to criminality (for example impulsiveness and need for excitement) are more pronounced and as such may encourage delinquency. We highlighted this in Chapter 2. Youngsters who have always possessed these traits to an extreme degree, will show them even more during the youth period and will have an even greater chance of becoming involved in delinquency.

NORMS

Norm Systems

Someone's norms, as inner rules for behaviour, form a frame of reference which guides behaviour. This set of norms does not only concern undesirable behaviour —the topic of this book— but also desirable conduct. It is not only involved in "thou shall not", but also in "thou shall". One tends to show behaviour that is consistent with one's own norm system and to avoid behaviour that is not.

Norm systems may vary widely. Mapes (1968) mentioned an angry phone call someone received from the father of his son's friend. The father complained that this son always stole pencils from his friend. "Don't get me wrong, it is a matter of principle" he said, "I myself can take as many pencils home from the office as I like".

The main focus of this book is the question of the degree to which someone's personal norms deviate from the conventional ones. Some (general) norms are found all over the world to an extent that it appears that they are genetically based (Kohlberg, 1976; Piaget, 1965). Biological explanations for norms are found in the works of, among others, Crombag (1983), Dawkinds (1976) and Wilson (1978). Perhaps, some norms originally have an instinctive basis, possibly related to an evolutionary need for survival (Campbell, 1975). This could explain why one usually spontaneously adheres to these norms (Wright, 1974). However, norms are particularly acquired through the experiences one has with other people in one's milieu and society.

The acquisition of norms has an intellectual and an affective aspect (Arbuthnot et al., 1987). In concrete cases the emphasis sometimes lies on the one aspect and sometimes on the other. The *intellectual* facet, for instance, is more pronounced when on the basis of information and discussion one concludes that a certain behaviour is desired or undesired (Krebs and Miller, 1985). This requires an ability to compare and weigh several behaviour possibilities. One has to be able to estimate what the consequences of the behaviour would be for not only oneself but also for others. To do the latter, one has to be able to put oneself in the place of those others (Rest, 1983). As far as the *affective* aspect is concerned, the more emotionally attractive norms are, the greater the probability that one will adopt them. For the transference of norms within one's own milieu this means that one adopts norms especially from persons with whom one feels emotionally connected (Ewin-Smith, 1984). For the transference of societal norms this means that the more one feels part of society, the more one will adopt its norms. Youngsters do not differ much from adults in this respect (Social and Cultural Planning Bureau, 1985).

Adoption of Norms

Youngsters are confronted with norms in their own milieu as well as in the broader framework of society. They learn norms in the first place from groups they associate with on a daily basis, such as the family, the school, and their circle of friends. However, it should be noted that being a member of a group does not automatically mean that one will adopt its norms. Rather, one must feel an affinity with the group before norm transfer will take place (Wright, 1974).

Within the groups, youngsters particularly adopt norms from significant others (Hirschi, 1969; Piaget, 1965). The latter influence their behaviour in four ways:

1. They are in a good position to supervise youngsters. They are aware of their behaviour, know their ideas, and usually are in frequent con-

tact with them.
2. Youngsters usually care about this supervision, because they do not want to disappoint these significant others.
3. Even if the latter ones would not be able to personally notice any undesirable behaviour, youngsters will (probably) abstain from it anyhow because of a sense of loyalty to these persons whom, they know, would disapprove. In such cases it seems as if these persons are present even though they are not.
4. Significant others contribute —especially by their example— to the formation of the norm system of youngsters because the latter adopt their norms.

The *family*, as the most prominent primary group in our culture, is the institution from which children derive most of their norms. The parents in particular serve as examples. Children's norm systems therefore usually resembles those of the parents (Friedlander, 1952; Hudgins and Prentice, 1973).

This process proceeds easier if the child has a good relationship with the parents; especially, if that relationship is so good that the child identifies with them. Because most children get along well with their parents and thus identify with them, they will adopt their norms. Because most parents have rather conventional norms and behave in an adjusted manner, most youngsters consequently will behave in a similar way (Arbuthnot et al., 1987; Holstein, 1976; Hudgins and Prentice, 1973; Olejnik, 1980; Peterson et al., 1979; Wright, 1974).

As far as juvenile delinquents are concerned, we will see that they often come from disharmonious families where the internal relationships leave a lot to be desired. These youngsters do not feel part of the family and do not feel involved in its functioning. They do not get along very well with their parents; there is no real close parent-child relationship. The youngsters ignore their parents, do not think much of their authority, and are not prepared to follow their advice or example. In such cases there is no smooth transference of norms. Consequently, delinquent youths differ in their norms from their parents to a greater extent than do other youngsters (Arbuthnot et al., 1987; Canter, 1982a; Jurkovic and Prentice, 1974; Nye, 1958; Snyder and Patterson, 1987).

Besides in the family, youngsters are also exposed to norms at *school*, norms which may differ from those they know from home. This in itself may cause problems. In most cases youngsters generally adhere to the norms of their parents. The influence of the school happens to be less strong than that of the family, it plays more of a supplementary role. The more similarity there is between the norms of the family and those of the school, the greater the influence of the school will be. The influence is also more pronounced if, on a personal level, there is a good relationship with fellow students and teachers. In general, schools are more geared toward transferring knowledge than toward contributing to the personality formation of their students. The school does not have much influence on delinquent youths in particular. The latter do not feel very involved in what is happening at school, neither in class nor during extracurricular activities. In such cases, transference of norms is rather impaired (Angenent, 1988).

As far as the influence of *friends* is concerned, it depends on what kind of friends the youngsters have. Friends may have a negative influence if they adhere to norms that are less disapproving of criminality than is the case in the dominant culture (Sutherland and Cressey, 1978). We will see that delinquent youngsters often have delinquent friends. The weaker the influence of the family and the school, the greater will be the influence of friends on the norm system of youngsters.

So far we have discussed youths who grow up in a milieu with conventional norms. If they conform to this milieu, which most youngsters do, they will embrace the conventional norms and grow up to be well-adjusted persons. If they do not accept these norms, problems may arise, although this is not inevitable. It is very well possible that youngsters distance themselves from the customary conventional norms and adopt other norms which do not lead to illegal or maladaptive behaviour. Nevertheless, the probability that youngsters who reject conventional norms will participate in delinquency is relatively great.

Not all milieus adhere to acceptable norms. There is a lot of variation in this respect. In some milieus, one is not too concerned with conventional norms and one disapproves less of criminal behaviour. When youngsters grow up in such an environment, matters are rather complicated. Those who have good relationships within such a milieu, appear to run the risk of becoming maladapted individuals, even though in reality this is not always necessarily the case (Hirschi, 1969). But also for youths who do not conform to such milieus, the prognosis is not all that favourable. In psycho-social terms, one could consider these youngsters to be doubly disadvantaged.

As we noted earlier, youths also come in contact with norms in the larger setting of society. As far as the adoption of these norms is concerned, one important aspect is the extent to which youngsters feel part of society. If they feel that they belong, they will identify with society and will accept the moral significance of the norm and value system of the dominant culture. Then, they will be inclined to conform, to listen to what authorities and institutions have to say, and to recognize their power. If involvement is lacking, youngsters are more inclined to disregard society's norms and not bother with rules and regulations.

One might ask at this point whether the examples youths observe in society can always be regarded as positive. Does society know its responsibilities in this respect? Are adults usually good models? We are not just talking here about the familiar examples of misery and aggression youngsters may see on television. There are more simple examples closer to home. For example, what percentage of people adheres to speed limits? How widespread is fraud? How creative are people in filling out their income tax returns? Youngsters often hear via the media about important people who commit fraud, and they note how lightly those people often get off. This does not encourage faith in society, solidarity with the community, and adoption of social norms. On the contrary, it invites one to become rather "flexible" oneself.

Old and New Norms

When they enter the youth period, youngsters characteristically begin to question the norms they have learned as children (see Chapter 2). This process is sometimes referred to as emancipation and the erosion of norms. This moving away from accepted norms happens at a time when youngsters have not yet acquired new ones. They find themselves in a *moratorium*, a period of exploration during which a reorientation takes place (Erikson, 1950, 1980). Thus, to a certain extent they live in a moral vacuum and therefore are temporarily vulnerable to delinquent influences. Usually, however, this vacuum is not that bad because most adhere to a large extent to the norms they learned at home. In the long run, most youths acquire a new norm system (identity achievement). Often, they more or less come back to their old norms. Youngsters who distance themselves from the conventional norms generally derive their norms in part from friends and subcultures (Cloward and Ohlin, 1960; Cohen, 1955). Their criminal inclination in that case depends on the norms adhered to by these friends and subcultures.

Among the youths who distance themselves from conventional norms there are some who do not manage to develop a new set of norms, or who possibly are not looking for it (identity diffusion). These are youngsters in whose life norms are not important. They usually are aware of norms, but these have no bearing on their behaviour. Such youths have a vaguely defined identity and are open to all sorts of influences, including those of a criminal nature (Blasi, 1980; Matza, 1964).

Finally, there are youngsters who unquestioningly adhere to the norms they learned at home and for whom therefore very little changes (foreclosure). They are not very susceptible to criminal influences (Adams et al., 1985; Marcia, 1966; Todor and Marcia, 1973).

Norm Levels

The norm system one maintains is not fixed, but develops over the years with increasingly higher levels of moral judgment (Piaget, 1965). This development may be illustrated by the model of Kohlberg (1964). According to this model, one passes through three levels of moral judgment, each consisting of two stages, for a total of six. Each subsequent stage involves a more complex and abstract way of moral reasoning.

The first level is the *preconventional* or premoral level. At this level, moral values do not yet have an independent significance. The child does not distinguish between moral and self-satisfying values.

In the first stage (reward and punishment), the morality of behaviour is judged on the basis of its consequences. Good behaviour is behaviour that is rewarded and bad behaviour is behaviour that is punished. To the child, good behaviour consists of looking for rewards and avoiding punishment.

The second stage (egoism) is hedonistic-individualistic. The morality criterion of behaviour is the degree to which needs are satisfied. Good is what the behaving person experiences as pleasant.

The second level is the *conventional* or conformistic level. Moral values are viewed in the light of social adjustment. This level is reached in later childhood. The needs of the individual become subservient to the needs of society. Good is whatever the environment dictates it is. The child comes to understand, accept, and uphold social rules and expectations.

In the third stage (interpersonal harmony), the morality of behaviour depends on the approval of others. Establishing good relationships with others is central.

In the fourth stage (law and order), the criterion of morality is the extent to which behaviour agrees with the conventional social order. Central is the acceptance and maintenance of the social system, including authority relationships.

The third level is the *postconventional* or principled level where the morality of behaviour is weighed against personal formulations of the basic moral principles which underlie the rules. This level is reached in the youth period. The external orientation is replaced by an internal one. One's own responsibility gains in importance. In every situation one evaluates whether and to what degree general rules are applicable, and whether or not one agrees with these. One begins to differentiate between rules based on social agreements and norms based on moral principles. Social conventions lose their absolute character. Universal norms are placed above social agreements.

In the fifth stage (social contract), the morality of behaviour is judged in terms of individual rights and democratically accepted rules. Central are concepts such as social usefulness and wellbeing.

In the sixth stage (universal ethical principles), the moral criterion is the individual's personal conscience. Central are concepts such as mutual respect, trust, justice, and equality.

In the process of moral development one progresses through the various stages, although not everybody reaches the last stage. The fact that one reaches a higher level does not mean that one completely loses the values of the preceding ones. In fact, a person's level of moral judgment varies depending on the question under consideration. Regarding juvenile delinquents it has been found that particularly where it concerns their own criminal behaviour, their moral judgement functions at a lower level (Jurkovic, 1980).

It is sometimes assumed that juvenile delinquents generally lag behind other youngsters in their moral development. In other words, juvenile delinquents are thought to possess an immature moral judgment (Fodor, 1972; Ruma and Mosher, 1967). Their orientation is more egocentric in nature and they are primarily interested in the satisfaction of their own needs and desires. Behavioural constraints will have to come from their own milieu (Hudgins and Prentice, 1973). However, research findings are not unanimous on this point (Jurkovic and Prentice, 1974).

Moreover, according to some authors this question is in fact rather complicated. It appears that juvenile delinquents who are involved in criminal behaviour primarily because of their maladjusted personality (aggressive delinquents, psychopaths), function at the preconventional level. Other juvenile delinquents, however, function at the conventional level. Among the latter we find relatively greater feelings of guilt and shame (Campagna and Harter, 1975; Fodor, 1973; Jurkovic and Prentice, 1977; Ruma and Mosher, 1967).

In light of what has been said thus far about child rearing and the family in connection with the transference of norms, one might expect that there would be a relationship between the parents' level of moral reasoning and that of their children. Indeed, several studies have found that mothers of delinquents have a lower level of moral judgement than do mothers of non-delinquent youths (Hudgins and Prentice, 1973). Research in this area, however, is not unanimous (Jurkovic, 1980).

Norms and Juvenile Delinquency

The readiness of youngsters to get involved in delinquency depends in part on the norms they follow (Arbuthnot et al., 1987; Brennan et al., 1978; Chandler, 1973; Elliott and Voss, 1974; Glueck and Glueck, 1950; Gordon et al., 1963; Heather, 1979; Hepburn, 1977; Hirschi, 1969; Lawrence, 1985; Schwabe-Holein, 1984; Sutherland and Cressey, 1978; Thompson and Dodder, 1983).

Criminal behaviour which poses no problems for one youth will be rejected by another. Norms may act as internal constraints on delinquency. The more youngsters accept conventional norms, the more one normally can appeal to their sense of norms in the fight against delinquency. In some cases this may have a greater effect than sanctions (Schwartz and Orleans, 1967; Tittle and Rowe, 1973).

As far as knowledge of conventional norms is concerned, delinquent youths differ little from non-delinquent ones. Some acknowledge the legitimacy of conventional norms and recognize their moral value. Others acknowledge the legitimacy of conventional norms, but don't accept their moral value. For others again, norms are merely verbal conventions which have little to do with behaviour (Briar and Piliavin, 1965). What is remarkable is that delinquent youngsters do not condemn criminal behaviour, particularly the kind in which they themselves are involved (Angenent, 1972; Hindelang, 1970, 1974a; Siegel et al., 1973).

The criminal norm system, to coin a term, often exists already *before* the youngster actually commits criminal behaviour (Hepburn, 1977; Liska, 1975; Sutherland and Cressey, 1978). On the other hand, it is also the case that the more one is involved in delinquency, the less one will condemn it. A gradual weakening of the influence of conventional norms takes place because of habituation (Merton, 1968).

La Pierre (1934) concluded in his —by now classic— publication that there is considerable difference between the opinions people have about norms (their moral judgment) and the way in which they express norms in their behaviour. At issue here is the phenomenon that people say that they will behave in one way, but in reality act in a different way (Wicker,

1969). There are authors (e.g., Blasi, 1980), by the way, who believe that this phenomenon is not that widespread. Nevertheless, people vary greatly in this respect. Some are reasonably faithful to their moral judgment, whereas in others the relationship is far from easy to find. The difference between moral judgment and behaviour —between theory and practice— usually is remarkably large among juvenile delinquents (Jurkovic, 1980; Matza, 1964; Mitchell and Dodder, 1983).

Neutralization

A small group of very deviant youths chooses more or less consistently for deviant norms. These norms are often diametrically opposed to those of the dominant culture. These youngsters usually belong to a criminal subculture which may be thought of as an anticulture.

In the lives of most delinquent youths, however, both the norms of the dominant, conventional culture and those of the delinquent subculture play a role. These youths usually view these cultures as two separate worlds. The norms of these two worlds often can not be combined because they conflict with one another. Both cultures are available simultaneously; the youngsters as it were "float" between the two cultures (Cernkovich, 1978a; Matza, 1964). In particular cases they sometimes choose one direction and sometimes the other. Conventional norms occasionally are temporarily ignored under the influence of adventure, excitement, and so forth. (Buffalo and Rodgers, 1971; Matza, 1964; Regoli and Poole, 1978; Siegel et al., 1973; Velarde, 1978).

In light of the above, it is possible that an individual's criminal behaviour clashes with his or her (conventional) norm system (deviancy-conflict). In such cases, the need may arise, possibly to prevent impairment of self-evaluation, to rationalize the behaviour by ignoring its negative value (Mitchell and Dodder, 1983). The criminality is blamed on factors over which one has no control, and responsibility for the delinquency is denied (it often involves an expanding or creative application of excuses that would be rather acceptable in a different context). We speak in those cases of verbalization (Cressey, 1953) or neutralization (personal neutralization) (Sykes and Matza, 1957). Thus, juvenile delinquents may, for instance, point out that criminal behaviour *in general* is wrong, but that it was unavoidable *in their situation*.

These reasons may and in many cases should be considered excuses. In other cases, self-deception is at work. But, in other cases again a sense of guilt and feelings of shame may be present (Sykes and Matza, 1957). Sometimes, what seems to be neutralization is not neutralization at all, but merely an explanation of the motives of the delinquents as these relate to their deviant sense of norms (Minor, 1981).

Neutralization may occur after the fact, as a kind explanation for oneself and others. It may, however, also take place prior to the criminal behaviour. Neutralization then becomes a motive to engage in criminality. The latter occurs, for example, in the case of recidivism. After the fact neutralization following a previous crime becomes prior neutralization in a subsequent crime. Therefore, neutralization may encourage recidivism (Bandura, 1977; Hindelang, 1973; Hirschi, 1969; Killias, 1981; Merton, 1968; Minor, 1981, 1984). The literature identifies five forms of neutralization (Amelang et al., 1988; Ball, 1983; Ball and Lilly, 1971; Hindelang, 1973; Hirschi, 1969; Matza, 1964; Mitchell and Dodder, 1983; Sykes and Matza, 1957):

1. The youngsters avoid taking responsibility by claiming circumstances beyond their control. For example, they point at conditions which left them no way out (e.g., peer pressure); at coincidence (e.g., having had too much to drink); at their background (e.g., lack of knowledge, poor parental child rearing, bad friends); and at mistakes ("it was an accident"; "it was not meant that way").
2. The youngsters deny that people or agencies have been (seriously) harmed. The bike was not stolen, but merely borrowed and forgotten to be returned. The store can always claim the theft-damage from the insurance company.
3. The individuals blame the victims (to a certain extent); they only got what they deserved. If people are so careless with their possessions (e.g., do not properly lock their house or car), or if they behave so stupidly (e.g., girls walking alone in the woods at night), then they also must carry full responsibility for the consequences. Moreover, the youngsters may suggest that the criminal behaviour is a justified retaliation against victims who well deserve their punishment (e.g., overly strict teachers, annoying shopkeepers), or that the victims are just unimportant individuals (e.g., homosexuals, ethnic minorities).
4. The individuals accuse people who criticize their behaviour of being bad themselves (attack is the best defense!). Those people are hypocrites, tricky in many ways, are looking for personal gain, and so forth. Parents take their frustrations out on their children, teachers have their pets, the police are unfair and stupid. The lack of respect delinquents often show towards the police is partly based on neutralization. Sometimes it precedes contact with the police and is subsequently reinforced by such contact (Hirschi, 1969).
5. The youngsters allude to their loyalty to friends. The behaviour was not done in the first place for themselves. This loyalty is placed above

the law and transcends the loyalty toward other groups and social obligations. In a broader sense, the norms of the subculture are placed
above those of the dominant culture.

The number of possible forms of neutralization is not exhausted with
these five examples. For instance, youngsters may point out that they
behave well so often and that they break the law so infrequently, that this
in fact compensates for their criminal behaviour (Minor, 1981).

Whatever the case may be, the various forms of neutralization often
occur simultaneously. In such cases we do not deal with separate factors
any more, but rather with a general syndrome (Amelang et al., 1988).

The higher the level of moral judgment of the delinquents and the more
conventional the norms they have incorporated, the more neutralization one
may expect (Amelang et al., 1988; Ruma and Mosher, 1967).

The more serious the crimes, the less the youngster feels the need for
neutralization. Youths who commit serious crimes are too far removed
from conventional norms to be overly concerned with the moral implications of their deviant behaviour. Scandal, guilt, and shame are concepts
which do not concern them very much (Egg and Sponsel, 1978; Mitchell
and Dodder, 1980; Velarde, 1978). A case in point is the (semi)-criminal
youngster who has a deviant identity. Sometimes, such youngsters do not
really experience their behaviour as deviant.

Girls neutralize to the same extent as boys. This is consistent with the
fact that neutralization particularly occurs with respect to crimes that are
not too serious, and in youngsters who (still) have some ties with
conventional norms (Mitchell and Dodder, 1983).

Neutralization is not unique to juvenile delinquents. After all, norms are
elastic and flexible; they are not categorical and always and under all circumstances valid. They are guidelines for behaviour. As such, they are
limited in their application depending on place, time, and person. Norms,
after all, are by definition abstract, and play a different role in different
situations.

An example: Box (1971) observed that members of a jury in England
falsified their expense declarations for amounts varying between three to
twenty-five pounds. Shortly before, these jury members had found a youngster guilty of theft of goods worth about 50 shillings. They had morally
disapproved of his behaviour and agreed with the judge's sentence of nine
months in jail.

Such a double standard is more the rule than an exception. In different
milieus, criminal behaviour is viewed differently depending on the circumstances. In every circle certain crimes are perceived as less serious. These
are the offenses which frequently occur in the milieu in question. Among

entrepreneurs one has greater understanding for not paying social benefit costs than is elsewhere the case; business people do not regard tax evasion as a major crime; labourers do not mind being paid under the table; and professional drivers do not worry too much about exceeding the speed limits. These people are aware of the fact that they are breaking rules and regulations, but in certain instances (especially when it concerns minor offenses) they consider it acceptable (Bandura, 1977; Cohen, 1970a; Lemert, 1972). Of course, it all depends on how far one is willing to go with this. And thus everybody interprets norms according to one's own particular background, thereby claiming all kinds of special circumstances and exceptions. Juvenile delinquents are no different in this respect; except for the fact that a number of them have made the neutralization process into an art form (Empey and Lubeck, 1971; Minor, 1984; Mitchell and Dodder, 1980).

IDENTITY, SELF-IMAGE AND SELF-ESTEEM

Identity

We have seen in Chapter 2 that young people develop an identity of their own. Most of the time this is an adjusted identity which results in social responsibility, obedience to authority figures, conformity to societal rules, avoidance of social conflicts, and so forth. For many reasons (which are discussed in this book), some youths do not develop such an adapted identity, particularly because they do not sufficiently acquire norms and methods needed to go through life in an adjusted fashion.

Those who can not or will not develop a conventional identity may opt for an alternative one. This alternative identity may be an adjusted one (e.g., one joins a religious group), but it may also be maladjusted or deviant. Kaplan (1976) provides several examples of maladjusted identities, such as personalities characterized by cheating, dishonesty, drug abuse, alcoholism, suicide, psychiatric symptoms, and also criminality. The criminal identity often already exists before the youngster actually shows criminal behaviour. On the other hand, participation in delinquent behaviour may contribute to the development of a criminal identity (Gold, 1978; Gold and Mann, 1972; Hall, 1966; Kaplan, 1975, 1980; Reckless et al., 1957; Scarpitti, 1965; Schwartz and Tangri, 1965).

If youngsters are not able to create an identity by themselves, there is the danger that they will submit all too easily to group influences, and that they will identify with the identity of the group. In the context of this book, the influence of deviant groups should especially be noted.

Self-Image

One's identity is not a very coherent whole. One only has to think of the many roles one plays in the various groups to which one belongs (family, school, friends, peers, etc.), and the diverse situations one encounters. Nevertheless, one usually has a pretty constant picture of one's identity. This is called the self-image (De Levita, 1965).

There is some confusion in the literature about what is meant by self-image. In fact, it appears to refer to all sorts of things. Sometimes, it seems as if each author has his or her own definition. Hence, self-image is referred to by terms such as self-acceptance, self-control, self-consciousness, self-reflection, self-understanding, self-confidence, and self-criticism. This apart from the fact that it is already an abstract, hard to define concept to begin with, and that obtaining reliable and valid information about this abstraction is not an easy task (Jensen, 1972a; Schwarz and Tangri, 1965; Tangri and Schwarz, 1967).

In this book, we interpret the concept of self-image as the reflection of how one experiences one's own identity. It is, as it were, the theory one has about oneself. The self-image provides the feeling that (the organization of) one's personality is consistent over time, and that one has control over mental processes and social behaviour (Cattell and Child, 1975). The consistent self-image enables people to bridge the various and sometimes contradictory roles they play. The self-image is present in the background of every thought and action.

Even though segments of the self-image are continuously changing, it generally is a conservative, stable entity. New experiences are interpreted against the frame of reference of the self-image. Experiences that are consistent with the self-image (consonance) are integrated, whereas those that are not (dissonance), are rejected. One strives for internal consistency, which results in an integrated system of behaviours, norms, and opinions. Consequently, people tend to behave in ways that correspond with their self-image (Festinger, 1957; Markus, 1977).

The self-image plays a crucial role in personality development and in the formation of a personal identity (Kelly, 1971). It determines to a large extent one's outlook on life.

If criminality is an important element in someone's self-image (i.e., if someone sees oneself as a delinquent) one speaks of a delinquent self-image. A delinquent self-image may be the result of delinquent behaviour, but it may also be the cause of it. In the latter case, the criminal behaviour is preceded by the delinquent self-image because people normally act according to their self-image (Foster et al., 1972; Jones, 1973).

Studies of the self-image of delinquent youths do not always give the same results, in part because of the different definitions that are used. Nevertheless, some general conclusions may be drawn. Noticeable, but not unexpected, is that criminal behaviour assumes a relatively important position in this self-image. Furthermore, compared to non-delinquent youths, family and school have less of an influence on self-image, whereas relatively greater influence is exerted by friends, appearance, and physique (Lund and Salary, 1980; Montemayor and Eisen, 1977). Arbuthnot et al. (1987) concluded that the self-image of delinquent youths is unclear, confused, and contradictory. This suggests an insufficiently differentiated and inconsistent self-image. Noteworthy, moreover, is that if one compares the self-image of juvenile delinquents with the way they think other people view them, there are clear differences implying an unrealistic self-image (Chasen and Young, 1981; Deitz, 1969).

Self-Esteem

Appreciation of one's self-image, thus appreciation of one's self, is referred to as self-esteem. Self-esteem depends on two closely related criteria: self-respect and social status. If one is accepted by others, then this contributes to high self-esteem. If one is not, the result will be low self-esteem. We noted this already in Chapter 2.

People's relative self-esteem can be determined by comparing their level of self-esteem with that of others. The higher one's self-esteem in such a test, the more positive this should be evaluated. It should be noted, however, that some people have an unrealistically high self-esteem, in which case we speak of self-overestimation. In reality, these individuals often suffer from a covert underevaluation of self and feelings of inferiority.

Another method of assessing someone's relative self-esteem is to compare that person's actual self-image with his or her ideal self-image. In other words, by comparing actual self-esteem with ideal self-esteem. When making such a comparison it is usually assumed that the smaller the discrepancy between the two aspects of self, the more stable the personality (Gold and Mann, 1972; Hepburn, 1977).

To some extent, self-esteem is already determined early in the youth period. During the preceding years it has developed under the influence of the parents, and this influence continues during adolescence (Lauer and Handel, 1977). Although friends also exert a great influence at that time, their influence is less than that of the family (Dinitz et al., 1962; Jensen, 1973). Usually, self-esteem increases gradually during the youth period, and it is relatively stable near the end (Lively et al., 1962; Savin-Williams and Demo, 1984).

High self-esteem is associated with positive mental health (Fitch, 1970). People with high self-esteem accept themselves with their faults and weaknesses without this leading to feelings of inferiority. They have ego-strength, are sure of themselves, have an opinion of their own, don't doubt their own value and capacities, and have a high tolerance for frustration (are able to absorb much without losing their balance). They have no problems with their role in society, have stable social relationships, and do not easily harbour hostile feelings. Generally, they have an optimistic outlook on life. Negative self-esteem, on the other hand, is associated with insecurity, maladaptation, inferiority feelings, and fear of failure.

If one has high self-esteem, one is also inclined to think positively of others and to at least give them the benefit of the doubt. Low self-esteem is associated with aloofness and suspicion; one easily feels threatened and shortchanged (Friedberg, 1982; Geist and Borecki, 1982; Goldfried, 1963).

According to some theorists, striving for high self-esteem (and the avoidance of low self-esteem) is the most important motive underlying human behaviour (Adler, 1930; Kaplan, 1980; Rosenberg and Rosenberg, 1978).

Negative self-esteem leads to defensive behaviour. Matters which threaten the self-image are denied or suppressed. There is *alienation* from norms and customs, from the institutions, groups, and persons one holds responsible for the low self-esteem. It should be noted, however, that it is not absolutely necessary that alienation is preceded by low self-esteem. Alienation happens in every situation where youngsters do not feel comfortable. In what follows we are, however, dealing with alienation as a reaction to low self-esteem.

As a result of alienation, youngsters begin to display avoidance behaviour and escape behaviour.

Avoidance behaviour means that a tendency develops to search for a different identity by rearranging matters in a different order and by seeking experiences that lead to greater self-esteem. One opts for different norms and customs. Many people attempt to affirm their self-esteem through conventional behaviour (for example, in caretaking professions), whereas others turn to deviant behaviour (Kaplan, 1975, 1980).

Escape behaviour means that one avoids the threatening situation. One distances oneself from institutions, groups, and persons who threaten the self-esteem and instead associates oneself with institutions, groups, and persons who augment the self-esteem (including the possibility to vent frustrations). In the case of youngsters, friends, peer groups, and subcultures are worth mentioning. As far as friends are concerned, these are usually comrades who have experienced similar frustrations and who have comparable attitudes.

Juvenile delinquents on the average do not appear to have very high self-esteem. They believe that they have had many negative experiences in life and that they live in a not so pleasant but rather threatening world. Therefore, they have less respect for themselves and for others (Ball, 1983; Berzonsky, 1978b; Brynner et al., 1981; Eyo-Isidore, 1981; Glueck and Glueck, 1950; Hirschi, 1969; Jensen, 1972a; Kaplan, 1980; Lund and Salari, 1980; Nye, 1958; Reckless and Dinitz, 1967; Reckless et al., 1957; Rosenberg and Rosenberg, 1978; Schwabe-Holein, 1984).

Even though relationships between low self-esteem and juvenile delinquency (recorded as well as survey delinquency) have been reported by many authors, it should be noted that these associations are not very strong and sometimes have not been confirmed by other researchers (Aultman and Welford, 1979; Deitz, 1969; Zieman and Benson, 1983). Therefore, it is certainly not the case that all juvenile delinquents have a very low self-esteem.

The assumption that low self-esteem can contribute to juvenile delinquency is supported by the fact that low-esteem often already exists before the youngsters begin to show criminal behaviour (Elliott and Voss, 1974; Gold, 1978; Gold and Mann, 1972; Kaplan, 1975, 1976, 1978, 1980; Mann, 1981; Patterson, 1986; Reckless et al., 1956a,b, 1957; Rosenberg and Rosenberg, 1978; Wright, 1974).

Delinquency then could be viewed as a response to a threat to the individual's self-esteem, as a compensation for feelings of inferiority, as a defense mechanism (Freud, 1956; Jacobson, 1957; Stott, 1950). A positive self-esteem therefore may inhibit juvenile delinquency (Jensen, 1973; Reckless and Dinitz, 1972).

Juvenile delinquency often leads to an increase in self-esteem. In such cases, self-esteem increases because the youth's self-image is enhanced by the respect he or she gets from friends when committing criminal acts (Akers et al., 1979; Cohen, 1955; Elliott and Voss, 1974; Kaplan, 1980; Matsueda, 1982).

The more one rebels against conventional norms and groups and the more one identifies with delinquent friends, the more delinquency will lead to an increase in self-esteem. The initially negative relationship between self-esteem and juvenile delinquency will then change into a positive one (Kaplan, 1975, 1976, 1978, 1980; McCord, 1978; Rosenberg and Rosenberg, 1978; Zieman and Benson, 1983).

In light of the weak relationships discussed here, it is uncertain for how many juvenile delinquents this process is valid. Some have suggested that the increase in self-esteem takes place particularly or even exclusively in delinquents with an initially very low self-esteem (e.g., Bynner et al., 1981; Kaplan, 1978). Others are of the opinion that the more serious juvenile delinquents do not have low self-esteem to begin with, so that in them this process does not take place (Deitz, 1969).

We have seen that relationships have been found between self-esteem and juvenile delinquency. If we combine this with the fact that self-esteem and delinquency both find their origin to a large degree in the person and his or her personal background (family, school, and friends), then one might very well conclude that the relationship between self-esteem and delinquency similarly is caused by factors found in the person and his or her background (common cause theory) (Bynner et al., 1981; Dinitz and Pfau-Vicent, 1982; Jensen, 1973; Kaplan, 1980; McCord, 1978; Wells and Rankin, 1983).

Gold (1978) and Mann (1981) distinguished between conscious and unconscious self-esteem. According to this theory (which still lacks sufficient empirical validation), delinquency causes the conscious self-esteem to increase, but not the unconscious one. The former is the result of increased status and prestige among friends and peers. The latter relates to the fact that deviant behaviour (usually) does not solve the problems which lead to low self-esteem. Delinquents, in the long run, would therefore have high conscious and low unconscious self-esteem.

The above discussed relationship between self-esteem and juvenile delinquency applies to boys. Self-image and self-esteem play a lesser and different role in the delinquency of girls (Kaplan, 1978; Porteus, 1985). For girls, delinquency is not as attractive, and well for three reasons. First, people generally regard delinquency in girls more negatively than they do in boys (see Chapter 1). Second, friends and peers also do not rate delinquency in girls very highly; they tend to regard girls who overtly participate in it with suspicion. Third, girls generally attach less importance to prestige, particularly if it is gained by such unconventional means. Whereas in boys self-image is very much determined by competition and achievement, in girls it is more based on harmony and friendly relationships. Consequently, for girls delinquency is not an obvious way to increase self-esteem (Bynner et al., 1981; Gold, 1978; Hindelang, 1974a; Kaplan, 1977a,b, 1978; O'Malley and Bachman, 1979; Rosenberg and Rosenberg, 1978).

We have seen that young people may be alienated from their milieu and may develop a criminal identity. It is possible that negative self-esteem acts as an intermediating factor in this process. Many authors regard negative self-esteem as a *necessary* intermediary step. It is feasible that some youngsters commit criminal acts as a result of, among others, negative self-esteem. Hence, the combination of identity, self-image, and self-esteem, as discussed in the above paragraph, is certainly worthy of attention. It has, however, not been proven that negative self-esteem is an inevitable step toward juvenile delinquency. Moreover, in view of the relatively weak relationships that have been reported, it is also not very likely. There are youths who, notwithstanding the fact that they do not have too many personal problems, peculiarities, or too much damage to their self-esteem, nevertheless show delinquent behaviour (Empey and Lubeck, 1971; Jensen, 1972a; Tangri and Schwarz, 1967).

4. THE FAMILY

THE FAMILY AND CHILD REARING

The family plays an important role in the development of children's personality. The security and shelter it provides gives youngsters the opportunity to mature and grow in a protective and safe environment. Their development progresses more easily when they feel at home and relaxed. This is particularly the case when they feel accepted by their parents and experience their child rearing as warm and friendly. Under such circumstances children will develop good relationships with their parents and will feel close to other family members.

The family is the most significant agent of socialization in our culture. It is the place where children develop a large part of their identity and self-image, where they learn to interact with others, are taught what is right and what is wrong, internalize conventional norms and customs, and are instructed how to behave accordingly. As agents of society, parents prepare their children to take their place in the community (Kohnstamm, 1987). Moreover, more than anybody else they are aware of the activities of their youngsters and consequently are in a position to properly guide them and keep them from getting into trouble. Should the latter nevertheless happen, then the family is the proper place to take corrective action and find a solution to the problem, whether the trouble originated inside or outside the family. Required measures can easily be taken within and by the family, because parents have a legal and (more important) usually also a personal authority over their children, as a result of which the latter tend to be more responsive to parental actions.

THE FAMILY AND JUVENILE DELINQUENCY

Because the family plays such an important role in the personality development of children, negative consequences are virtually predictable when less than optimal family conditions prevail. Juvenile delinquency is an example (Gove and Crutchfield, 1982; Junger-Tas, 1983; Loeber, 1986; McCord, 1979; Ouston, 1984; Patterson, 1980; Patterson and Dishion, 1985; Riley and Shaw, 1985; Rosen, 1985; Rutter and Giller, 1983; Wadworth, 1979; Wells and Rankin, 1986; West and Farrington, 1973, 1977;

Wilson, 1980a,b, 1983; Wilson and Herrnstein, 1985).

One of the most frequently reported findings of criminological studies is that adverse family circumstances contribute to the cause and maintenance of delinquent behaviour (Leeuw, et al., 1987). Loeber and Dishion (1983) identified family functioning and parental child rearing practices as best predictors of juvenile delinquency.

The relationship between family and juvenile delinquency has a long history. Since the early 1900s —particularly following the appearance of the classic publication *The Delinquent Child and the Home* (Breckinridge and Abott, 1912)— many books and articles have been written on this topic (e.g., Gruhle, 1912; Postma, 1931; Shideler, 1981). The interest in the influence of the family on juvenile delinquency which emerged at that time was related to a general preoccupation with the nuclear family which around the turn of the century had gained in importance and had become subject of study. Concern for youngsters and their place in society also increased in those years, and, as we have seen in Chapter 2, there was a corresponding rise in attention given to juvenile delinquency. It is therefore not surprising that one began to study the possible role of the family in juvenile delinquency.

Initially, the emphasis was on structural aspects (family size, birth order, family incompleteness), but gradually it became apparent that these characteristics were less important to juvenile delinquency than functional aspects such as family atmosphere, family relationships, and child rearing (Glueck and Glueck, 1959; Laub and Sampson, 1988; McCord, 1982; Nye, 1958; Van Voorhis et al., 1988). At present it is acknowledged that the interaction between structural and functional factors in conjunction with factors external to the family forms the basis for understanding and explaining juvenile delinquency (Rosen, 1985).

The younger the delinquent, the more one must seek the causes of his or her criminality within the family. This is of even greater importance when it concerns misbehaviour of children under the age of 12. In those cases, lack of family warmth and protection are often identified as antecedents of the delinquent behaviour.

In the following paragraphs we will first discuss the structural factors and then the functional ones.

FAMILY SIZE

There is a modest but noticeable relationship between family size and juvenile delinquency (Biles and Challinger, 1981; Farrington et al., 1975;

Fisher, 1984; Glueck and Glueck, 1950; Hirschi, 1969; Mannheim, 1965; Nye, 1958; Rahav, 1980, 1982; Rutter and Giller, 1983; Wadworth, 1979; West, 1982; West and Farrington, 1973; Wilson, 1982; Wilson and Herrnstein, 1985).

The following explanations have been suggested for this association:

1. In larger families, financial resources must be shared by a larger number of people. Children in such settings enjoy fewer material benefits than their counterparts in smaller families. This does not only pertain to clothing and food, but also to matters such as education, travel, club memberships, hobbies, and so forth. This could mean that, particularly at the lower socioeconomic level, family size and juvenile delinquency are associated. Farrington and West (1981) reported this indeed to be the case; Rosen (1985), on the other hand, found no differences between socioeconomic levels.

2. Children in large families enjoy less space and privacy (Galle et al., 1972; Glueck and Glueck, 1950). They have to share with many family members, and chances are that they get into each other's way. Feij (1979) suggested that the relatively high level of activity in such families provides great stimulation. Exposure over a number of years results in an increase in tolerance. Consequently, children from large families often experience the average stimulation level of the general culture as insufficient. They may become impulsive individuals with a higher than average need for excitement; characteristics which, as we have seen in Chapter 3, are related to juvenile delinquency.

3. In large families, parental attention must be shared with more siblings. Parents can devote less individual time to their children, and the latter become each other's rivals for attention (Boer, 1986; Hirschi, 1983; Marjoribanks, 1979; Zussman, 1980). They experience fewer expressions of parental affection, there is less supervision, and they are raised in a relatively strict manner (Feij, 1979). On the other hand, in larger families children raise each other, but this appears to be less effective than parental child rearing.

4. Society and its agencies are more readily inclined to regard large families as troubled (Angenent, 1990; Biles and Challinger, 1981). In problem cases, particularly those involving girls, intervention is more rapid because it is assumed that large families are less capable of solving problems.

These factors —material disadvantage, limited space, less parental supervision, discrimination by society and its agencies— have as a result that the socializing ability of large families is less than that of small ones.

Compared to children of small families, those of large ones encounter greater difficulties in internalizing norms, in forming an identity, and in developing a positive self-image. This makes them more vulnerable to delinquency (Bossard, 1953; Kohnstamm, 1987). Some authors have suggested that the small family may be regarded as a buffer against delinquent behaviour (Biles and Challinger, 1981; Rahav, 1980; Werner, 1987).

BIRTH ORDER

Over the years, the literature on birth order and juvenile delinquency has reflected an interesting change in thinking. Early publications suggested that first born children run a greater risk of becoming delinquents (Breckinridge and Abott, 1912; Goring, 1913). More recent reports indicate that it is middle and —to a lesser extent— last born children and not firstborns who show delinquency (Biles, 1971; Dentler and Monroe, 1961; Glueck and Glueck, 1950; Hirschi, 1969; McKissack, 1974; Rahav, 1980; Syrotuik, 1978; West and Farrington, 1973).

Several reasons have been suggested for this phenomenon:

1. Because there are no siblings to distract the parents, firstborns receive greater attention and supervision and are raised in a more consistent manner (Angenent, 1990; Kohnstamm, 1987; Rahav, 1980). They adhere more strongly to what has been taught at home. Because of the rather intensive contact with their parents, they learn to adapt socially. Furthermore, many parents involve their firstborns in raising the children that follow; sometimes, oldest children themselves choose this role. Consequently, firstborns develop very early in life a sense of responsibility and concern for others, and they often serve as models for younger siblings. To be able to set credible examples they must orient themselves to the conventional adult world, something which girls do with greater ease than boys (Abramovitch et al., 1979; Sutton-Smith and Rosenberg, 1970).

2. Middle —and to a lesser extent last born— children are more often delinquent than firstborns, notwithstanding the fact that they have the benefit of the latter's example. By observing the firstborn, later born children can learn how to behave and discover which behaviour is successful and which is not (Sutton-Smith and Rosenberg, 1970; Wilkinson, et al., 1982). The example set by the older sibling will certainly have an effect, but may be overshadowed by the younger children's desire to develop their own identity and to be noted in the family. Because the oldest child is already so well-adjusted, younger siblings

can not set themselves apart and draw attention by behaving in a similar way. They must come up with a different approach. They may resist conforming and may reject the firstborn's style of life (Forer, 1969; Grotevant, 1978; Leventhal, 1970; Schachter et al., 1976).

3. There appears to be an interaction between birth order and family size. Oldest and youngest children grow up in relatively small families; the firstborns are already older or have left home when the youngest ones are still growing up. Middle children, however, are raised in relatively large families with older and younger siblings. Hence, the greater participation in delinquent behaviour by middle-borns may in fact be the result of factors associated with family size (Kidwell, 1983).

Thus, it appears that it is difficult to differentiate the effects of birth order and family size on delinquency. There is a clear relationship between the two variables (i.e., the larger the family, the greater the influence of birth order), and the birth order effect may be explained to a large extent by the effect of family size (Hirschi, 1969; West and Farrington, 1973).

A few words about the only child. The only child is the oldest and the youngest at the same time, and by definition grows up in a small family. This seems to be a good position to be in. Indeed, such children tend to be intelligent, achievement oriented, autonomous, and sociable; they have a positive self-image and leadership abilities (Falbo, 1987; Falbo and Pilot, 1986; Snow et al., 1981). Very few are delinquent (Hirschi, 1969).

Questions remain about the effect of birth order on juvenile delinquency. For instance, it is not clear whether there is a gender effect, although Wilkinson et al. (1982) suggested that the influence is stronger in boys. Furthermore, it is not clear whether there are differences between first-borns and later-borns in terms of the kind of delinquent behaviour they show. Perhaps, older children commit more often individual crimes, and younger ones more often group offenses (Lerner and Lindner, 1975).

Finally, there is an inverse relationship between spacing of births and juvenile delinquency (Markus and Zajonc, 1975; Rahav, 1980; Werner, 1987); that is, the shorter the interval between births, the greater the chance that children get involved in delinquency. Children born in close intervals grow up in a relatively large family with all its limitations.

FAMILY INCOMPLETENESS

Families with both biological parents present are referred to as complete families. Incomplete or single-parent families are families where only one of the parents (most often the mother) is present. Besides these two types of family, there is a third one, characterized by the fact that one of the two biological parents has been replaced by a step-parent (e.g., remarriage). A fourth family form is one in which neither parent is a biological parent, as is the case in adoptive and foster families.

Besides permanently incomplete families, there are families where the incompleteness is temporary in nature (e.g., as a result of marital conflict, professional demands, illness requiring hospital admission, imprisonment, and so forth). This form of single-parenthood has received less attention in the literature than prolonged or permanent incompleteness (Wells and Rankin, 1986).

Complete families with mothers who are employed outside the home are often lumped together with single-parent families. When mothers leave the house to work they are, of course, for a specific period of time not available to help or supervise their children. The results of studies of the effect of employment of mothers on their children are not always congruent. On the average, there appears to be a small relationship with juvenile delinquency (Hirschi, 1969). It is clear that this relationship depends on a large number of factors. An example is the length of time the mother is away from the family; it seems that a limited number of hours is most beneficial. Furthermore, the kind of work the mother does (light, heavy, interesting, boring) is of importance. If the mother enjoys her work, it appears that maternal employment outside the home has a positive effect on children. Negative effects, including delinquency, may result when the mother is forced to work in order to supplement a family income that is insufficient. This is more often the case at the lower socioeconomic level where many mothers are employed as janitors, cleaning ladies, factory workers, waitresses, and so forth. Moreover, the effects depend on the circumstances at home (family atmosphere), the manner in which the children are cared for during the mother's absence, and the gender and age of the children involved. Concerning the latter, girls appear to benefit more from the positive effects than do boys, but also seem to suffer more from the negative effects, if any. The older the children, the fewer the negative influences (Angenent, 1990; Glueck and Glueck, 1950).

The fact that a family is not physically complete does not necessarily mean that it can not function properly as a group (Angenent, 1990). Boss (1980) noted that it is psychological rather than physical completeness that matters. Parents may be physically present, but psychologically absent. Nevertheless, the effect of family incompleteness on children generally is not positive (Rankin, 1983; Rijksen, 1955). Incomplete families often are at a disadvantage in material terms because of limited income, and single parents often are preoccupied with survival. Consequently, their children may receive less affection and guidance, and may lack a person with whom they can identify (Brandwein et al., 1974; Burgess, 1980). Matsueda and Heimer (1987) pointed out that there may be less supervision; children may spend more time in the streets where the chances of being exposed to delinquency are greater. Of course, many of these problems may be compensated for by other factors, as often happens (Rosen, 1985).

The early literature on family status and juvenile delinquency suggested that young delinquents tend to come from incomplete families (e.g., Cavan, 1934). Monahan (1957), summarizing the earlier literature, estimated that twice as many delinquents come from incomplete rather than from complete backgrounds. More recent studies paint a more complex picture (Wells and Rankin, 1986). Weak relationships have been found between family status and criminal behaviour reported by children in surveys. However, clear associations have been found between family incompleteness and recorded juvenile delinquency (contact with the police, convictions, etc.) (Burchard and Burchard, 1987; Gove and Crutchfield, 1982; Johnson, 1986; Johnstone, 1980; Rankin, 1983; Van Voorhis et al., 1988).

These associations may be explained in part by the labelling process. People in the neighbourhood and agency officials (school, police, justice system) tend to regard children from incomplete families differently than they view those from "normal" families. Teachers often judge such children as delinquent, even if it evidently is not the case (Blechman, 1982; Johnson, 1986; Santrock and Tracy, 1978). Action (e.g., removing children from the home or bringing them to the attention of the police) is taken more readily when it involves children of incomplete families, particularly when it concerns girls (Datesman and Scarpitti, 1975; Herzog and Sudia, 1973; Robins and Hill, 1966; Smart, 1976; Wilson and Herrnstein, 1985).

Incomplete family status may be the result of the death of a parent (in some cases, of both parents), divorce or separation (or abandonment), or voluntary single-parenthood. The relationship between these three family circumstances and juvenile delinquency varies with each type. Families where incompleteness is caused by the death of a parent do not substantially differ from intact families in terms of delinquency. However, families that are incomplete as a result of divorce are particularly implicated (Gold, 1970; Rosen, 1970; Rutter and Giller, 1983; Sterne, 1964; West and Farrington, 1973; Wilson and Herrnstein, 1985). In fact, Loeber and Dishion (1983) regarded divorce as a rather reliable predictor of criminal behaviour among children. Not much is known about the relationship in voluntary single-parent families.

Although children may experience the divorce itself as traumatic, it appears that preceding and subsequent experiences are of greater importance (Rosenfeld and Rosenstein, 1973). Parental conflicts prior to the divorce may have serious consequences for the children and may lead to all sorts of behaviourial problems such as impulsiveness and aggression (Block et al., 1986). Following the divorce —which, depending on the circumstances, may be experienced as positive by the child— contact with the absent parent is of great importance. The quality of such contact is directly related to the manner in which the parents interact. Thus, it may be concluded that the relationship between divorce and juvenile delinquency is not a direct one, and that divorce may be viewed as a symptom that reflects other causative factors in delinquent behaviour (Rutter, 1979a).

The effect of family incompleteness on juvenile delinquency depends very much on the extent to which the absence of a parent affects the identity and particularly the self-image of the child. It concerns here —as is always the case with such matters— not only the specific family status, but also a conglomerate of factors, of which socioeconomic considerations, the social background of the family, and internal family relationships are the most important (Blechman, 1982; Cicourel, 1976; Hess and Camera, 1979; Kaplan and Pokornov, 1971; Wilkinson, 1980).

The relationship between family incompleteness and delinquency varies with age and gender. The younger the child when the family becomes a single-parent family, the more serious the consequences (Bowlby, 1946; Toby, 1957; Wells and Rankin, 1986). Furthermore, the association is stronger in girls (Austin, 1978; Datesman et al., 1975; Elliott, 1988; Monahan, 1957; Morris, 1964; Wattenberg and Saunders, 1954). It has been speculated that because family life is more important to girls, their deviant behaviour, including delinquency, is more closely related to family circumstances (e.g., incompleteness). However, this speculation is not universally accepted (Canter, 1982a,b; Dornbusch et al., 1985; Gove and Crutchfield, 1982; Hennessy et al., 1978; Rosen and Nielson, 1982).

The question may be raised as to whether it makes any difference which parent is absent. In cases where the father is absent, *compulsive masculinity* could be an issue (Brownfield, 1987a; Parsons and Shils, 1951). *Boys* in these circumstances may lack an identification figure who could teach them how to come to terms with their masculinity; this may lead to role confusion. These youngsters may be inclined to deliberately demonstrate their masculinity through aggressive and criminal behaviour. Santrock and Warshak (1979) and Rosen (1985) determined that absence of the father leads to greater delinquency. On the other hand, Monahan (1957) concluded that in the long term, boys from single-mother families are less delinquent than those from families with a father as the single parent. Rankin

(1983) felt that it does not make a difference which parent is absent.

The incomplete family can be made complete again if the single parent finds a partner. Kohnstamm (1987) suggested that stepfathers are more easily accepted than stepmothers. However, families with a biological mother and a stepfather are more frequently found in the backgrounds of delinquent *boys*. It has been suggested that the latter do not accept the stepfather as part of the family, and that this results in greater interpersonal distance and possible alienation (Dornbusch et al., 1985; Gold, 1970; Johnson, 1986; Junger-Tas et al., 1983; Hirschi, 1969; Rankin, 1983).

FAMILY ATMOSPHERE

Families function better when they are characterized by a positive internal atmosphere. In this respect one may differentiate between harmonious and disharmonious families (Angenent, 1990).

Members of *harmonious families* generally get along very well; they like each other and treat each other in a friendly manner. Level of cooperation, consultation, and mutual understanding is high; parent-child interactions are warm in nature. The family forms a cohesive unit while maintaining good contact with the external world. Tensions and conflicts are rare.

In *disharmonious families* interpersonal relationships are problematic; the members do not get along very well and do not care about each other. There is little cooperation and much mutual criticism. Parental attitudes are cold and neglecting, and supervision is inadequate. The children do not feel comfortable at home; in relative terms, many are unwanted and victim to child abuse and incest.

Juvenile delinquents often come from disharmonious homes where there are many conflicts between the two parents, between the parents and the children, and between the children themselves. Anger, irritations, and disagreements are expressed in behaviours such as fighting, blaming each other, and avoiding responsibilities (Alexander, 1973; Alkire et al., 1971; Emery and O'Leary, 1982; Faunce and Riskin, 1970; Hanson et al., 1984; Hetherington et al., 1971; Hirschi, 1969; McCord, 1979; Nye, 1958; Porter and O'Leary, 1982; Riskin and Faunce, 1970a,b; Rutter, 1971a; Schneider, 1987; Snyder and Patterson, 1987; West and Farrington, 1973; Wilson, 1974).

The atmosphere in the family depends on many internal and external factors, but the personalities and personal circumstances of the parents and the children are of major importance. If the parents are easily upset, disinterested, depressed, ill, drug dependent (alcohol, etc.), or unemployed, then the atmosphere will suffer. Similarly, children's delinquent behaviour may disturb the family climate (Elliott and Voss, 1974; Thornberry and Christenson, 1984).

ALIENATION, ESCAPE AND AVOIDANCE BEHAVIOUR

Children who grow up in disharmonious families may gradually come to the conclusion that the family is not a very rewarding place. They do not feel at home any more and experience *alienation*. They devote less time and energy to the family, their relationships with the others become less intense, they distance themselves from the norms and customs of the family, and, most importantly, their affective ties with the others weaken (Keniston, 1960). As part of this alienation, the children may show escape and avoidance behaviours.

Escape behaviour means that the children increasingly focus their interests and activities outside the family. They are home less often and seek the company of others with a similar frame of mind. Usually, these others are friends, but they may also be members of certain institutions, organizations, religious groups, or subcultures (Hawkins and Lane, 1987).

Avoidance behaviour may take a variety of forms and may be adjusted or maladjusted (e.g., delinquent activities) in nature. It may be expressed in a passive, active, or reactive manner, or in a combination of these three forms.

In *passive* avoidance behaviour, children basically withdraw from the family situation and ignore what is going on around them. They may turn inwards and display clinically maladaptive behaviour (e.g., neurotic, psychotic, or psychosomatic symptoms; excessive use of prescription drugs; suicidal behaviour; anorexia, bulimia, or obesitas). Juvenile delinquency in these cases usually involves individual covert criminal activities (e.g., theft) (Glueck and Glueck, 1970; Mawby, 1980; Reckless et al., 1957; Stott, 1965; Toby, 1960).

In *active* avoidance behaviour, children try to make the best of their life situation, either within or outside the family. Characteristically, they begin experimenting with activities that actually belong to the world of adults (alcohol and other drug use, gambling, sex, staying out late, and so forth). It may also be expressed in overt delinquent behaviour (e.g., vandalism, assaults), often in groups and under the influence of alcohol.

Reactive avoidance behaviour is aimed directly at the parents and may take the form of pestering and embarrassing the parents through a variety of criminal behaviours (Stott, 1950).

Which form of avoidance behaviour the children adopt depends on a large number of factors. Among others, it appears to be gender and personality related. Boys more often opt for active avoidance behaviour and girls tend to choose the passive form. Introverts tend to display the passive approach and extraverts choose the active form (Brennan et al., 1978). Moreover, modelling plays a role: in present society, children are exposed to a multitude of good and bad examples and some children model themselves on delinquent examples. *Chance* contacts play a role here (Adams, 1973; Akers et al., 1979), as do friends.

Alienation precedes juvenile delinquency which in turn increases alienation (secondary alienation). Over time, juvenile delinquents realize that their behaviour is not congruent with the norms of their elders. They are aware that they have crossed the line and that they are involved in activities that are not acceptable to their parents. This creates distance. Furthermore, these children often commit crimes as members of peer groups and subcultures that adhere to deviant norms and customs, and which in a variety of ways criticize parents. This also creates distance. Thus, juvenile delinquency is not only caused by alienation from the family, but also contributes to this state of isolation.

FAMILY RELATIONSHIPS

The atmosphere in a family is to a large extent a function of the quality of the relationship between the parents; that is, the more positive and warm the interaction, the better the family climate. It has been found that the relationship between the parents of juvenile delinquents often leaves much to be desired (Duncan, 1971; Farrington, 1980a; Hetherington et al., 1971; Nye, 1958; Porter and O'Leary, 1982; Rodrick and Henggeler, 1982; Rutter, 1971b; Rutter and Giller, 1983; Sroufe, 1984; Werner, 1987).

Sibling relationships also play a role in juvenile delinquency, because children of a family tend to interact much (Allen, 1977; Boer, 1986; Dunn, 1984; Wilkinson et al., 1982). Like parents, older children often serve as examples for the younger ones who may imitate their behaviour. However, as is the case between parents and children, younger siblings sometimes go against their older brothers or sisters. As we have seen, older children sometimes assist their parents in raising their siblings, either because they have been asked to do so or on a voluntary basis (e.g., when the parents fail to do their part). Most of the time, however, the relationship between brothers and sisters is one of equals. They provide each other with advice and support, and sometimes unite against the parents in various coalitions. They help each other with concrete problems (homework, lending money or clothing, etc.), but can also be rivals. Particularly when close in age, they do a lot of things together, and the relationship between siblings very much resembles the one between friends, as will be discussed in Chapter 6. Therefore, it is not surprising that youngsters who are involved in delinquent activities often have brothers or sisters who have similar inclinations (Hanson and Henggeler, 1984; Wilkinson et al., 1982).

Rosen (1985) reported that the interaction between parents and children emerges as an important factor in all investigations pertaining to juvenile delinquency, independent of the definition of delinquency that is used and the subject groups under consideration. It appears that juvenile delinquents do not enjoy good relationships with their parents. This bad interaction is directly related to their criminal behaviour (Andry, 1970; Canter, 1982a,b; Empey and Lubeck, 1971; Glueck and Glueck, 1950; Gold, 1963; Gove and Crutchfield, 1982; Hindelang, 1973; Hirschi, 1969; Nye, 1958; Slocum and Stone, 1963).

Hirschi (1969) regards the bad relationship between juvenile delinquents and their parents as one of the best documented findings of delinquency research. The image juvenile delinquents have of their parents usually is not a very positive one; as a result, they often do not care about what the latter might think (Andry, 1957, 1960; Elifson et al., 1983; Meddinus, 1965; Riege, 1972).

CHILD REARING

The relationship between parents and children expresses itself in concrete terms in child rearing. Child rearing is not a simple, unidimensional process, but rather involves a complex combination of many interacting forces. The relative importance of individual forces and the resulting approach to child rearing varies from family to family. For example, there are parents who are very restrictive in their child rearing attitudes, whereas others allow their children a great deal of freedom. Some parents are very interested in the activities of their youngsters and spend much time with them, whereas others are less interested and tend to leave them alone. Furthermore, approaches to child rearing not only differ from family to family, but may also vary from child to child within the same family.

Notwithstanding this diversity, it is possible to differentiate two basic dimensions or patterns of child rearing: *warmth* and *dominance*. It concerns basic characteristics of child rearing that are analogous to the basic characteristics we differentiated in the personality. They may be used as models, as a frame of reference with which one may describe and compare child rearing practices and ideas (Angenent, 1990; Maccoby and Martin, 1983; Rollins and Thomas, 1979).

Warmth reflects the affectional aspect of the parent-child relationship. This basic attitude is related to the previously discussed family atmosphere, which of course also expresses itself in child rearing. *Dominance* refers to the manner in which parents transfer their norms and customs to their children. This may or may not happen in a domineering manner. Warmth and dominance are used as basic patterns in many publications about child rearing, although under different names and not always defined in the same way (Goldin, 1969). The following paragraphs present ideal descriptions of warmth and dominance on the basis of findings of various investigations (Angenent, 1990).

In *warm* child rearing, the parents accept their children as they are. They are emotionally involved with their youngsters and provide a lot of care and attention. The children feel safe and protected in the family. Parents and children share many interests and spend a great deal of time together. The children trust their parents and know that the latter will support them and help them when they encounter difficulties or problems. Warm child rearing is particularly found in harmonious families.

The opposite of warm child rearing is *cold* child rearing in which the emotional distance between parents and children is large. The attitude of cold parents toward their children is superficial, indifferent, negative, rejecting, critical, and in some cases even hostile. Children do not feel at home in the family; they may feel neglected, superfluous, and rejected. In extreme cases, very cold child rearing may involve neglect, exploitation, sexual abuse, and child abuse. Cold child rearing is primarily found in disharmonious families.

In *domineering* child rearing, parents demonstrate a need to control their children. They try to force their ideas and customs on them. They want to be informed about virtually everything their youngsters do, and they want to supervise their actions. In this kind of child rearing the children are restricted in their activities and have little opportunity to develop independently from the parents.

Dominant child rearing is especially found in closed families where there is little contact with the external world. These families to a certain extent live in isolation; family life is centripetal, that is, focused on and largely restricted to the family. There is a solid family structure with a clear hierarchy. The parents occupy a central position in this type of family.

Permissive child rearing is the opposite of dominant child rearing. The parents leave their children a great deal of freedom and hardly control them. They demand very little of their youngsters and provide few rules and limitations.

Permissive child rearing is primarily found in families where there are few strong ties between family members, little family cohesiveness, and few family activities. The children seek their social contacts predominantly outside the family.

In general, the manner in which parents raise their children remains rather constant over the years. Nevertheless, changes do occur for the simple reason that parents and children change (they get older and more experienced). Hence, parents of young children express warmth especially by providing security and comfort, whereas parents of older children —the group of interest to this book— express it more by solidarity and by accepting and respecting their youngsters. Dominance takes the form of protection with young children, and of rules and regulations with older ones.

CHILD REARING AND JUVENILE DELINQUENCY

Classic and more recent publications indicate that there is a strong relationship between particular approaches to child rearing and juvenile delinquency (Andry, 1960; Bowlby, 1951; Burchard and Burchard, 1987; Faunce and Riskin, 1970; Glueck and Glueck, 1968, 1970; Göppinger, 1976, 1983; Hanson et al., 1984; Hetherington et al., 1971; Hewitt and Jenkins, 1946; Hindelang, 1973; Hirschi, 1969, 1983; Johnson, 1979; Laub and Sampson, 1988; Marcus, 1961; McCord, 1979; McCord and McCord, 1964; McCord et al., 1959; Merrill, 1947; Nye, 1958; Olweus, 1980a; Riege, 1972; Riskin and Faunce, 1970b; Rutter and Giller, 1983; Snyder and Patterson, 1987; Sutherland and Cressey, 1978; Taft, 1950; West and Farrington, 1973, 1977; Wilson and Herrnstein, 1985).

There are very few delinquents among children who have experienced warm child rearing. Lack of warmth in the parent-child relationship, on the other hand, seems to be a major factor in the development of juvenile delinquency. Delinquent children perceive their parents as cold and deficient in their provision or expression of love. They believe that their elders are not interested in them and often feel treated unjustly or rejected. One of the most important complaints of juvenile delinquents is that they feel disadvantaged and discriminated against (Aultman and Wellford, 1979; Göppinger, 1976; Mannheim, 1965). This cold attitude is mutual; the children on their part reject the parents, seek little contact with them, and do not confide in them when troubled (Andry, 1957, 1960; Glueck and Glueck, 1950; Nye, 1958).

The inverse relationship between parental warmth and juvenile delinquency is based on the fact that warm child rearing facilitates positive personality development in children (Angenent, 1990; Rodick and Henggeler,

1982). Warm parents may make major mistakes in child rearing without necessarily producing disastrous results. Because of the good interpersonal relationships which exist in warm families, the children can accept and cope with their parents' mistakes and shortcomings. Youngsters who are raised warmly develop a basic sense of personal security (Erikson, 1968); they feel that they belong and that they are accepted as individuals (Bowlby, 1979).

Warmly raised children generally become individuals with a clear sense of identity as well as social and intellectual independence. They have a stable personality, are self-assured, and self-controlled. They assume that life to a certain extent is predictable and believe that they control the outcomes of their lives; that is, they have internal locus of control (Dusek and Litovsky, 1985).

Children raised in this manner have a positive self-image and seldom suffer feelings of inferiority, guilt, or anxiety. The security they enjoy in the family gives them the courage to explore the environment. They are not easily discouraged and do not feel insecure in new situations. New experiences are assimilated without too much difficulty. These children are spontaneous and socially well-adjusted; their relationships generally are free of deep-going conflicts (Feij, 1979; Fromm, 1941; Langeveld, 1979).

Warmly raised children develop a close relationship with their parents. They follow their example and internalize their norms and customs (Elifson et al., 1983; Snyder and Patterson, 1987). Because most parents behave in an adjusted manner, children who enjoy a good relation with their parents will do the same. Moreover, because of this closeness, the parents are in a good position to supervise their children and to take corrective action should this be necessary, for instance in the case of criminal behaviour shown by their youngsters. The children on their part are more open to this attention and will respond more readily to measures taken by their elders.

A cold parent-child relationship as compared to a warm one leads to opposite results (Angenent, 1990). Children from a cold family often have an identity problem, suffer low self-esteem, and feel insecure. They believe that life is largely determined by factors over which they have no control (external locus of control). Sometimes they develop into introverted, anxious, and aggressive individuals who are inhibited in their emotional expressions (Feij, 1979; George and Main, 1979; Herbert, 1975).

The poor relationship with the parents often leads to a limited ability to empathize with others and to establish social contacts. They are not interested in other people, but are suspicious and feel easily threatened. As a result they encounter a great number of problems in their relations with other people and institutions (Freedman, et al., 1978).

Coldly raised children are indifferent to their parents, reject them, and even rebel against them. This hampers identification and transference of norms and customs. In cold child rearing we find at a young age already all kinds of deviant behaviour and other conduct disorders (e.g., feeding problems, bed wetting, attention-seeking, and so on). Also, later on in life coldly raised children are overrepresented in all areas of deviant behaviour, including delinquency (Brennan, et al., 1978).

Nevertheless, coldly raised children often have a rather intense —albeit negative— relationship with their parents which expresses itself in the sometimes fervent way in which they rebel against their parents (Mury and De Gauléjac, 1974).

Even in some cases of extremely cold child rearing (e.g., unwanted, exploited, or abused children) the youngsters are still attached to their parents. This may be explained by the fact that these children have known too little security and comfort in order to develop even the smallest degree of independence (Rutter, 1972).

Although cold child rearing usually precedes juvenile delinquency, the reverse may also be true. Problematic behaviour in children may decrease their parents' love for them. Even though parents usually disapprove of their children's criminal behaviour, they still accept them. But sometimes delinquency may cause such an interpersonal distance that the parent-child relationship is damaged and the parents reject their children. Some parents give up, others deliberately distance themselves and evict the child (Gove and Crutchfield, 1982; Patterson, 1986; Rutter and Giller, 1983; Thornberry and Christenson, 1984).

Dominance in child rearing is related to juvenile delinquency in a somewhat more complicated manner (Laub and Sampson, 1988; Wells and Rankin, 1988; Wilson, 1980a, 1982; Wilson and Herbert, 1978).

A child rearing regime characterized by an average level of dominance is most favourable to the prevention of juvenile delinquency. In those cases the parents provide clear rules and regulations and are not afraid to make the necessary demands of their children. They bring their own ideas to the attention of their children, but do not force these on them. They are not overly strict, but adequately supervise their children's actions (Weiss, 1980).

However, overly dominant as well as overly permissive child rearing is associated with juvenile delinquency (Glueck and Glueck, 1950). In very dominant child rearing, children often develop a rigid lifestyle to which they strictly adhere. They conform to conventional norms and customs and strictly follow rules and regulations; life becomes a routine. These children may develop feelings of anxiety and inferiority because they may think that they are inadequate. This makes them feel insecure (Hewitt and Jenkins, 1946; Kohnstamm, 1987; Rodick and Henggeler, 1982). They, in fact, fail constantly (in the eyes of their parents and their own if they accept the strict norms of the latter, which is normally the case) because they can not meet the demands of their elders. This may lead to an identity crisis and a negative self-image (Erikson, 1980; Eskilson et al., 1986).

With respect to juvenile delinquency, it may be expected in the first instance that dominantly raised youths —who have learned to conform— will cause few problems. Should they develop delinquent behaviour, it usually happens at a later age (Buikhuisen and Meijs, 1983). There are however two possible dangers associated with the personality development of dominantly raised children as discussed above. *First*, because they have never learned to form their own opinions, assume responsibilities, or behave autonomously, they may run into trouble if they have to act independently, something they do not feel comfortable doing. Under those circumstances they are more inclined to follow the majority in the groups with which they associate. This means that they have little resistance against delinquent influences should these be present. Because they are inclined to submit to the authority and influence of dominant people, they may be overwhelmed by delinquent peers. Parents and others may be surprised that their "good" children so easily turn to criminal behaviour under the influence of "bad" friends. Dominantly raised youngsters may be particularly receptive to the authoritarian leadership that is frequently found in youth groups (gangs). *Second*, it often happens that children try to escape from the restrictions of an extremely dominant child rearing regime and go their independent way (Elliott, et al., 1979). This frequently causes problems because they have never learned how to be independent. They may experience an identity crisis with as a possible result that they —as a reaction to their child rearing experiences— choose a negative and sometimes criminal identity. In some cases such youngsters become completely lost, unattached, and do not care about anything or anybody.

One characteristic of dominant child rearing is that there normally are many rules in the family. It is surprising that this particular aspect is *not* found in families of juvenile delinquents. There is little emphasis on rules concerning, for example, the acquisition of skills, achievement, consideration for others, and so forth. Child rearing in these families is more oriented toward immediate obedience (Göppinger, 1976; Junger-Tas, 1972; Kohn, 1959; McCord et al., 1959; Peterson and Becker, 1965).

Juvenile delinquents often come from families where both parents, but especially the mother, subscribe to a permissive child rearing approach (Bandura and Walters, 1959; Bennett, 1960; Glueck and Glueck, 1950;

McCord et al., 1959; Mannheim, 1965; Merrill, 1947; Peterson and Becker, 1965; Sutherland and Cressey, 1978; Wilson, 1980a,b, 1987).

Permissively raised children usually know how to find their way in life; they are active, sociable, and take initiative. However, if child rearing is too permissive, then the children do not learn to meet any demands or to exert themselves, which leads to superficiality, laziness, and opportunism. Generally, youngsters from such a family environment have trouble giving direction to their lives. Sometimes they are anxious because they do not feel in control of themselves (Herbert, 1975). The main cause of delinquency in permissively raised youngsters is that they have never learned to follow rules and to be considerate of other people (Bandura and Walters, 1959; Nye, 1958). It is remarkable that they often participate in delinquency at an early age and show recidivist tendencies (Wilson, 1980a). The influence of delinquent friends generally is considerable (Hewitt and Jenkins, 1946; Stanfield, 1966).

FATHERS AND MOTHERS

Traditionally, the literature on child rearing emphasized the role of the mother, and little attention was paid to the role of the father. Peterson et al (1959), in a literature review spanning the period from 1919 to 1956, found 169 publications about mother-child relationships, but only 12 about father-child relationships. Since that time, however, the importance of the father in child rearing has become more recognized. It may be assumed that a comparable review covering more recent years would produce a more balanced distribution.

Similarly, the literature on juvenile delinquency regarded the influence of the mother as paramount (e.g., Bowlby, 1946, 1951). More recently, it has become apparent that whether or not children become delinquent is to a large extent determined by paternal influences (Bruce, 1970; Johnson, 1987; Nye, 1958; Peterson et al., 1959; Winder and Rau, 1962).

Research increasingly suggests that the contact between juvenile delinquents and their fathers is disturbed (Andry, 1957; Bandura and Walters, 1959; Glueck and Glueck, 1950; Grygier et al., 1969; Hirschi, 1969; Janes, 1958; McCord and McCord, 1964). Juvenile delinquents themselves often report that this relationship is troubled and that their fathers fail in their child rearing (Andry, 1957, 1960; McCord et al., 1959; Meddinus, 1965; Riege, 1972).

The importance of the role of fathers with respect to juvenile delinquency lies in the fact that children, particularly through the relationship with their fathers, learn how to behave independently, how to adjust socially, and how to build contacts outside the family (Lamb, 1979; Smith and Walters, 1978; Weiss, 1980).

Focusing on warmth and dominance, we have seen that these two dimensions may be regarded as basic child rearing concepts. Child rearing, of course, is a special form of interpersonal relationships; indeed, it has been found that warmth and dominance are distinctive aspects of all interpersonal relationships (Angenent, 1990). Moreover, these two basic concepts are also found in all groups, particularly in relation to group leadership.

One may distinguish two orientations in group functioning: an instrumental approach (in which the task which confronts the group is central) and an expressive approach (which emphasizes mutual relations) (Parsons and Bales, 1956). These orientations require two different types of leadership: instrumental and expressive leadership which respectively reflect dominance and warmth.

Dominance expresses itself in guiding and supervisory activities, whereas warmth is reflected in leaders' appreciation of and attention given to subordinates (Marmet and Meyer, 1988). Some leaders prefer to act dominantly, whereas others favour a warm approach. Sometimes, one leader is specifically expected to take the dominance route and another is required to use the warmth approach (Zeldith, 1956). In such cases, the instrumental leader (task leader) focuses on the goals of the group and determines its external relations, whereas the expressive leader (sociometric star) functions as the emotional centre and is responsible for the atmosphere in the group. Both kinds of leadership are needed for a group to function well.

In our culture, the instrumental and the expressive leadership positions in the family are respectively assumed by the father and the mother. Children perceive their father more as the dominance-figure and their mother more as the warmth-figure (Angenent, 1990). The contact children maintain with their mother is usually more intense and more intimate than the one they have with their father (Curtis, 1975; Stevenson et al., 1967). However, when parents share each others' roles, this difference disappears (Lamb, 1979).

Traditionally, lack of maternal warmth (maternal deprivation) has been viewed as a cause of delinquency (Bowlby, 1946; Krohn and Massey, 1980). More recently, it has been discovered that paternal warmth inhibits the development of delinquency (Glueck and Glueck, 1950; Hirschi, 1969; Johnson, 1987; Nye, 1958; Stagner, 1974). In fact, paternal warmth appears to be as important as maternal warmth (Gold, 1963; Hirschi, 1969; Smith and Walters, 1978).

Delinquent *boys* tend to feel that they do not receive sufficient warmth, especially from their fathers (Andry, 1960). This relationship between delinquency and lack of paternal warmth is not surprising. Fathers serve as identification figures to their sons and in that capacity contribute to the development of the boys' norm structure. Of course, it is easier to identify with a father who is warm than with one who is cold. Poor relationships with the father is also a basis for faulty social relationships in general.

With respect to dominance, the situation is less clear. It is often found that the fathers of juvenile delinquents are very domineering, whereas the mothers are rather permissive (Bandura and Walters, 1959; Buikhuisen and Meijs, 1983; Glueck and Glueck, 1950; Junger-Tas, 1972; Mannheim, 1965; Merrill, 1947). In the long run, the affected children do no longer accept the domineering attitude of their father, particularly because their mother does not support the behaviour of her partner.

LABELLING

Many parents attribute the delinquent behaviour of their children to external causes such as the infamous "delinquent friends". However, there are also elders who (in the long run) can not deny any more that their children in fact are directly responsible for their criminal activities. These parents then often distinguish between "criminal behaviour" and "being criminal"; they blame their children for their criminal behaviour, but do not ascribe a criminal identity to them ("my son does steal, but that does not mean that he is a thief"). In cases of repeated and serious criminal behaviour, the possibility exists that the parents (and others) start labelling their children as delinquent with all the stereotyping that is associated with such a designation. If the children identify themselves with the criminal identity assigned to them by the labelling process, they will develop a delinquent self-image. This self-image, as a self-fulfilling prophecy, will place them at risk for delinquency (Merton, 1968).

CHILD REARING POLICY

Child rearing policy refers to the combination of rules, regulations, agreements, and associated measures parents consider of importance to successful child rearing. A child rearing policy may be regarded as the concrete expression of the child rearing style of the parents which aims to influence the behaviour of the children so that they grow up in accordance with specific norms and customs.

It is not unreasonable to assume that when a family fails in its child rearing policy, the road to delinquency is wide open (Gold, 1970; Hanson et al., 1984; Loeber and Schmaling, 1985a; Snyder and Patterson, 1987; West and Farrington, 1973).

Two approaches may be differentiated with respect to parental child rearing policies (Gerris, 1988; Rollins and Thomas, 1979). The first one focuses on immediate behavioural consequences; reward and punishment are central to this method. The parents may manipulate the behaviour of their children by using warmth, emotional support, and affection; they may also take measures that are physical or material in nature. The effects of this approach are usually limited and temporary in nature. The second approach aims to influence the personality of the child, and thus focuses only indirectly on behavioural consequences. Parents may present and explain norms to their children and may discuss with them the advantages and disadvantages of following or disregarding norms. They may explore their children's motives for maladaptive behaviour and appeal to their sense of responsibility. This approach tends to have a positive and generally long-lasting effect. Families of juvenile delinquents have been found to emphasize the first approach (Kohn, 1959).

Consistency

A good child rearing policy by definition is a consistent policy. It is very important for children to know what their parents expect of them and how they will respond to their behaviour. It gives them a sense of security and self-confidence, and provides them with norms they can follow.

Inconsistent child rearing may be the result of a *structural* inconsistency in the family. Such inconsistency may result from a change in family composition (e.g., divorce, death, new family member) or a change in socioeconomic status (e.g., unemployment, change in job, moving). As has been discussed previously, problems of this nature may to a certain extent be related to juvenile delinquency (Brennan et al., 1978).

Functional inconsistency occurs when parents (or one of the parents) vary their child rearing from situation to situation (e.g., they alternate between warm and cold or between dominance and permissiveness) or when they do not present a common approach to child rearing (e.g., one parent is cold and the other is warm).

There is a clear relationship between inconsistent child rearing (particularly by the father) and juvenile delinquency (Andry, 1960; Glueck and Glueck, 1950; Göppinger, 1976; Junger-Tas, 1972; McCord et al., 1959; Nye, 1958; Patterson and Stouthamer-Loeber, 1984; Rutter and Giller, 1983; Schwabe-Holein, 1984; Stanfield, 1966; Wilson, 1980b). If a particular behaviour is randomly approved of in one situation and condemned in another, the child will become insecure. The behaviour will take on conflicting values. When approved, the behaviour will be associated with positive feelings, when disapproved it will be linked with negative emotions. In the first situation, the child will try to repeat the behaviour, whereas in the latter instance the behaviour will not be repeated. In other words, in the case of an inconsistent child rearing policy, positive and negative feelings are intermixed. This makes the child insecure, confused, and, in extreme situations, neurotic (Kohnstamm, 1987). A sense of "learned helplessness" may develop (Klein, et al., 1976). As a result, the youngster becomes alienated from the parents and attempts to solve the dilemma by means of escape and avoidance behaviour. The influence of the parents is reduced, and relationships are sought outside the family, particularly with friends (Stanfield, 1966).

Supervision

Parental supervision of children's behaviour very much inhibits the development of juvenile delinquency (Glueck and Glueck, 1968; Gold, 1963; Hanson et al., 1984; Hirschi, 1969, 1983; Jensen, 1972b; Laub and Sampson, 1988; Laybourn, 1986; Loeber and Dishion, 1983; Loeber and Schmaling, 1985b; McCord, 1979; Olweus, 1980a; Patterson and Stouthamer-Loeber, 1984; Reckless et al., 1957; Riley, 1987; Rutter and Giller, 1983; Snyder and Patterson, 1987; Snyder et al., 1986; Stanfield, 1966; West and Farrington, 1973, 1977; Wilson, 1980a).

Because children spend a great deal of time outside the family, providing such supervision is not an easy task. However, this task is an important one because there is a direct relationship between delinquency and the amount of time children spend away from the family (Nye, 1958; West and Farrington, 1973).

In order to exercise a certain degree of control over the behaviour of their children, it is of primary importance that parents *know where the latter are* and what they are doing. Parents of delinquent youngsters often are rather incognizant of what their children are up to (Hirschi, 1969, 1983; McCord, 1979; Mutsaers, 1987; Patterson and Stouthamer-Loeber, 1984; West and Farrington, 1977; Wilson, 1980a).

The manner in which parents *respond* to delinquent behaviour is also of great importance (West, 1969; West and Farrington, 1973). They may disapprove of certain behaviours of their children, counsel them against associating with certain peers, or disapprove of the behaviour of *other* youths. This approach allows them to indicate that certain behaviours are unacceptable and at the same time warn against delinquent peers. If their children accept this advice, they will not only discontinue the behaviours in question but also avoid contact with delinquent others. This way there will be a relationship between parental supervision and the kind of friends the children will seek (Jensen, 1972b; Patterson and Dishion, 1985; Wilson, 1980a).

The families of juvenile delinquents often do not actively intervene at the right time with the right measures. Some parents take surprisingly little action against unacceptable behaviour of their offspring. For example, they ask no questions when they come home with all kinds of goods they clearly can not afford on their own. Others tend to rationalize ("my child did this because he was forced by delinquent peers") or attempt to cover up what their children did ("my child could not have done that because he was at home with me when it happened"; "my child did not steal this, I gave it to him as a present"). This shows that the information parents have about their children often is incorrect (Stagner, 1974). Moreover, parents and other family members often fail to recognize the seriousness of delinquent behaviour, in part because they are not well informed (Janes, et al., 1979).

The relationship between supervision and delinquency appears to be particularly strong in older children (Snyder, et al., 1986). Younger children by definition are supervised more closely, whereas with older children there is greater variation in the amount of parental supervision. Of course, adequate supervision does not necessarily guarantee that things will not go wrong, but the chances of this happening are greatly reduced.

Strictness

A strict child rearing policy has been found to be related to juvenile delinquency (Glueck and Glueck, 1968; Gold, 1970; Hollerman et al., 1982; Kraus, 1977; Lobitz and Johnson, 1976; Loeber et al., 1983; McCord, 1979; Nye, 1958; Olweus, 1980a; Rutter and Giller, 1983; Schwabe-Holein, 1984; Snyder, 1977; West and Farrington, 1973). Of course, extremely permissive child rearing probably does not promote adjusted behaviour in children either, but there is less evidence for that in the literature (Schaefer, 1965; Stanfield, 1966).

The strict character of a policy is, among others, expressed in the manner, frequency, and severity of *punishment*. Punishment is sometimes necessary, but should be used with caution. The pedagogical effects of punishments are limited; they emphasize that particular behaviours are not allowed, but do not indicate what should be done instead. Families of juvenile delinquents tend to rely on physical punishment, verbal abuse, and threats, rather than on giving attention, reasoning, praise, and disapproval (Bandura and Walters, 1959; Glueck and Glueck, 1970).

Juvenile delinquents themselves feel that they are more often and more severely punished than their siblings, and as a result tend to feel rejected by their parents. Of course, some of this punishment is in response to their own delinquent behaviour (Duncan, 1971). In may be noted that *severe punishment* is not a good way to prevent delinquency or to curtail the behaviour should it occur. Such punishments often are counterproductive, especially if applied unjustly in the eyes of the recipients. They result in the suppression of behaviour, but not in the elimination of the tendency toward such behaviour. As a result, the consequences of strict discipline are temporary and uncertain. In most cases, the children only learn that they should not show the undesired behaviour in the presence of their parents. The effect may be that the behaviour intensifies, although out of sight of the parents (Church, 1963). Severe physical punishment is particularly counter-productive. It may cause antipathy toward the punisher, and may elicit aggression in children (Maurer, 1974; Sears et al., 1957; Wells, 1976). If combined with aggression on the part of the parent, it may act as an example, and the chance exists that the children will imitate this aggression (Snyder and Patterson, 1987). This may lead to *circular aggression* between parents and children. Of course, such learned aggressive behaviour will not be confined to the family.

The relationship between strict punishment and juvenile delinquency is bi-directional in nature: strictly punished youngsters are more often delinquent (Reckless et al., 1956a, b) and delinquent children are more often punished severely. In this context, it is worth noting that hard-core delinquents often have a history of strict punishment (Stagner, 1974).

The relationship between severe punishment in child rearing and juvenile delinquency sometimes does not develop when the punishment is extremely severe in nature. In such cases, almost all overt forms of deviant behaviour disappear (girls are possibly more affected in this respect than are boys) because the children develop a neurotic inhibition (Asumi, 1963; Bennett, 1960; Gibbens, 1963; Hewitt and Jenkins, 1946; McCord et al., 1959; Peterson and Becker, 1965; Sears et al., 1957).

CRIMINALITY OF PARENTS AND CHILDREN

Transferring Criminality

Despite the fact that delinquency is so prevalent among youngsters, it appears that some families contribute to it in a big way. Therefore, criminality of family members is a good predictor of juvenile delinquency (Loeber and Dishion, 1982; Schneider, 1987).

Often, there is an *intergenerational effect* in delinquent families; that is, a greater involvement in delinquency by children whose parents are not free of such behaviour themselves (Farrington et al., 1975; Loeber and

Dishion, 1982; Osborn and West, 1979; Robins et al., 1975; West, 1969, 1982; West and Farrington, 1973, 1977; Wilson, 1980b, 1982).

In some families, criminal behaviour is something of a tradition which is passed on, as it were, from generation to generation (Cloninger and Guze, 1970; Ellis, 1987b, Glueck and Glueck, 1974; Robins et al., 1975; Schneider, 1987). We find similar family traditions with respect to other forms of deviant and maladapted behaviour such as child abuse, negligence, running away, and so forth.

The correlation between the criminality of parents and that of their children may be the consequence of *child rearing traditions, modelling, assortative partner choice,* or *heredity.*

Child Rearing Traditions

The experiences parents have accumulated during their lives influence the way in which they raise their children. Of particular importance is the child rearing they themselves were exposed to during their own childhood (Angenent, 1990). Usually, parents will use child rearing methods that relate to and are a continuation of the way in which they themselves were raised. This "repetition through the generations" phenomenon may be referred to as a child rearing tradition. The presence of such a tradition can be easily demonstrated by comparing the child rearing approaches of successive generations.

Conscious imitation of their own child rearing is found in parents who believe that they have been raised well and who want to provide their children with a similar experience. On the other hand, parents who experienced their own child rearing as negative may make a conscious effort to raise their children in a way that is different from the manner in which they were raised themselves. This is referred to as *compensation child rearing.* But even in those cases is it possible to find striking similarities between the way the parents were raised and the way they raise their own children. Child rearing traditions are hard to break and are in fact mostly subconscious. Such a subconscious tradition may be observed, for example, in parents who have been neglected during their youth and who now unintentionally neglect their own children. The reason for this is that they have not personally experienced nor learned how to build a good relationship with a child. A striking example of a subconscious tradition is the abuse of children by parents who themselves were victims of child abuse when they were young. As far as juvenile delinquency is concerned, there are child rearing traditions in which approaches to raising children that have been found to be related to juvenile delinquency —which have been discussed in this chapter— are passed on from generation to generation (Patterson, 1986; Ricks, 1985).

Modelling

We have seen that good parent-child relationships inhibit juvenile delinquency. A good relation facilitates the adoption of parental norms and behaviours by children. In this context we noted the prime importance of role models. One should not forget, however, that children can also learn criminal behaviour from their parents (Adams, 1973; Elliott and Voss, 1974; Killias, 1981; Poole and Regoli, 1979; Rutter and Giller, 1983; Sutherland and Cressey, 1978; West and Farrington, 1973). Bad examples (deviations from the norm) work just as well as good ones. There are even indications that maladaptive examples have more of an impact. The reason for this is that maladaptive behaviour is rewarded irregularly, and that irregular rewards have greater effects than regular ones (Bandura, 1977; Killias, 1981). Of course, youngsters are not restricted to maladaptive examples provided by family members, but also meet maladapted adults outside the family. In any case, juvenile delinquents have more contact with adult delinquents than do other youngsters (Short, 1958; Sutherland and Cressey, 1978; Voss, 1964).

Parents who were or are delinquents themselves, sometimes are not concerned about the example they are setting for their children. In such cases, their children learn delinquency on a firsthand basis. However, these are exceptions; parents who are (or were) involved in criminality often do their best to hide this from their children (Hirschi, 1969; Sykes and Matza, 1957; West, 1982; West and Farrington, 1973). This is probably the reason for Hirschi's (1969) finding that even with delinquent parents, if there is a good parent-child relationship, a favourable prognosis is justified.

Assortative Partner Choice

The issue of whether interpersonal relationships are fostered by complementarity or similarity of the partners has engaged the interest of social psychologists for many years. *Complementarity theory* suggests that people who differ a lot from each other are attracted to each other and seek to form mutual relationships ("opposites attract"). Generally, they get along very well because of the complementary nature of their affiliation (Winch, 1958). *Similarity theory*, on the other hand, states the opposite. People seek to form relationships with others whose personality resembles their own ("birds of a feather flock together"). Such relationships will be smooth because they recognize so much of themselves in their partners (Meyer and Pepper, 1977). The bulk of research evidence favours the similarity point of view (Cattell, 1982; Meyer and Pepper, 1977).

Applied to marriage, similarity theory implies that one searches for a partner who is rather similar to oneself. Such a relationship is referred to as an *assortative* relationship. Hence, an assortative affiliation is one in which the partners display a great deal of similarity. It has been found that marriage partners tend to be more alike (homogamy) than is the case with people in general (panmixia). The similarities may involve, for instance, age, ethnic background, socioeconomic status, values, norms (religion), social and political attitudes, intelligence, education, personality, and physical characteristics, as well as neurotic tendencies, alcoholism, and psychiatric symptoms (Cattell, 1982; Murstein and Christy, 1976; Rushton et al., 1985; Vandenberg, 1972).

The question remains whether or not this homogamy also includes criminal behaviour. In other words, do delinquent man and delinquent women gravitate toward each other? Do men who have criminal characteristics more often than not marry women with similar qualities? This question thus far has not received a great deal of attention in the literature. However, Guze et al. (1970) found that wives of convicted delinquents have problematic family backgrounds that resemble those of their husbands.

The question of homogamy and criminality is especially important because homogamy influences the children of a family in a variety of ways (Miller and Rose, 1982). In the first place, it influences the relationship between the parents and thus the family atmosphere (Rushton et al., 1985). The greater the similarity between the parents (especially, the more they believe that they resemble each other) the better and more stable the marriage (Bentler and Newcomb, 1978; Cattell and Nisselroade, 1967, Meyer and Pepper, 1977; Pickford et al., 1967). The latter is, as we have seen, beneficial to child rearing. Moreover, characteristics that are shared by the parents have a greater possibility of being transferred to the children. In other words, the more the parents resemble each other, the more the children will resemble the parents. This similarity between parents and children is facilitated by child rearing, the example set by the parents, and by heredity. The latter factor appears because in homogamous marriages there is a certain concentration of hereditary material as a result of the fact that the partners resemble each other also in genetic terms to a greater extent than is the case with complementary partners (Buss, 1984). The relationship between homogamy as a result of assortative partner choice and juvenile delinquency has not yet been researched very much.

Heredity

Hereditary studies of criminal behaviour thus far have mainly focused on recorded criminality, serious criminal behaviour, adults, and males. We will discuss two evidence-gathering procedures used to study the degree of genetic influence on delinquent behaviour: namely, twin studies and adoption research.

Twin studies make use of the fact that there are two types of twins; namely, fraternal or dizygotic twins and identical or monozygotic twins. Most twins (about 3 out of 4) are fraternal. They result from the fertilization of two eggs by two different sperm cells at the same time. Thus, fraternal twins are no more alike than non-twin siblings. The remaining quarter are identical twins. The latter result from the splitting of one fertilized egg and have exactly the same genetic makeup. They are, for example, of the same sex.

Because identical twins have identical genes, they are physically and behaviourally more similar than fraternal twins. If there are differences between identical twins, these should be due to the environment, whereas differences between fraternal twins may be due to genetic as well as environmental factors. If there is greater similarity with respect to a particular characteristic (e.g., delinquent behaviour) between identical twins than there is between fraternal twins, this should be due to the impact of the former's identical genetic makeup.

Lange (1929) was the first person to use a twin study to gather evidence regarding criminality. Among 13 delinquents who were part of an identical twin pair there were 10 who had a twin brother who had been in jail. This degree of similarity is called *concordance*. Among 17 delinquents who were part of a fraternal twin pair there were only 2 such cases. Thus, the concordance was 77% and 12% respectively. Montagu (1959) reported percentages of 67% and 33% for earlier investigations. However, questions may be raised concerning the samples that were used in these earlier studies and the reliability of the method used to determine twin-type. In more recent investigations the differences between concordance rates have been less dramatic (Ellis, 1982; Forde, 1978; Trasler, 1987). Research conducted in Denmark by Christiansen (1977a, b) found concordance rates of 36% versus 13%; in Norway, Dalgaard and Kringlen (1976) found ratios of 22% versus 18% and 26% versus 15%.

The higher concordance for criminality between identical twins as compared to fraternal twins suggests that a genetic factor is operating in delinquency. However, the conclusions about genetic influence in such studies are compromised. The reason for this is that identical twins normally live in more similar milieus than do fraternal twins whose environments, even though they share the same family, may still be different. For example, identical twins tend to be treated in the same way, because they look so much alike and are of the same sex. Parents of fraternal twins, because the children do not look the same and may be of different sex, may treat one twin differently than the other. The greater concordance between identical twins may therefore in part be ascribed to environmental factors. Thus, twin studies do provide suggestions about the influence of heredity, but do not lead to definite conclusions.

In an attempt to systematically control for milieu factors, some researchers have studied adopted children. In *adoption research*, people who have been separated from their biological parents shortly after birth and who subsequently have been raised in a foster family that has no blood relationship with the natural family are studied. To study criminality, these investigations examine the delinquent behaviour of adopted children as compared to that of their respective biological and adoptive parents. If heredity is important in the development of delinquency, one would expect that the incidence of criminality shown by the children would resemble that shown by their biological rather than their adoptive parents.

It has indeed been found that biological parents of delinquents show a higher incidence of criminal behaviour than do adoptive parents (Bohman et al., 1982; Hutchings and Mednick, 1977; Sigvardsson et al., 1982; Trasler, 1987). Thus, it appears that delinquent behaviour of adopted children may be better predicted on the basis of the criminal activities, if any, of their natural parents rather than that of their adoptive parents.

There is a problem, however, because adoption agencies are selective in their choice of potential foster families. They tend to prefer foster parents who resemble the natural parents in terms of ethnic background, socioeconomic status, appearance, and so forth. As a result the concordance is influenced by this selection, and thus by milieu factors.

Because of these difficulties, the question as to the extent to which genetic factors play a role in the development of delinquent behaviour has not yet been answered conclusively. A preliminary inference may be that genetic makeup may in some way contribute to criminality (Rowe, 1983; Rowe and Osgood, 1984; Walters and White, 1989). It is not so much the case that criminality itself is inherited, but that particular personality characteristics that are related to delinquency are to a certain extent genetically determined. Such a genetic influence would express itself in the functioning of the nervous system, and, related to this, hormonal factors (Cattell, 1982; Ellis, 1982; Eysenck, 1977).

In fact, the low concordance for delinquency between identical twins (notwithstanding their identical genes), and the relatively small number of adopted children who resemble their biological parents in this respect, indicate that environmental influences are of greater importance to the development of delinquency than are genetic factors (Füllgrabe, 1978).

The few investigations which include juvenile delinquents in their considerations, give the impression that heredity plays an even less important role in the delinquent behaviour of youngsters than it does in the criminality of adults. In other words, the environment has a relatively greater influence on juvenile delinquency (Eysenck, 1977; Miller and Rose, 1982; Trasler, 1987).

5. THE SCHOOL

YOUTH AND THE SCHOOL

Probably the most important role youths play in today's society is that of student. What work is to adults, school is to youths. For many years they spend many hours in school where they develop intellectually, emotionally, as well as socially. As a result, school forms an important part of their environment.

Because of developments in society, the school has become more and more important. Society increasingly requires better educated people who can handle the problems it faces. Consequently, great demands have been placed on the schools, which has led, among others, to a differentiated system of education.

Moreover, recently an increasing number of tasks in the areas of child rearing and formation has been transferred to the school, thereby enlarging its range of responsibilities. Modern view, in theory at least, no longer regards the school as just an institute for training, but sees it more as an institution that also fosters general development (Liazos, 1978; Timmermans, 1987).

School is a place where youngsters acquire knowledge, but it is also a place where they are trained in social relations and where they are exposed to various societal norms, rules, and customs. At school, youngsters learn to function in an achievement-oriented system; they learn about ambition, competition and the struggle for life. Also, they will meet friends and peers, learn to function in groups, and form all sorts of practical alliances in order to collectively cope with life at school. All in all, school is an important frame of reference for youngsters (Brentjens, 1978; Mannheim and Steward, 1964).

In fact, the school is the first institution of society, besides the family, with which youngsters come into real contact. It may be considered as a kind of pre-societal world: those who can cope with school have a fair chance of surviving in society. The type of education one has received and the educational level one has achieved are of vital importance to future opportunities in society. In a broader context, youngsters' performance in school determines to a large extent their subsequent social status and identity, and thus how they will fare in life (Elliott, 1972).

DELINQUENCY BY STUDENTS

Both recorded and surveyed delinquency data indicate that between the ages of 12 and 14 years, youngsters begin to display noticeably more criminal behaviour. Reckless and Shoham (1963) speak of a "fast rising storm". For a number of years, youths account for a substantial part of criminality; a significant number of these are students.

There is a relationship between school type and delinquency. It is an international phenomenon that students who follow less advanced forms of education commit relatively more crimes than students who follow higher levels (Hartnagel and Tanner, 1982; Junger-Tas et al., 1983; McDonald, 1969; Mutsaers, 1987; Schafer et al., 1972; Toby, 1982, 1983). This relationship is sometimes attributed to the selection process that takes place at the end of elementary school. At that time, students are selected for specific forms of continued schooling on the basis of their abilities and academic success, but also on the basis of socioeconomic milieu, gender, and ethnic background (Brentjens, 1978; Gamoran and Mare, 1989; Johnson, 1979; Kelly, 1974, 1975, 1978; Pink, 1984; Polk and Schafer, 1972; Schafer et al., 1972; Tygart, 1988; Wesselingh, 1979). Because of this selection process, children who have been rated at the lower end tend to be directed toward vocational training or a similar type of schooling. Once students have been classified as such by this *early, negative selection process*, transfer to a higher form of education is almost impossible (Hargreaves, 1967; Rutter et al., 1979). The lower-rated students end up in a school that has lower status. Moreover, these students, as compared to their peers in more advanced school types, much less perceive the value schooling has for their future. This is not conducive to their performance in school, and inadequate performance may, as we will see shortly, lead to delinquency.

Some authors have suggested that a lower classification affects a youngster's self-esteem, and that low self-esteem may lead to delinquency; others believe that low self-esteem is not needed as intermediary variable (e.g., Kelly, 1978). They note that the low self-esteem is limited to performance in school, especially to academic achievement. Outside the school setting, "lower-track" students do not necessarily feel inferior, possibly because they do not regard school achievements as very important (Byrne, 1988).

Lower-rated students are given fewer opportunities than their higher-rated peers, even when they attend the same type of school. They are treated more critically, are less appreciated by school administrators and teachers who have high hopes for the better students and who give them more attention (Pink, 1984). Lower-rated students are also treated less positively by their peers (Byrne, 1988).

This discrimination of lower-rated children contradicts the myth that the school is an institution which offers everybody the same chances and which takes care of students who are weaker to begin with. In reality, this is not and has never been the case (Adams and Looft, 1977).

The above mentioned discrimination does not promote adaptation to school, but instead leads to loss of motivation. Students who are victims of this bias run the danger of becoming fringe figures inside and outside school, and of coming into contact with less adjusted youths who sometimes are involved in delinquency (Hargreaves, 1967; Hartnagel and Tanner, 1982; Kelly and Pink, 1973; Ogbu, 1974; Polk, 1969).

JUVENILE DELINQUENCY AND FUNCTIONING IN SCHOOL

If so many students are guilty of delinquent behaviour, one may well ask what the association is between school and delinquency. This question has interested many since the beginning of this century (e.g., Healy, 1915). In trying to answer it, the focus has been primarily on how students function in school (e.g., Dijksterhuis and Nijboer, 1984; Dishion et al., 1984; Elliott and Voss, 1974; Frease, 1973; Glueck and Glueck, 1959; Gold and Mann, 1972; Hartnagel and Tanner, 1982; Junger-Tas, 1987; Junger-Tas et al., 1983, 1985; LaGrange and White, 1985; Lawrence, 1985; Loeber and Dishion, 1983; Ouston, 1984; Polk, 1969, 1975; Rutter et al., 1979; Wadworth, 1979; West and Farrington, 1973; Wiatrowski et al., 1981; Wilson and Herrnstein, 1985; Wolfgang et al., 1972). The less well youngsters function in school in terms of academic achievement and conduct, the greater the probability that they will show criminal behaviour.

School records show that juvenile delinquents tend to score relatively low in school achievements (Hirschi and Hindelang, 1977; Jensen, 1976). Conduct problems involve annoying and disturbing behaviours, which often result in punishment, including dismissal from class or temporary expulsion from school. Behavioural problems are particularly evident when youngsters do not get along with teachers and fellow-students, which may lead to disagreements and arguments. Students who (later in life) commit crimes often are described by teachers as annoying and disturbing. This judgement by teachers therefore is a reliable predictor of subsequent delinquency (Farrington and West, 1971; Feldhusen and Benning, 1972; Venezia, 1971).

It may be noted that girls usually function better in school than boys. They are better integrated and feel greater affinity with the school. This is related to the fact that girls adapt easier, are less achievement oriented than boys, are better able to cope with frustrations, and have their family and friends to fall back on. Performance in school therefore is more related to delinquency in boys than in girls (Gold; 1970; Zinnecker, 1982).

FUNCTIONING IN SCHOOL

Taking the relationship between functioning in school and juvenile delinquency as point of departure, we will first address the question of how youngsters function in school and which problems they may encounter. Because it is not only the juvenile delinquents who have trouble with functioning in school, we will first deal with this question in a more general sense. Later on we will come back to the more specific relationship between functioning in school and juvenile delinquency.

The causes for the fact that some students function poorly in school may be sought in the school as well as in the students, and especially in the interaction between the two. It is noteworthy that schools (administration, teachers) blame the problems mainly on shortcomings of the students, whereas students —and not only the poorly functioning ones— attribute it to imperfections of the school (Mooij, 1980). The main complaint schools have about students is their poor motivation. Youngsters, it is said, often lack interest in school; their interests lie outside. They do not show much initiative either, rather they are inactive and weak and lack the necessary perseverance. Furthermore, many students have difficulties accepting authority. Leadership based on authority is not appreciated and is undermined in many ways. Another complaint is that many students can not cope well, are easily frustrated, and subsequently react either by withdrawing or by becoming aggressive. Finally, there are more general complaints about the chaotic and disturbing conduct of students who are difficult to control.

The other side of the coin is that a student's daily life at school is bleaker (Matthijssen, 1986) than is apparent from the official curriculum and school regulations. The school's organization, the manner in which the students are approached, the teaching methods, and the content of the lessons have a discouraging effect on many students. Studies often suggest that students are not entirely enthused about school; moreover, the longer they stay in school, the more negative their perception. This is, understandably, particularly the case with students who function poorly (Brentjens, 1978; Matthijssen, 1986).

The school has an instrumental as well as an expressive task with respect to students. The former means that the school has to equip the students with the necessary cognitive, social, and emotional knowledge and skills, whereas the latter means that the school must provide an atmosphere in which this is possible. The characteristics of a good school are derived from this. We will review the most important ones:

1. A good school is one where there is a good climate, a warm ambience which excludes nobody. This means, among others, that every student

gets a chance to have positive learning experiences, relationships, and identifications.

2. The school atmosphere is moderately controlling: that is, not too regulated and not too permissive. On the one hand there is room for responsibility and autonomy on the part of the students, on the other hand they have to meet reasonable expectations.
3. School policy is consistent; consequently, the students know where they stand. The procedures are clear and are regarded as fair by the students. This applies in particular to the policy on punishment.
4. Learning is central; the content of the lessons is relevant and presented in an satisfactory way. Students are well aware that learning comes first at school and through it gain self-esteem (Rutter et al., 1979).

Schools with such characteristics instill in their students a sense of affiliation and at the same time decrease the attractiveness of behaviours and life styles that are incompatible with school (Rubel, 1978a,b; De Vries, 1987).

Ad 1. School atmosphere is to the school what family atmosphere is to the family. For students it would be ideal if the atmosphere of their school complements the (positive) atmosphere of their family (Hartup, 1985). A harmonious school atmosphere allows good relationships between teachers and students and among students themselves. The school is better able to influence the students in a personal way and to supervise them. Students can go to their teacher not only with their school problems but also with their personal difficulties. As far as the latter is concerned, relationships with a teacher may compensate for inadequate relationships with parents. As such, the school's influence on students may be regarded as supplementing that of the family. Many teachers, though, limit themselves to transferring knowledge, so that their influence on the personal life of their students is minimal (Hellman and Beaton, 1986; Rubel, 1978a,b).

Ad 2. A positive school atmosphere entails a not too controlling attitude on the part of the school. The school has the final responsibility, but within limits gives students sufficient freedom. Generally, however, the input of students is rather restricted. They are forced into a passive role (Brentjens, 1978), are not actively involved in the curriculum, and hardly have any responsibilities. Inside and outside the classroom there prevails a domineering atmosphere with teachers and school administration in control. Participation by students (in the organization, in designing the curriculum, and so on) is rare. This is a difficult environment for youngsters who are in an active phase of life. At school, youths are treated as adults in miniature rather than as individuals with an identity of their own. This is the more frustrating because elsewhere (at home, during leisure time) they are more treated like adults (Adams and Looft, 1977; Zinnecker, 1982). This discrepancy is greater with boys than with girls. Outside school, youths sometimes already have responsibilities, whereas in school all that is demanded of them is obedience and conformity (Graham, 1988a; Grunsell, 1980).

Of course, the other extreme is not advisable either. A too permissive attitude has its problems too. It creates an atmosphere in which too much responsibility is put on the shoulders of the students. Furthermore, there is the danger that domineering and aggressive students can do what they want, and that shy, naive students are victimized (Kohnstamm, 1987).

Ad 3. The way life at school turns out to be in reality depends on the school policy which is reflected in the rules and the way in which these are enforced. Many students perceive the policy as too strict. This elicits aggressive feelings which they direct not only toward the school but also toward peers. It may also negatively affect their conduct; they may show all sorts of deviant behaviour, in and outside the school (Rubel, 1978a,b).

Ad 4. In school, students function within the framework of the school organization. The anonymity of large organizations is often viewed as a negative factor (Marwijck Kooij, 1984; Schuurman, 1985). Whereas some think that students at large schools have less of a sense of belonging and that such schools are less able to deal with problem students (Willems, 1967), others feel that it is not so much the size of the school as the size of classes which makes school less attractive to students (Baerveldt, 1987).

Within the context of its mission to transfer knowledge, the school has developed into an achievement oriented system in which the element of competition takes an important place (Adams and Looft, 1977; Gold, 1978). In no other milieu (at home, at work, during leisure time, etc.) are the achievement norms so evident and pronounced as they are at school. This is accompanied by incessant testing, weighing, and comparing. Experiences of success and failure follow one another. Student very much resemble top athletes in this respect. The marks-culture so prevalent in many schools does not make life any more attractive. As a result, many students are too preoccupied with earning good marks and show little interest in what goes on in class (Matthijssen, 1986).

Most students resign themselves to this state of affairs. They realize that a diploma is important, particularly because it increases the chances of landing a good job. For this they gladly suffer somewhat (Stinchcombe, 1964). And yet, there is much opposition among students to this achievement orientation and the rivalry among themselves. The greater the discrepancy between the achievement demands and the possibility and will to comply, the easier students will lose the motivation to exert themselves (Csikszentmihalyi and Larson, 1978).

As far as teaching is concerned, students generally have clear expectations. They expect, for example, that their teachers know their job, as reflected in the way they teach. As such, the latter will have to prove themselves time after time (Rutter et al., 1979).

Students are very critical of the contents of the lessons. They regard the material as too theoretical, poorly related to social reality, and certainly not consonant with their personal experiences and interests. The lessons therefore are often characterized as boring and of little importance (Matthijssen, 1986). Reason for Liazos (1978) to observe that the school in this respect is a good preparation for the kind of work the students will be doing later on, which in most cases will be just as mind-numbing as school!

Thus, it is clear that students may have enough problems functioning in school. Students who function well are usually prepared to put up with things, particularly because they understand that their future depends on their career at school. Moreover, they are able to compensate for the frustrations in school by their achievements, interest in learning, good relations with teachers, popularity among their peers, and so forth. For nonfunctioning students this is more difficult. In the first place, the school is oriented toward students who function well. This means that those who function less well experience more frustrations and also receive less support from the school in overcoming these frustrations. In the second place, these students know the above mentioned and other compensating factors only from hearsay. Reasons why they gradually alienate from school.

PEERS AT SCHOOL

Besides factors such as the ones we discussed in the previous section, the way in which students function in school also depends on their relations with other students, especially with those in the same class. We refer here to the school as a social system, which is just as important to students as the school as a learning system (Wiatrowski and Anderson, 1987).

Even though students, as we have seen, usually have little input into the instrumental aspect of the school (teaching), their influence on the expressive aspect is relatively large. Daily life at school and how it is experienced is to a large extent determined by the students themselves. They influence each other's behaviour greatly. We have already discussed some aspects of this mutual influence in Chapter 2. We will discuss it more extensively in the next chapter which deals with friends and peers. We will see, among others, that a flexible relationship with friends and peers is no luxury, but rather an essential condition for adequate identity formation and social development. The relationships with fellow students may also contribute to these aspects of development. Students like to interact with others; they do their utmost to be part of the group. There is much imitation in appearance (hairstyle, clothing), behaviour, language, and norms. Popular students in particular may have a large influence. This popularity is determined by intelligence and achievement, but also by sport accomplishments, social skills, and appearance (Cavior and Dokecki, 1973).

Youths who do not function very well in school gradually end up on the fringe of the group of well-adjusted students. Initially, this may not be a problem, but over time being "different" leads to a separation of minds. Moreover, less well functioning students can hinder other students in their learning process, for instance by creating chaos in the classroom. Even though well-adjusted students on occasion enjoy a certain amount of excitement, they do not like it if it happens too often. Non-functioning students who are too disruptive therefore are regarded as annoying by their fellow students. The result is that they are ignored. This lack of acceptance by fellow students may be a large handicap. Non-functioning students often become alienated from not only the school as institution but also from their fellow students (Barclay, 1966; Parker and Asher, 1987).

ACHIEVERS AND FAILURES

Youngsters who do not function well in school usually do not like it there nor feel involved. They do not only feel alienated from what goes on in the classroom but also from extracurricular activities. Their relationship with the school is cool and distant and they sometimes even hate the place, especially because they are discriminated against by administrators, teachers, and fellow students (Brennan et al., 1978; Brusten and Hurrelmann, 1973). They receive less attention from teachers who prefer to work with better students, they are excluded from all kinds of activities, and, as we have seen, they are not very popular among their classmates. To place this in perspective, however, it should be noted that studies have shown that in reality the consequences of discrimination within the school are not that serious (Bezamore, 1985; Farrington et al., 1978). Poorly functioning students may interpret the discrimination as a warning, and may subsequently behave in a more acceptable manner. This probably occurs only in less severe cases. In most instances, the youngsters in question will distance themselves even more from school. Particularly because the school offers them little opportunity to succeed and gain status in areas other than academics, for example in the school organization (committees), in sports, or recreational activities (school parties) (Mooij, 1984).

This means that students who function poorly in school by definition end up in a vicious circle, and one may well expect that —unless effective counter measures are taken— their adaptation to school will deteriorate over time. Thus, in black and white terms, we see a segregation between "achievers" and "failures", "successful individuals" and "duds", "winners" and "losers" "adjusted and maladjusted ones", "conformists and non-conformists" or whatever they are called. The "failures" lose interest in school, adopt a rejecting attitude, do not adopt the conventional norms of the school and over time do no longer respect its moral authority, and increasingly behave as fringe figures. And thus they become more and more marginalized and alienated from school (Hargreaves et al., 1967; Polk and Schafer, 1972; Van der Linden and Roeders, 1983).

ALIENATION, ESCAPE AND AVOIDANCE BEHAVIOUR

Alienation is not so much the result of non-functioning in school as it is the result of the way in which youngsters deal with this. According to many authors, we find alienation particularly in youths whose self-esteem has been undermined by poor functioning in school (Cattell and Child, 1975; Empey and Lubeck, 1971; Gold and Mann, 1972; Jensen, 1972a; Junger-Tas, 1983; Polk and Schafer, 1972; Van der Linden and Roeders, 1983). And self-confidence is just as important for success in school as learning ability (Klein et al., 1976). Some authors (e.g., Gold, 1978) consider a negative self-image a necessary mediating factor between poor functioning in school and alienation. Others (e.g., Kelly, 1971) note that alienation may also be a direct result of poor functioning. Often, negative self-image is further reinforced by the response of fellow students and teachers (Offord et al., 1978). Poor functioning in school has a greater influence on a student's self-image if the latter regards school as important.

Students respond to alienation in the habitual way, namely, by escape behaviour and avoidance behaviour.

In school, *escape behaviour* consists of associating oneself with fellow-sufferers. Thus, the school has two subcultures. Besides the official school culture there is an alternative one which exists inside as well as outside the classroom (Coleman, 1961; De Vries, 1987; Hargreaves, 1967; Mooij, 1982; Noblit, 1976; Polk and Pink, 1971; Reinert and Zinnecker, 1978; Rutter et al., 1979; Sugerman, 1967). This alternative school culture is an opposing pole of the official school culture.

The official school culture depends on matters such as the type of school, its ideological orientation, its pedagogical viewpoint, the neighbourhood in which the school is located and —not in the least— the composition of the student body (which depends on the admission policy of the school). The official school culture is an extension of the dominant culture we discussed in Chapter 2. The school represents this culture; it adheres to its norms and customs. For the students this means that they are expected to follow the rules, earn good marks, and participate in all sorts of activities.

The alternative culture is a reaction to school and is characterized by rebellion against school norms and rejection of conformity (Willis, 1977). It relates to the hedonistic youth culture (see Chapter 2). Unlike the official school culture, the alternative culture is immediate in nature. It is oriented toward activities that are more attractive to students than school is. Central are a good atmosphere and fun activities and everything that allows one to escape from frustrations experienced at school. One of the most important motives for the development of the alternative culture is the youngsters' tendency to imitate each other. Students copy one another's behaviour, including deviant behaviour. Some students take this further than others. The scope of the alternative culture therefore depends very much on the make-up of the student body (Davis, 1966; Rutter, 1980; Rutter et al., 1979).

The particular culture chosen by the students leaves its imprint on their identity and self-image (Erikson, 1974). Well-adjusted students who embrace the dominant school culture develop an "in school" identity, the maladjusted ones an "out of school" one.

In this context, it should be noted though that well-functioning students do not per definition completely reject the alternative culture. Often, they participate in it (to a certain extent and temporarily). Even well-functioning students are sometimes fed up with school, and the alternative culture has its attractions for them too. Sometimes, they also clown around in class and skip school. However, they keep this behaviour within limits because of the important issue at stake (success at school) and their background-related inhibitions regarding too boisterous behaviour. An example of such an inhibition is the parents' pressure to behave in school (Gold, 1978).

The escape behaviour usually does not end at the school's borders. Outside school, non-functioning students look for subcultures which in terms of norms and customs resemble the alternative school culture and in a broader context the hedonistic youth culture (Cohen, 1970a; Strodtbeck and Short, 1964). These are the same subcultures which attract youngsters who are alienated from their family. In these leisure-time subcultures, as is the case in the alternative school culture, one rejects the values of the dominant culture and (thus) those of the dominant school culture, and becomes involved in matters far removed from life at school. The attitude toward juvenile delinquency is less rejecting than is the case in the school culture (Brennan et al., 1978; Cernkovich, 1978). The possibility that students meet delinquent friends in this subculture is not fictitious (Patterson and Dishion, 1985). This subculture is a milieu that is attractive to youngsters who do not do well in school because it provides them with an environment in which they can vent the frustrations resulting from their school problems (Brusten and Hurrelmann, 1973; Empey and Lubeck, 1971; Starr, 1981).

Avoidance behaviour in school may take a passive, active, and/or reactive form (Elliott and Voss, 1974; Stinchcombe, 1964). In passive avoidance behaviour, students try to escape from the situation by withdrawing, by letting things slide by, and by generally being inactive. In class they tend to daydream and doze off, and they do not participate in extracurricular activities. Active avoidance behaviour is found in students who, in spite of school, are determined to have fun. They are interested in entertainment, clowning and fooling around, and all kinds of bravura behaviour. Reactive avoidance behaviour consists of subversive behaviour that is directed against the school; being difficult, criticizing teachers, overtly showing disinterest, and disturbing the peace. The three forms of avoidance behaviour are often shown in combination.

In school, the most apparent forms of escape behaviour and avoidance behaviour include school delinquency, truancy, and dropping out. These three topics will be discussed at the end of this chapter. Outside school, avoidance behaviour is expressed in the forms normally associated with alienation that were discussed in the previous chapter (Aronson and Mettee, 1968; Brusten and Hurrelmann, 1973; Philips and Kelly, 1979).

FUNCTIONING IN SCHOOL AND JUVENILE DELINQUENCY

There are three explanations for the relationship between poor functioning in school and delinquency:

1. Juvenile delinquency may, as we have seen, be a reaction to poor functioning in school. This has been discussed in the previous section.
2. Although poor functioning in school may lead youths to get involved in delinquency, the reverse also happens, although to a lesser degree (Elliott and Voss, 1974; Thornberry and Christenson, 1984). Delinquent students may have less time and energy available to devote to school. They may experience delinquent behaviour as something positive: an interesting way to spend time, an activity that yields valuable returns and fills their life, a way to prove themselves (to themselves and others). In that case, their attention will shift and their interest in school matters will diminish. Furthermore, if the school learns of their criminal activities it is possible that they will be labelled and (to protect other students) marginalized, which will not benefit their functioning in school (Glueck and Glueck, 1950; Liska and Reed, 1985).
3. In most cases, the relationship between non-functioning in school and

delinquency must be ascribed to deeper causes which foster both problems at the same time. These causes should be sought in the personality and background of the individual concerned (common cause theory) (Glueck, 1966; McMichael, 1979; Offord et al., 1978; Schuurman, 1984; Snyder and Patterson, 1987; Wilson and Herrnstein, 1985). In such cases, poor functioning in school and delinquency are as it were two aspects of one factor, the *deviancy syndrome* we discussed in Chapter 1. This explains why many youths already show criminal behaviour and other deviant conduct before they begin to have problems in school (Wiatrowski et al., 1982; Wilson and Herrnstein, 1985).

The extent to which personality traits contribute to juvenile delinquency has been discussed in the preceding chapter. The same factors are the cause of the fact that youngsters do not succeed in school. In this chapter we limit ourselves to personality traits that are expressed in school, particularly learning disabilities. The latter will be discussed in the following section and personal background factors will be addressed in the section following.

LEARNING DISABILITIES

Since the late sixties the literature has increasingly shown an association between juvenile delinquency and learning disabilities (Grande, 1988; Hubble and Groff, 1981; Offord et al., 1978; Satterfield et al., 1982; Wolff et al., 1982; Zimmerman et al., 1981). The latter include problems in concentrating, listening, thinking, talking, reading, writing, spelling, and arithmetics. In short: problems in information processing. Studies done in various countries consistently estimate the percentage of students with learning disabilities to be between ten and fifteen percent. Learning disabilities are more frequently found in boys than in girls (Coons, 1982).

There is a clear relationship between learning disabilities and recorded juvenile delinquency. Roughly between a quarter and three-quarters of recorded juvenile delinquents are youths with learning disabilities (Zimmerman et al., 1981). It is remarkable that the association is less strong if we consider survey-reported criminality. In Chapter 4 we described a similar, albeit less extreme, discrepancy between recorded and reported criminality as it related to the incomplete family. There, we decided that the difference is mainly the result of the fact that certain groups of youngsters are more readily subjected to all sorts of social measures. In this case, we could conclude that learning-disabled youths are not necessarily more criminal than others, but are more likely to get caught (Broder et al., 1981; Zimmerman et al., 1981). Perhaps this is because they make a poorer impression because of their lower verbal and other communication abilities, awkwardness, and disturbed motor skills. Another possibility is that learning-disabled youths do not understand the questions of the questionnaires as well, and therefore report fewer crimes. It is also conceivable that these youngsters are less open when responding to surveys, something which, judging from their experiences in and outside school, is quite possible.

The greatest learning difficulty is the concentration problem. Concentration problems are particularly found in hyperactive students. These students have an attention span that is extremely short. They have a high activity level, react impulsively, and can not sit still. They have a low frustration tolerance and may act aggressively. Some researchers blame hyperactivity on minimal brain damage which leads to decreased excitability of the central nervous system. The hyperactivity then aims to increase the chronically lowered (proprioceptive and exteroceptive) input. However, this neurological explanation is questioned by many (Rutter, 1977). Whatever the case may be, there is a clear relationship between hyperactivity and juvenile delinquency (Rutter and Giller, 1983).

Concentration problems are also found in students who close themselves off from everything that falls outside a restricted sphere of attention. These are introverted, internally oriented students (daydreamers).

Concentration problems, for that matter, are not limited to learning disabled students. Half of the students at the secondary level have trouble concentrating (Matthijssen, 1986). Teachers as well as students complain about this. Many of the difficulties in classroom discipline may be traced back to this problem. Concentration problems are related to the extent to which students perceive their lessons as relevant. We have seen earlier that students do not always experience the school milieu as stimulating. In fact, the classroom is the place students associate most with boredom. When in class, much of the time their thoughts are elsewhere rather than on the material being presented (Csikszentmihalyi and Larson, 1978). In class, high demands are made of students in terms of attention and concentration, and many are not able to deliver (Schuurman, 1984). It is these students in particular who experience education as dull and tedious and who out of sheer boredom will look for other kinds of stimulation (Berlyne, 1960). Of course, deviant behaviour in class (Watson, 1980) and outside (Csikszentmihalyi and Larson, 1978) may provide exciting stimulation. It appears that delinquent youngsters have greater concentration problems than others (Gibbens, 1963; Voorhees, 1981; Yeudall et al., 1982).

The demands made by the school render it difficult for learning-disabled students to function adequately (Menard and Moore, 1984). They are in the same predicament as less intelligent students. The fact that their achievements are not impressive is already frustrating, but it is the reaction of the school on top of that which causes deviant behaviour. As we previously noted, the school is in actuality an institution that is geared to the average (in reality often the better) student. Consequently, youngsters who deviate from the norm by definition will encounter difficulties. Not only are students with learning disabilities stigmatized because of their poor achievements (they are often labelled as "dumb"), they themselves also realize that they have little to gain (Lawrence, 1985). As a result, these students end up in the previously described vicious circle that is the fate of poorly functioning students, with the well-known result that they become more and more alienated from school (Hirschi and Hindelang, 1977). Here too, we find the same reaction: escape behaviour and avoidance behaviour. They turn for support to fellow-sufferers who similarly have been marginalized and show all kinds of deviant behaviour, including delinquency.

We have noted earlier that the deviant behaviour of students often is already apparent before they start school (in the family). There are indications that this is also the case with learning-disabled students. Already at an early age do they display deviant behaviour, of which delinquency during the youth period is (only) a special manifestation (McMichael, 1979; Rutter and Giller, 1983).

PERSONAL BACKGROUND AND FUNCTIONING IN SCHOOL

Particularly in a developed, technological society is the school a necessary socialization institute where youngsters learn about how society operates and how they should behave. This unavoidably means that, in the first place, students are taught to adapt to the dominant culture. The school is a representative of this culture, and thus its culture will reflect the dominant one. Therefore, students must not only have the necessary intellectual abilities but also a certain amount of cultural knowledge to be able to benefit from their education. This cultural knowledge has been acquired in the family during child rearing. It is in the family where the primary socialization takes place; the secondary socialization in school should correspond with this. In that sense, the school has an influence which supplements that of the family, particulary because youngsters care more about their parents than about school and view school and family as two different environments (Torsell and Klemke, 1972).

The nature and level of youngsters' cultural knowledge depend on the socioeconomic level of the family, and the educational level, ideology, and social orientation of the parents.

It remains to be seen whether the cultural knowledge acquired in the family corresponds with that of the school. The knowledge students have gained at home, but also the norms, customs and habits they have acquired, may deviate to a greater or lesser degree from those of the school. Youngsters who are not familiar with the school culture simply because they did not learn it at home are at a disadvantage. Students may fail because of limited learning ability but also because of an inability to cope with rules and customs at school (Hirschi, 1969). A child may be handicapped, for example, by the fact that the language used at school differs from that used at home. The language used at the lower socioeconomic levels in particular is simpler and in any case differs from that used at school. This limits not only social communication but also the cognitive functioning of students coming from these backgrounds (Henggeler et al., 1982).

Youngsters whose background does not conform with the school milieu often lack an intrinsic, at home acquired motivation to learn. Moreover, they are discriminated against by teachers and students because they do not know the rules of behaviour (Offord et al., 1978). An important problem is that the school does not offer alternatives (extrinsic motivation) to youngsters who lack an appropriate background (Short and Strodtbeck, 1965). These youths easily develop adjustment problems, become alienated from school, and may resort to escape and avoidance behaviour, including delinquency (Debuyst, 1960; Starr, 1981; Van Kerckvoorde et al., 1984).

It is perhaps the capacity to adapt to school rather than learning ability which determines whether or not youngsters will become delinquents (Mannheim, 1965).

The manner in which youngsters manage at school is not only influenced by cultural factors but also by their family's structural characteristics (see preceding Chapter). From what we have seen, it may for example be expected that children from larger families will not do as well in school as children from smaller ones, because they have received less supervision and therefore are not as prepared to accept school discipline. The same applies to children from single-parent families. School achievements are particularly lower in cases where the father is absent, because the children have lost an example and stimulator (Kohnstamm, 1987).

Family structure may also have consequences for school achievement because of its relationship with intelligence. Children from smaller families generally are more intelligent than their peers from larger ones. Low birth order also is related to intelligence. This may be explained by the greater intellectual stimulation such children receive from their parents (Bellmont and Marolla, 1973; Marjoribanks, 1979; Markus and Zajonc, 1975).

However, it is especially the atmosphere within the family and particulary the type of child rearing received at home which determine how youngsters will do in school (Friday and Hage, 1976; Gold, 1970; Johnson, 1979; Klein et al., 1976; Kohnstamm, 1987; Philips and Kelly, 1979).

Youngsters from harmonious families —as opposed to their peers from disharmonious families— will do well in school. These youngsters have sufficient self-confidence not to be frustrated too readily. They know how to interact with others and how to deal with rules in a flexible way. Youths who have enjoyed warm child rearing and who consequently have develop- ed the kind of personality we discussed in the previous chapter, stand a good chance of finishing school without problems. They will try to estab- lish relationships with others (teachers, students) that are similar to the good relationship they enjoy with their parents. On the other hand, children who have been raised in a cold manner easily run into problems because of their inadequate ability to make contacts and their sensitive attitude. Dominant child rearing is favourable to a smooth school career. Dominant- ly raised children are obedient in school, just like they are at home; except, of course, for those youngsters who at a certain moment break free from the dominant straitjacket. Permissively raised children probably have the hardest time at school because they have hardly learned how to behave in an environment such as the school milieu.

The relationship between family and poor functioning in school may be explained as follows. Because of experiences at home, youngsters may be socially handicapped by a negative self-image, a deviant set of norms, and a fear of failure. Under such circumstances they will not be able to estab- lish an identity with which they can maintain themselves at school (Brennan et al., 1978). The problems surface in school because the student is preoc- cupied and may not be able to concentrate or may misbehave. These problems also leave their traces in the family; for example, if parents are disappointed with the school achievements of their children. Whatever the case may be, family problems and school problems often are intertwined. Youngsters with problems at home frequently have them at school as well and also get more often involved in delinquency. The basis for these relationships should be sought in the general deviancy syndrome discussed in Chapter 1. The main cause of the problems usually originates from the home and not the school. Many youngsters who have not been able to make it at home usually do not make it anywhere else either. These are youngsters who are inclined to reject all conventional institutions. Some demonstrate already at an early age behavioural problems at home as well as at school (McMichael, 1979; Offord et al., 1978; Perry et al., 1979).

These briefly described effects of family factors on functioning in school are self-evident, but have not yet been studied much. Investigations usually focus on either the family or the school. However, cross-institutional studies confirm the thesis (Brennan et al., 1978; Timmermans, 1987).

SCHOOL DELINQUENCY

Juvenile delinquency does not stop at the school gate; it is also found in the school (referred to as school delinquency). The extent of school delinquency varies from institution to institution. There are schools where it occurs only seldom, but there are also institutions where it is rampant. This is true notwithstanding the fact that some schools are quite frank as far as the subject of school delinquency is concerned, whereas other schools prefer to keep this information under wraps.

Larger schools suffer more from school delinquency —and also from delinquency which originates from outside (breaking and entering)— because they own more (and more expensive) equipment. Consequently, there is more to be wrecked and stolen, and there are more opportunities for violence. The average damage per student, however, does not seem to be higher than that in smaller schools (Rubel, 1978a,b).

Delinquency in school very much resembles that in the outside world (McDermott, 1983). It appears that youths —mainly boys— who behave criminally in school, behave in a similar manner outside school and vice versa. In other words, to the extent that juvenile delinquents are students, we find the same offenders inside and outside school. School delinquency, therefore, is a good predictor of delinquency outside the school (Spivack and Cianci, 1987). This is all the more significant because it is easier to observe and record deviant behaviour that takes place in school than is the case with deviant behaviour that takes place outside school.

Viewed in a broader context, the causes of school delinquency do not differ from those of delinquency in general (as discussed in this book). They must be sought in the person and in the individual circumstance of the offender. Personality, child rearing, intelligence, and learning disabilities, for example, play an important role in this respect (Harlan and McDowell, 1980; Hellman and Beaton, 1986; McDermott, 1983).

The causes that may be traced to the school, such as its structure, organization, curriculum, atmosphere, and so forth, are more specific. They are usually the same causes we previously discussed with respect to poor functioning in school. School delinquency is committed by students who are not very happy in school and who are critical of the way in which order is maintained. They think that the school is strict, that the school regulations are not right, and that the punishments are unfair. This is probably related to the fact that they often behave deviantly and thus receive a lot of punishment. They also obtain poor results in school, whereby it is not always so much a question of not being able to do the work but of not wanting to do it. Their limited interest in school is demonstrated by the fact that they are often truant and often drop out early.

The students who are involved in school delinquency are rather evenly distributed over the various grades, even though the lower and higher grades are somewhat underrepresented. That is understandable, because the younger students are not yet daring enough, and the older ones are seriously involved in their studies (others have quit school already by this time) and stand to lose too much. A bad reputation or possible dismissal from school is something they can not afford.

Since *theft* has become a part of our culture, a lot of stealing goes on in the schools as is the case everywhere else in society. There is a lot to be stolen at school; from the school itself (these may be little things, but also expensive audio-visual equipment, and so forth) and from the students who come to school with expensive clothes, accessories, school supplies, and bicycles. Theft at school is possibly the crime, besides bicycle theft outside school, which strikes students the most (Junger and Zeilstra, 1989).

That theft is a problem is evident from the measures taken by the schools. In many schools, students are not allowed any more to hang their coats in the halls; clothing and other articles must be taken into the classroom or put in lockers. When classrooms are vacated, they are locked. In some schools, television cameras have been installed to oversee activities in and around the school. These measures are not superfluous because school seems to be a good place to lose one's things.

Schools suffer a lot from *vandalism* (Angenent, 1988). There is external and internal vandalism. External vandalism involves the exterior of the building or the school premises (bicycle storage). Much of this vandalism is done by youngsters who are not students of the school, even though the contribution of the school's own students should not be underestimated. Internal vandalism, inside the school, is usually committed by students. In instances where this is not the case, the perpetrators are youngsters who have illegally entered the school, for example to commit theft. In classrooms (laboratories), hallways, corridors, stairways, elevators, and washrooms a lot of damage can be done, to the building as well as the furniture.

School delinquency is mainly limited to theft and vandalism. *Violence* occurs less frequently. Usually it is of an incidental nature and a result of daily frictions in school which on occasion escalate, especially at times when there is no supervision (Garafalo et al., 1987). Violence at school is often committed by students from backgrounds where violence is not uncommon. It is part of the habitual manner in which these youngsters maintain themselves in school and elsewhere. These youths (among them we find three times as many boys than girls) also commit much violence aimed at one another (McDermott, 1983). They are not only aggressive towards fellow students but also towards others, such as their parents, siblings, teachers, and so forth. Studies suggest that certain types of child rearing may be responsible for the development of aggressive personality traits that are expressed at a young age already. These youngsters appear to have been raised in a very cold manner. Their child rearing seems to be characterised by too much permissiveness, with great tolerance for aggressive behaviour, and by emotional outbursts and physical punishment.

Violence is sometimes a part of *harassment*. It should be kept in mind that there is a great deal of such behaviour among youngsters, and thus also in school. This harassment —of weaker victims who allow themselves to be bullied by physically and mentally stronger students— can go quite far. It sometimes even begins to resemble a reign of terror. Usually the perpetrators do not realize the kind of mental damage they cause their victims. For example, the victims are often ostracised and ignored by other students (one pretends they are not present). Or the victims are used as targets for ridicule; sometimes as the victim of funny (at least meant to be funny) pranks, sometimes only to embarrass them. Other forms of harassment include intimidation, name calling, teasing, insulting, pushing, hitting, kicking, beating, grasping, blaming, locking up, and —victims mind this the most— humiliation (Olweus, 1978, 1987; Starr, 1981).

The victims are often marginal characters who are not accepted (Perry et al., 1988). They are usually students who are unable to defend themselves. They have been taught at home that name calling and physical violence is not acceptable. Other students as it were "smell" this defencelessness and abuse it. Often it concerns students who differ in appearance or behaviour, if only in the eyes of the other students. Most victims would give anything to belong. As a result they are often pushed into doing things they do not enjoy, such as making themselves look foolish or delinquency.

It is especially these students who are often the victims of school delinquency; it is their belongings that are stolen (or hidden or lost), their things that are destroyed (bicycle), and they are especially at the receiving end of school violence. The victims' reaction is often one of despair and sadness. They develop feelings of inferiority combined with fear of failure and suspicion, they develop problems in establishing and maintaining relationships and do not know how to behave in groups. Something they certainly do not do is discussing their problems with parents or teachers. It may reach the point that these students do not dare to go to school any more, or, in extreme cases, commit suicide.

Contrary to what is the case with school delinquency in general, the perpetrators of harassment generally are not students who do not function very well in school. Pestering is therefore not so much a reaction to frustrations encountered at school, but more and expression of the personality traits of the youths in question.

Remarkable is also that parents and teachers often remain unaware of the fact that harassment is taking place, even if it transpires over an extended period of time. In some instances, teachers even participate by ridiculing the youths in question. This means in the first place that the students concerned feel even more humiliated. It further means that it intensifies the attitudes of the other students toward the victims.

Of a different nature than pestering of students is the harassment of teachers (Wells, 1978). This kind of pestering happens quite frequently and is usually done by the whole class, especially with teachers who are incapable of maintaining order. Physical violence toward teachers occurs less frequently and is done mainly by youths (boys) who attend school against their will and are only serving time. They often come from incomplete and disharmonious families. They also show other kinds of abnormal behaviours and act criminally outside of school. It is not so that violence against teachers is the prerogative of students; this kind of violence is often done by non-students (e.g., angry parents) (Kratcoski, 1985; Toby, 1983).

TRUANCY AND DROPPING OUT

Two phenomena that are associated in a special way with juvenile delinquency are truancy and dropping out behaviour (Dijksterhuis and Nijboer, 1984; Farrington, 1986; Hauber et al., 1986b, 1987b,c; Junger-Tas, 1983; Ouston, 1984; Parker and Asher, 1987; West and Farrington, 1973, 1977).

Truancy or *absenteeism* occurs just as much among boys as among girls. The older the student, the more absenteeism takes place. The relationship between truancy and delinquency also increases with age.

In absenteeism a distinction can be made between occasional and habitual truants. Occasional truants are students who skip class once in a while or are absent for a day. It usually involves students who are normal in every way, but who take advantage of an opportunity. Because there are no structural problems at work in these students, reducing this kind of absenteeism is primarily a question of effective control. Adequate record-keeping (automatized, if possible) and a swift response to truancy are usually enough to deter occasional absentees from future truant behaviour (Berg, 1985). Habitual truants are frequent absentees who on a regular basis stay away from school for hours or days at a time. In surveys, usually an approximately equal number of occasional absentees and non-absentees report that they have committed offenses. Among habitual truants there are many more (almost all of them) who report having committed crimes. Besides, they commit offenses more frequently and their crimes are more varied in form. They also come more often in contact with the police and the justice system (Junger-Tas et al., 1983; Mutsaers, 1987).

Youngsters who were absentees as children, often continue to be so during the youth period. Absenteeism during childhood is therefore a good predictor of absenteeism during the youth period. Possibly, it involves here especially habitual absentees (Fogelman et al., 1980).

The relationship between absenteeism and delinquency is not valid for the special group of *neurotic* absentees (Gibbens, 1961; Miller, 1961). These individuals are afraid of school, a fear which may have gradually developed over time. At a certain moment this fear becomes so intense that these students can no longer cope with the insecurity and threat of life at school and can no longer bring themselves to go to school. They fear the teachers or their fellow students. They may, for example, fear being called upon in class or being harassed by fellow students (Berg, 1980; Nielson and Gerber, 1979). This problem is referred to as a school phobia which may be accompanied by a variety of psychosomatic complaints such as headaches, irritability, sleep disturbances, and digestive upsets (e.g., nausea, vomiting, stomach ache). Fear of school is sometimes attributed to an overly protective child rearing (Conger, 1977; Eisenberg, 1958).

Absenteeism often precedes *dropping-out behaviour*. Youths who leave school before obtaining their diploma are at greater risk for delinquency than youngsters who finish their education. We are not talking here about the relatively small group that quits school prematurely because of illness, family circumstances, pregnancy, marriage, and so forth, but about youths whose frustrations with the situation at school has led them to drop out.

These premature school drop-outs commit more crimes (and more school delinquency) before dropping out than youngsters who complete their education. Criminality therefore precedes dropping out. One might expect (Elliott and Voss, 1974) that once drop-outs have left school their delinquency would decrease because they no longer have to cope with the frustrations of school. This, however, is not the case. On the contrary, drop-outs stand out because of their delinquency even after leaving school. It is also remarkable that they continue this behaviour much longer, even at an older age (Thornberry et al., 1985). This is due to the fact that, after leaving school, they end up in an unfavourable milieu. They are not easily absorbed by the labour force, because one is not that interested in youths with limited education. If they do find work at all, it is usually work of an unskilled, unpleasant, and poorly paid nature. Normally, dropping out means unemployment, and delinquency among unemployed drop-outs is extremely high (Farrington, 1986).

How can we explain the relationship between absenteeism, dropping out, and juvenile delinquency?

1. Absenteeism and dropping out means that the students have more free time on their hands and therefore have more opportunities to commit offenses. It should be pointed out, however, that committing crimes during absenteeism does not happen that often (Belson, 1975; De Vries et al., 1985; Hirschi, 1969; Jaspers et al., 1986). Students frequently are at home during their truancy. Another thing is that absenteeism and dropping out may contribute to delinquency because the youngsters in question are labelled as such (in the case of absentees, for example, by the school) and therefore are forced into a delinquent corner. Via the detour of discrimination, absenteeism and dropping-out therefore may lead to delinquency.

2. On the other hand, juvenile delinquency may lead to absenteeism and dropping out. Criminal activities may make it desirable to stay away from school or to drop out. Another possibility is that once the delinquency becomes known at school, labelling results. This may cause the youngsters involved to withdraw from the situation, to skip school, or to drop out completely. In some cases, delinquency may lead to dismissal from school.

3. In many cases, poor performance at school may be the common cause of absenteeism, dropping out, and delinquency. They are expressions of school avoidance and compensation for school frustrations.

4. The deeper causes of absenteeism and dropping out, however, usually lie —like in delinquency and poor performance in school— in the person and his or her personal background (De Vries et al., 1985; Dijksterhuis and Nijboer, 1984; Farrington, 1980a; Mawby, 1977; Reynolds, 1980; Rutter et al., 1979). Absentees and drop-outs in this sense very much resemble (based on the deviancy syndrome) delinquents (De Vries, 1987; Farrington, 1980a; Hauber et al., 1987b,c). It should be mentioned that the influence of personal and background factors seem to be more central in the case of juvenile delinquency. This is understandable: absenteeism and dropping out are more direct reactions to the school, and therefore more related to the school than to juvenile delinquency (Rutter et al., 1979).

How absentees and drop-outs fare later on in life has been studied by Kandel et al. (1984) in a 10 year longitudinal study. Compared to youngsters who regularly attended school and finished their education, absentees were more often unemployed, changed jobs more frequently, were more often divorced, were in poorer health, and more often committed crimes. Drop-outs fared even worse in this respect. These expectations for the future do not differ much from those of delinquent youngsters.

6. FRIENDS AND PEERS

FRIENDS AND PEERS DURING THE YOUTH PERIOD

With the beginning of the youth period, adolescents enter a phase during which they gradually begin to loosen the ties with their families and take the first steps toward independence. In the course of this process they develop a new orientation. It is a time of relative insecurity, during which they seek contact with other youths who are in similar circumstances. There is no room for adults in these relations, which have "being-young-together" as central theme. Friends and peers, therefore, play an important role in the lives of youths, a role that has become more prominent over the past decades (Lasseigne, 1975).

There are youngsters who reserve the term friend for their closest confidants; others interpret the idea in broader terms and include among their friends, youths who perhaps more correctly should be called acquaintances or peers. Therefore, it is difficult to determine what differentiates friends and peers. We can only note at this point that the difference is determined by the personal character of the relationship: that is, with friends there is a stronger personal bond. Friendship is an exclusive relationship characterized by intimacy, respect, affection, closeness, loyalty, acceptance, support, sharing, doing things together, and having the same interests and ideals (Berndt and Perry, 1986; Buunk, 1983).

Brennan et al. (1978) identified the need for friends as one of the most fundamental needs of youths. For youngsters it is important to be able to choose their own friends, something that is not really possible in the family or at school.

As far as number of friends is concerned, boys and girls differ: girls have fewer friends (two or three on the average) than boys (an average of five). Girls, more often than boys, have **one** good (female) friend. Generally, the more friends people have, the less important they are to them (Maccoby and Jacklin, 1974; Wiatrowski and Anderson, 1987).

In contrast to friendships, relationships with peers may be superficial (e.g., going out for an evening or attending a rock concert together) and more abstract. Whenever the terms friends and peers are used in this book, one should be aware of the unclear boundary between these two concepts.

The attention the criminological literature has given to friends and peers has largely been limited to the youth period. Although the influence of friends and peers indeed increases during that period, this does not mean that such relationships were not important during the preceding years. On the contrary, a child's development is influenced by friends and peers at an early age already. This is particularly of interest because young children who cannot get along with agemates may at a later age show adjustment problems and deviant behaviour (e.g., delinquency) (Asher et al., 1981).

Relationships with peers develop at school where from the first day on contacts are established with other students, and in other institutionalized settings (e.g., clubs, associations, churches) where youngsters meet. They particularly develop in one's own neighbourhood where the street corner or a nearby park serves as a meeting place. Later, the location shifts to public places such as shopping malls, bars, discos, snackbars, and so forth; initially in the neighbourhood, but later on elsewhere.

Relationships with peers over the years change in nature and quality. During childhood, children meet in large same-sex groups. Relationships are primarily instrumental: they need one another to play certain games. During the youth period, affiliations assume a more personal character and become increasingly independent from traditional settings (e.g., neighbourhood, school, club) (Parker and Asher, 1987). Besides the instrumental aspect which continues, the emphasis is more and more on mutual understanding and support (Kurdek and Krile, 1982). Therefore, it is only during the youth period that one can really begin to speak of intimate friendships.

It is not so that the initiative to fraternize lies solely with the individual youth. Peers and particularly friends put pressure on the individual to participate, to assimilate, to adopt their norms and ideals, and to be loyal (Brown, 1982; Kandel, 1978).

The amount of pressure that is exerted varies with the *circumstances*. For instance, peer pressure plays an important role in deviant behaviour (Berndt, 1979; Bixenstine et al., 1976; Brown, 1982). The amount of pressure is also related to *age*: for example, pressure to use alcohol or drugs, to be sexually active, or to be delinquent increases rapidly in the beginning of the youth period (Polk, 1971). There are also *sex* differences. There is greater pressure to conform among boys, but girls are more susceptible to the influence of friends and peers (Collins and Thomas, 1972; Costanzo and Shaw, 1966; Giordano et al., 1986; Landsbaum and Willis, 1971). Furthermore, the pressure that is exerted is qualitatively different for each gender; it follows the notion of the stereotypical sex roles. Girls experience greater pressure related to their appearance (clothing, hairstyle) and sociability (parties, dates); boys more regarding sexuality and the use of alcohol and drugs (Brown, 1982). In terms of delinquency, boys are more influenced by friends and peers than are girls (Berndt, 1979).

With respect to the extent to which juvenile delinquency is motivated by friends, there are positive as well as negative influences depending on the norms and customs followed by these friends (Cloward and Ohlin, 1960; Cohen, 1971; Poole and Regoli, 1979). Therefore, the kind of friends a youth has is very important. Are they adjusted friends, or friends who do not shy away from delinquency? If they are adjusted, the mutual influence is usually positive. They may for instance encourage each other to listen to their parents or to do their best in school. If they are delinquent, then the youngster's set of norms, self-esteem, and ties with the family and other conventional institutions will have to compete with the pressure exerted by friends to participate in delinquency. Non-delinquent friends inhibit delinquency, whereas delinquent friends do the opposite. The influence of friends should not be underestimated. In some instances it is just as strong as that of the family. This influence is greater in cases of more serious delinquency (Emmerich et al., 1971; Kraus, 1977; Snyder et al., 1986).

It is also through friends that youngsters come into contact with the youth culture and subcultures. These cultures may reject the dominant culture and its norms and customs, and may be delinquent (Brennan et al., 1978; Cohen, 1970a; Empey and Lubeck, 1971).

Youngsters who opt for delinquent companions and a delinquent subculture thereby sever their ties with regular friends and the conventional culture. In that case, society may label them as deviant, delinquent, no good, and so forth. Thus, there is mutual alienation.

The influence of friends and peers peaks halfway the youth period around the age of sixteen (Bixenstine et al., 1976; Constanzo and Shaw, 1966; Iscoe et al., 1963), when contacts with friends and peers are strongest. The youngsters are far removed from conventional norms, parental influence is low, and there are many conflicts with elders, school, and so forth (Berndt, 1979; Biddle et al., 1980; LaGrange and White, 1985). We have seen that around this time delinquency also reaches its greatest intensity. The influence of groups (e.g., gangs) may be especially strong at this point (Short and Strodtbeck, 1965).

Near the end of the youth period, the influence of friends and peers declines (Collins and Thomas, 1972; Landsbaum and Willis, 1971). The many friends are replaced by a few intimate confidants, a single boyfriend or girlfriend, and, later, a family. Youths begin to act more autonomously. They have developed their own norms, interests, and ambitions. This makes them independent from friends and peers and they have less need to conform. Older youths are more characterized by personal (e.g., higher education, higher status, expertise in certain areas) rather than group characteristics (Costanzo and Shaw, 1966).

The youth culture also declines in importance; older youths are increasingly assimilated by the dominant culture. Like the youth culture, subcultures fade into the background, including criminal subcultures to which youngsters may have belonged. Soccer vandals are a good example. When these individuals grow a bit older they acquire the status of veteran and no longer personally participate in vandalism. Sometimes, they stay in the same section of the stands, though clearly separated from the vandals. More often, they disassociate themselves and move to another section.

Youths who continue to commit crimes are a different story. They remain part of large groups of friends, the youth culture and delinquent subcultures, for a longer time (West, 1982; West and Farrington, 1977).

PARENTS AND FRIENDS AND PEERS

The family occupies a central position in the lives of children. Younger children are able to differentiate between the norms and behaviours of their parents and those of their peers, but their behaviour is guided by those of their parents. This changes around the age of twelve when the influence of friends and peers increases and that of the parents decreases (Berndt, 1979; Bixenstine et al., 1976; Brittain, 1963; Greenberg, 1977; Hartup, 1970).

From that moment on, friends may compete with parents, although the decrease in parental influence should not be exaggerated (Lasseigne, 1975). The family continues to occupy an important position in the world-view and experiences of youngsters, and the influence of parents usually remains significant (Fasick, 1984; Smith, 1980; Wiatrowski et al., 1981).

Even during the youth period, youngsters continue to pay considerable attention to their parents. Moreover, the influence of peers is only temporary and usually concurs with that of the parents because the family generally determines the kind of friends one has (Briddle et al., 1980; Elliott and Voss, 1974; Patterson and Dishion, 1985; Snyder et al., 1986).

That does not take away from the fact that friends may have an important influence, an influence which —as we have already seen— may be just as great as that of the parents (Lasseigne, 1975). Also, distancing from the parents happens not only because of the influence of peers, but also because of a need for personal independence (Curtis, 1975; Piaget, 1965).

This distancing is more true for boys than for girls who even during those years remain closely attached to the family. In Chapter 1 we have already discussed the background of this phenomenon.

Youths view the world of their parents and the world of their friends and peers as two separate entities (Douvan and Adelson, 1966; Emmerich et al., 1971; Fasick, 1984). Parents belong more to the dominant culture; friends, naturally, more to the youth culture. Youngsters orient themselves towards both worlds. They want to be with their friends, but do not want to give up their parents (Hartup, 1970; Parker and Asher, 1987). In most cases they are quite successful in this respect, because they usually choose friends who are compatible not only with themselves but also with their families (assortative principle). In some cases, the two worlds may influence one another. Parents may criticize the behaviour of friends, whereas youths who have been spoilt by their parents may be told by their friends that they cannot always have it their way. Conflicts may arise when the opinions of parents and friends are too different. In that case, youngsters try to postpone confrontations and, if possible, avoid them.

The question as to whether parents or friends have more influence on the behaviour of youngsters has been widely discussed in the pedagogical literature. However, the usefulness of such a discussion seems to be limited considering the fact that the respective influence of parents and friends varies depending on the situation (Briddle et al., 1980; Douvan and Adelson, 1966; Greenberg et al., 1983).

Youths seek autonomy in two areas: they want to have their own norms and values (normative autonomy), and they want to develop their own activities in their own circle (associative autonomy). They look for and obtain autonomy especially in the latter area.

To understand this, we have to return to what we stated before: namely, that youngsters usually experience family and friends as two separate worlds. In that sense, parents and friends constitute two separate groups of reference. Parents serve more as a *normative reference group*; they provide guidelines for behaviour. Friends are more a *comparative reference group*; they serve as examples for concrete behaviour (Breznitz, 1975; Briddle et al., 1980; Merton, 1968).

Where it concerns norms, values, and issues that are of long-term importance, youths put great weight on their parents' opinion (Brittain, 1963; Panella et al., 1982). For girls especially, parental influence remains strong. This is, among others, because of the close bond girls usually have with their parents and the greater parental supervision to which they are subjected. Girls spend a great deal of their leisure time at home, whereas boys spend more time away. Moreover, when girls socialize with (particularly girl) friends, it is usually in private or under more formal circumstances, often supervised by adults; whereas boys fraternize. Besides, girls participate less in youth subcultures (Box, 1981; Panella et al., 1982).

Friends and peers particularly affect concrete behaviour. Their influence covers a variety of general issues such as society, politics, and sexuality, but mainly affects the manner in which these issues are expressed in everyday life. Moreover, it concerns specific matters such as clothing, hairstyle, music, smoking, alcohol and drug use, and delinquency (Briddle et al.,

1980; Clasen and Brown, 1985; Liska and Reed, 1985; Sebald, 1968; Smith, 1980).

It is normal that during the youth period the influence of friends and peers increases at the expense of the family. This development is necessary for identity formation (Erikson, 1980). The extent to which this change takes place depends on the relationship youngsters have with their family. The influence of friends and peers will be greater if this relationship is lacking in some respect (Box, 1981; Coleman, 1979; Conger, 1973; Empey and Lubeck, 1971; Glueck and Glueck, 1950; Johnson, 1979; Poole and Regoli, 1979; Stanfield, 1966). We have seen that youths in that case alienate from the family and begin to show escape and avoidance behaviour. They turn away from the family, seek contact with other youths, and become more dependent on them. The latter relationships assume an autonomous nature; that is, relatively independent of family influences (Hartup, 1985). A similar process —we discussed this earlier— develops when youngsters become alienated from other conventional institutions (e.g., school) (Hepburn, 1976; Hirschi, 1969). If the relationship with such institutions leaves much to be desired, the influence of friends will be greater than would normally be the case. In such situations any delinquent tendencies these friends may have, may have great consequences.

THE IMPORTANCE OF FRIENDS AND PEERS

Youngsters have each other a lot to offer: companionship and sociability, cohesiveness and solidarity, understanding and support, advice and comfort, protection and security, status and prestige. Youths do things together they consider important: talking (about important as well as trivial things), playing (fooling around), being active (doing fun things), experimenting (exploring the world), looking for excitement (sensation), and so on. The need for these activities is insufficiently satisfied elsewhere (e.g., the family, school, society in general), or is not satisfied in a way that appeals to youngsters (Wagner, 1971).

Youths, therefore, have a fundamental need to "belong", that is to say, to be with other youths. This explains why many do their utmost to be accepted by friends and peers (in the neighbourhood, at school, in clubs). It also explains why they resent being uprooted. Leaving a familiar environment (e.g., changing schools, moving) may mean a lot of stress for them.

Two things are central to the self-image of the average youth. First, they do not want to look silly. They prefer to maintain their image or, even better, make an impression. To look foolish in the eyes of others is a disaster. Second, they do not want to be rejected. They want to be accepted or, even better, be popular. Because they so desperately want to belong, rejection may lead to mental and physical complaints (Cowen et al., 1983).

Being like one's peers is a sign that one belongs. Youngsters therefore have a strong need to imitate. This is quite obvious from the way they dress and their use of language. But the imitation goes further and deeper. Youths want to resemble the others in behaviour; they also adopt one another's ideas and ideals. In short, they are very conforming.

On the other hand, youths want to be their own person with a unique personality, different from anyone. Although this seems to contradict their conformity, this is not the case. The psychological explanation for this apparent paradox is that the security found in conformity (and the related positive self-image) gives them the courage to strive for uniqueness. Conformity and originality often mix and are both appreciated (Ausubel, 1954).

Self-assertion and popularity among friends may be achieved by acts of bravura. This may involve behaviour that is funny but also actions that reveal insight, originality, nerve, skill, sturdiness, or cockiness. The more extreme the behaviour, the better. It may be expressed in, for instance, school achievements but also in bluffing, macho behaviour, playing tricks, and so forth. Rules are sometimes forgotten and limits exceeded; deviant and criminal behaviour may be the result.

SOCIAL RELATIONSHIPS AMONG YOUTHS

The social relationships youngsters have with friends and peers are not superfluous. They contribute to a large degree to their identity formation (Erikson, 1968). The reactions of other youths, in particular those of friends, determine identity, self-image, and self-esteem (O'Donnell, 1979). Moreover, social relationships with other youths are a necessity for adequate social development, because it is through these relationships that youngsters learn to behave socially.

Girls have an easier time with social relationships than boys. Their social contacts tend to be expressive in nature. They are more socially inclined, have a greater ability to accommodate, and are better able to understand human relations and empathize with others (Iscoe et al., 1963). They look for responses, and are attracted to community, unity, and belonging. From a very young age, they show more cooperative behaviour than boys. They also have more long-lasting relationships and intimate friendships than boys do.

Boys, on the other hand, are more instrumental in their social relationships. They look for contacts with others with whom they can produce something. But they also seek individual status. Therefore, they use social relationships to set themselves apart from others; they do not stress similarities, but rather differences. As a result they, more than is the case with girls, opt for short-term, opportunistic relationships.

In summary, it may be stated that girls are more relation-oriented, whereas boys are more status-oriented. Girls think more along horizontal lines, that is, in terms of similarities. Boys in think more along vertical lines, in hierarchies. In reference to the child-rearing model we discussed in Chapter 4, warmth plays a larger role in the relationships of girls, whereas dominance characterizes those of boys.

The criterion whether or not youngsters are successful in their social relations is the status they enjoy among other youths, a status that is reflected in their *popularity*. In mixed groups, the most popular youths usually are boys. And yet, girls on the average are respected more highly than boys. Furthermore, it is noticeable that girls speak of boys in more positive terms than vice versa, and especially that girls speak of other girls more positively than do boys of each other (Asher and Dodge, 1968; Kurdek and Krile, 1982).

If we list the characteristics of popular youths, it is evident that it involves two kinds of attributes: horizontally oriented qualities that are more characteristic of girls and vertically oriented attributes that are more particular to boys (i.e,, expressive and instrumental characteristics).

Popular youngsters maintain good and frequent contacts with other youths. They are verbally gifted and communicate well. They are cognizant of norms, rules, and customs of the individuals and groups with whom they interact. They understand the social consequences of their behaviour and are able to put themselves in other people's positions (for instance, they are quite capable of reading the mood of another person). They adapt easily, are cooperative, and know how to share.

Popular youngsters show leadership, they point out possibilities, rules, and customs to other youths, make suggestions, and in part devise the rules themselves. They act as "opinion makers" and "taste makers". They are active, independent, and achieve much (e.g., at school). They are not aggressive, but know how to defend themselves if necessary.

Popular youngsters are respected by their peers and are, for example, less often the target of aggression. They get away with things. If they behave negatively, this is easily accepted by other youngsters (Coie and Kuperschmidt, 1983; Coie et al., 1982; Newman and Newman, 1976).

Popularity is strongly related to *appearance* (Cavior and Dokecki, 1973; Dodge, 1983; Eme et al., 1979; Kleck et al., 1974; Langlois and Stephan, 1977; Lerner and Lerner, 1977). The basis for this is that attractive people

generally are ascribed relatively more positive and fewer negative characteristics by others. One expects more positive things from attractive people,
for instance at school, in marriage and career, and one expects less deviant
behaviour from them (Dion et al., 1972). It appears that one thinks that
what is attractive is also good, and that external attractiveness is a sign of
internal beauty. In short, the psychosocial milieu is relatively favourable
for attractive people. As a result, their interpersonal relationships are less
complicated and they enjoy an easier life (Dion and Berscheid, 1974). This
already begins in early childhood (Dion, 1972, 1973; Dion and Berscheid,
1974; Dion et al., 1972; Langlois and Stephan, 1977). Attractive children
are more highly regarded by their peers. The question is whether the latter
merely parrot their elders (young children regard the same children as
attractive as adults do) or primarily respond to the exterior or to the behaviour (attractive children behave differently than unattractive ones). If attractive children behave deviantly, their behaviour is not as much resented by
other children (Dion, 1972). Adults more easily blame deviant behaviour
of attractive children on circumstances, whereas similar behaviour shown
by unattractive children tends to be viewed as chronic and reproachable.

The above described mechanism is strongly at work in youths, to whom
physical appearance is so important, for girls even more than for boys
(Conger, 1977; Kleck et al., 1974; Langlois and Stephan, 1977).

The more attractive one is, the more status one enjoys among peers, and
the more friends one has. Besides, adults too (parents, teachers) judge
youngsters among others on the basis of their appearance, they overrate
those who look attractive and favour them over others (Clifford and
Walster, 1973; Lerner and Lerner, 1977). We pointed out in Chapter 1 that
delinquent youngsters put relatively much emphasis on their appearance
(clothes, hairstyle, tattoos). The better one looks, the higher one's status,
also in delinquent circles (Glueck and Glueck, 1950).

Less popular youngsters for a long time have been regarded as one
group. Closer study, however, has shown that a distinction should be made
between rejected youngsters and youngsters who do not count (Kafer and
Shannon, 1968; Peery, 1979; Shannon and Kafer, 1984).

Rejected youths are not popular and are not accepted. Peers have few
positive and many negative things to say about them (Coie and Kuperschmidt, 1983; Coie et al., 1982; Parker and Asher, 1987). *Youths who do
not count* similarly are not popular, but they *are* accepted. Their peers have
few positive but also few negative opinions about them. Youngsters who
do not count do not differ much from normal youths. Usually there is little
friction in their relations with other youngsters (Asher and Wheeler, 1985;
Boivin and Begin, 1989; Coie et al., 1982; Dodge, 1983; Dodge et al.,
1982; French and Waas, 1985). They look less for contact with others,

often entertain themselves, and show little problem behaviour. They are viewed by their peers as timid, shy, and less active (Coie et al., 1982; French, 1988; Parker and Asher, 1987). When frustrated, they ignore the problem or withdraw from the situation. The prognosis for the future of these youngsters is not unfavourable (Coie and Kuperschmidt, 1983). It has been suggested that some youths who do not count in one group may play a more central role in another. Moreover, it may be that the emphasis of their social relationships is not on peers, but on family, animals, and so forth (Parker and Asher, 1987).

Rejected youngsters are socially removed from other youths. They have fewer social skills, as is demonstrated by the fact that they do not easily interact with others, that they don't know very well how to make friends, that they are unable to integrate in a group, and that they are less attuned to the norms and customs of their peers. They feel less affinity with other youngsters and do not care much about them (Walsh and Kurdek, 1984). Rejected youths show much deviant behaviour, such as hyperactivity, restlessness, irritability, and asocial and aggressive behaviour (Coie and Kuperschmidt, 1983; Coie et al., 1982; Dodge, 1983; Dodge et al., 1982). Rejected youngsters participate to an unusually large degree in delinquency, particularly the more serious forms. Boys who have been rejected and have become delinquent often show aggressive behaviour (Cowen et al., 1983; French and Waas, 1985; Janes et al., 1979; Parker and Asher, 1987; Roff and Wirt, 1984; Walsh and Kurdek, 1984; West and Farrington, 1977).

The deviant behaviour of rejected youths is due in part to a lack of self-confidence which makes them feel insecure and vulnerable. They are not at peace with themselves and have low self-esteem. They feel easily threatened and tend to be suspicious and defensive. This, with a need to assert themselves, often causes them to behave in a violent and obstinate way (Waas, 1988). Peers see rejected youths as belligerent and aggressive. Their restless and uninhibited behaviour repeatedly causes conflicts with others, who get fed up with it (Asher and Wheeler, 1985; Coie and Kuperschmidt, 1983; Dodge, 1983; French and Waas, 1985). Their lack of popularity also affects their behaviour at school. Success in school requires not only intellectual capacities but also an ability to adapt to school life. One has to live with the school as institution, the teachers, and fellow-students. Rejected youths do not make the grade in this respect (Coie and Kuperschmidt, 1983; Green et al., 1980; Parker and Asher, 1987).

The poor relationship between rejected youngsters and their peers has as result that rejected youths become alienated from their peers. The effects of alienation are well known: escape behaviour and avoidance behaviour. Regarding escape behaviour it may be noted that rejected youngsters and peers avoid one another; peers ignore rejected youths and the latter withdraw and feel relatively lonely, more lonely than youngsters who do not count. Furthermore, rejected youths seek the company of fellow-sufferers. The avoidance behaviour rejected youngsters show is the same behaviour which caused the rejection in the first place. However, as a result of the alienation, that behaviour increases and intensifies.

A separate type is the *controversial type*. These youngsters have much contact with others, a contact that is sometimes (very) positive and sometimes (very) negative. On the one hand, these youths interact socially with peers and cooperative well, sometimes assuming a position of leadership. On the other hand, they stand out because of quarrelling, name calling, obstructionism, and aggressive behaviour. In short, they simultaneously show the behaviour of a youngster with high status and with low status. Generally, these youths have low self-esteem. Their behaviour is unpredictable, partly because of a lack of self-control (Boivin and Bégin, 1989; Coie et al., 1982; Dodge, 1983; Newcomb and Bukowski, 1983). It appears that these youngsters may be dominant figures in delinquent groups.

Status among peers is fairly constant. It already exists more or less in early childhood and does not change much over time. An exception are youngsters who do not count; when placed in a new situation they may make a fresh start and may escape their marginal position (Coie and Kuperschmidt, 1983; French and Waas, 1985). The status of rejected youths seems to be particularly resistant to change; once rejected, always rejected (Asher et al., 1979; Asher and Dodge, 1986; Coie et al., 1982; Coie and Kuperschmidt, 1983; Kafer and Shannon, 1986; Newcomb and Bukowski, 1983). If one combines this information with the fact that the incidence of delinquency is relatively high among rejected youngsters, it appears to be possible to predict at an early age already subsequent delinquency on the basis of a child's rejected status (Cowen et al., 1973; French and Waas, 1985; Janes et al., 1979; Parker and Asher, 1987; Roff, 1961; Roff and Wirt, 1984; Walsh and Kurdek, 1984).

FRIENDS OF DELINQUENT YOUTHS

Delinquent youths often have delinquent friends, just as non-delinquent youngsters tend to have non-delinquent friends. This applies to recorded as well as surveyed delinquency (Bruinsma, 1985; Elliott and Voss, 1974; Elliott et al., 1985; Erickson and Empey, 1965; Glueck and Glueck, 1950; Hindelang, 1973; Hirschi, 1969; Jensen, 1972b; Johnson, 1979; Junger-Tas, 1983; Rankin, 1977; Wilson, 1987). This relationship is not only found in boys but also in girls (Berndt, 1979; Brown et al., 1986;

Bruinsma, 1985; Hauber et al., 1987a; Johnson, 1979). It appears that one
of the most reliable indications that a youngster is involved in delinquency,
is his or her contact with delinquent friends. The more delinquent friends,
the greater the probability of delinquency (Elliott and Voss, 1974; Jensen,
1972b; Johnson, 1979; Mitchell and Dodder, 1980; Voss, 1964).

PARENTS AND FRIENDS OF DELINQUENT YOUTHS

Juvenile delinquents spend less time with their parents and other family
members and more time with friends in (relatively large) groups. They
participate less in activities in and around the family, but instead seek their
entertainment somewhere else where there is less supervision. Thus, delinquent youngsters are in a position where on the one hand they are less
under the control of their families and on the other hand are more exposed
to the influence of friends (Junger-Tas, 1972; Hirschi, 1969; Wiatrowski
et al., 1981). This is more true for boys than for girls (Bruinsma, 1985;
Hauber et al., 1987a).

We have already seen that the last word has not yet been said as to who
exercises greater influence over youths (parents or friends). The same
applies to the more specific question as to whether parents or friends play
the more important role in juvenile delinquency. There is still a lot of
discussion about this, whereby it is often forgotten that we are dealing with
a two-stage process (Patterson and Dishion, 1985).

The first stage concerns the background of youngsters, which allows
them to develop either a defence against or an interest in delinquency. In
this stage, which begins during early childhood, parental influence is great.
A bad relationship with parents and limited supervision leads to negative
identity, normlessness, and deviant behaviour. This may cause problems
at school and less than optimal contact with friends and peers.

The explicit step of getting involved in delinquency marks the transition
to the second stage. The influence of (delinquent) friends plays hereby an
important role. The latter model deviant norms and values, and support and
instigate deviant activities. From them, youngsters learn where and when
to commit crimes, and which methods and techniques may be useful. They
may learn that delinquency can be fun and exciting, and that it may be
financially lucrative. At the same time, any negative consequences are
pushed to the background (Riley, 1987).

The above described "distribution of tasks" between parents and friends
is not only found in delinquency, but also in other forms of deviant behaviour (e.g., alcohol and drug use) (Halebsky, 1987; Sheppard et al., 1987).

RELATIONSHIP OF DELINQUENT YOUTHS AND FRIENDS

We have seen that as far as deviant behaviour is concerned the influence of friends is relatively large. Delinquent youths, as compared to non-delinquent ones, are more influenced by their friends (Box, 1981; Giordano et al., 1986; Hindelang, 1973; Hirschi, 1969; Jensen, 1972b; Junger-Tas, 1983; Kraus, 1977; Poole and Regoli, 1979).

Delinquent youngsters generally are very dependent on their friends. They will, therefore, make an above average effort to impress the latter. Often, as is customary among youngsters, this takes the form of bravura behaviour; macho-behaviour, which may include aggression (e.g., fighting). Status may be achieved by behaviour that is usually found among adults, such as smoking, drinking, sex, and so on. Even though this type of behaviour does not necessarily lead to criminality, we find it more often among delinquent than among non-delinquent youths. And, of course, criminality may mean prestige in some cases (Glueck and Glueck, 1950; Hirschi, 1969; Matza and Sykes, 1961).

Because juvenile delinquents spend much of their time with their friends and are relatively dependent on them, one might expect that they also have good relationships with them. For many years this has been the assumption. According to earlier authors, headed by Thrasher (1927), juvenile delinquents maintain warm relations with their friends, bonds that are characterized by solidarity, loyalty, support, and mutual understanding (Cohen, 1971; Coleman, 1961), aspects which have been identified as characteristic of relationships between good friends. The good relations juvenile delinquents have with their friends may be explained by the *compensation-principle*. That is, the relationship delinquents have with their friends contrasts the one with their parents; it is a compensation for the bad relationship with the latter. Youngsters turn to each other to find what their parents do not offer (DiLalla et al., 1988).

Giordano et al. (1986) wondered whether these authors did not idealize the relationship somewhat by creating an image of "a noble brotherhood, characterized only by comradeship and a 'we'-feeling". Hirschi (1969) called the good relationship between delinquent youngsters and their friends "a romantic myth". He suggested that the opposite is true: that the relationships are rather cool and fragile. Others point at the instability and changeability of the relations between juvenile delinquents (Velarde, 1978), and the relatively frequent differences of opinion and conflicts (Giordano et al., 1986). Hartup (1985) considered the inability to get along socially to be one of the most important characteristics of juvenile delinquents. Others have confirmed this less than optimal relationship between delinquents and their friends (Freedman et al., 1978; Rothstein, 1962; Short and Strodt-beck, 1965; Wiatrowski and Anderson, 1987). It is also consistent with what was stated earlier in this chapter, namely, that one finds many delinquents among rejected youngsters (who have few social skills).

The not-so-good relationship between delinquents and their friends may be explained by the *analogy-principle*. According to this principle, youngsters interact with their friends the same way they interact with their parents. The ties youths have with their friends may be viewed as an extension of the bond with the parents. Youngsters who get along well with their parents also get along well with their friends. If the contact with parents leaves something to be desired, then the relationship with friends similarly is not optimal (Henggeler, 1982; Hill, 1987; Poole and Regoli, 1979).

Because juvenile delinquents often have poor relationships with their parents, they may not be able to enjoy good relations with friends either. This is because the poor relationship with the parents inhibits their socialization, so that they have trouble establishing long-lasting, mutual relationships. This has as result that many delinquent youngsters are relatively isolated and enjoy fewer social contacts than non-delinquent youths. Therefore, they look for contacts with others who are in a similar position. One should not have too high expectations of these contacts. Two observations are necessary here for the purpose of nuance:

1. In some cases the relationship delinquent youngsters have with their friends may indeed compensate for a poor relation with their parents. This is the case when the parents have *very* little to offer and the youngster has to depend on his friends. Such a compensation phenomenon is sometimes found among members of youth-gangs.
2. The relationship of juvenile delinquents with their friends probably depends to a large extent on their personality. Hewitt and Jenkins (1946) already noted this. For instance, sociable delinquents get along very well with their friends, whereas emotional and aggressive delinquents do not.

These observations perhaps explain why some authors observe few differences in the way in which delinquent and non-delinquent youngsters get along with their friends (Giordano et al., 1986; Hindelang, 1973).

DELINQUENT FRIENDS AND JUVENILE DELINQUENCY

As far as the relationship between juvenile delinquency and delinquent friends is concerned, we are, as is the case with many relationships discussed in this book, faced with the familiar problem of the chicken and the egg. What came first: the delinquent friends or the delinquency? There are two contrasting points of view regarding this question.

According to the *social-cause-theory* or socialization theory, youngsters become delinquent because they associate with delinquent friends. This point of view is popular among sociologically oriented authors (Cohen, 1971; Johnson, 1979; Sutherland and Cressey, 1978). It states that behaviour (in this case, delinquency) is a function of social attitudes that are formed in social relations (in this case, with friends). These social relations are often formed, especially among the young, in groups where there is pressure to conform (coalition theory). According to this point of view, youths who do not come in contact with deviant youngsters will rarely get involved in criminality. Regardless of how important friends may be, this appears to be a somewhat unrealistic viewpoint in light of the many different ways in which youngsters may be exposed to all sorts of criminal examples in society which may motivate them toward delinquency (Hindelang, 1973; Hirschi, 1969).

The *social-selection-theory* or social situation theory assumes that youngsters acquire delinquent friends because of their delinquency, thereby finding social support. Psychologically oriented authors in particular defend this point of view (S. and E. Glueck, 1950, 1962, 1972; Hirschi, 1969; Johnson, 1979; Short and Strodtbeck, 1965). One refers to the *assortative-principle* which states that people who are alike look for contact with one another (birds of a feather flock together), to subsequently behave in an even more similar manner (interpersonal balance theory). We already came across this assortative behaviour in the chapter about the family as it relates to the partner choice of the parents. As married people tend to resemble one another, so do friends. Youngsters, as it were, look for themselves in their friends (Kandel, 1978). Apart from the fact that physical proximity (neighbourhood, school, class) plays a role, youngsters prefer friends who are similar in age, gender, and ethnic background, and who resemble them in terms of abilities, interests, personality, and appearance (Gibson, 1971; Kurdek and Krile, 1982; Rushton et al., 1985). They particularly look for friends among like-minded individuals who live in comparable circumstances. The assortative orientation not only influences the choice of friends but also the course of the friendship. The more assortative the choice, the more lasting, intense, and harmonious the friendship will be. Moreover, the similarity between friends seems to increase as the friendship evolves. If the similarity turns out to be less than optimal, one either accommodates or one breaks off the friendship. Therefore, if friends part their ways it is usually because the similarity has decreased (Kurdek and Krile, 1982).

Assortative behaviour also plays a role in juvenile delinquency. Delinquent youngsters look for friends that are like them. Delinquency is one criterion, but personality traits, norms, attitudes and interests related to delinquency are just as important (Kandel, 1978; Snyder et al., 1986).

Liska (1975) pointed out that the controversy between the social-cause-theory and the social-selection-theory is not limited to juvenile delinquency, and provided examples illuminating the contrast.

The social-cause-theory attributes the relationship between psychiatric illness and (low) socioeconomic status to the unfavourable circumstances in which people from lower milieus are living. The social-selection-theory, on the other hand, states that people suffering from a mental disease are less capable of functioning in higher socioeconomic milieus and gravitate to a milieu where fewer social demands are made of them. Thus, they descend the socioeconomic ladder. Research has shown that the social-selection-theory is right in this respect. Psychiatric illness therefore seem to be more the cause of unfavourable socioeconomic conditions than the result. The social-selection-theory is confirmed by the results of studies by Alexander and Campbell (1968) of the relationship between alcohol use among youngsters and the presence of friends who drink. This research indicates that youngsters usually start drinking first and then come in contact with friends who drink. With respect to marihuana smoking, Krohn (1974) found a reverse relationship: a poor relationship with parents causes youngsters to seek contact with drug using friends which leads to the smoking of marihuana.

Returning to the question of whether juvenile delinquency leads to having delinquent friends or vice versa, it may be noted that both positions are valid. As is usually the case in such relationships we are dealing with a reciprocal affiliation (Thornberry and Christenson, 1984).

The assumption that youngsters get involved in delinquency because of delinquent friends is an obvious one. The delinquent friends of their (good) son parents often refer to, are a well-known example. We have encountered this example several times already in this book. And indeed it is true that delinquent friends may lead a youngster astray (Hepburn, 1977; Hirschi, 1969; Liska, 1978; Sutherland and Cressey, 1978; Voss, 1964).

The opposite, that delinquency precedes delinquent friends, also occurs. Prior to making delinquent friends many youngsters have already committed all kinds of offenses and misdemeanours. This behaviour brings them in contact with other delinquents whom they meet, as it were, as colleagues on the job (store theft), the fencing market, and so forth (Glueck and Glueck, 1950, 1962, 1972).

In short, delinquent friends may be the cause as well as the result of delinquency. Possibly there are differences in nuance depending on the type of delinquent. It is conceivable that occasional delinquents often have been led astray by friends, whereas habitual delinquents, particularly (semi)-criminal youths, generally have a tendency to get involved in delinquency first and only subsequently come into contact with delinquent friends.

Perhaps there is also a difference depending on the type of crime. According to Liska (1975), in youngsters who steal, the behaviour usually precedes association with delinquent friends; in vandalism and violent crimes, on the other hand, contacts with delinquent friends usually precede the crimes.

In most cases, however, matters are more complex and should the explanation for the relationship between juvenile delinquency and delinquent friends be sought in other factors which cause the delinquency as well as the delinquent friendships (common cause theory). These causes lie mainly in the person and the personal circumstances of the youth. Because of these factors, the youngster develops attitudes that either strengthen or weaken the appeal of delinquency and delinquent friends (Hirschi, 1969; Liska, 1975). Youngsters with strong negative attitudes toward delinquency will not easily get involved in such behaviour and also will avoid contact with delinquent youths. Youngsters with strong positive attitudes toward delinquency will be drawn toward the behaviour as well as toward delinquent friends. In youngsters who are more or less neutral toward delinquency, it will depend on the kind of friends they meet. In fact, according to Liska (1969), in the latter cases the influence of friends is the determining factor.

In Chapter 3 we have seen that personality traits may foster juvenile delinquency. Many of these characteristics also influence the social contacts youngsters have and the friends they choose. For example, a youngster with a great need for excitement may be drawn to delinquency and also to delinquent peers with adventurous inclinations.

As far as personal circumstances are concerned, it should be noted that prior to their involvement with delinquency and delinquent friends, many youngsters already have problems with conventional institutions such as the family and school (as discussed in previous Chapters) and with other non-delinquent youths (as discussed in this Chapter). These problems may lead them to participate in delinquency as well as look for delinquent friends.

YOUTH GROUPS

Whether or not one regards human beings as social creatures or herd animals, it is a fact that people look for relationships with others. This is very much the case with youngsters who, as we have seen, are strongly oriented towards other youths. Thus, group formation is very prominent among youngsters. The groups originate spontaneously. Adults (parents, school) have little control over their formation. Generally, they accept them as a natural phenomenon, at least as long as the behaviour of the members does not get out of hand.

There may be overlap between youth groups because youngsters may belong to more than one circle. Also, youngsters sometimes change groups. There may be cooperation, but also rivalry between groups (Brown et al., 1986; Coleman, 1974; Dunphy, 1963).

The place groups occupy in the life of youngsters varies with age and runs parallel to the above discussed influence of friends and peers. Groups are formed early, during childhood, at school and in the neighbourhood. These groups consist of boys **or** girls. At that age level there are more boys' groups than girls' groups. Moreover, the former groups are usually (much) larger than the latter ones. Besides, girls more often than boys team up with one other person. Sometimes, girls are part of boys' groups, where, in terms of numbers, they are in the minority, and often play a secondary role. At the beginning of the youth period, the groups become more heterogenous genderwise.

Boys in particular, are drawn to youth groups (Coleman, 1974). Girls are more interested in quality than in quantity in their relationships with friends and peers. This relates to the fact that they attach greater importance to a real, close friendship than boys do. Girls look for other things in groups than do boys. They are interested in intimacy and affection, relationships and friendship, understanding one another, and sharing emotions. They adapt better than boys do; at least they conform more readily to the norms and behaviour of the group (Feldman, 1972; Kurdek and Krile, 1982). Boys use the group more, as they do with friendships, to achieve status and to establish a reputation.

After the age of 15 or 16, the importance of the youth group declines. Youngsters begin to experience the ties with the group as limiting, and, as we have seen, begin to associate with only a few friends (Brown et al., 1986; Feldman, 1972; Newman and Newman, 1976).

It is in youth groups where the things youngsters have to offer one another (i.e., friendship, security, confidence, support, activity, sport and games, adventure and excitement, status) find their concrete expression. As such, the group gives meaning to youths' behaviour. Therefore, it is especially in youth groups where youngsters find their identity and develop their self-image and self-esteem. In that sense, youth groups are "self-help groups". They are almost indispensable in order to deal with the youth period (Brown et al., 1986; Krisberg, 1974; Newman and Newman, 1976).

Group norms and motivations, related or not to subcultural factors, are manifestly present in youth groups (Briar and Piliavin, 1965; Costanzo and Shaw, 1966; Velarde, 1978). Youngsters conform; in fact, the group demands conformity. Too much individuality will lead to expulsion. Because youngsters conform to the group, their own norms and motivations may be at risk. This is one of the reasons why youths behave differently when they are in a group than when they are on their own. The groups' norms are usually somewhat more liberal than those held by the individual youngster, which are closer to the conventional norms. Consequently, in delinquent groups, criminal group norms and motives weigh more heavily than its members individually would allow. Because they believe that the other youngsters totally subscribe to the group norms even in their private lives, and that they themselves are mere exceptions, juvenile delinquents regard their friends as more delinquent than themselves (Breznitz, 1975; Buffalo and Rodgers, 1971; Matza, 1964). Outwardly, however, they conform and imitate their friends. Juvenile delinquents play, as it were, a delinquent game with one another. They behave in a way they think the group expects them to behave, and usually pretend to be more delinquent than they actually are. They will not readily admit to their friends that in reality they adhere to more conventional norms and motives. This discrepancy between personal norms and group norms is one of the reasons why delinquency declines when, toward the end of the youth period, the influence of groups decreases (Matza, 1964; Velarde, 1978).

To the outsider, youth groups often appear to be loose entities. This, however, is only appearances (Savin-Williams, 1979). Within groups there is a more differentiated structure than would appear at first sight. This consists of a network of personal relationships. One knows one another's capacities and knows what to expect from one another. The position one occupies within the group is related to this.

Most youth groups have a natural leadership with leaders and sub-leaders, bosses and sub-bosses, though the leaders are not necessarily regarded as such by the members of the group. It is therefore an informal leadership. Leaders are *popular* youths, as we described them earlier. Others identify them as a friend more often than is the case vice versa. They personify the ideals of the group. They have a coordinating, integrating, and stimulating role. Leaders are active, show initiative, come up with proposals, take decisions, and know how to persuade others. They take care of the relations with the outside world (parents, school), and are also regarded and accepted by these outsiders as representing the group. Leadership in groups is characterized by social mobility with many contacts inside and outside the group. Group members assume that leaders possess much information (youngsters ask them a lot of questions), they take them into their confidence, and in many cases expect them to lend support and assistance.

When leaders assume the role of "task leader" and stress the instrumental goal of the group, there may be tensions if the mutual relationships and the interests of individual group members suffer as a result. It is in these cases that youngsters who play an expressive role in the group ("sociometric stars") come forward. These are youths who, often with humour and jokes, manage to ease the tension. Their task becomes more involved when leaders act dominantly and as a result cause opposition among the group members. Because they draw a lot of attention, these sociometric stars are often seen as the leaders of the group by outsiders. They should, of course, not be confused with boys who constantly play the clown. Even though at first sight there may be some resemblance, these individuals normally are low on the social ladder and can only maintain their status by their clownish behaviour.

We may conclude that there are vertical as well as horizontal relationships in youth groups. The structure very much resembles that of the family. In the group, the leaders and the sociometric stars assume responsibilities which in the family would be assumed by the parents. Leaders fulfil instrumental tasks, as does the father in the family. The sociometric stars, like the mother in the family, perform the expressive tasks. The similarity with the family is also apparent from the youngsters' identification with these prominent figures.

Youth groups are comprised of smaller groups often called cliques. These are small groups of at the most ten youngsters who are close friends and who spend, relatively speaking, a lot of time together. There is a difference in emphasis between the youth group and the clique. The youth group satisfies youngsters' need to belong and it provides the necessary action. In the clique the accent lies more on personal alliance and friendship, affection, and intimacy. Cliques are formally organized in the same way as youth groups are. The relationships between the cliques within the youth group specifically take place through the leaders of the cliques, who have the same task and position as the leaders of youth groups. Between the cliques which form a youth group there is a hierarchical relationship which usually is determined by the (average) age of the members of the respective cliques.

Finally: within cliques there are small groups rarely consisting of more than two youngsters whom may be considered bosom friends.

There are large differences in the extent to which youth groups are structured (O'Hagan, 1976). One the one hand, there are highly structured groups. These are circles of a closed nature where the group comes first and where the individual is subservient to the group. Decisions are made by the leaders; there is instrumental leadership. Members of the group have relatively limited freedom of action. There is a division of labour, a group code, and many rules. Such groups are dominant in character.

On the other hand, there are loose, informal groups in which there is hardly any structure. They function spontaneously, without any clear leadership. As far as there is leadership, it is rather expressive. There is a lack of rules: a lot is left to the individual members who collectively determine the workings the group. There is a large turn-over in membership; these groups are usually temporary in nature. When we discussed child rearing, we used the word permissive in describing similar attitudes. With respect to youth groups, spontaneity seems to be a better term. As far as their structure is concerned, youth groups fall between the two extremes.

The classic example of a structured delinquent youth group is the gang (Dubet and Lapeyronnie, 1985; Jackson, 1989; Kreuzer, 1972; Miller, 1983; O'Hagan, 1976; Robert and Lascoumes, 1974).

The suggestion is often made, for example in the media, that the larger part of juvenile delinquency and certainly delinquency committed as a group, may be attributed to gangs. This, however, is a misconception. Even though gangs are responsible for a fair share of criminal behaviour, most juvenile delinquency is committed by youth groups with a much looser structure (Curry and Spergel, 1988; Schneider, 1987).

That means that current theories about gangs are less useful in explaining the delinquent behaviour of groups than are the more general theories about group processes (Marash, 1986).

It is, for that matter, not that easy to define what a gang is. In the literature we come across descriptions in which —to quote Schneider (1987)— myths, ideological stereotypes, and unclear concepts cloud the picture. To begin with, it is not easy to determine at which point a youth group becomes a gang. Similarly, it is not easy to demarcate gangs from groups of adults involved in organized crime.

We would like to define a gang as a highly structured group with a criminal identity which expresses itself in the (criminal) vision of its members and the (criminal) norms to which they adhere. These are groups that are regularly and systematically involved in (more serious forms of) delinquency. This is a rather strict description in which two characteristics are central: structure and criminality.

The ideal-typical image of the gang is as follows. The gang has a hierarchical structure. There are leaders, sub-leaders, fringe figures, and hanger-ons. Leaders stand out because of their intelligence, daring attitude, resourcefulness, physical strength, or a combination thereof. In any case, they must have authority, either because they elicit admiration or because they instill fear. Leaders determine the area of operation, assign tasks, plan actions, and decide who does what; they are the boss.

The gang has a fixed distribution of roles. Everybody has an assigned position in a hierarchy which may be construed as a pecking order. One is constantly busy defending one's place in the group, or attempting to improve one's position in the hierarchy.

The gang is rigidly organized and sometimes cast in a military mould. There are established codes and rules that are strictly enforced, and there are heavy punishments for transgressions. Furthermore, the gang has all kinds of conventions and practices that are expressed in rituals, ceremonies, and insignias. Group consciousness and solidarity play a very important role. Thus, every gang has its own subculture. Youths wishing to join often have to earn their acceptance and must subject themselves to initiation rites. Sometimes they have to prove themselves by submitting to a test of strength whereby they have to do something that will impress the others. This may involve committing a crime.

Sometimes, gangs attract fringe followers consisting of younger children who perform all kinds of services and hope to become members at some time in the future (O'Hagan, 1976). That way the gang is assured of a steady supply of new members. Juvenile delinquents often follow this route. A good example is soccer vandalism. Soccer vandals normally range in age from 16 to 19 years. Youngster between the ages of 12 and 14 years join the group and undergo, as it were, a kind of training where they learn the job by example. In the stands, these "pupils" are, at least for insiders, easy to recognize. They stand away from the real vandals (usually closer to the field). By shouting loudly and other kinds of noisy behaviour they try to impress the older vandals whom they admire. For the rest, they limit themselves to verbal violence and foolish behaviour.

Youth gangs are mostly found in large cities. They range in size from a few dozen to a few hundred members. They are usually organized on the basis of neighbourhood affiliation or ethnic background, and usually have names reflecting this background. Gangs exist at all socioeconomic levels, but are particularly found in the lower milieus which appear to come into contact with the police more often (Chambliss, 1973; Miller, 1973).

Gangs usually compete with other gangs. Each group has its own territory which is fiercely defended against intrusion. The violence that takes place between gangs is often enormous. The criminality of these gangs particularly involves crimes against property, often accompanied by violence: violent theft, threats, abuse, blackmail, fraud, breaking and entering, robbery, pickpocketing, purse theft, and dealing in hard and soft drugs.

Even though youth gangs seldom are part of the world of real organized crime, there sometimes is contact with professional criminals. For example, a gang may deal with fences or may collect protection money from businesses on behalf of professional criminals. On occasion they steal to order. Organized crime tends to recruit its future members from these youth gangs (O'Hagan, 1976).

The gang means a lot to its members. It may even compensate for conventional institutions. The gang provides youths with a security that resembles that of the family, and an opportunity to learn that parallels that of the school. Of course, this security is of a different nature than that of the family, and what they learn in the gang is quite unlike what they would learn in school. This security and learning may compete with that provided by the family and school, whereby the gang usually is considered to be more important than family and school. This does not bode well for the acquisition of conventional norms and a career at school. In the gang, youngsters learn how too take care of themselves in life. There are opportunities for identity formation and growth of self-esteem. Usually, there is a negative attitude toward society and identifiable groups such as homosexuals, foreigners, the police, and so on.

The gang also offers protection. Anyone who harms a gang member knows that he may have to face the whole gang. Gang membership protects youngsters against becoming victims of criminality (for example being attacked by youths of another gang). At least, that is the way it is perceived. However, research shows that gang members run a greater risk of becoming victims of criminality than others.

All this means that the gang's influence on youngsters is more extensive than that of youth groups in general. A lot of pressure may be exerted by a gang to commit crimes, including more serious and aggressive offenses (Friedman et al., 1976; Savitz, et al., 1980).

Gangs are primarily a boys' affair, girl-gangs are exceptions (Giordano, 1978; McClelland, 1982; Miller, 1973, 1974). Consequently, little attention has been paid in the literature to girl-gangs, although interest in the phenomenon has increased lately. Girl-gangs usually are less criminally oriented than boy-gangs. This does not preclude the fact that there are girl-gangs which very much resemble boy-gangs, also in criminal behaviour.

Boy-gangs often include a few girls. The position of these girls in the gang is determined by the usually conservative role expectations that exist in these groups and which make it difficult for a girl to achieve equality with the boys. Girls who show boyish behaviour (e.g., fighting) are regarded with suspicion. On the other hand, if they act ladylike, they are not taken seriously either and are even more regarded as sex objects. Because of this, girls remain fringe figures. As fringe figures they are only marginally involved in delinquency. They may indirectly and often unconsciously foster the criminal behaviour of gang members because their mere presence may promote bravura behaviour and jealousy among the boys. The few girls who do manage to achieve a position of equality in the gang, are completely accepted as such and may even achieve positions of leadership (Bowker et al., 1983; Campbell, 1984; Schneider, 1987).

GROUP BEHAVIOUR

It is understandable that youths who seek one another's company and who subsequently form a group, in reality also function as a group.

The coherence of youth groups may differ greatly. It may vary from groups where there are strong interpersonal relationships (e.g., the above discussed gangs) to groups where the members hardly know one another. Generally, it is true that the larger the group, the less it functions as a group.

In light of the fact that youngsters so often operate in groups, it should not be surprising that much delinquency takes place in groups (Emler et al., 1987; Erickson and Jensen, 1977; Farrington, 1987; Hindelang, 1976; Hood and Sparks, 1972; Sehli, 1971; Zimring, 1981). However, this does not mean that juvenile delinquency is almost always committed in groups. It has been estimated that about two thirds of the behaviour takes place in cooperation with others (Erikson, 1971; Hindelang, 1971b). The distribution is somewhat more skewed in recorded criminality than in survey reported delinquency. Youths operating in groups behave, as we will see, more daringly and blatantly than when operating alone. Therefore, they stand out more and their criminal behaviour is more often known to the police. Moreover, the police possibly are more likely to take action when groups are involved (Hindelang, 1976).

The fact remains that many crimes are committed by individual youths, even though there are few youngsters who work completely alone. Youths who commit crimes alone differ from youths who operate in groups. They generally are more intelligent, come from higher socioeconomic milieus, and suffer more frequently from background related difficulties (e.g., poor family relationships) and emotional problems (e.g., neuroticism) (Brigham et al., 1967; Emler et al., 1987; Randolph et al., 1961; Wattenberg and Balistrier, 1950; Wilcock, 1964).

Group behaviour is found in all forms of juvenile delinquency, although it is more frequent in some than in others. Vandalism is a typical group activity. It hardly ever happens that youngsters destroy property on their own. If it occurs at all, it is usually out of revenge. Similarly, although one would not expect this to be the case, theft is often a group activity. Shop-lifting, for instance, is in only a third of the cases committed by individual youngsters; most times it takes place in smaller or larger groups. Breaking and entering also is often a group activity, as are traffic violations. More than is the case with adults, young traffic offenders tend to be in the company of friends when apprehended. Even though the driver has to face the consequences as an individual, his friends are usually to blame in part for his dangerous driving or driving under the influence. Even sexual crimes are, albeit to a lesser degree than other violations, sometimes committed as a group. For instance, gang rapes are not an exception (Robert et al., 1970).

Fights involving youths often take place between groups. Farrington et al. (1982b) have compared group fighting with individual fighting. They found that the reasons for fighting differ. Youngsters who fight alone feel that they have been challenged and insulted, they get angry and begin fighting. Group fights are more often motivated by a sense of threat and a need to help friends. Group fights tend to involve the use of weapons, there are more injuries, and the police frequently have to intervene. Youths who fight in groups, fight more often and have an aggressive attitude. Farring-ton et al. (1982b) identified a special type of aggressive and frequent fighters who were found to have background problems (economically disadvantaged, large family) and a deviant lifestyle (juvenile delinquency and subsequent adult criminality, drug use, sexual promiscuity, problems at work). Possibly it concerns here the type of (semi)-criminal youngster we discussed in Chapter 1.

Generally, group crimes are more serious in nature than offenses perpe-trated by individual youngsters. Groups destroy more in vandalism than individuals do, they steal larger amounts, and there are more victims when fighting take place. On the other hand, serious crimes involving grave bodily harm most often are committed by individuals (Hindelang, 1976).

Juvenile delinquency in many cases is a direct result of processes that take place within a group. In the first place, youth-related characteristics and motives such as impulsiveness and need for excitement which may cause matters to get out of hand, are easily expressed in a group. More-over, youngsters are quite capable of provoking one another. Under those circumstances, youngsters may, in order to save face, show behaviours that are unacceptable.

Moreover, acting in groups has all kinds of practical advantages. In a group one can do things which require cooperation and which otherwise would not be possible. One can complement one another and perform all kinds of services. Whatever one person cannot do, another one can; whatever one does not know, the other knows. Furthermore, the group lends moral support. As far as juvenile delinquency is concerned, it is significant that with a group (in numbers alone already) one has more physical power. One can risk more and there is no need to be afraid of others (other youths, bystanders, police). One is therefore more inclined to take risks when in a group. This also as a result of the fact that persons with a need for excitement have relatively greater influence in a group and are able to steer its members in a particular direction. (Wallach et al., 1962, 1964).

The group offers youngsters the protection of anonymity. Because of this, it is hard to be identified. One acts as a group, and it is often not that apparent who does what. One can escape responsibility by hiding behind the others. This hiding, by the way, is to be taken literally at times. Youths who have done something wrong and are called to account for their behaviour by bystanders, the police or whoever, may be observed to literally disappear in the group, covered by their mates.

In anonymous situations de-individuation easily takes place. That is to say, one loses to a certain extent one's individuality and is present as part of the group and not so much as an individual (Darley and Latané, 1968; Festinger et al., 1952; Singer et al., 1965).

The result of de-individuation is that personal responsibility decreases. Responsibility becomes a shared responsibility, which may become so diffuse under certain conditions that nobody feels responsible and a group spirit takes over. On occasion this may cause the group to go too far, resulting in serious violence, senseless destruction, and wanton theft. It may start as something minor, but gradually control over the situation is lost and matters go from bad to worse. Sometimes, because of motives that are not really clear, the situation may also suddenly explode and unpredictable serious criminality may occur.

The literature generally emphasizes that group membership may lead to de-individuation. It should be kept in mind, however, that groups may also provide a good opportunity to individuate (Festinger et al., 1952). In a group, youngsters may be able to express their originality and thus gain status and prestige. Thus, both individuation and de-individuation may be found in groups.

7. SOCIAL CIRCUMSTANCES

JUVENILE DELINQUENCY AS SOCIAL PHENOMENON

Juvenile delinquency is a social phenomenon. It is expressed in social behaviour, and the motives for the delinquency and the way in which it takes shape are related to the social position and circumstances (demographic, social, and economic) of the youngsters in question. We discussed the social position of youths and the way it has evolved historically in Chapter 2; this chapter focuses on social circumstances.

SOCIAL FACTORS

Demographic Relationships

Juvenile delinquency rates are related to the composition of the population (Block, 1986; Jackson, 1981; Leeuw et al., 1987; Van Tulder, 1985; Wilson and Herrnstein, 1985). That is, the more youths there are, the greater the number of potential delinquents.

The presence of a relatively large number of youths means that these young people have to share the opportunities that exist with many peers, not only in the society-at-large but also in their own milieu. In the family, at school, and elsewhere in society, youngsters are faced with greater competition in times when there are many youths (Burchard and Burchard, 1987; Easterlin, 1987; Kalacheck, 1973; Leeuw et al., 1987; Levy and Herzog, 1974; O'Brien, 1989; Van Fulpen, 1985). This leads to frustrations which impede identity formation and transference of norms. This, in turn, leads to alienation, avoidance behaviour, and escape behaviour, all at the expense of social integration (Peters, 1985; Wallimann and Zito, 1984).

Therefore, when a lot of children have been born during a particular period of time one may expect an increase in juvenile delinquency some ten years later and a decrease following another decade. This also applies to other behaviours (deviant and others) related to the youth period (Maxim, 1985; Siegal, 1984). Thus, the increase in juvenile delinquency that followed the Second World War may be attributed to, among others, a post-war birth-wave (Leeuw et al., 1987; Wolfgang, 1970).

Socio-Economic Milieu

The social behaviour of youths is related to the socioeconomic milieu in which they grow up. Socioeconomic status is usually assessed by indicators such as family affluence (income, home ownership), educational level of family members, and the neighbourhood in which one lives. A criterion that is often used to assess the socioeconomic status of a youngster's milieu is the professional level of his or her father. Of course, one may use other criteria, the end result is usually the same (Linden, 1978).

Many criminological theories assume that juvenile delinquency is a characteristic of the lower socioeconomic milieus; some are even exclusively geared toward youths from these backgrounds (Cloward and Ohlin, 1960; Cohen, 1971; Council of Europe, 1960; Healy and Bronner, 1936; Merton, 1968; Miller, 1958; Quinney, 1977; Shaw and McKay, 1969; Thrasher, 1963; Yablonsky, 1962). These theories usually presume that social circumstances related to delinquency are more pronounced in lower socioeconomic milieus. They note that youths from such backgrounds in many ways enjoy fewer opportunities for realizing their wishes and for acquiring status. Materially as well as otherwise these children have less to fall back on. They are less able to cope with social problems, and, compared to youths from higher milieus, they have less to lose (schooling, career). On this basis, one might expect that there would be more juvenile delinquency at the lower socioeconomic level. However, this expectation is not supported by research findings.

Studies of recorded criminality have only found a weak relationship between (low) socioeconomic level and juvenile delinquency (Hathaway and Monachesi, 1963; Havighurst, 1962; Hindelang et al., 1979, 1981; Ouston, 1984; Polk et al., 1974; Wadworth, 1979; West and Farrington, 1973; Williams and Gold, 1972). In only a few cases has a substantial relationship been found (Braithwaite, 1981; Reiss and Rhodes, 1961).

Similarly, most survey studies show an even weaker relationship between (low) socioeconomic milieu and juvenile delinquency (Akers, 1964; Arnold, 1965; Blomme, 1983; Casparis and Vaz, 1973; Clark and Wenniger, 1962; Dentler and Monroe, 1961; Empey and Lubeck, 1971; Gold, 1970; Hindelang, 1973; Hindelang et al., 1981; Hirschi, 1969; Johnson, 1979, 1980; Junger-Tas and Kruissink, 1987, 1990; Kelly and Pink, 1975; Krohn and Massey, 1980; Krohn et al., 1980; Linden, 1978; Matsueda, 1982; McDonald, 1969; Polk et al., 1974; Stark, 1979; Thornberry and Farnworth, 1982; Tittle et al., 1978; Williams and Gold, 1972; Wolfgang et al., 1972). Exceptions include findings by Braithwaite (1981), Briar and Piliavin (1965), Bytheway and May (1971), Clelland and Carter (1980), Elliott and Ageton (1980), Elliott and Huizinga (1983), Elliott and Voss

(1974), Johnstone (1978), McDonald (1969), Reiss and Rhodes (1961), Short and Strodtbeck (1965).

In cases where a relationship has been found, it has been observed that youths from lower milieus are somewhat more involved in delinquency. There is not much difference between the socioeconomic levels in terms of minor offenses, but a greater proportion of youngsters from lower milieus has been found to be implicated in more serious crimes. Possibly, a small group of habitual delinquents is responsible for this finding (Braithwaite, 1981; Clark and Wenniger, 1962; Elliott and Ageton, 1980; Elliott and Huizinga, 1983; Gibbons, 1970; Gold, 1987; Hagan et al., 1985; Johnson, 1980; Johnstone, 1978; Linden, 1978; McDonald, 1969; Wadworth, 1979).

The fact that the relationship is somewhat stronger for recorded delinquency than for survey-reported delinquency is perhaps due to the unequal distribution of serious offenses over the various socioeconomic levels. Because such offenses are reported more often and solved more often by the police, they appear with a higher frequency in data of recorded criminality.

Rutter and Giller (1983) assumed that the relationship between socioeconomic milieu and juvenile delinquency is not a direct one, but rather should be ascribed to differences between socioeconomic milieus that trace back to the family and child rearing.

The —limited— overrepresentation of lower milieus in recorded criminality is, according to some authors (e.g., Bonger, 1916; Lemert, 1972; Sampson and Castellano, 1982; Schur, 1971), caused by the fact that the police focus more on these milieus. They make the rounds more often in these neighbourhoods, and resort more readily to arrest. As far as such a selective attitude of the police is concerned, the literature is not unanimous, thereby suggesting local differences. The socioeconomic milieu certainly does not seems to have much influence on actual intervention (apprehension, arrest) by the police (Elliott and Voss, 1974; Gould, 1969b; Hindelang, 1978; Hindelang et al., 1979; Johnstone, 1978; Kleck, 1982; Lundman, 1974; Sherman, 1980; Weiner and Willie, 1971; Williams and Gold, 1972; Wolfgang et al., 1972).

In the administration of justice, youngsters from lower socioeconomic milieus may expect a somewhat less favourable treatment than their peers from higher milieus (Jongman, 1971; Newton et al., 1975; Sampson, 1986). This is not because of intentional discrimination. The way the police and the justice system treat youngsters depends mainly on the seriousness of the crime, recidivism, age, and gender (Cohen and Kluegel, 1978; Wolfgang et al., 1972). The somewhat less favourable treatment of lower socioeconomic youths is caused by the fact that the police and justice system possess limited knowledge of their background and consequently do not quite know how to deal with them and what measures would be most suitable. Youths from lower milieus are, so to speak, not treated more negatively than other youngsters, but rather less positively.

At every stage of the judicial process, youngsters from lower socio-economic milieus are subjected to a (slightly) negative bias. This has a cumulative effect which in the course of the judicial process causes delinquent youths from lower socioeconomic milieus to be increasingly disadvantaged (Liska and Tausig, 1979; Wellford, 1975).

Returning to the question of the relationship between socioeconomic milieu and juvenile delinquency, there is a discrepancy between expectations regarding this relationship that are based on theory and expectations that are based on empirical research. This finding has led to a broad discussion of the milieu-delinquency relationship (Braithwaite, 1981; Clelland and Carter, 1980; Elliott and Ageton, 1980; Hindelang et al., 1979, 1981; Hirschi, 1969; Thornberry and Farnworth, 1982).

As part of this discussion, the problems associated with survey-research —which we reviewed in the first Chapter— have been reviewed at length. In particular, it has been noted that different studies have defined the concept of socioeconomic milieu in different and often unclear ways (Empey and Lubeck, 1971; Johnson, 1980; McDonald, 1969; Rutter and Giller, 1983). Furthermore, it has been suggested that youngsters from higher socioeconomic milieus provide better reports of their deviant behaviour than their lower socioeconomic peers (Wiatrowski et al., 1981). Youths from higher milieus supposedly cooperate better because they have a less defensive attitude toward survey situations. They remember their (less frequent) crimes better, and when surveyed enjoy the advantage of a superior verbal ability. As a result, surveys do not adequately reflect the relationship between juvenile delinquency and (low) socioeconomic level (Braithwaite, 1981; Hardt and Peterson-Hardt, 1977; Kleck, 1982; Nettler, 1978; Toby, 1960). It is also possible that in survey-research, youths more likely report less serious offenses (the opposite is also claimed to be true). If that were the case, the previously discussed milieu difference in terms of serious criminal behaviour may not be completely revealed.

Another argument is that surveys often are conducted in secondary schools where the lower socioeconomic milieus may be underrepresented (Johnson, 1980). Moreover, school populations tend to be rather homogeneous socioeconomically. In that case, it would by definition be difficult to determine milieu differences (Kleck, 1982).

These criticisms aim to underscore that surveys lead to an *underestimation* of the relationship between socioeconomic milieu and juvenile delinquency, and that this relationship in fact is greater than is apparent from such research. An important counter-argument is of course that in recorded data there is also little influence to be detected from the socioeconomic milieu on delinquency.

On the other hand, juvenile delinquency surveys are more often conducted in cities than in the country, and in cities socioeconomic milieu plays a more significant role. This means that the relationship between socioeconomic milieu and delinquency is stronger in cities than in the country, and that surveys *overestimate* the relationship (Box and Ford, 1971).

Notwithstanding these objections, it is generally assumed that survey data present an adequate picture of the misconduct of youths (we already saw this in Chapter 1), and that they fairly reflect the relationship between socioeconomic milieu and juvenile delinquency. Of course, two limitations apply. First, the relationship concerns less serious forms of criminality. Second, it concerns youngsters who have been integrated into society to some degree (Hindelang et al., 1981).

The conclusion therefore remains that there is only a weak relationship (Elliott and Huizinga, 1983). This conclusion is also valid for deviant behaviour in general; other forms of deviant behaviour such as running away and risky habits (e.g., alcohol, drugs, gambling) similarly lack a substantial relationship with socioeconomic milieu.

The socioeconomic milieu provides youths with an *ascribed status* which is related to the social status of their family, particularly with their father's profession and social position. More important to the question of delinquency is the *achieved status* youngsters acquire within the family, at school, among friends, and so forth. The lower this status, the greater the chance that they get involved in delinquency (Blomme, 1983; Braithwaite, 1981; Brusten and Hurrelmann, 1973; Hirschi, 1969; Junger-Tas et al., 1985; Stark, 1979; Thornberry and Farnworth, 1982).

The question is sometimes asked whether in recent history there has never been a substantial relationship between socioeconomic milieu and juvenile delinquency, or whether this relationship did exist at some point, but subsequently declined. Such a decline could have been caused by two factors. First, the dividing lines between milieus have blurred in recent times. As a result any difference in criminal behaviour between the various milieus may have decreased in magnitude. Second, as far as recorded delinquency is concerned, it is possible that agencies (police, justice, social workers) have to some extent abandoned the discriminating way in which they treated the different milieus. In the past, significant associations have been found between socioeconomic milieu and juvenile delinquency, but usually on the basis of studies which upon closer examination did not warrant such a conclusion because of methodological limitations (Hindelang et al., 1981). In retrospect, it is difficult to determine the exact nature of the relationship. According to some, there has been a decline (Greenberg, 1977; Tittle et al., 1978); others have not been able to confirm this (Blomme, 1983; Hindelang et al., 1981).

The differences in delinquency of youths from diverse socioeconomic milieus are more qualitative than quantitative in nature, even though these differences are not very large either. These dissimilarities are related to the fact that different socioeconomic milieus view (certain) crimes from different perspectives (Quensel, 1971). In higher milieus one finds more individual delinquents, whereas youths from lower milieus tend to operate in groups. This is, in part, because the latter have stronger ties with their friends than their peers from higher milieus (Hirschi, 1969; Wattenberg and Balistrieri, 1950). In higher milieus one more often finds crimes without direct victims (e.g., vandalism); in lower milieus there is a tendency toward crimes with direct victims (violence) (Braithwaite, 1981).

The explanation for the criminal behaviour of youngsters from lower milieus is commonly sought in socio-cultural factors, whereas the delinquency of higher milieu youths is mainly explained by socio-psychological factors. However, this differential approach is not congruent with research findings which show that sociocultural factors have only a limited influence on juvenile delinquency, and that there are no differences between youngsters from different socioeconomic levels in terms of personality problems (Brownfield, 1987b; Casparis and Vaz, 1973; Conger and Miller, 1969; Gibbons, 1970; Hirschi, 1969).

We have seen that most youths abandon their delinquent behaviour near the end of the youth period. A small number continues into adulthood. As far as the behaviour of the latter is concerned, there is a difference in emphasis that is related to socioeconomic background. Youths from lower milieus who continue tend to be youngsters who previously have been involved in more serious criminal activities and who may be regarded as habitual or even (semi-)criminal delinquents; they simply continue their criminal career. It is different for youths from higher milieus. If they continue their delinquency, it usually involves crimes of a different nature, such as white-collar crime, tax evasion, milieu fraud, and so on. In other words, there is less of a qualitative change in the criminal career of recidivists from lower milieus than there is in the career of those from higher milieus.

We may conclude that there is little difference between youths from the different socioeconomic levels as far as delinquency is concerned. There is hardly any difference in terms of minor offenses; there is only a weak association between serious crime and low socioeconomic status.

The picture is distorted by youngsters from the traditional substratum of society. This substratum consists of populations which for generations have remained at the bottom of society and have no access to the normal social opportunities. Youths from this substratum, engage to a large degree in delinquency.

These youngsters hardly ever participate in surveys of delinquency. As a result, this lowest socioeconomic level is rarely represented in such studies. These youths, of course, do show up in recorded criminality. It is plausible that this contributes to the somewhat stronger relationship that has been found for recorded criminality. And yet, even recorded criminality does not adequately reflect this group's contribution. The standard procedure is to compare the delinquency of all milieus. The total number of milieus included in investigations varies and may be as high as ten. In such a comparison, the substratum's criminality becomes insignificant. However, in studies where separate comparisons are made between this substratum and the other milieus, differences are found. This is the case with reported as well as recorded criminality (Braithwaite, 1981; Clelland and Carter, 1980; Elliott and Ageton, 1980; Elliott and Huizinga, 1983; Elliott and Voss, 1974; Hirschi, 1969; Rutter and Giller, 1983; Thornberry and Farnworth, 1982; Williams and Gold, 1972).

Youngsters from society's substratum are a risk group as far as delinquency is concerned. They have a greater chance of getting involved.

Prosperity

Traditionally, criminological theories have assumed a direct causal relationship between level of prosperity and criminality (Beccaria, 1764; Von Mayr, 1877); that is, low prosperity was thought to be associated with greater criminality. However, attempts to empirically prove this assumption (e.g., Bonger, 1916: Durkheim, 1951, 1966) have not been very successful. It certainly seems that it is not valid at present (Cohen, 1981; Cohen and Felson, 1979; Godefroy and Laffargue, 1984; Gould, 1969a; Mansfield et al., 1974; Orsagh and Witte, 1981; Van Kerckvoorde et al., 1984).

Low prosperity and high criminality are not necessarily related. The global economic crisis between the two World Wars demonstrated this (Taft and England, 1964). Similarly, high prosperity does not always go hand in hand with low criminality. We saw this at the end of the 19th and the beginning of the 20th century. More recently, the high prosperity following the second World War coincided with high criminality in general and juvenile delinquency in particular. This criminality primarily involved crimes against property. Vandalism, violence, and traffic offenses occurred to a lesser degree, followed by homicide and sex offenses. The final conclusion has to be that there is no simple relationship between level of prosperity and juvenile delinquency, nor between level of prosperity and other forms of deviancy. The exception is suicide, which more often occurs in times of low prosperity (Clinard, 1968; Glaser, 1979).

In so far as there is a relationship between prosperity level and juvenile delinquency, the picture is rather complicated. In times of low prosperity the number of serious crimes increases, whereas in times of high prosperity there is an increase in the number of less serious offenses. The incidence of juvenile delinquency and, more generally, of petty crime usually is highest during periods of high prosperity (Cantor and Land, 1985; Clinard, 1968; Cohen and Felson, 1979; Cohen et al., 1980; Gould, 1969a; Leeuw et al., 1987; Mansfield et al., 1974; Stack, 1982; Toby, 1982).

Some assume that in years of prosperity much criminality is perpetrated by frustrated groups who either do not or only to a lesser degree benefit from the economic circumstances (Taft and England, 1964). Another suggested explanation for the increase in juvenile delinquency during times of prosperity is that when prosperity is high there are more (valuable) goods and these are more readily accessible, legally or illegally. More people are working and one is therefore less able (more often away from home) to keep an eye on one's own and other people's possessions. Generally people are more mobile, which increases the chances of becoming either the perpetrator or the victim. Also, many mothers work outside the home, which decreases parental supervision. This also is the case with respect to the supervision exercised by other people. Furthermore, because in affluent times youths generally have more disposable income, commercial recreation and its associated delinquency (recreational criminality) also increases.

However, as far as these data are concerned, it is difficult to establish to what degree there is a causal relationship. Fluctuations in prosperity are associated with developments in social welfare, training programs, education, leisure activities, health care, professions, and so on, which individually and in combination (may) influence delinquency.

The following appears to be an important explanation for the increase in juvenile delinquency in times of prosperity. When there is an increase in prosperity and material opportunities, youngsters' wishes increase accordingly. It seems that in times of high prosperity the discrepancy between needs and desires on the one hand and the satisfaction of these on the other, becomes larger rather than smaller. Level of need is namely not only determined by what one really requires, but also by what one feels entitled to in comparison to others (Bandura, 1977; Chester, 1976; Johnstone, 1978). Think only of Marx's labourer who lived happily in his little house until a wealthy man built a mansion in the neighbourhood.

People, including youths, are not very modest as far as rights are concerned. Durkheim (1897) already chose as one of the starting points of his theory the fact that people's needs know no limits. This leads to frustrations and may lead to criminality. These frustrations are not the prerogative of people who are less well off. Those who enjoy prosperity also complain about social injustices of which they believe themselves to be the victim. This sometimes leads to illegal practices of which tax fraud is a classical example. People who are relatively well-off have more means but also have higher demands, while poorer people adjust their desires to what is possible (Blake and Davis, 1964; Hyman, 1953).

Thus, the old thesis (Bonger, 1932; Colajanni, 1887; Turati, 1883) that desires generated by higher prosperity do increase criminality does seem to have validity. For juvenile delinquency in particular it is true that the criminality is more prosperity-related (greed criminality) than poverty-related (misery criminality) (Bonger, 1954).

Poverty

For centuries, poverty has been regarded by many (e.g., Xenophon, Plato, Aristotle, Virgil, Horace, Thomas of Aquino, Thomas More, the French encyclopedists) as an important cause of criminality. These authors wrote mainly about *absolute poverty* where one is unable to provide for one's most basic needs. We must distinguish this from *relative poverty* ("social poverty" or "modern poverty"), where one can not adequately benefit from or take part in society, and where one is limited to one's own little world. This rarely leads to criminality.

There are youngsters who live on welfare or otherwise have a minimal income and who better their material circumstances by illegal means. This, of course, concerns primarily crimes against property. Generally, however, juvenile delinquency is not related to poverty. Wootton (1959) concluded that poverty is more related to honesty than to criminality.

Poverty is not directly related to juvenile delinquency, but it is part of the framework of social conditions in which the delinquency occurs (Dinitz et al., 1982; Lane, 1986; Rutter and Giller, 1983).

Unemployment

Research findings are not unanimous as to whether there is a lot of juvenile delinquency in times of unemployment. Some studies have found a positive relationship, others have found no association, and others again have found a negative correlation (Chiricos, 1987; Cohen and Felson, 1979; Farrington et al., 1986; Glaser, 1979; Leeuw et al., 1987; Parker and Horwitz, 1986; Rutter and Giller, 1983; Wilson and Herrnstein, 1985).

This inconsistency may perhaps be explained in part by the suggestion that unemployment may have a positive as well as a negative effect on criminality (Cantor and Land, 1985). Unemployment increases the *motivation* to commit crimes, but in times of high unemployment the *opportunity* to do so decreases. Unemployment increases in times of low prosperity when there is less to be stolen and when what is worth stealing is more closely guarded (Cohen et al., 1980, 1981). It all depends on the balance of these and other factors at the time.

When we speak of youth unemployment, we mean unemployment in relation to work that enables youngsters to (somewhat) provide for themselves. Thus, we do not mean part-time jobs youths may have while still in school; that is a totally different matter. By the way, it appears that there is no relationship between having or lacking such a job and juvenile delinquency (Gottfredson, 1985).

The temporal relationship between unemployment and juvenile delinquency says, of course, little about unemployment as a cause of criminality. If there is more delinquency in times of great unemployment, it does not mean that unemployed youths are (largely) responsible. The question as to whether unemployed youths are more involved in delinquency is often raised in publications that are based on deprivation theories, including (neo) marxist theories. The literature, however, does not provide a conclusive answer (Allan and Steffensmeier, 1989; Leeuw et al., 1987; Thornberry and Christenson, 1984; Wilson and Herrnstein, 1985).

Generally, however, it apears that there is a weak relationship between youth unemployment and juvenile delinquency. This association is stronger for recorded than for reported criminality, and mainly concerns crimes against property. The latter take place especially during the periods that a youngster is out of work. The fact that the connection between unemployment and delinquency is relatively weak is the result of the fact that this relationship is only valid for certain *groups* of unemployed youths. We will return to this later (Cantor and Land, 1985; Chiricos, 1987; Farrington et al., 1986; Hirschi, 1969; Leeuw et al., 1987; Martens and Steinhilper, 1978; Neustrom et al., 1988; Orsagh and Witte, 1981; Parker and Horwitz, 1986; Thornberry and Christenson, 1984; Thornberry and Farnworth, 1982; West, 1982, 1986; Wilson and Herrnstein, 1985).

The relationship between unemployment and criminality varies over time (Parker and Horwitz, 1986). Hoch (1974) concluded that in years of low unemployment the relationship with criminality is higher than in years with high unemployment. He assumed that in times of low unemployment there are just the chronically unemployed, whereas in periods of high unemployment the ranks also include a higher number of employment-seeking, non-criminal unemployed (Leeuw et al., 1987).

Allan and Steffensmeier (1989) suggested that the association between unemployment and crimes (against property) has decreased because of the improved (financial) provisions that have been created for the unemployed.

The most tangible consequence of unemployment is that one has less money, at least less than those who do have a job. One may compensate for this by borrowing money; however, this offers only temporary relief. The latter is not the case if one were to generate income by committing crimes against property on a regular basis.

Furthermore, unemployment may cause some social isolation which may lead to alienation from conventional institutions. This is not conducive to integration. Socially speaking, unemployment leads to dependence on the parents, financially (the parents are usually the first to be approached for help) and otherwise. This dependency may lead to all sorts of frictions. Moreover, unemployed youths miss the contacts at work —particularly the interaction with adults— and the opportunity to take on responsibilities. Thus, they may also miss out on the socializing influence this may have on their identity formation.

Often there is a certain estrangement from friends who do have a job. They may feel excluded and seek contact with others who are in a similar position. This is why many unemployed youths have unemployed friends. Such youngsters are more susceptible to influences from subcultures than are youngsters with a job (Allan and Steffensmeier, 1989; Donovan and Oddy, 1982; Hamilton and Crouter, 1980).

Being unemployed means that one has a lot of free time. Many youngsters do not know how to fill this time in a productive way, and this may result in boredom. In their search for activities to alleviate this boredom, they may become less discriminating. Unemployed youths spend a good deal of their time out of doors (the streets, youth centres, bars, etc.). There, they may come in contact with delinquent peers.

The criminality of unemployed youths is sometimes attributed to low self-esteem and feelings of powerlessness, uselessness, and depression (Donovan and Oddy, 1982; Jaspers and Heesink, 1987). Work and income provide status and form an intrinsic part of the identity experience, especially in boys with a distinctive sense of male identity. If this identity is tampered with, compensation is sought in all sorts of ways (including delinquency) to impress oneself and others. Girls are thought to suffer less from this problem because home and family are relatively more important in their lives than work. In some cases, low self-esteem causes youngsters to be discouraged and to adopt an indifferent and maladapted life-style, which leads them into a downward spiral (Furnham, 1985). The fact that the better educated suffer fewer negative consequences from unemployment at the personal level may be explained by their higher self-esteem and belief in their own abilities (Schaufeli, 1988). To place the self-esteem hypothesis in perspective, it should be noted that most youths have largely completed their identity formation by the time they become unemployed (Social and Cultural Planning Bureau, 1980).

As a counter-argument to the self-esteem hypothesis, it may be stated that for many youths being employed is not always related to high self-esteem. Work may indeed offer prestige because one feels productive, is respected by others, and has a higher income. However, if one does low-level, unschooled, or unpleasant work (and this is what is in store for many youngsters), these advantages may not be there, and work may have a negative effect on self-esteem (Berk et al., 1980; Covington, 1986; Gottlieb, 1979; Holzman, 1982; Knox, 1981; Liker, 1982; Sviridoff and Thompson, 1983). This negative effect increases with age. When young, the important thing is to have a job at all; as one grows older, the quality of the job becomes more important (Allan and Steffensmeier, 1989; Thornberry and Christenson, 1984).

Generally, the psychological consequences of youth unemployment do not seem to be that disastrous. Many youths see the advantages of unemployment, such as having lots of free time for themselves and for hobbies and being able to do useful and enjoyable volunteer work. But at the same time they are aware of the disadvantages, particularly the financial ones. As well, many unemployed youngsters feel rather insecure about the future and have a less optimistic outlook than employed youths (Feather and Barber, 1983; Feather and Davenport, 1981; Feather and O'Brien, 1986; Goede and Maassen, 1986a,b; Jackson et al., 1983; Schaufeli, 1988).

The consequences of unemployment become more pronounced *the longer it lasts*. In the beginning one often thinks that the unemployment is only temporary. Often, it is welcomed as an opportunity to take a holiday, to do things one would not otherwise do, and so forth. Financially too, one is able to get by. But often this does not last too long. Soon all kinds of psychological and social disadvantages begin to play a role. In particular, being rejected time after time when searching for a job is frustrating and may lead to feelings of insecurity and depression. The association with criminality is therefore stronger in cases of long-term unemployment (Leeuw et al., 1987; Orsagh and Witte, 1981).

The *older* the youngster, the more negative he or she experiences the consequences of unemployment. At a younger age one knows better how to entertain oneself, and one finds it less problematic to ask parents and other people for financial help. Moreover, the younger one is, the more other people are inclined to accept the fact that one is unemployed.

A distinction may be made between *active* and *passive* unemployed.

Active unemployed people are "job-oriented"; they keep on looking for work, keep on applying. They are enterprising and inventive when it comes to improving their income status (through temporary and black market work) and taking advantage of all sorts of provisions. Passive unemployed people are more likely to adopt a wait-and-see attitude. In this group we also find drop-outs and social marginals such as addicts. Active unemployed youths have fewer problems and get less involved in delinquency. This seems to be related with staying active and high self-esteem (Leeuw et al., 1987; Schaufeli, 1988).

Does providing jobs to young people lower delinquency? That remains to be seen. If juvenile delinquents find a job, it often involves work that does not pay very well and is not very pleasant. The question is whether or not this kind of work decreases delinquency. This apart from the fact that youngsters who have unpleasant work on a regular basis opt for voluntary unemployment because they are fed up with the job. What is important is not so much the relation between delinquency and having or not having a job, but between delinquency and having a *good* job (i.e., well-paid *and* pleasant). Such a job means that youths are financially better off and that they feel better. This, in turn, increases their self-esteem and involvement in society, which keeps them from delinquency (Orsag and Witte, 1981).

If unemployment causes juvenile delinquency, the reverse is also true. Sometimes, criminality offers such good financial opportunities that looking for a job is not attractive (e.g., drug dealers). A totally different case is when one is fired because one has committed crimes, whether or not in connection with the kind of work one did. Furthermore, for people with a record it is difficult to find work (Pirog-Good, 1986; Schwarz and Kolnick, 1962; Thornberry and Christenson, 1984).

The relationship between unemployment and juvenile delinquency is, however, especially caused by factors that are found in the person and the personal circumstances of the youngsters involved. These factors already surfaced earlier in, for example, their relationships with their parents, behaviour at school, and their social integration in general. In this respect, many unemployed youths who commit crimes already did so when they were still employed. Unemployment may even be part of a delinquent lifestyle (Buikhuisen and Meijs, 1983; Dahrendorf, 1985; Glaser, 1979; Van Kerckvoorde et al., 1984; Martens and Steinhilper, 1978; Rutter and Giller, 1983; West, 1982; Wilson and Herrnstein, 1985).

When studying juvenile delinquency one should consider the employment status of the father of the family. If he is unemployed, it may act as an important factor in the delinquency of his children (Brownfield, 1987a; Cantor and Land, 1985; Hirschi, 1969; Rutter and Giller, 1983).

If the father is out of work, there is less income and the children enjoy fewer material opportunities. This is frustrating and may lead to compensation via crimes against property (Cantor and Land, 1985). Furthermore, an unemployed father usually is more involved in the daily routine of the family. The effect of this depends on a lot of factors such as the kind of job the father had, his level of education, the reason why he was fired, age and gender of the children (girls are more easily influenced), and how the father is taking his dismissal. In harmonious families, a father's unemployment may result in a deeper and improved relation with his family. In disharmonious families, it more often than not does not benefit the relationship. Moreover, even if the relationship within the family is good, a father who is constantly (or at least often) present and who concerns himself with everything, may negatively influence the family atmosphere. In that case, his unemployment may lead to all kinds of family problems (including child abuse) and to problems among the children (absenteeism, poor school performance, and delinquency) (Baarda, 1983; Steinberg, 1981).

Cities

Juvenile delinquency is unequally distributed over the various regions (Angenent, 1988; Clinard, 1968; Fagan et al., 1987; Friday and Hage, 1976; Horn, 1989; Rutter, 1980). In areas where there is a lot of delinquency, there are also other kinds of criminal behaviour, other forms of deviant behaviour, and other social problems. Some assume that there is a link between population density in a region and juvenile delinquency (Gilles, 1974; Shichor and Kelly, 1979; Traulsen, 1988). Others have not been able to confirm this relationship (Choldin, 1978; Freedman, 1977; Kvalseth, 1977).

There is more juvenile delinquency in cities than in rural areas, and the larger the city the more criminality there is. In cities, the accent lies relatively more on offenses such as fare-dodging on public transport, theft (shoplifting, bicycle theft), fencing, and graffiti. Factors that have been proposed to explain the concentration of juvenile delinquency in cities include: more opportunity to commit offenses, the heterogenous structure of the population, and the turnover of people due to greater mobility. A relatively large number of youths live in cities. There is anonymity in large groups which leads to social isolation and less supervision. There are more family problems and there are problems with how the police system operates (Crutchfield et al., 1982; Horn, 1989; Lambooy, 1988; Leeuw et al., 1987).

Moreover, there tends to be a higher concentration of risk groups in cities. These are groups whose members run a greater risk of getting involved in delinquency: runaways, homeless youths, youths in prostitution, youths from the social substratum, rebelling youths, and youths with dangerous habits (alcohol, drugs, gambling). Besides, in cities much juvenile delinquency takes place in entertainment areas. More about this later.

Neighbourhoods

In cities, juvenile delinquency is more or less concentrated in certain neighbourhoods. In many larger metropolitan areas there are neighbourhoods one preferably should avoid; for example, areas populated by drug addicts, alcoholics, dropouts, and so forth. It should be noted that the extent to which juvenile delinquency is recorded is determined not only by the criminal behaviour that actually takes place but also by the reputation of the neighbourhood in the eyes of the people and the police. This reputation may inflate crime statistics because citizens report more readily and there may be more surveillance by the police. Consequently, youths who misbehave in these neighbourhoods are apprehended more quickly and will therefore be overrepresented in the official records (Gold, 1987; Horn, 1989; Jacobs, 1979; Landau, 1981).

Generally, the rate of juvenile delinquency in cities is higher downtown than in the suburbs, except for certain neighbourhoods we will discuss in a moment. In the downtown area one especially notices activities such as fare-dodging, shoplifting, bike theft, street robbery. It usually, but not exclusively, involves local youths.

Juvenile delinquency is particularly found in neighbourhoods where there is plenty of opportunity to commit crimes: shopping areas, entertainment districts, and socially troubled neighbourhoods (Baker and Donelly, 1986; Brown and Altman, 1981; Cusson, 1989; Harries, 1980; Hesseling 1987; Horn, 1989; Johnstone, 1978; Lahaye et al., 1982; Rubinstein et al., 1980). These areas are primarily located in and around the centres of cities, although socially troubled neighbourhoods are also found in the suburbs. In *shopping districts*, the most often committed crimes are —rather obvious seen the nature of these areas— crimes against property, such as shoplifting, pickpocketing, bicycle and car theft, swindling, fraud, and robbery. In *entertainment districts* the emphasis is less on crimes against property and more on violent crime, sometimes related to alcohol abuse.

Socially troubled neighbourhoods generally are either old neighbourhoods in need of improvement or more modern apartment districts. Characteristic of social problem neighbourhoods is the low percentage of privately owned homes, the inferior housing conditions, and the poor maintenance of the dwellings. There are many open spaces and abandoned buildings, and the future of the homes and other structures is often uncertain. There are few basic amenities such as shops, schools, and recreational facilities. Many households have a low income and often rely on welfare. Arrears in rent are common. The health of people in these neighbourhoods is often below average, resulting in, among others, lower life expectancy. There is unemployment and drug and alcohol abuse. People with an education, a higher professional level, and a reasonable income (middle class and skilled labourers) move away. The ones who stay or move in are the elderly, people who live alone, incomplete families, transient youths, and people from ethnic minorities. These are mostly individuals who did not really choose the neighbourhood and who certainly would not have selected it if they had other options. These are people with varied backgrounds. This, in combination with a large mobility (many relocations), leads to a lack of homogeneity in life style and norms. In such neighbourhoods there are feelings of alienation, uncertainty, and insecurity, and possibly racial tensions. The people do not identify with the area, they do not feel involved nor responsible for it. There is little social intercourse, one retreats into one's own quarters, one's own home. Isolation and social disruption render the neighbourhood susceptible to all kinds of deviant behaviour. Level of criminality (juvenile as well as adult) is high (Fagan et al., 1986; Simcha-Fagan and Schwarz, 1986; Stark, 1987).

Besides in the above mentioned neighbourhoods —where there is much opportunity for delinquency— many youngsters commit crimes in their *own neighbourhood*. The emphasis lies thereby more on vandalism, breaking and entering, and arson, and less on crimes against property (except for fencing which is more prevalent here) (Baldwin and Bottoms, 1976; Fiselier, 1972; Junger-Tas and Kruissink, 1990; Screvens, 1981; Willemse, 1989).

The relationship between area of residence and delinquency is also based on the fact that a neighbourhood is a social network, just as the family and the school are. It should be noted, however, that the influence of the neighbourhood on older youths is rather limited; more limited than was assumed in the past. This is related, among others, to their greater mobility, which causes them to feel less attached to the neighbourhood. They are "cosmopolitans" rather than "locals" (Merton, 1968). The influence of the neighbourhood on youngsters is less in large-scale residential areas where one tends to have fewer personal relationships.

The relationship between residential area and juvenile delinquency is established along two lines. On the one hand there are the contacts with *friends and peers* in the neighbourhood. As we discussed in Chapter 6, youths meet age-mates in their immediate environment, and these peers may influence their behaviour. On the other hand there are the *opportun-*

ities for delinquency that are present in the neighbourhood. We discussed these opportunities in Chapter 1. These two lines converge in the neighbourhood. This explains why youths commit relatively much criminality in their own neighbourhood (Clark and Wenniger, 1962; Dentler and Monroe, 1961; Erickson and Empey, 1965; Gold, 1970; Johnstone, 1978; Nye et al., 1958).

Church Affiliation

Youths who are believers, youths who belong to a church, and youths who attend church are less involved in delinquency. Thus, there is a, albeit small, negative association between church affiliation and juvenile delinquency (Bainbridge, 1989; Donovan and Jessor, 1985; Elifson et al., 1983; Ferguson, 1952; Glueck and Glueck, 1950; Higgins and Albrecht, 1977; Miller, 1965; Nye, 1958; Rhodes and Reiss, 1970; Stark et al., 1982; Tittle, 1983). It should be noted, however, that some studies have failed to confirm this negative relationships (Conger and Miller, 1969; Elifson et al., 1983; Hirschi and Stark, 1969; McDonald, 1969; Middleton and Putney, 1962).

The extent to which the church inhibits juvenile delinquency depends on the social framework. The influence would be especially great in societies where the social setting supports religious beliefs and where churches have already much influence (Stark et al., 1982). It would also be great in societies where social institutions are failing and where churches fill the vacuum (Tittle and Welch, 1983).

The fact that churches inhibit juvenile delinquency is probably more the result of being a member of an adjusted group than of the specific religious character of that group. *Churches as institutions* usually preach conformity to society and defend norms which forbid criminality. *Local congregations* (religious communities and parishes) offer their members security, encourage them to conform, and have a supervisory function. But it is particularly the *personal relationships* with parents and friends that are coloured by the shared religious affiliation which cause youngsters to participate less in delinquency (Elifson et al., 1983).

Wright (1974) suggested that church affiliation inhibits serious criminal behaviour, but that it does not influence less serious crimes.

Leisure Time

Juvenile delinquency takes particularly place during leisure time (Agnew and Peterson, 1989; Buikhuisen et al., 1973a; Junger-Tas and Kruissink, 1990; Kruissink, 1988; Riley, 1987). The more leisure time youngsters have, the more delinquency there is. It is not difficult to see why it is primarily during their free time that youths are involved in criminal behaviour. During that time there is much opportunity and incentive to commit crimes. One is mobile, one moves from one situation to another, and one meets many people. Motives for participating in criminal activities (to entertain oneself, excitement seeking) are more readily realized during leisure time. Also, there is less supervision. What is important here is the balance between the amount of free time one has and the opportunities that are available to fill this time. If adequate opportunities to entertain oneself are lacking, boredom (which we previously identified as a cause of delinquency) may result.

Juvenile delinquency is directly related to the way in which one spends one's spare time (including where and when this takes place and with whom). It has been reported (Cohen et al., 1956) that delinquents differ from other youngsters in that they have fewer opportunities to satisfy their recreational needs in a conventional way. To some youngsters delinquency is in fact a form of recreation (Angenent, 1988).

Juvenile delinquents spend their time relatively more often in ways which encourage delinquency, in the company of other youths who do not shy away from deviant behaviour, and in places where there is little supervision. We saw in Chapter 6 that juvenile delinquents spend less of their leisure time within the family. They seek it more outside the home, often in less conventional milieus. They do not spend much of their spare time in organized activity, but more in the company of friends. They less often belong to societies, clubs, and action groups. They prefer passive forms of recreation (playing cards, pool). They are just as interested in music as other youngsters, but usually do not play an instrument themselves. Also, like other youths they show an interest in sports, but their interest lies mainly in physical, exciting, and risky sports (motor-crossing, go-carting, [kick]-boxing).

Juvenile delinquents prefer freedom. They loiter a lot downtown and enjoy going out. They frequently visit recreational establishments such as discos, bars, and amusement halls where they spend relatively large amounts of money. Visiting such establishments correlates with involvement in delinquency and with the possibility of becoming a victim of criminality (Wilson, 1987).

Delinquency that is related to the way in which youths spend their free time is referred to as *recreational delinquency* (Angenent, 1988; 1989a). This kind of delinquency usually takes place during weekends and holidays. It occurs throughout the year, but particularly during the summer and special holidays such as New Year's Eve. The action takes primarily place in the entertainment districts. Local conditions play thereby an important role (e.g., does one have easy access to establishments, how far does one have to travel, and so forth). The kind of entertainment offered is central because particular forms elicit particular types of behaviour, including criminal behaviour. Moreover, a specific type of amusement attracts a particular audience, which in turn will have repercussions for the qualitative and quantitative aspects of the delinquency one may expect.

Recreational delinquency resembles regular juvenile delinquency as outlined in Chapter 1, but it also has unique characteristics. In the first place, there is a high incidence of vandalism, usually committed in groups. Youngsters in an excited (or frustrated) mood are capable of destroying plenty in a short period of time. Furthermore, the amount of violence involved is remarkable, varying from threats and arguments to smaller and larger fights to abuse. The victims are normally other youths. Usually, one fights with bare hands or with whatever one can find. However, there are quite a few youngsters who walk around with special equipment, to defend themselves so to speak, including knives and, to a lesser extent, firearms. A popular item is the baseball bat which is kept in the trunk of the car, just in case. A large percentage of the violence in recreational areas must be attributed to a very small group of youths who are out to fight. We noted this type in Chapter 1. Traffic offenses are also common, especially reckless driving (showing off), having too many people in the car, and driving under the influence. Crimes against property mainly involve shoplifting (if there is opportunity), bicycle theft, and theft from cars. Car theft often entails the "borrowing" of a vehicle to get home after, for example, having missed the last bus. Finally, there is "dealing" in soft and hard drugs.

Recreational delinquency is not limited to entertainment districts. On the way home after an evening on the town, a small number of youngsters causes trouble in the public transit system. However, these few may cause quite a stir. Especially the last few rides in the weekends are disturbed by this behaviour. As a result the police has to act regularly, and occasionally drivers refuse that particular shift because they feel threatened.

Several causes of recreational delinquency may be noted. When relaxing in a less restrictive atmosphere, youngsters feel more free than is the case in daily life, and less bound by rules and regulations. They throw off the straitjacket of everyday life and are less inhibited. They are among peers and wish to be freed from the adult world which they must take into account when at home, school, and work. This is especially the case when recreation serves as compensation for a less than happy existence (disagreements with parents, poor functioning at school, boring work, unemployment). As such, the diversion permits them to vent their frustrations. Sometimes, the recreational situation leads them to collectively go wild.

Furthermore, the recreational situation offers greater anonymity than is normally the case. And in anonymous situations norms are less defined and one may behave in ways one ordinarily would not in everyday life.

It is particularly during recreational activities when youths look for fun and excitement. They want to experience something. Therefore, they usually go to places where "something is happening". Important hereby is the contact with other youths. The recreational situation is ideal for bravura behaviour. The latter may get out of hand on occasion, especially in situations where one competes with one another. Confrontation between (groups of) youngsters is often the result. They especially want to impress the opposite sex. Picking up a partner is namely an important part of recreational activities. To the majority of youths in recreation areas, meeting the opposite sex is of primary importance. This may give rise to tensions between youngsters if they feel frustrated or outmanoeuvred in this respect.

The main cause of recreational criminality is without a doubt the impressive alcohol consumption that takes place while unwinding. It may be noted that alcohol consumption (usually beer) fits in with bravura behaviour and may accord a certain status. In some circles, the amount of beer one can consume in a limited period of time without dropping to the ground may raise the drinker's prestige. It shows that one "can handle it", which is a valued macho characteristic. Being drunk also may increase one's prestige, because this is also viewed as a positive male characteristic. Drinking a lot, therefore, always brings success, whatever the outcome. Only youngsters who show bad effects after having consumed only a little amount of alcohol are treated with disdain because they "can't handle it".

Alcohol use has as result that almost all the causes of recreational delinquency which we have discussed are amplified. Alcohol may lead to excessive euphoria, or it may cause all kinds of frustrations to surface. In both cases the result may be the same: one loses sight of what is proper and sometimes control over the situation may be lost.

SOCIAL BACKGROUNDS OF JUVENILE DELINQUENCY

Social Factors and Juvenile Delinquency

The relationships between social factors and juvenile delinquency found in studies seem to be weaker than is assumed by some theories —among them many traditional deprivation theories— which assign an important position to these factors. This has consequences for theory development because reformulation and revalidation is required.

Generally, the relationships between social factors and recorded juvenile delinquency are stronger than those between social factors and survey-reported delinquency. This indicates that social factors have more influence on how society reacts to juvenile delinquency than on the delinquency itself (Reinarman and Fagan, 1988).

Discussing only one social factor at a time, as we did above, actually does injustice to these variables because in reality multiple interacting factors are involved. It is the whole of social factors that constitute the social background of a youngster which influences whether or not he or she participates in criminality. If this whole is negative in nature, a youngster may be considered to be socially handicapped and he or she will run a greater risk of getting involved in delinquency (Wilson, 1975). This, however, is not necessarily inevitable. A similar social handicap exists, for example, for youngsters growing up in oriental neighbourhoods (Chinatown) as they are found all over the world. And criminality among these youths is conspicuously *low* (Wilson and Herrnstein, 1985).

Social factors are usually indirectly related to juvenile delinquency. Their influence on youngsters —particularly at a younger age— takes place mainly via their own milieu (family, school, friends, peers) (Angenent, 1990; Friday and Hage, 1976; Hepburn, 1976; Hirschi, 1969; Wiatrowski and Anderson, 1987; Wiatrowski et al., 1981). They form as it were a frame of reference for behaviour. They are represented in the youngsters' daily life by intermediating factors such as participation in social life and the fulfilling of social roles. If there is something wrong with the social factors, then these intermediating factors will cause youths to be less integrated into society (Cernkovich, 1978b; Roff and Wirt, 1984; Simcha-Fagan and Schwarz, 1986).

Social Integration

Integration into society goes hand in hand with conforming to the conventional culture (acculturation), to conventional institutions, norms and customs. In light of what we have seen in Chapter 2 regarding the youth period, it seems that youngsters are not fundamentally predisposed towards social integration. We have seen that the search for identity and the striving for independence clash with such an integration. Youths are critical of society, point out mistakes and shortcomings, and are usually not very willing to compromise. This is not to say, however, that they turn away from society. They grumble and complain, but follow the rules anyway, just like regular people. They do not rebel actively nor passively; rebelling is only done by a small minority. In this context, youngsters' relationship with society resembles the one they have with their parents. In the latter relationship we also notice a certain detachment during the youth period, without this leading to real conflicts or a break-up. On the contrary, this relationship remains characterized by solidarity and loyalty. Something like that also applies to the relationship between youngsters and society. Even though youths are critical, they do not turn away from society, but rather try to integrate, particularly towards the end of the youth period. This is related to the fact that by that time youngsters develop greater social interests and responsibilities. This integration, by the way, is also demanded from them by other people. Deviant behaviour —at least if it concerns less serious deviant behaviour— is tolerated to a certain degree. After all, they do have to sow some wild oats. Usually, this type of behaviour is viewed as a part of normal development, but the older youngsters are, the less deviant behaviour is accepted and the more they are held accountable.

The integration of youths into society depends on the *norms* to which they personally adhere. The more these norms agree with the dominant norms, the greater the probability that they will discern the reasonableness and legitimacy of the dominant culture, and that they will adapt to its customs and regulations. If the differences are too great, deviant behaviour, including criminality, is a possible consequence. As we have seen in Chapter 3, it is not so much which norms one knows, but rather the extent to which one adheres to norms (beliefs). Of course, integration does not necessarily mean than one completely adopts the norms and customs of the dominant culture. However, it does mean that one behaves in such a way as to avoid social friction (Box, 1981).

Integration is facilitated by involvement in *conventional activities*, such as attending school, doing homework, reading, having a hobby, and so on. Youths involved in conventional activities are less drawn to criminal behaviour and also have neither the time nor the energy for it. They are less likely to come in contact with persons with a certain affinity for criminal behaviour, and less easily end up in situations leading to criminality. They also less readily get in contact with deviant subcultures, among others because they do not know the norms and customs of the latter. Conversely, delinquent youths for the same reasons do not have access to adjusted youth groups and subcultures (Brennan et al., 1978).

Integration is also related to what youngsters have *invested* —via school and occupation— in an adjusted life (commitment). These investments, which are an good measure of social integration, may be jeopardized if they get involved in delinquency (see the utility-principle as discussed in Chapter 2). Many youngsters do not wish to risk their interests (future) in that way. Perhaps it is for this reason that the more educated they are, the less they participate in delinquency (Cernkovich, 1978b; Cohen, 1967; Hirschi, 1969; Junger-Tas et al., 1983).

The integration of youths into society also depends strongly on the bonds they have with their own milieu. We have seen that social functioning is an extension of the way in which one functions within one's own environment.

Even though youngsters in our society are probably better off than ever before, the circumstances under which they live are accompanied by a few phenomena which may render their integration difficult.

Because of the considerable *openness* of our society, youths become aware of varying norms and customs. This gives them the opportunity to orient themselves extensively. This is necessary in a pluriform society which in most areas offers many —sometimes contradictory— opportunities. This *pluriformity*, which for example is clearly expressed in the media, means that youngsters must (learn to) live in a complex network of social relationships in which they have to play varying roles in various circles and at various levels. Associated with this pluriformity is a fragmentation which expresses itself in a mosaic of institutions and groups which coexist, but which usually interact very little and do not collaborate. This pluriformity also leads to norms and customs which are not only dissimilar but sometimes difficult to reconcile. In such a state of fragmentation, it is not always easy for youngsters to gain a complete overview and to take a position.

Because of the *large-scale character* resulting from technological developments, industrialization, and urbanization, human existence is sometimes dominated by mass-culture, impersonality and anonymity. Abstract laws and regulations, institutions and commissions have the upper hand of personal relationships. Within the more complex and larger whole, the individual may easily be lost. Some youngsters have trouble recognizing themselves in this anonymous society and find it difficult to select from it norms which apply to them. In the personal area there is also much *anonymity*. One has quite a few relationships, but they are mostly anonymous. In cities one often does not know one's neighbour, at school one often does not know one's fellow students, and at work one often does not know one's colleagues. Contacts are fleeting, among others because of the greater mobility of people (moving, changing jobs). Anonymity has two consequences for delinquency. First, it limits the transfer of norms and supervision of youngsters. Second, people in anonymous situations feel less responsible for their own behaviour and that of others.

Democratic relations cause authority to be limited. The authorities' power is circumscribed as is their influence. With respect to youngsters this is true not only for institutions but also for parents, teachers, employers, churches, the law, and the police. Youths, therefore, enjoy much *freedom and autonomy*. This is also what they want. They want to determine their own lives, form their own opinions, set their own goals and try to reach these in their own ways. They also do not accept norms and values as a matter of course, but want to decide for themselves. Youngsters are indeed able to decide much for themselves because of the schooling they receive and the large amount of information that is made available to them. Meddling by persons and institutions is sometimes perceived as interference. However, the relatively greater freedom and autonomy youngsters are allowed, does demand a great responsibility. To a certain extent they have to determine their own limits. They have to supervise themselves, so to speak. In most cases they are quite successful. However, not all are capable of carrying such a heavy responsibility.

The fact that many *opportunities* for youngsters primarily exist in theory is detrimental to the integration of youths into society. In every society, government and social institutions raise expectations among youngsters about what society has to offer them. However, meeting these expectations is another matter. In reality, youngsters are often disappointed and face all kinds of frustrations in realizing their desires. For example, in theory everybody may choose his or her own housing, schooling, and profession. There is, however, a housing shortage, too few educational opportunities that appeal to youngsters, and unemployment. It goes without saying that, if the discrepancy between expectation and reality is too large, youngsters will feel shortchanged and will turn away from society. Exactly because there are, in principle, so many possibilities to reach all kinds of social goals, it is twice as hard if one is frustrated in one's efforts.

Congruent with Merton (1968), the literature sometimes suggests that youths are especially frustrated because they can not realize the goals of the *dominant* culture by lawful means and therefore opt for illegal ways to realize these goals. However, it is unclear whether youngsters in general and delinquent youths in particular do experience this discrepancy that strongly (Elliott and Voss, 1974; Liska, 1971; Tittle, 1983). Working against Merton's idea is the fact that delinquent youngsters usually are not strongly oriented towards the goals of the dominant culture (diploma, job). There are, besides similarities, quite a few differences between the goals of the dominant culture and those of the hedonistic culture of delinquent youths. Moreover, the goals of the dominant culture are in the future and delinquent youngsters are often not that preoccupied with the future. They have a short time-perspective and are mainly oriented towards short-term goals. Parents and schools encounter great difficulties in making them see the value of future goals (Cohen, 1971). Furthermore, choosing illegal behaviour to reach goals of the dominant culture does not seem to be sensible. These goals are not reached by unlawful means; the opposite is true. School career and professional success, for example, are *negatively* related to delinquency (Glueck and Glueck, 1950). Delinquency increases the distance between youngsters and the dominant culture. Only organized crime leads to social success. Illegal trade in drugs, antiques, cars, women and so on, may result in such financial gains that social status may be bought. In juvenile delinquency this is only true in exceptional cases. Youngsters who save their earnings from robberies, break-ins, or drug dealings can be counted on the fingers of one hand. Juvenile delinquency is not a good way to gain social status. It only leads to short-term satisfaction.

Finally, in spite of the imperfections and injustices in society it is a little bit too easy to claim that juvenile delinquency is only a matter of rebellion against a society which is imperfect. If that were the case, youngsters from lower socioeconomic milieus would participate (much) more in criminality than youngsters from higher milieus. We have seen that this is not the case. In fact, there are not too many feelings of injustice in the lower socio-economic milieus. As far as they do exist they more often lead to resignation than rebellion (Berger and Berger, 1973; Freire, 1979; Langeveld, 1975). Moreover, many juvenile delinquents are not disadvantaged and most do not feel very shortchanged. They have had opportunities —and most of them are fully aware of this— that are not any less than those of others who have not become delinquents (Braithwaite, 1981; Peterson, 1969). Juvenile delinquency causes more social problems than the other way around.

Criminal Sanctions

The most obvious response of society to juvenile delinquency consists of criminal sanctions. The latter should be mainly seen as measures of last resort, only to be used if other social measures fail to control youngsters (Angenent, 1988). It must be made clear that the law will run its course and that infractions will lead to sanctions that will be applied consistently. From a social standpoint it is important that these sanctions be viewed not so much in terms of their punishment value, but more in terms of their function of confirming norms: as instruments which emphasize the norms of society and indicate its limits. Essential is that youngsters are confronted with the consequences of their behaviour. To achieve this, an effective criminal justice policy is needed which guarantees a clear and consistent judicial processing on the basis of the following:

1. Sanctions cannot be viewed independent from the likelihood of getting caught. As we pointed out before, especially within the framework of delinquency prevention, the chance of getting caught seems to be more important to youngsters than the punishment. In this respect it is worth

mentioning that with many offenses the chance of getting caught is rather small, and that youngsters are fully aware of this.

2. The sanctions should follow the crime as soon as possible. If possible, quick legal action should be taken. We already saw that youths often are short-term thinkers. The shorter the interval between crime and sanction, the more of an impression it will make.

3. Sanctions should be applied in adequate doses. Sanctions that are too light are easily dismissed by youngsters. Moreover, there is a chance that they feel that they are not being taken seriously. This does not mean that youths should be given Draconian punishments. It is generally known that severe punishments do not work better than moderate punishments and that they may harm the self-image and self-esteem of youngsters, and may evoke feelings of revenge.

4. The perpetrator must, to the extent to which this is possible, be held liable for any damage caused. This way, the fact that youngsters are responsible for their behaviour is emphasized.

5. Sanctions should fit the crime as much as possible; that is to say, they should be clearly related. Alternative punishments are in order here. This means, for example, that a youngster who defaces a bus with graffiti would be required to clean a bus, ideally the same bus. In this way delinquents realize the consequences of their behaviour. It has been found that such punishments are very effective, not in the least because youngsters experience them as fair and just.

The effect of criminal sanctions is most easily measured by the extent to which they deter youngsters from again getting involved in crime. Sanctions do not appear to be that successful in this respect. Contacts with the police and the judicial system (arrests, criminal record, convictions) usually do not go hand in hand with a decrease in criminal behaviour. Of survey respondents who report similar number of offenses, those youths who have more frequent contacts with the police and the courts also tend to commit more subsequent crimes (Ageton and Elliott, 1974; Farrington, 1977; Farrington et al., 1978; Gold, 1970; Gold and Williams, 1969; Junger-Tas, 1976; Miller and Gold, 1984; Werner, 1987; West and Farrington, 1977).

Various, not necessarily mutually exclusive, explanations have been proposed for these counterproductive effects of contacts with the police and the judicial system. Reference has been made to a labelling effect (Becker, 1963), suggesting that youths because of their contacts with the police and judicial system are, or at least feel, labelled as official delinquents. As a result, they will begin to view themselves as delinquent (delinquent self-image) and act accordingly (self-fulfilling prophecy). Another explanation is that youngsters who come in contact with the police and the judicial system have a greater chance of also coming in contact with other delinquents. These may motivate them to behave criminally, and they may learn some tricks of the trade from them. Prison is a classic example of such a training school. Furthermore, contacts with the police and the judicial system may give rise to feelings of resentment and revenge which subsequently may be expressed in criminal behaviour. Finally, youngsters may learn from their contacts with the police and the judicial system that the consequences of criminal behaviour are not that serious.

Social Involvement

The integration of youngsters into society depends first and foremost on the way in which they personally experience their position in society, and —related to this— the extent to which they feel part of society (Matza, 1964; Reckless, 1961). The concept of involvement was briefly mentioned in Chapter 3 in the paragraph about adoption of norms.

Social involvement has an expressive and an instrumental aspect. The *expressive*, emotional aspect concerns the degree to which youngsters feel that they belong, that they are accepted and especially that they are taken seriously. This is the case when they are able to achieve a status in society that is satisfactory to them. They certainly must have the feeling that they are treated fairly in the sense that their concerns are being considered and that there is an equal (in this context a fair) distribution of opportunities. Youngsters' solidarity with society depends on the extent to which society is in solidarity with them. The *instrumental*, rational aspect concerns the concrete opportunities society offers to youngsters. Central are the regulations and measures that may promote or limit their interests. Youngsters weigh the advantages and disadvantages integration offers (utility principle). The question of what society may expect from them is answered, taking the one-good-turn-deserves-another approach, in light of what society has to offer them (Williamson, 1978).

Youths who do not feel part of society are less convinced of the moral significance of the dominant system of norms and values, of the validity of social rules, and the usefulness and importance of social regulations. Therefore, they are at a greater risk for delinquency.

Alienation, Escape and Avoidance Behaviour

Youths who do not feel that they belong become alienated from society, from its norms and customs, and from conventional institutions, groups and persons. And alienation leads, as is well-known, to escape behaviour and avoidance behaviour. *Avoidance behaviour* in most cases is rather passive and fatalistic, and is limited to negative feelings towards society. As far as delinquency is concerned, those who get at all involved limit themselves to less serious offenses (vandalism, theft). In active avoidance behaviour, youngsters opt for behaviours that fall outside the conventional pattern, such as deviant behaviour, including delinquency. It usually involves more overt forms of criminal behaviour, mostly committed in groups (vandalism and violence). Finally, reactive avoidance behaviour is found among youths with an anti-establishment attitude who openly rebel against society. Reactive avoidance behaviour may be accompanied by all kinds of criminal behaviour (Hirschi, 1969; Leeuw et al., 1987; Merton, 1968).

Escape behaviour means that youngsters withdraw from conventional institutions and groups. As we have pointed out on previous occasions, youths who are alienated from society look for peers who live under similar circumstances and who experience the same frustrations as they do. They tend to become affiliated with the hedonistic youth culture in general, and deviant subcultures in particular. Besides the fact that they are able to satisfy their own desires and wishes through these contacts with peers, the latter also enables them to vent their social frustrations (Cohen, 1970a; Hargreaves, 1967; Keniston, 1960; Strodtbeck and Short, 1964).

SOCIAL CHANGE

Society may be viewed as a stable entity. This stability, however, is relative. Developments constantly take place in all sectors and at all levels. This does not mean that completely new social developments appear out of the blue; it is more a reshaping of old arrangements. It involves a continuing process in which the social structure and the corresponding cultural patterns are changing. Most of the time at a slow rate, but sometimes quite rapidly.

Periods of relative balance and peace in which relationships are more or less fixed and in which there is general consensus concerning the prevailing norms and customs, alternate with less stable times in which rapid changes take place. This goes hand in hand with disintegration of the social structure and the cultural pattern: regulatory mechanisms fail and social disintegration results. In times like these, existing provisos become unsettled. There is uncertainty and disagreement regarding norms and customs, and one searches by trial-and-error for new social rules and relationships. The ultimate result is an integrated and balanced society in which new relationships replace the old ones. The decades following the Second World War are an example of an unstable era with rapid and major social changes.

A problem is that in times of social change there is a certain friction between various elements of society which do not change at the same rate. More specifically, there is the phenomenon that changes in the social structure proceed more rapidly than changes in the culture. This is referred to as a "cultural lag" or an "institutional lag" (Ogburn, 1950; Ogburn and Nimkoff, 1946). For instance, the changes in norms, expectations, and goals of institutions such as the family and school trail structural changes.

In times of rapid social change there is a shift in the norms that govern social intercourse. The consistent conglomeration of agreed upon norms becomes blurred (Durkheim, 1951). A complicating factor is that old norms are questioned while new norms have not yet been clarified, or have not yet been agreed upon. Stable moorings in society and in the lives of its members disappear. Many traditional values are abandoned, whereas others are reexamined. Moreover, norms become less absolute. The general validity of norms is less obvious, especially because in a rapidly changing society many certainties are rather shortlived. Generally speaking, norms are taken less seriously. One becomes more tolerant in many areas. Because of this development, the established pattern of (traditional) norms which serves as a frame of reference and a source of support for many people, is eroded. A condition of normlessness, called anomie by Durkheim (1951), develops. The result is that people do no longer feel bound nor protected by an established cultural pattern. One no longer knows how to behave and what kind of behaviour to expect from others. There is uncertainty about what is possible and what is not, what is allowed and what is not. Conflicting norms and customs lead to role conflicts. People become less concerned with norms and regulations and begin behaving according to their own preferences. A certain aloofness from society may develop which sometimes may result in a crisis of authority and trust. Consequently, in times of rapid social change people do not bother much with rules and regulations. Behaviour which the dominant culture considers to be deviant emerges, and there is a greater chance that fringe groups will appear and flourish. In times such as these, criminality increases (Campbell and Converse, 1972; Dahrendorf, 1985; Durkheim, 1951; Hobart, 1978; Krohn and Wellford, 1977; Tobias, 1967; Wright, 1981).

What influence does rapid social change have on youngsters? Youths generally experience unstable times as interesting. These are times in which a lot is possible and in which there is a lot actually happening. The large, fluctuating supply of norms and customs offers them the opportunity to orient themselves extensively and to develop in a direction they choose. It also means, however, that they may become confused by the diversity of what is offered and may experience difficulties in finding their own way in this complex whole. The fact that in such times youngsters are not sufficiently provided with fixed norms and customs they can use as guidelines, will then come home to roost.

And yet, rapid social change in itself fits in well with the rapid pace of life of youngsters who usually have little trouble adapting to new relations. Older people have a much harder time in this respect. That means that in times of rapid change there is, per definition, a greater distance between youths and older people. As well, if the youth period is the time of life during which one picks up most of one's ideas, then those held by older people per definition are a generation or more behind (Matza, 1961). Furthermore, older people are realists who consider what is attainable and who are willing to compromise, whereas youths are idealistic and critical at the same time. It should not be forgotten that, unlike their elders, youngsters have (not yet) completely embraced or learned to live with the social order.

The greater distance between youths and older people also means that the transfer of norms becomes more complicated. In fact, we see an increase in juvenile delinquency in times of rapid social change, and the reasons for this may be summarized as follows (Durkheim, 1951; Lane, 1986):

1. Traditional certainties have disappeared. The legitimacy of many of the old rules and regulations is questioned because the norms on which they are based have become blurred or have disappeared. New norms have not yet been created or have not been sufficiently finalized.
2. There is confusion about norms and customs which makes it hard for youngsters to choose their own guidelines.
3. The ties between people and social institutions and among people themselves are looser. Hence, the transfer or norms is less smooth.
4. There is a weak response to transgressions of norms. There is a great tolerance in many areas. One of the consequences is that there is a decline in the effectiveness of the application of criminal law.

Thus, we find that it is not only the social factors in themselves which must be considered in connection with juvenile delinquency, but also the *changes* in social factors.

8. CONCLUDING COMMENTS

Juvenile delinquency is, as has been shown in this book, a multivariate phenomenon; many factors are needed to adequately describe its background. The first task of an integrated theory is to identify these factors (still an ongoing process). We have concerned ourselves with factors which cause criminality and factors which maintain the behaviour. Often, but not always, these factors are one and the same (Paternoster and Triplett, 1988). Furthermore, we have discussed factors which prevent delinquency and factors which inhibit this criminality. We have seen that there are internal factors which may be found in the personality of youths (traits, norm systems, identity, self-image, and self-esteem), and external factors which exist in their own milieu (family, school, friends) and in society. These factors together form a conglomerate of variables which interact and which may contribute to the fact that youngsters do or do not engage in delinquency. Within this conglomerate of factors many paths leading to delinquency may be identified. Although in reality each youth will follow his or her own path, it is possible to distinguish routes that are followed relatively more often, thereby bringing some structure to the network of factors. The second task of an integrated theory is to discover these main routes. They form the backbone of the theory. It should be noted that criminology is still in its infancy as far as the discovery and description of these routes are concerned.

Of course, the routes in question only lead to probabilities because criminological theories can never provide absolutes. Findings apply to a greater or lesser extent to groups; individual youths may always be exceptions to the rule. It is not the case that youngsters who have followed particular routes —who meet a certain profile— inevitably end up as either straight individuals or as delinquents (West and Farrington, 1973). There are youths who have all the background factors to avoid delinquency, who under certain circumstances nevertheless engage in the behaviour. The latter cases usually involve lighter forms of delinquency. There are also youngsters who have a bad prognosis but who nevertheless stay on the right path. However, for many of these youths the future is not too promising. Later on in life they tend to show the same handicaps we find among their delinquent peers, such as impoverished living conditions, limited social contacts, unemployment, divorce, and so on. On the other hand, there are youths who notwithstanding a bad prognosis do not engage in delinquency and who personally and socially become quite successful.

These youngsters are competent and able to cope and adjust. They believe that they have control over their lives, they are efficient, and possess a clear self-image and positive self-esteem. It appears as if they are steeled against delinquency (Van Lieshout, 1987; Ooyen-Houben and Berben, 1988; West, 1982).

One must guard against forcing youths to fit a particular theoretical model. Theoretical knowledge may or may not apply to an individual youngster because each youth —delinquent or not— is a unique individual with his or her own history and course of life. Some theorists and adults who do not seem to remember that once they were young themselves, tend to forget this.

REFERENCES

Abramovitch, R., Corter, C., & Lando, B. (1979). Sibling interaction in the home. *Child Development, 50,* 997-1003.

Ackerson, L. (1942). *Children's behavior problems II.* Chicago.

Adams, G. R. (1980). Runaway youth project: Comments on care programs for runaways and throwaways. *Journal of Adolescence, 3,* 321-334.

_____, & Looft, W. R. (1977). Cultural change: Education and youth. *Adolescence, 12,* 137-150.

_____, Ryan, J. H., Hoffman, J. J., Dobson, W. R., & Nielson, E. C. (1985). Ego identity status, conformity behavior, and personality. *Journal of Personality and Social Psychology, 47,* 1091-1104.

Adams, R. (1973). Differential association and learning principles revisited. *Social Problems, 20,* 458-470.

Adelson, J. (1979). Adolescence and the generation gap. *Psychology Today, 13,* 33-37.

Adler, A. (1930). *The pattern of life.* New York: Little and Ives.

Adler, F. (1975). *Sisters in crime: The rise of the new female criminality.* New York: McGraw-Hill.

_____ (1977). The interaction between woman's emancipation and female criminality: A cross-cultural perspective. *International Journal of Crime and Penology, 5,* 101-112.

Ageton, S. S., & Elliott, D. S. (1974). The effectiveness of legal processing on delinquent orientations. *Social Problems, 22,* 87-100.

Agnew, R. (1985). Social control theory and delinquency: A longitudinal test. *Criminology, 23,* 47-61.

_____, & Peterson, D. M. (1989). Leisure and delinquency. *Social Problems, 36,* 332-310.

Ajzen, I., & Fishbein, M. (1980). *Understanding attitudes and predicting social behavior.* Englewood Cliffs, NJ: Prentice-Hall.

Akers, R. L. (1964). Socio-economic status and delinquent behavior: A retest. *Journal of Research in Crime and Delinquency, 1,* 38-46.

_____, Krohn, M. D., Lanza-Kaduce, L., & Radosewich, M. (1979). Social learning and deviant behavior: A specific test of a general theory. *American Sociological Review, 44,* 636-655.

Akumatsu, T. J., & Farudi, P. A. (1978). Effects of model status and juvenile offender type on the imitation of self-reward criteria. *Journal of Consulting and Clinical Psychology, 46,* 187-188.

Alexander, C. N., & Campbell, E. Q. (1968). Balance forces and environmental effects: Factors influencing the cohesiveness of adolescent drinking. *Social Forces, 46,* 367-375.

Alexander, J. F. (1973). Defensive and supportive communication in normal and deviant families. *Journal of Consulting and Clinical Psychology, 40,* 223-231.

Alkire, A. A., Goldstein, M. J., Rodnick, E. H., & Judd, L. L. (1971). Social influence and counter influence within families of four types of disturbed adolescents. *Journal of Abnormal Psychology, 77,* 32-41.

Allan, E. A., & Steffensmeier, D. J. (1989). Youth, underemployment and property crime: Differential effects of job availability and job quality and young adult arrest rates. *American Sociological Review, 54,* 107-123.

Allen, G. (1977). Sibling solidarity. *Journal of Marriage and the Family*, 39, 177-184.
Allport, G. W., & Odbert, H. S. (1936). Trait-names: A psycho-lexical study. *Psychological Monographs*, 47, No. 211.
Allsop, J., & Feldman, M. (1976). Personality and antisocial behaviour in schoolboys. *British Journal of Criminology*, 16, 337-351.
Amelang, M., Schahn, J., & Kohlmann, D. (1988). Techniken der neutralisierung: Eine modeltestende untersuchung auf der basis offizieller und selbstberichteter delinquenz. *Monatschrift für Kriminologie und Strafrechtsreform*, 71, 178-191.
Andry, R. G. (1957). Faulty paternal and maternal child relationships, affection and delinquency. *British Journal of Delinquency*, 8, 34-48.
_____ (1960). *Delinquency and parental pathology*. London: Methuen.
_____ (1970). Parental affection and delinquency. In M. E. Wolfgang, L. Savitz, and N. Johnston (Eds.), *The sociology of crime and delinquency*. New York: John Wiley and Sons.
Angenent, H. L. W. (1972). Moral judgement. *Abstracts on Criminology and Penology*, 12, 529-537.
_____ (1974). *Opvoeding, persoonlijkheid en gezinsverhoudingen in verband met criminaliteit*. Groningen: Tjeenk Willink.
_____ (1976a). De basisdimensies in de opvoeding, gemeten met een vragenlijst. *Gedrag*, 4, 39-51.
_____ (1976b). Achtergronden van vrouwencriminaliteit. *Maandblad voor Geestelijke Volksgezondheid*, 31, 22-34.
_____ (1985). *De criminologische theorie van H. J. Eysenck*. Groningen: Umiv. of Groningen.
_____ (1988). *Kleine criminaliteit: Een beschrijving van veel voorkomende vormen van criminaliteit*. Amsterdam-Meppel: Boom.
_____ (1990). *Opvoeding en persoonlijkheidsontwikkeling*. Nijkerk: Intro.
Arbuthnot, J., Gordon, D. A., & Jurkovic, G. J. (1987). Personality. In H. C. Quay (Ed.), *Handbook of juvenile delinquency*. New York: John Wiley and Sons.
Archer, J., Pearson, N. A., & Westemann, K. E. (1988). Aggressive behavior of children aged 6-11: Gender differences and their magnitude. *British Journal of Social Psychology*, 27, 371-384.
Ariès, P. (1960). *L'enfant et la vie familiale sous l'Ancient Régime*. Paris: Plon.
Arnold, W. A. (1965). Continuities in research: Scaling delinquent behavior. *Social Problems*, 13, 59-66.
Aronson, E., & Mettee, D. R. (1968). Dishonest behavior as a function of differential levels of induced self-esteem. *Journal of Personality and Social Psychology*, 4, 121-127.
Asher, S. R., & Dodge, K. A. (1986). Identifying children who are rejected by their peers. *Developmental Psychology*, 22, 444-449.
_____, & Wheeler, V. A. (1985). Children's loneliness: A comparison of rejected and neglected peer status. *Journal of Consulting and Clinical Psychology*, 53, 500-505.
_____, Markell, R. A., & Hymel, S. (1981). Identification of children at risk in peer relations: A critique of the rate of interaction approach to assessment. *Child Development*, 52, 1239-1245.
_____, Singleton, L. C., Tinsley, B. R., & Hymel, S. (1979). A reliable sociometric measure for preschool children. *Developmental Psychology*, 15, 443-444.
Asumi, T. (1963). Maladjustment and delinquency: A comparison of two samples.

Journal of Child Psychology and Psychiatry, 4, 219-228.

Aultman, M. G., & Wellford, C. F. (1979). Toward an integrated model of delinquency causation: An empirical analysis. *Sociology and Social Research*, 63, 316-327.

Austin, R. L. (1978). Race, father-absence and female delinquency. *Criminology*, 15, 487-504.

Ausubel, D. P. (1954). *Theory and problems of adolescent development*. New York: Grune and Stratton.

Baerveldt, C. (1987). *School en delinquentie*. The Hague: Staatsuitgeverij.

Baker, D., & Donelly, P. G. (1986). Neighbourhood criminals and outsiders in two communities: Indications that criminal localism varies. *Sociology and Social Research*, 71, 59-61.

Baldwin, S., & Bottoms, A. E. (1976). *The urban criminal: A study in Sheffield*. London: Tavistock Publications.

Ball, I. L., Farnhill, D., & Wangeman, J. F. (1984). Sex and age differences in sensation seeking: Some national comparisons. *British Journal of Psychology*, 75, 257-265.

Ball, R. A. (1983). Development of basic norm violation. *Criminology*, 21, 75-94.

_____, & Lilly, J. R. (1971). Juvenile delinquency in a rurban county. *Criminology*, 9, 69-85.

Bandura, A. (1964). The stormy decade: Fact or fiction. *Psychology in the Schools*, 1, 224-231.

_____ (1965). Influences of model's reinforcement contingencies on the acquisition of imitative responses. *Journal of Personality and Social Psychology*, 1, 589-595.

_____ (1973). *Aggression: A social learning analysis*. Englewood Cliffs, NJ: Prentice-Hall.

_____ (1977). *Social learning theory*. Englewood Cliffs, NJ: Prentice-Hall.

_____, A., & Walters, R. H. (1958). Depending conflicts in aggressive delinquents. *Journal of Social Issues*, 14, 52-65.

_____, & Walters, R. H. (1959). *Adolescent aggression*. New York: Ronald.

Barclay, J. R. (1966). Sociometric choices and teacher ratings as predictors of school dropout. *Journal of Social Psychology*, 4, 40-45.

Beccaria, C. (1764). *Dei delitti e delle pene*.

Becker, H. S. (1963). *Outsiders*. New York: The Free Press.

Bellebaum, A. (1972). *Soziologische Grundbegriffe*. Stuttgart: Kohlhammer.

Bellmont, L., & Marolla, F. A. (1973). Birth order, family size and intelligence. *Science*, 182, 1096-1101.

Belson, W. A. (1975). *Juvenile theft: The causal factors*. London: Harper and Row.

Bengtson, V. (1970). The generation gap: A review and typology of social-psychological perspectives. *Youth and Society*, 2, 7-32.

Bennett, I. (1960). *Delinquent and neurotic children*. New York: Tavistock Publications.

Bentler, P. M., & Newcomb, M. D. (1978). Longitudinal study of marital success and failure. *Journal of Consulting and Clinical Psychology*, 4, 1053-1070.

Berg I. (1980). School refusal in early adolescence. In L. Hersov and I. Berg (Eds.), *Out of school*. London: Wiley.

_____ (1985). The management of truancy. *Journal of Child Psychology and Psychiatry*, 26, 325-331.

Berger, P., & Berger, B. (1973). *Sociologie, een biografische opzet*. Bilthoven: Ambo.

Berk, R., Lenihan, K. J., & Rossi, P. (1980). Crime and poverty: Some experimental evidence from ex-offenders. *American Sociological Review*, 45, 766-786.

Berlyne, D. E. (1960). *Conflict, arousal and curiosity*. New York: McGraw-Hill.

Berman, A., & Siegal, A. (1976). A neuropsychological approach to the etiology, prevention and treatment of juvenile delinquency. In A. Davids (Ed.), *Child personality and psychopathology: Current topics*. New York: John Wiley and Sons.

Berndt, T. J. (1979). Developmental changes in conformity to peers and parents. *Developmental Psychology*, 15, 606-616.

_____, & Perry, T. B. (1986). Children's perceptions of friendships as supportive relationships. *Developmental Psychology*, 22-5, 640-648.

Berzonsky, M. D. (1978b). Formal reasoning in adolescence: An alternative view. *Adolescence*, 13, 279-290.

Bettelheim, B. (1966). Obsolete youth: Toward a psychograph of adolescent rebellion. *Encounter* (september).

Bezamore, G. (1985). Delinquent reform and the labelling perspective. *Criminal Justice and Behavior*, 12, 131-170.

Biddle, B. J., Bank, B. J., & Klein, M. M. (1980). Parental and peer influence on adolescents. *Social Forces*, 58, 1057-1079.

Biles, D. (1971). Birth order and delinquency. *Australian Psychologist*, 6, 189-193.

_____, & Challinger, D. (1981). Family size and birth order of young offenders. *International Journal of Offender Therapy and Comparative Criminology*, 25, 60-66.

Binder, A. (1987). A historical and theoretical introduction. In H. C. Quay (Ed.), *Handbook of juvenile delinquency*. New York: John Wiley and Sons.

Bixenstine, V. E., DeCorte, M. S., & Bixenstine, B. A. (1976). Conformity to peer-sponsored misconduct at four grade levels. *Developmental Psychology*, 12, 226-236.

Black, D. J., & Reiss, A. J. (1970). Police control of juveniles. *American Sociological Review*, 35, 63-77.

Blake, J., & Davis, K. (1964). Norms, values, and sanctions. In R. E. L. Paris (Ed.), *Handbook of modern sociology*. Chicago: Rand McNally.

Blasi, A. (1980). Bridging moral cognition and moral action: A critical review of the literature. *Psychological Bulletin*, 88, 1-45.

Blechman, E. (1982). Are children with one parent at psychological risk? *Journal of Marriage and the Family*, 44, 179-195.

Block, J. (1982). Assimilation, accommodation and the dynamics of personality development. *Child Development*, 53, 281-295.

_____ (1983). Differential premises arising from differential socialization of the sexes: Some conjectures. *Child Development*, 54, 1335-1354.

Block, J. H., & Block, J. (1980). The role of ego control and ego-resiliency in the organisation of behavior. In W. A. Collins (Ed.), *Development of cognition, affect, and social relations*. New York: Erlbaum.

_____, Block, J., & Gjerda, P. F. (1986). The personality of children prior to divorce: A prospective study. *Child Development*, 57, 827-840.

Block, R. C. (1986). Tijd, leeftijd en misdaad: Een analyse van levensmisdrijven in Chicago. *Justitiële Verkenningen*, 12, 161-189.

Blomme, J. (1983). Sociale klasse en jeugdmisdadigheid. Een secundaire analyse van de empirische onderzoeksliteratuur. *Tijdschrift voor Criminologie*, 25, 173-188.

Blücher, V. G. (1966). *Die Generation der Unbefangenen*. Düsseldorf: Eugen Diederich Verlag.

Boer, F. (1986). Broers en zusters. De betekenis van siblings in de normale en gestoorde ontwikkeling. *Kind en Adolescent*, 7, 55-76.

Bohman, M., Cloninger, C. R., Sigvardsson, S., & Von Knorring, A. L. (1982). Predisposition to petty criminality in Swedish adoptees I. Genetic and environmental heterogeneity. *Archives of General Psychiatry*, 39, 1233-1241.

Bohnsack, R. (1973). *Handlungskompetenz und Jugendkriminalität*. Neuwied: Luchterhand.

Boivin, M., & Bégin, G. (1989). Peer status and self-perception among early elementary school children: The case of the rejected children. *Child Development*, 60, 591-596.

Bol, M. W. (1975). Vrouwen en criminaliteit. *Justitiële Verkenningen*, 1, 190-200.

Bonger, W. A. (1916). *Criminality and economic conditions*. Boston: Little Brown.

_____ (1932, 1954). *Inleiding tot de criminologie*. Haarlem: Bohm.

Bontekoe, E. H. M. (1984). Criminaliteit en geslacht. *Tijdschrift voor Criminologie*, 26, 18-31.

Bosma, H. A. (1986). Identiteitsontwikkeling in de adolescentie. *Nederlands Tijdschrift voor de Psychologie*, 41, 268-274.

Boss, P. (1980). Normative family stress: Family boundary changes across life-span. *Family Relations*, 29, 445-450.

Bossard, J. H. (1953). *Parent and child*. Philadelphia, PA: Umiv. of Pennsylvania Press.

Bourduin, C. M., Henggeler, S. W., & Pruitt, J. A. (1985). The relation between juvenile delinquency and personality dimensions of family members. *Journal of Genetic Psychology*, 146, 563-565.

Bowker, L. H., & Klein, M. W. (1983). The etiology of female juvenile delinquency and gang membership: A test of psychological and social structural explanations. *Adolescence*, 18, 739-751.

Bowlby, J. (1946). *Forty-four juvenile thieves: Their characters and home-life*. London: Bailliere, Tindall and Cox.

_____ (1951). *Maternal care and mental health*. Geneva: World Health Organization.

_____ (1979). *The making and breaking of affectional bonds*. London: Tavistock Publications.

Box, S. (1971, 1981). *Deviance, reality, and society*. New York: Holt, Rinehart and Winston.

_____, & Ford, J. (1971). The facts don't fit: On the relationship between social class and criminal behavior. *Sociological Review*, 19, 31-53.

Braithwaite, J. (1981). The myth of social class and criminality reconsidered. *American Sociological Review*, 46, 36-57.

Brandwein, R., Brown, C., & Fox, F. M. (1974). Women and children last: The social situation of divorced mothers and their families. *Journal of Marriage and the Family*, 36, 498-514.

Breckinridge, S. P., & Abott, E. (1912). *The delinquent child and the home*. New York: Russell Sage.

Brennan, T., Huizinga, D, & Elliott, S. S. (1978). *The social psychology of runaways*. Lexington: Lexington Books.

Brentjens, H. (1978). *Visies op jeugd*. Deventer: Van Loghum Slaterus.

Breznitz, T. (1975). Juvenile delinquents perception of own and other's commitment to delinquency. *Journal of Research in Crime and Delinquency*, 12, 124-132.

Briar, S., Piliavin, I. (1965). Delinquency, situational inducements, and commitment to conformity. *Social Problems*, 13, 35-45.

Briddle, B. J., Bank, B. J., & Marlin, M. M. (1980). Parental and peer influence on adolescents. *Social Forces*, 58, 1057-1079.

Brigham, J. C., Ricketts, J. L., & Johnson, R. C. (1967). Reported maternal and paternal behavior of solitary and social delinquents. *Journal of Consulting Psychology*, 31, 420-422.

Brittain, C. V. (1963). Adolescent choices and parent-peer cross-pressures. *American Sociological Review*, 28, 395-391.

Broder, P. K., Dunivant, N., Smith, E. C., & Sutton, L. P. (1981). Further observations on the link between learning disabilities and juvenile delinquency. *Journal of Educational Psychology*, 73, 838-850.

Bronson, W. C. (1966). Central orientations: A study of behavior organization from childhood to adolescence. *Child Development*, 37, 125-156.

Brown, B., & Altman, I. (1981). Territoriality and residential crime. In P. J. Brantingham and P. L. Brantingham (Eds.), *Environmental Criminology*. Beverly Hills: Sage.

Brown, B. B. (1982). The extent and effects of peer pressure among high school students: A retrospective analysis. *Journal of Youth and Adolescence*, 11, 121-133.

_____, Clasen, D. R., & Eicher, S. A. (1986). Perception of peer pressure, peer conformity dispositions, and self reported behavior among adolescents. *Developmental Psychology*, 22, 521-530.

_____, Eicher, S. A., & Petrie, S. (1986). The importance of peer group ("crowd") affiliation in adolescence. *Journal of Adolescence*, 9, 73-96.

Brown, W. K., & Gable, R. J. (1979). Social adaption of former delinquents. *International Journal of Offender Therapy and Comparative Criminology*, 23, 117-128.

Brownfield, D. (1987a). Father-son relationship and violent behavior. *Deviant Behavior*, 8, 149-176.

_____ (1987b). A reassessment of cultural deviance theory: The use of underclass measures. *Deviant Behavior*, 8, 343-359.

_____, & Sorenson, A. M. (1987). A latent structure analysis of delinquency. *Journal of Quantitative Criminology*, 3, 103-124.

Bruce, N. (1970). Delinquent and non-delinquent reactions to parental deprivation. *British Journal of Criminology*, 10, 270-276.

Bruinsma, G. J. M. (1985). *Criminaliteit als sociaal leerproces: Een toetsing van de differentiële associatietheorie in de versie van K. D. Opp*. Arnhem: Gouda Quint.

Brunt, L. (1989). In de schaduw van het stedelijk elan: Angst en criminaliteit in de grote stad. *Justitiële Verkenningen*, 15, 8-24.

Brusten, M., & Hurrelmann, K. (1973). *Abweichendes Verhalten in der Schule*. München: Juventa.

Brynner, J., O'Malley, P., & Bachman, J. (1981). Self-esteem and delinquency revisited. *Journal of Youth and Adolescence*, 19, 407-411.

Buffalo, M. D., & Rodgers, J. W. (1971). Behavioral norms, moral norms, and attachment: Problems of deviance and conformity. *Social Problems*, 19, 101-113.

Buikhuisen, W. (1985). *Kriminaliteit. Uitgangspunten voor het verklaren van krimineel gedrag*. Deventer: Kluwer.

_____, & Lachmann, I. G. M. (1985). Vroegdelinquenten en strafgevoeligheid: Een theorie. *Delikt en Delinkwent*, 15, 918-932.

_____, & Meijs, B. W. G. P. (1983). Het belang van een differentieel criminologische benadering van criminaliteit. *Delikt en Delinkwent*, 13, 95-106.

_____, Bontekoe, E. H. M., Van der Plas-Korenhoff, C, & Van Buuren, S. (1984a). Studentencriminaliteit: Een oriënterend interdisciplinair onderzoek. *Delikt en Delinkwent*, 14, 615-630.

Burchard, J. D., & Burchard, S. N. (1987). *Prevention of delinquent behavior*. Beverly Hills: Sage.

Burgess, P. K. (1972). Eysenck's theory of criminality: A new approach. *British Journal of Criminology*, 10, 74-82.

Burgess, R. L. (1980). Family violence: Implications from evolutionary biology. In T. Hirschi and M. Gottfredson (Eds.), *Understanding Crime*. Beverly Hills: Sage.

Bursik, R. J., & Baba, Y. (1986). Individual variations in crime-related decisions. *Social Science Research*, 15, 71-81.

Burton, W. (1863). *Helps to education*. Boston: Crosby and Nichols.

Buss, A. H., & Plomin, R. (1975). *A temperament theory of personality development*. New York: John Wiley and Sons.

_____, Plomin, R., & Willerman, L. (1973). The inheritance of temperament. *Journal of Personality*, 41, 513-524.

Buss, H. B. (1984). Toward a psychology of person-environment (PE) correlations: The role of spouse selection. *Journal of Personality and Social Psychology*, 47, 361-377.

Buunk, B. (1983). *Vriendschap, een studie over de andere persoonlijke relatie*. Amsterdam: Bert Bakker.

Bynner, J. M., O'Malley, P. M., & Bachman, J. G. (1981). Self-esteem and delinquency revisited. *Journal of Youth and Adolescence*, 10, 407-441.

Byrne, B. M. (1988). Adolescent self-concept, ability grouping, and social comparison, reexamining academic track differences in high school. *Youth and Society*, 20, 46-67.

Bytheway, W. R., & May, D. R. (1971). On fitting the "facts" of social class and criminal behavior: A rejoinder to Box and Ford. *Sociological Review*, 19, 585-607.

Caesar, B., & Weber, I. (1979). Geschlechtstypische Entwicklungs-und Sozialisations bedingungen bei Neugeborenen: Eine Literaturüberblick. *Zeitschrift für Entwicklungspsychologie und Pädagogische Psychologie*, 11, 275-299.

Campagna, A. F., & Harter, S. (1975). Moral judgement in sociopathic and normal children. *Journal of Personality and Social Psychology*, 31, 199-205.

Campbell, A. (1984). *The girl in the gang*. New Society, 67, 308-311.

_____, & Converse, P. (1972). *The human meaning of social change*. New York: Russell Sage.

_____, A., Bibel, D., & Munce, S. (1985). Predicting our own aggression: Person, subculture or situation? *British Journal of Social Psychology*, 24, 169-180.

_____, Munce, S., & Galea, J. (1982). American gangs and British subcultures: A comparison. *International Journal of Offender Therapy and Comparative Criminology*, 26, 76-89.

Campbell, D. T. (1975). On the conflicts between biological and social evaluation and between psychology and moral tradition. *American Psychologist*, 30, 1103-1126.

Canter, R. J. (1982a). Family correlates of male and female delinquency. *Criminology*, 20, 149-168.

_____ (1982b). Sex differences in self report delinquency. *Criminology*, 20, 373-393.

Cantor, D., & Land, K. C. (1985). Unemployment and crime rates in the post World War II United States: A theoretical and empirical analysis. *American Sociological Review*, 50, 317-332.

Caplan, N. S. (1965). Intellectual functioning. In H. C. Quay (Ed.), *Juvenile delinquency*. Princeton: Van Nostrand.

Carey, G., Goldsmith, H. H., Telligen, A., & Gottesman, I. I. (1978). Genetic and personality inventories: The limits of replication with twin studies. *Behavior Genetics*,

8, 299-313.

Casparis, J., & Vaz, E. W. (1973). Social class and self reported delinquency among Swiss boys. *International Journal of Comparative Sociology*, 14, 47-58.

Cattell, R. B. (1946). *Description and measurement of personality.* New York: World Book.

_____ (1957). *Personality and motivation, structure and measurement.* New York: World Book.

_____ (1965). *The scientific analysis of personality.* Harmondsworth: Penguin.

_____ (1973). *Personality and mood by questionnaire.* San Francisco: Jossey Bass.

_____ (1982). *The inheritance of personality and ability.* New York: Academic Press.

_____, & Cattell, M. (1975). *Handbook for the High School Personality Questionnaire.* Champaign, Ill: Institute for Personality and Ability Testing.

_____, & Child, D. (1975). *Motivation and dynamic structure.* New York: Holt, Rinehart and Winston.

_____, & Nichols, K. E. (1972). An improved definition, from the researchers, of second order personality factors in Q data. *Journal of Social Psychology*, 86, 187-203.

_____, & Nisselroade, J. R. (1967). Likeness and completeness theories by sixteen personality factor measures on stable and unstable married couples. *Journal of Personality and Social Psychology*, 7, 351-361.

Cavan, R. S. (1934). *The adolescent in the family.* New York.

Cavior, N., & Dokecki, P. R. (1973). Physical attractiveness, perceived attitude similarity and academic achievement as contributors to interpersonal attraction among adolescents. *Developmental Psychology*, 9, 44-54.

Cernkovich, S. A. (1978a). Value orientations and delinquency involvement. *Criminology*, 15, 443-458.

_____ (1978b). Delinquency involvement: An examination of the non-intervention strategy. *Criminal Justice Review*, 3, 43-51.

_____, Giordano, P. C., & Pugh, M. D. (1985). Chronic offenders: The missing cases in self-report delinquency research. *Journal of Criminal Law and Criminology*, 76, 705-732.

Chambliss, W. J. (1973). Race, sex and gangs. The Saints and the Roughnecks. *Society*, 11, 24-31.

Chandler, M. (1973). Egocentrism and antisocial behavior: The assessment and training of social perspective-taking skills. *Developmental Psychology*, 9, 326-332,

Chasen, L., & Young, R. D. (1981). Salient self-conceptions in normal and deviant adolescents. *Adolescence*, 16, 613-620.

Chester, C. R. (1976). Perceived relative deprivation as a cause of property crime. *Crime and Delinquency*, 22, 17-30.

Chilton, R. J., & Spielberger, A. (1972). Increases in crime: The utility of alternative measures. *Journal of Criminal Law, Criminology and Police Science*, 63, 68-74.

Chiricos, T. G. (1987). Rates of crime and unemployment: An analysis of aggregate research evidence. *Social Problems*, 43, 187-212.

Choldin, H. M. (1978). Urban density and pathology. *Annual Review of Sociology*, 4, 91-115.

Christiansen, K. O. (1977a). A preliminary study of criminality among twins. In S. A. Mednick and K. O. Christiansen (Ed.), *Biosocial basis of criminal behavior.* New York: Gardner.

_____ (1977b). A review of studies of criminality among twins. In S. A. Mednick and K. O. Christiansen (Eds.), *Biosocial basis of criminal behavior*. New York: Gardner.

Church, R. M. (1963). The varied affects of punishment on behavior. *Psychological Review*, 369-402.

Cicourel, A. (1968, 1976). *The social organisation of juvenile justice*. New York: John Wiley and Sons.

Clark, J. P., & Tifft, L. L. (1966). Polygraph and interview validation of self reported delinquent behavior. *American Sociological Review*, 31, 516-523.

_____, & Wenninger, E. P. (1962). Socio-economic class and area as correlates of illegal behavior among juveniles. *American Sociological Review*, 27, 826-834.

Clasen, D. R., & Brown, B. B. (1985). The multidimensionality of peer pressure in adolescence. *Journal of Youth and Adolescence*, 14, 451-468.

Clelland, D., & Carter, T. J. (1980). The new myth of class and crime. *Criminology*, 18, 319-336.

Clifford, M. M., & Walster, E. (1973). The effect of physical attractiveness on teacher expectation. *Sociology of Education*, 46, 248-258.

Clinard, M. B. (1968). *Sociology of deviant behavior*. New York: Holt, Rinehart and Winston.

_____, & Quinney, R. (1967). *Criminal behavior systems: A typology*. New York: Holt, Rinehart and Winston.

Cloninger, C. R., & Guze, S. B. (1970). Female criminals: Their personal, familial and social backgrounds. *Archives of General Psychiatry*, 23, 554-558.

Cloward, R. A., & Ohlin, L. E. (1960). *Delinquency and opportunity: A theory of delinquent gangs*. Glencoe: The Free Press.

Cohen, A. K. (1955, 1971). *Delinquent boys. The culture of the gang*. Glencoe: The Free Press.

_____ (1966). *Deviance and control*. Englewood Cliffs, NJ: Prentice-Hall.

_____ (1967). Middle-class delinquency and the social structure. In E. W. Vaz (Ed.), *Middle-class juvenile delinquency*. New York: Harper and Row.

_____ (1970a). The delinquent subculture. In M. Wolfgang, L. Savitz, and N. Johnston (Eds.), *The sociology of crime and delinquency*. New York: John Wiley and Sons.

Cohen, L. E. (1981). Modelling crime trends: A criminal opportunity perspective. *Journal of Research in Crime and Delinquency*, 18, 138-164.

_____, & Felson, M. (1979). Social change and crime rate trends: A routine activity approach. *American Sociological Review*, 44, 588-608.

_____, & Kluegel, J. R. (1978). Determinants of juvenile court dispositions: Ascriptive and achieved factors in two metropolitan courts. *American Sociological Review*, 43, 162-176.

_____, Felson, M., & Land, K. C. (1980). Property crime rates in the United States: A macrodynamic analysis. 1947-1977. *American Journal of Sociology*, 86, 90-118.

_____, Kluegel, J. R., & Land, K. C. (1981). Social inequality and predatory criminal victimization: An exposition and test of a formal theory. *American Sociological Review*, 46, 505-524.

Coie, J. D., & Kuperschmidt, J. B. (1983). A behavioral analysis of emerging social status in boys' groups. *Child Development*, 54, 1400-1416.

Coie, J. D., Dodge, K. A., & Coppotelli, H. (1982). Dimensions and types of social status: A cross-age perspective. *Developmental Psychology*, 18, 557-570.

Colajanni, N. (1887). *Sociologica criminale*.

Cole, C. A. (1952). *The self-concept as a means of determining personality types in a population of delinquent boys*. Washington.

Coleman, J. C. (1974). *Relationships in adolescence*. London: Routledge and Kegan Paul.

_____ (1979). Who leads who astray? Causes of antisocial behavior in adolescence. *Journal of Adolescence*, 2 179-185.

_____ (1980). *The nature of adolescence*. London: Methuen.

Coleman, J. S. (1961). *The adolescent society*. New York: The Free Press.

Collins, J. K., & Thomas, N. T. (1972). Age and susceptibility to same sex peer pressure. *British Journal of Educational Psychology*, 42, 83-85.

Comrey, A. L. (1958). A factor analysis of items on the MMPI Psychopathic Deviate Scale. *Educational and Psychological Measurement*, 18, 91-98.

Conger, J. J. (1973, 1977). *Adolescence and youth. Psychological development in a changing world*. New York: Harper and Row.

_____ (1979). *Opgroeiende jeugd. De weg naar volwassenheid*. Amsterdam: Kosmos.

_____, & Miller, W.C. (1969). *Personality, social class and delinquency*. New York: John Wiley and Sons.

Coons, W. H. (1982). Learning disabilities and criminality. *Canadian Journal of Criminology*, 24, 251-265.

Cornelissen, J. (1970). *Jongeren over huwelijk en gezin*. Zeist: Nisso.

Costanzo, P. R., & Shaw, M. E. (1966). Conformity as a function of age level. *Child Development*, 37, 967-975.

Council of Europe (1960). *Juvenile delinquency in post-war Europe*. Strasbourg.

Council of Europe (1979). *Social change and juvenile delinquency*. Strasbourg.

Covington, J. (1986). Self-esteem and deviance: The effect of race and gender. *Criminology*, 24, 105-138.

Cowen, E. L., Pederson, A., & Babigian, H. (1973). Long-term follow-up of early detected vulnerable children. *Journal of Consulting and Clinical Psychology*, 41, 438-446.

_____, Pederson, A., Babigian, H., Izzo, L. D., & Trost, M. A. (1983). Long-term follow-up of early detected vulnerable children. *Journal of Consulting and Clinical Psychology*, 41, 438-446.

Cowie, J., Cowie, V., & Slater, E. (1968). *Delinquency in girls*. London: Heinemann.

Cressey, D. R. (1953). *Other people's money*. New York: The Free Press.

Crombag, H. F. M. (1983). *Een manier van overleven*. Zwolle: Tjeenk Willink.

Crutchfield, R. D., Geerken, M. R., & Gove, W. R. (1982). Crime rate and social integration: The impact of metropolitan mobility. *Criminology*, 20, 467-478.

Csikszentmihalyi, M., & Larson, R. (1978). Intrinsic rewards in school crime. *Crime and Delinquency*, 24, 322-335.

Curry, G. D., & Spergel, I. A. (1988). Gang homicide, delinquency and community. *Criminology*, 26, 381-405.

Curtis, R. L. (1975). Adolescent orientations toward parents and peers: Variation by sex, age, and socioeconomic status. *Adolescence*, 10, 483-494.

Dahrendorf, R. (1985). *Law and order*. London: Stevens.

Dalgaard, O. S., & Kringlen, E. (1976). A Norwegian twin study of criminality. *British Journal of Criminology*, 16, 213-232.

Damon, W. (1983). *Social and personality development*. New York: W. W. Norton.

Darley, J., & Latané, B. (1968). Bystanders intervention in emergencies: Diffusion of responsibility. *Journal of Personality and Social Psychology*, 8, 377-383.

Dasberg, L. (1975). *Groot brengen door klein houden*. Meppel-Amsterdam: Boom.

Datesman, S. D., & Scarpitti, F. R. (1975). Female delinquency and broken homes: A re-assessment. *Criminology*, 13, 33-55.

Davids A., & Falkof, B. B. (1975). Juvenile delinquents then and now: Comparison of findings from 1959 and 1974. *Journal of Abnormal Psychology*, 84, 161-164.

Davis, J. A. (1966). The campus as frog pond: An application of the theory of relative deprivation to career decisions of college men. *American Journal of Sociology*, 72, 17-31.

Dawkins, R. (1976). *The selfish gene*. New York: Oxford Univ. Press.

Debuyst, C. (1960). *Criminels et valeurs vécues*. Leuven: Publications Universitaires.

De Haas, G. C. (1975). *De jeugd van tegenwoordig*. Baarn: Ten Have.

Deitz, G. E. (1969). A comparison of delinquents with nondelinquents on self-concept, self-acceptance and parental identification. *Journal of Genetic Psychology*, 115, 285-295.

De Levita, D. J. (1965). *The concept of identity*. The Hague: Mouton.

Deluty, R. H., & Lopresto, C. T. (1988). Consistency of aggressive, assertive and submissive behavior in male adolescents. *Journal of Social Psychology*, 128, 619-632.

De Mause, L. (1976). *The history of childhood*. London: Psychohistory.

Demos, J., & Demos, V. (1969). Adolescence in historical perspective. *Journal of Marriage and the Family*, 31, 632-638.

Denkers, F. A. C. M. (1973). Persoonlijkheidsonderzoek bij delinkwenten. *Nederlands Tijdschrift voor Criminologie*, 15, 35-47.

Dentler, R. A., & Monroe, L. J. (1961). Social correlates of early adolescent theft. *American Sociological Review*, 26, 733-743.

De Vries, G. C. (1987). Schoolcultuur als uitdaging en als opgave: Over verzuim, delinquentie en de invloed van de school. *Justitiële Verkenningen*, 13, 64-84.

_____, De Kat, E., & Derriks, M. (1985). Schoolverzuim en voortijdig schoolverlaten in het voortgezet onderwijs. In A. M. van Wieringen (Ed.), *Beeld van het voortgezet onderwijs*. Assen: Van Gorcum.

De Wuffel, F. J., & Mönks, F. J. (1983). *Parent-adolescent interaction and adolescent interpersonal orientation: Development and implications for coping*. Nijmegen.

Dijksterhuis, F. P. H., & Nijboer, J. A. (1984). Spijbelen en delinquent gedrag: De signaalwaarde van spijbelen. *Tijdschrift voor Criminologie*, 26, 32-45.

DiLalla, L. F., Mitchell, C. M., Arthur, M. W., & Paglioca, P. M. (1988). Aggression and delinquency: Family and environmental factors. *Journal of Youth and Adolescence*, 17, 233-246.

Dinitz, S., & Pfau-Vicent, B. A. (1982). Self-concept and juvenile delinquency. *Youth and Society*, 14, 133-158.

_____, Scarpitti, F. R., & Reckless, W. C. (1962). Delinquency vulnerability: A cross-group and longitudinal analysis. *American Sociological Review*, 27, 515.

Dion, K. K. (1972). Physical attractiveness and evaluation of children's transgressions. *Journal of Personality and Social Psychology*, 24, 207-213.

_____ (1973). Young children's stereotyping of facial attractiveness. *Developmental Psychology*, 9, 183-188.

_____, & Berscheid, E. (1974). Physical attractiveness and peer perception among children. *Sociometry*, 37, 1-12.

_____, Berscheid, E., & Walter, E. (1972). What is beautiful is good. *Journal of*

Personality and Social Psychology, 24, 285-290.

Dishion, T., Stouthamer-Loeber, M., & Patterson, G. J. (1984). Skill deficits and male adolescent delinquency. *Journal of Abnormal Child Psychology*, 12, 137-154.

Dodge, K. A. (1983). Behavioral antecedents of peer social status. *Child Development*, 54, 1386-1399.

_____, Coie, J. D., & Brakke, N. P. (1982). Behavioral patterns of socially rejected and neglected preadolescents: The roles of social approach and aggression. *Journal of Abnormal Child Psychology*, 10, 398-410.

Donelly, P. (1981). Athletes and juvenile delinquents: A comparative analysis based on a review of literature. *Adolescence*, 16, 415-432.

Donovan, J. E., & Jessor, R. (1985). Structure of problem behavior in adolescent and young childhood. *Journal of Consulting and Clinical Psychology*, 53, 890-904.

Donovan, A., & Oddy, M. (1982). Psychological aspects of unemployment: An investigation into the emotional and social adjustment of school leavers. *Journal of Adolescence*, 5, 15-30.

D'Orban, P. T. (1972). Female crime. *Criminologist*, 23, 29-51.

Dornbusch, S. M., Carlsmith, J. M., Bushwall, S. J., Ritter, P., Leiderman, H., Hastorf, A. H., & Gross, R. T. (1985). Single parents, extended households, and the control of adolescents. *Child Development*, 56, 326-341.

Douvan, E., & Adelson, J. (1966). *The adolescent experience.* New York: John Wiley and Sons.

Downes, D., & Rock, P. (1982). *Understanding deviance: A guide to the sociology of crime and rule breaking.* Oxford: Oxford Univ. Press.

Dubet, F., & Lapeyronnie, D. (1985). Du gang à la galerie, les conduites marginales des jeunes. *Revue Suisse de Sociologie*, 11, 309-322.

Dublineau, J. (1964). Maturation et personalité criminelle. *Annales Internationales de Criminologie*, 2, 403-427.

Duncan, P. (1971). Parental attitudes and interaction in delinquency. *Child Development*, 42, 1751-1765.

Dunford, F. W., & Elliott, D. S. (1984). Identifying career offenders using self-reported data. *Journal of Research in Crime and Delinquency*, 21, 57-86.

Dunn, J. (1984). Sisters and brothers. In J. Bruner, M. Cole, and B. Loyd (Eds.), *The developing child.* London: Fontana.

Dunphy, D. C. (1963). The social structure of urban adolescent peer groups. *Sociometry*, 26, 230-246.

Durkheim, E. (1951). *Le suicide, Etude de sociologie*, 1897; Suicide, a study in sociology. New York: The Free Press.

Dusek, J. B., & Litovsky, V. G. (1985). Perception of child rearing and self-concept development during the early adolescent years. *Journal of Youth and Adolescence*, 14, 373-387.

Dworkin, R. H., Burke, B. W., Maher, B. A., & Gottesman, I. I. (1976). A longitudinal study of genetics of personality. *Journal of Personality and Social Psychology*, 34, 510-518.

Easterlin, R. A. (1987). *Birth and fortune: The impact of numbers on personal welfare.* Chicago: Basic Books.

Eaves, L., & Eysenck, H. J. (1975). The nature of extraversion: A genetical analysis. *Journal of Personality and Social Psychology*, 32, 102-112.

Egg, R., & Sponsel, R. (1978). "Bagatelldelinquenz" und Techniken der Neutralisie rung. Eine Empirische Prüfung der Theorie von Sykes und Matza. *Monatsschrift für Kriminologie und Strafrechtsreform*, 61, 38-50.

Eilenberg, M. D. (1961). Remand home boys: 1930-1955. *British Journal of Criminology*, 2, 111-131.

Eisenberg, L. (1958). Schoolphobia. *American Journal of Psychiatry*, 114, 712-718.

Eisenstadt, S. N. (1964). *From generation to generation: Age group and social structure.* Glencoe, ILL: The Free Press.

Elifson, K. W., Petersen, D. M., & Hadaway, C. K. (1983). Religiosity and delinquency: A contextual analysis. *Criminology*, 21, 505-527.

Elliott, D. (1988). *Gender, delinquency and society.* Aldershot: Avebury.

Elliott, D. S. (1972). *Delinquency and the school.* Washington D.C.: Youth Development and Delinquency Prevention Administration.

_____, & Ageton, S. S. (1980). Reconciling race and class differences in self reported and official estimates of delinquency. *American Sociological Review*, 45, 95-110.

_____, & Huizinga, D. (1983). Social class and delinquent behavior in a national youth panel. *Criminology*, 21, 149-177.

_____, & Huizinga, D. (1984). *The relationship between delinquent behavior and ADM problems.* Boulder: Behavioral Research Institute.

_____, & Huizinga, D. (1988). *Improving self-reported measures of delinquency.* Nato workshop on self-reported measures of delinquency. Congress Center, The Netherlands.

_____, & Voss, H. (1974). *Delinquency and dropout.* Lexington, DC: Heath.

_____, Ageton, S. S., & Canter, R. J. (1979). An integrated theoretical perspective on delinquent behavior. *Journal of Research in Crime and Delinquency*, 16, 3-27.

_____, Dunford, F. W., & Huizinga, D. (1987). The identification and prediction of career offenders utilizing self-reported and official data. In J. D. Burchard and S. N. Burchard (Eds.), *Prevention of delinquent behavior.* Beverly Hills: Sage.

_____, Huizinga, D., & Ageton, S. S. (1985). Explaining delinquency and drug use. Beverly Hills: Sage.

Ellis, L. (1982). Genetics and criminal behavior. *Criminology*, 20, 43-66.

_____ (1987b). Criminal behavior and r/k selection: An extension of gene-based evolutionary theory. *Deviant Behavior*, 8, 149-176.

Eme, R., Maisiak, R., & Goodale, W. (1979). Seriousness of adolescent problems. *Adolescence*, 14, 93-99.

Emery, R. E., & O'Leary, K. D. (1982). Children's perception of marital discord and behavior problems of boys and girls. *Journal of Abnormal Child Psychology*, 10, 11-24.

Emler, N., Reicher, S., & Ross, A. (1987). The social context of delinquent conduct. *Journal of Child Psychology and Psychiatry and Allied Disciplines*, 28, 99-109.

Emmerich, W., Goldman, K. S., & Shore, R. E. (1971). Differentiation and development of social norms. *Journal of Personality and Social Psychology*, 18, 323-353.

Empey, L. T. (1967). Delinquency theory and recent research. *Journal of Research in Crime and Delinquency*, 3, 28-41.

_____, & Lubeck, S. G. (1971). *Explaining delinquency.* Lexington: Lexington Books.

Erickson, K. (1972). Notes on the sociology of deviance. *Social Problems*, 9, 307-314.

Erickson, M. L., & Empey, L. T. (1963). Court records, undetected delinquency and decision making. *Journal of Criminal Law, Criminology, and Police Science*, 54, 456-469.

_____, & Empey, L. T. (1965). Class position, peers, and delinquency. *Sociology and Social Research*, 49, 269-282.

_____, & Jensen, G. F. (1977). Delinquency is still group behavior. Toward revitalizing the group premise in the sociology of deviance. *Journal of Criminal Law and Criminology*, 68, 262-273.

Erikson, E. H. (1950). *Childhood and Society*. New York: Norton.

_____ (1968). *Identity, youth and crisis*. New York: Norton.

_____ (1974). *Dimensions of new identity*. New York: Norton.

_____ (1980). *Identity and the life cycle*. New York: Norton.

Erikson, M. (1971). The group context of delinquent behavior. *Social Problems*, 19, 114-129.

Eskilson, A., Wiley, M. G., Muehlbauer, G., & Dodder, L. (1986). Parental pressure, self-esteem and adolescent reported deviance: Bending the twig too far. *Adolescence*, 21, 501-515.

Ewin-Smith, T. (1984). Sex and sibling structure: Interaction effects upon the accuracy of adolescent perceptions of parental orientation. *Journal of Marriage and the Family*, 901-907.

Eyo-Isidore, D. (1981). British delinquents and non-delinquents on seven domains of the self-concept. *Journal of Psychology*, 109, 137-145.

_____ (1947). *Dimensions of personality*. London: Routledge and Kegan Paul.

_____ (1956). The questionnaire measurement of neuroticism and extraversion. *Review of Psychology*, 50, 113-140.

_____ (1958). A short questionnaire for the measurement of two dimensions of personality. *Journal of Applied Psychology*, 14-17.

_____ (1959). *The Maudsley personality inventory manual*. London: Umiv. of London Press.

_____ (1977). *Crime and Personality*. London: Routledge and Kegan Paul.

_____, & Eysenck, S. B. G. (1964). *Manual of the Eysenck personality inventory*. London: Umiv. of London Press.

_____, & Eysenck, S. B. G. (1970). Crime and personality: An empirical study of the three factor theory. *British Journal of Criminology*, 10, 225-239.

_____, & Eysenck, S. B. G (1976). *Psychoticism as a dimension of personality*. London: Hodder and Stoughton.

_____, & Wilson, G. (1975). *Know your own personality*. London: Maurice Temple Smith.

_____, Eysenck, S. B. G., Hendrickson, A., Rachman, S., White, P. O., & Soueif, M. I. (1969). *Personality, structure and measurement*. London: Routledge and Kegan Paul.

Eysenck, S. B. G. (1960). Social class, sex and responses to a five part personality inventory. *Educational and Psychological Measurement*, 20, 47-54.

_____, & Eysenck, H. J. (1969). Scores on three personality variables as a function of age, sex and social class. *British Journal of Clinical Psychology*, 8, 69-76.

_____, & Eysenck, H. J. (1971). Crime and personality: Item analysis of questionnaire responses. *British Journal of Criminology*, 11, 49-62.

_____, & Eysenck, H. J. (1977a). Personality differences between prisoners and controls. *Psychological Reports*, 40, 1023-1028.

_____, & Eysenck, H. J (1977b). The place of impulsiveness in a dimensional system of personality description. *British Journal of Social and Clinical Psychology*, 16, 57-

68.

_____, & McGurk, B. J. (1980). Impulsiveness and venturesomeness in a detention center population. *Psychological Reports*, 47, 1299-1306.

Fagan, J., Piper, E., & Moore, M. (1986). Violent delinquents and urban youth. *Criminology*, 24, 439-471.

_____, Slaughter, E., & Hartstone, E. (1987). Blind justice? The impact of race on the juvenile justice process. *Crime and Delinquency*, 33, 224-258.

Falbo, T. (1987). Only children in the United States and China. *Applied Social and Psychological Annual*, 7, 159-183.

_____, & Pilot, D. F. (1986). Quantitative review of the only child literature: Research evidence and theory development. *Psychological Bulletin*, 100, 176-189.

Farley, F. (1986). The Big T in personality. *Psychology Today*, 20 (5), 44-52.

Farley, F. H., & Farley, S. V. (1972). Stimulus-seeking motivation and delinquent behavior among institutionalized delinquent girls. *Journal of Consulting and Clinical Psychology*, 39, 94-97.

Farrington, D. P. (1973). Self-reports of deviant behavior: Predictive and stable? *Journal of Criminal Law and Criminology*, 64, 99-110.

_____ (1978). The family background of aggressive youth. In L. A. Hersow, M. Berger, and D. Shaffer (Eds.), *Aggression and antisocial behavior in childhood and adolescence*. Oxford: Pergamon Press.

_____ (1979). Longitudinal research on crime and delinquency. In N. Morris and M. Tonry (Eds.), *Criminal justice: An annual review of research I*. Chicago: Umiv. of Chicago Press.

_____ (1980a). Truancy, delinquency, the home and the school. In L. Herder and I. Berg (Eds.), *Out of school*. Chichester: Wiley.

_____ (1980b). *Prevention of juvenile delinquency: An introduction*. Paper presented at the 14th Criminological Research Conference, Straatsburg.

_____ (1986). Stepping stones to adult criminal careers: Development of antisocial and prosocial behavior. In D. Olweus, J. Block and M. K. Radke-Yarrow (Eds.), *Development of antisocial and prosocial behavior: Research, theories, and issues*. New York: Academic Press.

_____ (1987). Epidemiology. In H. C. Quay (Ed.), *Handbook of juvenile delinquency*. New York: John Wiley and Sons.

_____, & West, D. J. (1981). The Cambridge study in delinquent development. In S. A. Mednick and A. E. Baert (Eds.), *Prospective longitudinal research: An empirical basis for the primary prevention of psychosocial disorders*. New York: Oxford Univ. Press.

_____, Biron, L., & LeBlanc, M. (1982a). Personality and delinquency in London and Montreal. In J. Gunn and D. P. Farrington (Eds.), *Abnormal offenders: Delinquency and the criminal justice system*. Chichester: Wiley.

_____, Berkowitz, L., & West, D. J. (1982b). Differences between individual and group fights. *British Journal of Social Psychology*, 21, 323-333.

_____, Gundry, G., & West, D. J. (1975). The familial transmission of criminality. *Medicine, Science and the Law*, 15, 177-186.

_____, Osborn, S. G., & West, D. J. (1978). The persistence of labelling effects. *British Journal of Criminology*, 18, 277-283.

_____, Snyder, H. N., & Finnegan, T. A. (1988). Specialization in juvenile court careers. *Criminology*, 26, 461-485.

_____, Callagher, B., Marloy, L., Ledger, R., & West, D. J. (1986). Unemployment, school leaving and crime. *British Journal of Criminology*, 26, 335-356.

Fasick, F. A. (1984). Parents, peers, youth culture and autonomy in adolescence. *Adolescence*, 19, 143-157.

Faunce, E. E., & Riskin, J. (1970). Family interaction scales II. Data analysis and findings. *Archives of General Psychiatry*, 22, 513-526.

Feather, N. T., & Barber, J. G. (1983). Depressive reactions and unemployment. *Journal of Abnormal Psychology*, 2, 358-390.

_____, & Davenport, P. R. (1981). Unemployment and depressive effect: A motivational and attributional analysis. *Journal of Personality and Social Psychology*, 41, 422-436.

_____, & O'Brien, G. E. (1986). A longitudinal analysis of the effects of different patterns of employment of school-leavers. *British Journal of Psychology*, 77, 459-479.

Feij, J. A. (1979). *Temperament. Onderzoek naar de betekenis van extraversie, emotionaliteit, impulsiviteit en spanningsbehoefte*. Lisse: Swets en Zeitlinger.

Feldhusen, J. F., & Benning, J. J. (1972). Prediction of delinquency, adjustment, and academic achievement over a five-year period. *Journal of Educational Research*, 65, 375-381.

Feldman, M. P. (1977). *Criminal behavior: A psychological analysis*. New York: John Wiley and Sons.

Feldman, R. A. (1972). Normative integration, alienation and conformity in adolescent groups. *Adolescence*, 7, 327-341.

Felice, M., & Offord, D. R. (1971). Girl delinquency, a review. *Correction, Psychiatry and Social Therapy*, 17, 18-33.

Festinger, L. (1957). *A theory of cognitive dissonance*. Stanford: Stanford Univ. Press.

_____, Pepitone, A., & Newcomb, T. (1952). Some consequences of deindividuation in a group. *Journal of Abnormal and Social Psychology*, 47, 382-389.

Feyerherm, W. H., & Hindelang, M. J. (1974). On the victimization of juveniles: Some preliminary results. *Journal of Research in Crime and Delinquency*, 11, 40-50.

Fischer, D. G. (1984). Family size and delinquency. *Perceptual and Motor Skills*, 58, 527-534.

Fiselier, J. P. S. (1972). Criminaliteit en buurt. *Nederlands Tijdschrift voor Criminologie*, 14, 93-105.

Fitch, G. (1970). Effect of self-esteem, perceived performance, and choice on casual attributes. *Journal of Personality and Social Psychology*, 16, 311-315.

Fitch, J. H. (1962). Two personality variables and their contribution in a criminal population: An empirical study. *British Journal of Social and Clinical Psychology*, 1, 161-167.

Floderus-Myrhed, B., Pedersen, N., & Rasmuson, I. (1980). Assessment of heritability for personality based on a short form of the Eysenck Personality Inventory: A study of 12,898 twin pairs. *Behavior Genetics*, 10, 153-162.

Fodor, E. M. (1972). Delinquency and susceptibility to social influence among adolescents as a function of level of moral development. *Journal of Social Psychology*, 86, 257-260.

Fodor, E. M. (1973). Moral development and parent behavior antecedents in adolescent psychopaths. *Journal of Genetic Psychology*, 122, 37-43.

Fogelman, K., Tibbenman, A., & Lambert, L. (1980). Absence from school: Findings from the National Child Development Study. In L. Hersov and J. Berg (Eds.), *Out of school*. New York: John Wiley and Sons.

Folker, D. W., Eysenck, S. B. G., & Zuckerman, M. (1980). A genetic and environ mental analysis of sensation seeking. *Journal of Research in Personality*, 14, 261-281.

Forde, R. A. (1978). Twin studies, inheritance and criminality. *British Journal of Criminology*, 18, 71-74.

Forer, L. (1969). *Birth order and life roles*. Springfield, Ill: Charles Thompson.

Forrest, R. (1977). Personality and delinquency: A multivariate examination of Eysenck's theory with Scottish delinquent and non-delinquent boys. *Social Behavior and Personality*, 5, 157-167.

Foster, J. D., Dinitz, S., & Reckless, W. C. (1972). Perception of stigma following public intervention for delinquent behavior. *Social Problems*, 20, 202-209.

Fraser, M., & Norman, M. (1988). Chronic juvenile delinquency and the "suspense effect": An exploratory study. *Journal of Offender Counseling, Services and Rehabilitation*, 13, 55-73.

Frease, D. E. (1973). Delinquency, social class and the schools. *Sociology and Social Research*, 57, 443-459.

Freedman, B. J., Rosenthal, L., Donahue, L. P., Schlundt, D. G., & McFall, R. M. (1978). A social-behavioral analysis of skill deficits in delinquent and non-delinquent adolescents. *Journal of Consulting and Clinical Psychology*, 46, 1448-1462.

Freedman, J. L. (1977). *Psychologie en overbevolking*. Utrecht: Het Spectrum.

Freeman, R. B. (1983). Crime and unemployment. In J. Q. Wilson (Ed.), *Crime and public policy*. San Francisco: ICS Press.

Freire, P. (1979). *Pedagogie van de onderdrukten*. Baarn: Anthos.

French, D. C. (1988). Heterogeneity of peer-rejected boys: Aggressive and nonaggressive subtypes. *Child Development*, 59, 976-985.

_____, & Waas, G. A. (1985). Behavior problems of peer-neglected and peer-rejected elementary-age children. *Child Development*, 56, 246-252.

Freud, A. (1956). *The ego and mechanisms of defense*. New York: International Univ. Press.

_____ (1958). Adolescence. In *The psycho-analytic study of the child*. London: International Univ. Press.

Friday, P. C., & Hage, J. (1976). Youth crime in postindustrial societies. *Criminology*, 14, 347-368.

Friedberg, R. D. (1982). Locus of control and self concept in a status offender population. *Psychological Reports*, 50, 298-290.

Friedenberg, E. (1969). Current patterns of generational conflicts. *Journal of Social Issues*, 25, 21-38.

Friedlander, K. (1952). *De jeugdige delinquent*. Haarlem: Tjeenk Willink.

Friedman, C. J., Mann, F., & Adelman, H. (1976). Juvenile street gangs: The victimization of youth. *Adolescence*, 11, 527-533.

Frisk, M., Tenhunen, T., Widholm, O., & Hortling, H. (1966). Psychological problems in adolescents showing advanced or delayed physical maturation. *Adolescence*, 1, 126-140.

Fromm, E. (1941). *Escape from freedom*. New York: Farrar and Rinehart.

Fülkrug, H. (1988). Manipuliertes Glück, Spiele an Geldspielautomaten, zugleich eine Entgegnung auf Steinke. *Kriminalistik*, 11, 587-610.

Füllgrabe, U. (1978). Gibt es kriminelle Erbanlagen? *Kriminalistik*, 32, 294-300.

Furnham, A. (1984). Personality, social skills, anomie and delinquency: A self-report study of a group of normal non-delinquent adolescents. *Journal of Child Psychology and Psychiatry and Allied Disciplines*, 25, 409-420.

Furnham, A. F. (1985). Youth unemployment: A review of the literature. *Journal of Adolescence*, 8, 109-124.

Galbraith, J. K. (1985). *The affluent society*. Boston: Houghton Mifflin.

Galle, O. R., Gove, W. R., & McPherson, J. M. (1972). Population density and pathology. *Science*, 176, 23-30.

Gamoran, A., & Mare, R. D. (1989). Secondary school tracking and education inequality, compensation, reinforcement, or neutrality? *American Journal of Sociology*, 94, 1146-1183.

Ganzer, V. J., & Sarason, I. G. (1973). Variables associated with recidivism among juvenile delinquents. *Journal of Consulting and Clinical Psychology*, 40, 1-5.

Garofalo, J., Siegel, L., & Laub, J. (1987). School related victimizations among adolescents: An analysis of National Crime Survey (NCS) narratives. *Journal of Quantitative Criminology*, 3, 321-338.

Gearing, M. L. (1979). The MMPI as a primary differentiator and predictor of behavior in prison: A methodological critique and review of the recent literature. *Psychological Bulletin*, 86, 929-963.

Geist, C. R., & Borecki, S. (1982). Social avoidance and distress as a predictor of perceived locus of control and level of self-esteem. *Journal of Clinical Psychology*, 38, 611-613.

George, C., & Main, M. (1979). Social interactions of young abused children: Approach, avoidance and aggression. *Child Development*, 50, 306-318.

Gerbing, D. W., Ahadien, S. A., & Patton, J. H. (1987). Toward a conceptualization of impulsivity: Components across the behavioral and self-report domains. *Multivariate Behavioral Research*, 22, 357-379.

Gerris, J. R. M. (1988). Bevordering van de socio-morele ontwikkeling. Een theoretische en een praktische uitwerking. *Justitiële Verkenningen*, 14, 60-89.

Ghali, M. A. (1982). The choice of crime: An empirical analysis of juvenile's criminal choice. *Journal of Criminal Justice*, 10, 433-442.

Giallombardo, R. (1980). Female delinquency. In D. Schichor and D. H. Kelly (Eds.), *Critical issues in juvenile delinquency*. Lexington: Lexington Books.

Gibbens, T. C. N. (1961). *Trends in juvenile delinquency*. Geneva: WHO.

_____ (1963). *Psychiatric studies of Borstal lads*. Oxford: Oxford Univ. Press.

Gibbons, D. C. (1970). *Delinquent behaviour*. Englewood Cliffs, NJ: Prentice-Hall.

_____ (1971). Observations on the study of crime causations. *American Journal of Sociology*, 77, 262-278.

Gibbons, H. B., Morrison, J., & West, J. (1970). The confessions of known offenders in response to a self-reported delinquency schedule. *British Journal of Criminology*, 10, 277-280.

Gibbs, J. P. (1981). *Norms, deviance and social control: Conceptual matters*. New York: Elsevier.

Gibson, H. B. (1971). The validity of the Eysenck Personality Inventory studied by a technique of peer-rating item by item, and by sociometric comparisons. *British Journal of Social and Clinical psychology*, 10, 213-220.

Gilles, A. R. (1974). Population density and social pathology: The case of building type, social allowance, and juvenile delinquency. *Social Forces*, 63, 306-314.

Giordano, P. C. (1978). Girls, guys and the gang: The changing social context of female delinquency. *Journal of Criminal Law and Criminology*, 69, 126-132.

_____, & Cernkovich, S. A. (1979). On complicating the relationship between liberation and delinquency. *Social Problems*, 26, 467-481.

_____, Cernkovich, S. A., & Pugh, M. D. (1986). Friendships and delinquency. *American Journal of Sociology*, 91, 1170-1202.

Gipser, D. (1975). *Mädchenkriminalität. Soziale Bedingungen abweichendes Verhaltens.* München: Juventa-Verlag.

Glaser, D. (1974). *Handbook of criminology.* Chicago: Rand McNally.

_____ (1979). Economic and sociocultural variables affecting rates of youth unemployment, delinquency, and crime. *Youth and Society*, 11, 53-82.

_____, & Rice, K. (1959). Crime, age, employment. *American Sociological Review*, 24, 679-686.

Glueck, E. T. (1966). Identification of potential delinquents at 2-3 years of age. *International Journal of Social Psychiatry*, 12, 5-16.

Glueck, S., & Glueck, E. (1950). *Unravelling juvenile delinquency.* Cambridge: Harvard Univ. Press.

_____, & Glueck, E. (1959). *The problem of delinquency.* Boston: Houghton Mifflin.

_____, & Glueck, E. (1962). *Family environment and delinquency.* London: Routledge and Kegan Paul.

_____, & Glueck, E. (1968). *Delinquents and non-delinquents in perspective.* Cambridge: Harvard Univ. Press.

_____, & Glueck, E. (1970). *Toward a typology of juvenile offenders.* New York: Grune & Stratton.

_____, & Glueck, E. (1972). *Identification of predelinquents.*

_____, & Glueck, E. (1974). *Of delinquency and crime.* Springfield: Illinois, Thomas.

Goddard, H. H. (1921). *Juvenile delinquency.* New York: Dodd-Mead.

Godefroy, T., & Laffargue, B. (1984). Crise économique et criminalité. Criminologie de la misère ou misère de criminologie. *Déviance et Société*, 8, 73-100.

Gold, M. (1963). *Status forces in delinquent boys.* Ann Arbor: Institute for Social Research, Umiv. of Michigan.

_____ (1966). Undetected delinquent behavior. *Journal of Research in Crime and Delinquency*, 3, 27-46.

_____ (1970). *Delinquent behavior in an American city.* Belmont: Brooks and Cole.

_____ (1978). Scholastic experience, self esteem and delinquent behavior: A theory for alternative schools. *Crime and Delinquency*, 24, 290-308.

_____ (1987). Social Ecology. In H. C. Quay (Ed.), *Handbook of juvenile delinquency.* New York: John Wiley and Sons.

_____, & Mann, D. (1972). Delinquency as defense. *American Journal of Orthopsychiatry*, 42, 463-479.

_____, & Petronio, R. J. (1980). Delinquent behavior in adolescence. In J. Adelson (Ed.), *Handbook of adolescent psychology.* New York: John Wiley and Sons.

_____, & Reimer, D. J. (1975). Changing patterns of delinquent behavior among Americans 13-16 years old: 1967-1972. *Crime and Delinquency Literature*, 7, 483-517.

Goldfried, M. R. (1963). Feelings of inferiority and the depreciation of others: A research review and theoretical reformulation. *Journal of Individual Psychology*, 19, 27-48.

Goldin, P. C. (1969). A review of children's report of parent behaviors. *Psychological Bulletin*, 11, 222-236.

Golding, S. L. (1975). Flies in the ointment: Methodological problems in the analysis of the percentage of variance due to persons and situations. *Psychological Bulletin*, 82, 278-288.

Göppinger, H. (1976). *Kriminologie*. München: Beck.

_____ (1983). *Der Täter in seinen sozialen Bezügen*. Berlin: Springer.

Gordon, D. A., Jones, R. M., & Nowicki, S. (1979). A measure of intensity of parental punishment. *Journal of Personality Research*, 43, 485-496.

Gordon, R., Short, J., Cartwright, D., & Strodtbeck, F. (1963). Values and gang delinquency: A study of street corner groups. *American Journal of Sociology*, 69, 109-128.

Goring, C. B. (1913). *The english convict: A statistical study*. London: Wyman and Sons.

Gottesman, I. I. (1963). Heritability of personality: A demonstration. *Psychological Monographs*, 77.

_____ (1966). Genetic variance in adaptive personality traits. *Journal of Child Psychology and Psychiatry*, 7, 199-208.

Gottfredson, D. C. (1985). Youth unemployment, crime and schooling: A longitudinal study of a natural sample. *Developmental Psychology*, 21, 419-432.

Gottfredson, M., & Hindelang, M. (1979). A study of the behavior of law. *American Sociological Review*, 43, 3-18.

_____, & Hirschi, T. (1986). The true value of lambda would appear to be zero: An essay on career criminals, criminal careers, selective incapacitation, cohort studies, and related topics. *Criminology*, 24, 213-233.

Gottlieb , D. (1979). Alienation and adjustment to limited prospects. *Youth and Society*, 11, 92-113.

Gough, H. G., Wenk, E. A., & Rozynko, V. V. (1965). Parole outcome as predicted from the CPI, the MMPI, and a base expectancy table. *Journal of Abnormal Psychology*, 70, 432-441.

Gould, L. (1969a). The changing structure of property crime in an affluent society. *Social Forces*, 48, 50-59.

Gould, L. C. (1969b). Who defines delinquency: A comparison of self reported and officially reported indices of delinquency for three racial groups. *Social Problems*, 16, 325-336.

Gove, W., & Crutchfield, R. D. (1982). The family and juvenile delinquency. *Sociological Quarterly*, 23, 301-319.

Graham, J. (1988a). *Schools, disruptive behavior and delinquency: A review of research*. London: HMSO.

_____ (1988b). *Amusement machines: Dependency and delinquency*. London: HMSO.

Grande, G. C. (1988). Delinquency: The learning disabled student's reaction to academic schoolfailure?. *Adolescence*, 23, 209-219.

Green, K. D., Forehand, R., Beck, S. J., & Vosk, B. (1980). An assessment of the relationship among measures of children's social competence and children's academic achievement. *Child Development*, 51, 1149-1156.

Greenberg, D. (1977). Delinquency and the age structure of society. *Contemporary Crises*, 1, 189-223.

_____ (1985). Age, crime and social explanation. *American Journal of Sociology*, 91,

1-12.

Greenberg, M. T., Siegel, J. M., & Leitch, C. J. (1983). The nature and importance of attachment relationships to parents and peers during adolescence. *Journal of Youth and Adolescence*, 12, 373-386.

Groenier, K. H., Hofstee, W. K. B., Kluiter, H., & Lutje Spelberg, H. C. (1973). Faktoren in een eigenschappenlijst. *Nederlands Tijdschrift voor de Psychologie*, 28, 249-257.

Grotevant, H. D. (1978). Sibling constellations and sex-typing of interests in adoles cence. *Child Development*, 49, 540-542.

Gruhle, H. W. (1912). *Die Ursachen der jugendlichen Verwahrlosung und Kriminalität*. Berlin.

Grunsell, R. (1980). *Beyond control? Schools and suspension*. Richmond: Chameleon Books.

Grygier, T., Chesley, J., & Tuters, E. W. (1969). Parental deprivation: A study of delinquent children. *British Journal of Criminology*, 9, 209-253.

Guilford, J. P. (1934). Introversion-extraversion. *Psychological Bulletin*, 31, 331-354.

Guze, S. B., Goodwin, D. W., & Crane, J. B. (1970). A psychiatric study of the wives of convicted felons: An example of assortative mating. *American Journal of Psychiatry*, 126, 115-118.

Hagan, J., Gilles, A. R., & Simpson, J. (1985). The class structure of gender and delinquency: Toward a power-control theory of common delinquent behavior. *American Journal of Sociology*, 90, 1151-1178.

Halebsky, M. A. (1987). Adolescent alcohol and substance abuse: Parent and peers. *Adolescence*, 22, 961-967.

Hall, P. M. (1966). Identification with delinquent subculture and level of self-evaluation. *Sociometry*, 29, 146-158.

Hamilton, J. A. (1983). Development of interest and enjoyment in adolescence: II. Boredom and psychopathology. *Journal of Youth and Adolescence*, 12, 363-372.

Hamilton, S. F., & Crouter, A. C. (1980). Work and growth: A review of research on the impact of work experience on adolescent development. *Journal of Youth and Adolescence*, 9, 321-328.

Hanson, C. L., Henggeler, S., Haefile, W., & Rodick, J. (1984). Demographic, individual and family relationship correlates of serious and repeated crime among delinquents and their siblings. *Journal of Consulting and Clinical Psychology*, 52, 528-538.

Hardt, R. H., & Peterson-Hardt, S. (1977). On determining the quality of delinquency self-report method. *Journal of Research in Crime and Delinquency*, 14, 247-261.

Hargreaves, D. H. (1967). *Social relations in a secondary school*. London: Routledge and Kegan Paul.

_____ (1982). *The challenge of the comprehensive school*. London: Routledge and Kegan Paul.

Harlan, J. P., & McDowell, C. P. (1980). Vindictive vandalism and the schools: Some theoretical considerations. *Journal of Police Science and Administration*, 8, 399-405.

Harries, K. D. (1974). *The geography of crime and justice*. New York: MacGraw-Hill.

_____ (1980). *Crime and environment*. Springfield, Ill: Charles C. Thomas.

Hartnagel, T. F., & Tanner, J. (1982). Class, schooling and delinquency: A further examination. *Canadian Journal of Criminology*, 24, 155-172.

Hartshorne, H., & May, M. A. (1928). *Studies in deceit*. New York: MacMillan.

Hartup, W. W. (1970). Peer interaction and social organization. In P. H. Mussen (Ed.), *Carmichael's manual of child psychology*. New York: John Wiley and Sons.

_____ (1985). Peer relations. In P. Mussen (Ed.), *Handbook of child psychology*. New York: John Wiley and Sons.

_____, Glazer, J. A., & Charlesworth, R. (1967). Peer reinforcement and sociometric status. *Child Development*, 38, 1017-1024.

Hathaway, S. R., & Monachesi, E. D. (1963). *Adolescent personality and behavior. MMPI patterns of normal delinquent, dropout and other outcomes*. Minneapolis: Umiv. of Minnesota Press.

Hauber, A. R., Toornvliet, L. G., & Willemse, H. M. (1986a). Persoonlijkheid en criminaliteit bij scholieren. *Tijdschrift voor Criminologie*, 28, 92-106.

_____, Toornvliet, L. G., & Willemse, H. M. (1986b). Spijbelen en criminaliteit. *Delikt en Delinkwent*, 16, 585-592.

_____, Toornvliet, L. G., & Willemse, H. M. (1987a). Achtergronden van criminaliteit bij meisjes. In G. Bruinsma, E. Leuw, E. Lissenberg, and A. Van Vliet, *Vrouw en criminaliteit*. Meppel-Amsterdam: Boom.

_____, Toornvliet, L. G., & Willemse, H. M. (1987b). De relatie spijbelen-criminaliteit nader bezien. *Justitiële Verkenningen*, 13, 41-63.

_____, Toornvliet, L. G., & Willemse, H. M. (1987c). De ene spijbelaar is de andere niet. *Pedagogisch Tijdschrift*, 12, 10-16.

Havighurst, R. J. (1962). *Growing up in River City*. New York: John Wiley and Sons.

Hawkins, J. D., & Lane, T. (1987). Teacher practice, social development and delinquency. In J. D. Burchard and S. N. Burchard (Eds.), *Prevention of delinquent behavior*. Beverly Hills: Sage.

Healy, W. (1915). *The individual delinquent*. Boston: Little-Brown.

_____, & Bronner, A. (1936). *New lights on delinquency and its treatment*. New Haven: Yale Univ. Press.

Heather, N. (1979). The structure of delinquent values: A reported grid investigation. *British Journal of Social and Clinical Psychology*, 18, 263-275.

Hellman, D. A., & Beaton, S. (1986). The pattern of violence in urban public schools: The influence of school and community. *Journal of Research in Crime and Delinquency*, 23, 102-127.

Hellmer, J. (1978). *Jugendkriminalität*. Neuwied-Darmstadt.

Henggeler, S. W., Urey, J. R., & Borduin, C. M. (1982). Social class, psychopathology and family interaction. In S. W. Henggeler (Ed.), *Delinquency and adolescent psychopathology*. Boston: John Wright.

Hennessy, M., Richards, P., & Berk, R. (1978). Broken homes and middle class delinquency: A reassessment. *Criminology*, 15, 505-527.

Hepburn, J. R. (1976). Testing alternative models of delinquency causation. *Journal of Criminal Law and Criminology*, 67, 450-460.

_____ (1977). The impact of police intervention upon juvenile delinquency. *Criminology*, 15, 235-264.

Herbert, M. (1975). *Problems of childhood*. Pan Books.

Herzog, E., & Sudia, C. (1973). Children in fatherless families. In B. M. Caldwell and H. N. Ricciuti (Eds.), *Review of child development research*, Chicago: Univ. of Chicago Press.

Hess, R. D., & Camera, K. A. (1979). Post-divorce family relationships as mediating factors in the consequences of divorce for children. *Journal of Social Issues*, 35, 79-

97.

Hetherington, E. M., Stouwie, R., & Ridberg, E. H. (1971). Patterns of family interaction and child rearing related to three dimensions of juvenile delinquency. *Journal
of Abnormal Psychology*, 78, 160-176.

Hewitt, L., & Jenkins, R. (1946). *Fundamental patterns of maladjustment, the dynamics
of their origin*. Springfield, Ill: State of Illinois.

Heymans, G. (1927). *Gesammelte kleine Schriften*. The Hague: Nijhoff.

Higgins, P. C., & Albrecht, G. L. (1977). Hellfire and delinquency revisited. *Social
Forces*, 55, 952-958.

Hill, K. A. (1987). Children's problems in peer relations and severity of behavior disorders. *Psychological Reports*, 55, 725-726.

Hindelang, M. J. (1970). The commitment of delinquents to their misdeeds: Do delinquents drift? *Social Problems*, 17, 502-509.

_____ (1971a). Age, sex and the versatility of delinquent involvements. *Social Prob
lems*, 18, 522-535.

_____ (1971b). The social versus solitary nature of delinquent involvements. *British
Journal of Criminology*, 11, 167-175.

_____ (1973). Causes of delinquency: A partial replication and extension. *Social
Problems*, 20, 471-487.

_____ (1974a). Moral evaluations of illegal behavior. *Social Problems*, 21, 370-385.

_____ (1974b). Decisions of shoplifting victims to invoke the criminal justice process.
Social Problems, 21, 580-593.

_____ (1976). With a little help from their friends: Group participation in reported
delinquent behavior. *British Journal of Criminology*, 16, 109-125.

_____ (1978). Race and involvement in common law personal crimes. *American
Sociological Review*, 43, 93-109.

_____ (1979a). Sex differences in criminal activity. *Social Problems*, 27, 143-156.

_____ (1979b). Variations in sex, race, age, specific incidence rates of offending.
American Sociological Review, 44, 999-1014.

_____, Hirschi, T., & Weis, J. G. (1979). Correlates of delinquency: The illusion of
discrepancy between self-report and official measures. *American Sociological Review*,
44, 995-1014.

_____, Hirschi, T., & Weis, J. G. (1981). *Measuring Delinquency*. Beverly Hills: Sage.

Hirschi, T. (1969). *Causes of delinquency*. Berkeley: Umiv. of California Press.

_____ (1983). Crime and the family. In J. Q. Wilson (Ed.), *Crime and public policy*.
San Francisco: ICS Press.

_____, & Gottfredson, M. (1983). Age and the explanation of crime. *American Journal
of Sociology*, 89, 552-584.

_____, & Hindelang, M. J. (1977). Intelligence and delinquency: A revisionist review.
American Sociological Review, 42, 571-587.

_____, T., & Stark, R. (1969). Hellfire and delinquency. *Social Problems*, 17, 202-213.

Hobart, C. W. (1978). Economic development, liquor consumption and offence rates in
the northwest territories. *Canadian Journal of Criminology*, 20, 259-279.

Hoch, I. (1974). Factors in urban crime. *Journal of Urban Economics*, 1, 184-229.

Hollerman, P. A., Littman, D. C., Freund, R. D., & Schmaling, K. B. (1982). A
signal detection approach to social perception: Identification of positive and negative
behavior by parents of normal and problem children. *Journal of Abnormal Child
Psychology*, 10, 547-558.

Holstein, C. (1976). Irreversible, stepwise sequence in the development of moral judgement: A longitudinal study of males and females. *Child Development*, 47, 51-61.

Holzman, H. R. (1982). The rationalistic opportunity perspective on criminal behavior. *Crime and Delinquency*, 28, 233-246.

Hood, R., & Sparks, R. (1972). *Key issues in criminology*. London: World Univ. Library.

Huba, G. J., & Bentler, P. M. (1982). On the usefulness of latent variable causal modelling in testing theories of naturally occurring events (including adolescent drug use): A rejoinder to Martin. *Journal of Personality and Social Psychology*, 43, 604-611.

Hubble, L. M., & Groff, M. (1981). Magnitude and direction of WISC-R Verbal Performance IQ discrepancies among adjudicated male delinquents. *Journal of Youth and Adolescence*, 10, 179-184.

Hudgins, W., & Prentice, N. (1973). Moral judgement in delinquent and non-delinquent adolescents and their mothers. *Journal of Abnormal Psychology*, 82, 145-152.

Huizinga, D., & Elliott, D. S. (1986). Reassessing the reliability and validity of self-report delinquency measures. Journal of Quantitative Criminology, 24, 293-327.

Hutchings, B., & Mednick, S. A. (1977). Criminality in adoptees and their adoptive and biological parents: A pilot study. In S. A. Mednick and K. O. Christiansen (Eds.), *Biosocial basis of criminal behavior*. New York: Gardner.

Hyde, J. S. (1984). How large are gender differences in aggression? A developmental meta-analysis. *Developmental Psychology*, 20, 722-736.

Hyman, H. H. (1953). The value system of different classes: A social psychological contribution to the analysis of stratification. In R. Bendix and S. M. Lipset (Eds.), *Class, status, and power*. Glencoe, Ill: The Free Press.

Iacovetta, R. G. (1975). Adolescent-adult interaction and peer-group involvement. *Adolescence*, 10, 327-336.

Iscoe, I., Williams, M., & Harvey, J. (1963). Modification of children's judgments by a simulated group technique: A normative developmental study. *Child Development*, 34, 963-978.

Jackson, P. G. (1989). Theories and findings about youth gangs. *Criminal Justice Abstract*, 12, 313-329.

Jackson, P. I. (1981). Opportunity and crime: A function of city size. *Sociology and Social Research*, 69, 173-190.

Jackson, P. R., Stafford, E. M., Banks, M. H., & Warr, P. B. (1983). Unemployment and psychological distress in young people: The moderating role of employment commitment. *Journal of Applied Psychology*, 68, 525-535.

Jacobs, D. (1979). Inequality and police strength: Conflict theory and coercive control in metropolitan areas. *American Sociological Review*, 44, 913-925.

Jacobson, E. (1957). Denial and repression. *Journal of the American Psychoanalytic Association*, 1, 61-92.

James, J., & Thornton, W. (1980). Women's Liberation and the female delinquent. *Journal of Research in Crime and Delinquency*, 7, 230-249.

Janes, J. A. (1958). The father's part in the development of personality. *Child Welfare*, 37, 12-15.

Janes, C. L., Hesselbrock, V. M., Myers, D. G., & Penniman, J. H. (1979). Problem boys in young adulthood: Teachers' ratings and twelve-year follow-up. *Journal of Youth and Adolescence*, 8, 453-472.

Janswoude, J. J., & De Mulder, R. V. (1980). Over de bruikbaarheid van CBS-gegevens. *Tijdschrift voor Criminologie*, 22, 264-272.

Jaspers, J. P. C., Schut, H. A. W., De Keijser, A., Gunnink, J. W., & Hüskin, F. A. H. (1986). Spijbelen en schoolbeleving in het voortgezet onderwijs. *Pedagogische Studiën*, 63, 61-73.

Jenkins, R. L. (1955). Adaptive and maladaptive delinquency. *Nervous Child*, 11, 9-11.

_____ (1957). Motivation and frustration in delinquency. *American Journal of Orthopsychiatry*, 27, 528-537.

_____, & Glickman, S. (1947). Patterns among personality organization among delinquents. *Nervous Child*, 6, 329-339.

_____, & Lorr, M. (1953). Patterns of maladjustment in children. *Journal of Clinical Psychology*, 9, 16-19.

Jensen, G. F. (1972a). Delinquency and adolescent self-conceptions: A study of the personal relevance of infraction. *Social Problems*, 20, 84-101.

_____ (1972b). Parent, peers and delinquent actions: A test of the differential association perspective. *American Journal of Sociology*, 78, 562-575.

_____ (1973). Inner containment and delinquency. *Criminology*, 64, 464-470.

_____ (1976). Race, achievement and delinquency: A further look at delinquency in a birth cohort. *American Journal of Sociology*, 82, 379-387.

Jessor, R., & Jessor, S. L. (1977). *Problem behavior and psychosocial development: A longitudinal study of youth.* New York: Academic Press.

_____, Graves, T. D., Hanson, R. C., & Jessor, S. L. (1968). *Society, personality, and deviant behavior.* New York: Holt, Rinehart and Winston.

Johanson, E. M. (1980). *Betrogene Kinder. Eine Sozialgeschichte der Kindheit.* Frankfurt am Mainz: Fischer.

Johnson, R. E. (1979). *Juvenile delinquency and its origins, an integrated theoretical approach.* Cambridge: Cambridge Univ. Press.

_____ (1980). Social class and delinquent behavior: A new test. *Criminology*, 18, 86-96.

_____ (1986). Family structure and delinquency: General patterns and gender differences. *Criminology*, 24, 65-84.

_____ (1987). Mother's versus father's role in causing delinquency. *Adolescence*, 22, 305-315.

Johnstone, J. W. C. (1978). Social class, social areas, and delinquency. *Sociology and Social Research*, 63, 49-72.

Johnstone, J. (1980). Delinquency and the changing American family. In D. Schochor and D. Kelly (Eds.), *Critical issues in juvenile delinquency*, Lexington: Lexington Books.

Jones, S. C. (1973). Self- and interpersonal evaluations: Esteem theories versus consistency theories. *Psychological Bulletin*, 79, 185-199.

Jongman, R. W. (1971). Verborgen criminaliteit en sociale klasse. *Nederlands Tijdschrift voor Criminologie*, 13, 141-154.

Jung, C. G. (1922). *Psychologische Typen.* Zürich: Rascher und Co.

Junger-Tas, J. (1972). *Kenmerken en sociale integratie van jeugddelinquenten.* Brussels: Studiecentrum voor Jeugdmisdadigheid.

_____ (1976). *Verborgen jeugddelinquentie en gerechtelijke selectie.* Brussels: Studiecentrum voor Jeugdmisdadigheid.

_____ (1983). *Jeugddelinquentie: Achtergronden en justitiële reactie.* The Hague:

Staatsuitgeverij.

_____ (1987). School en criminaliteit. *Justitiële Verkenningen*, 13, 7-33.

_____, & Kruissink, M. (1987). *Ontwikkeling van de jeugdcriminaliteit*. The Hague: Staatsuitgeverij.

_____, & Kruissink, M. (1990). *Ontwikkeling van de jeugdcriminaliteit, periode 1980-1988*. Arnhem: Gouda Quint.

_____, Junger, M., & Barendse-Hoornweg, E. (1985). *Jeugddelinquentie II: De invloed van justitieel ingrijpen*. The Hague: Staatsuitgeverij.

_____, Junger, M., Barendse-Hoornweg, E., & Sampiemon, M. (1983). *Jeugddelin quentie, achtergronden en justitiële reactie*. The Hague: Staatsuitgeverij.

Junger, M., & Zeilstra, M. (1989). *Deviant gedrag en slachtofferschap onder jongens uit etnische minderheden I*. Arnhem: Gouda Quint.

Jurkovic, G. J. (1980). The juvenile delinquent as a moral philosopher: A structural-developmental perspective. *Psychological Bulletin*, 88, 709-727.

_____, & Prentice, N. M. (1974). Dimensions of moral interaction and moral judgment in delinquent and nondelinquent families. *Journal of Consulting and Clinical Psychology*, 42, 256-262.

_____, & Prentice, N. M. (1977). Relations of moral and cognitive development to dimensions of juvenile delinquency. *Journal of Abnormal Psychology*, 86, 414-420.

Kafer, N. F., & Shannon, K. A. L. (1986). Identification of rejected and neglected children. *Psychological Reports*, 59, 163-168.

Kaiser, G. (1982). *Jugendkriminalität*. Weinheim-Basel: Beltz.

Kalacheck, E. (1973). The changing economic status of the young. *Journal of Youth and Adolescence*, 2, 125-132.

Kandel, D. B. (1978). Homophily, selection and socialization in adolescent friendships. *American Journal of Sociology*, 84, 427-436.

_____, & Lesser, G. (1969). Parental and peer influences on educational plans of adolescents. *American Sociological Review*, 34, 1969, 212-232.

_____, Ravels, V. H., & Kandel, P. E. (1984). Continuity in discontinuities -adjustment in young adulthood and former school absentees. *Youth and Society*, 15, 325-352.

Kaplan, H. B. (1975). Increase in self-rejection as an antecedent of deviant responses. *Journal of Youth and Adolescence*, 4, 281-291.

_____ (1976). Self attitudes and deviant response. *Social Forces*, 54, 788-801.

_____ (1977a). Increase in self-rejection and continuing/discontinued deviant response. *Journal of Youth and Adolescence*, 6, 77-87.

_____ (1977b). Antecedents of deviant responses: Predicting from a general theory of deviant behavior. *Journal of Youth and Adolescence*, 6, 89-101.

_____ (1978). Deviant behavior and self enhancement in adolescence. *Journal of Youth and Adolescence*, 7, 253-277.

_____ (1980). *Deviant behavior in defense of self*. New York: Academic Press.

_____ & Pokornov, A. D. (1971). Self derogation and childhood broken home. *Journal of Marriage and the Family*, 33, 328-333.

Karlen, A. (1971). *Sexuality and homosexuality: A new view*. New York: Norton.

Katchadourian, H. (1976). *The biology of adolescence*. San Francisco: Freeman.

Kelly, D. H. (1971). School failure, academic self-evaluation, and school avoidance and deviant behavior. *Youth and Society*, 2, 489-502.

_____ (1974). Track position and delinquent involvement: A preliminary analysis. *Sociology and Social Research*, 58, 380-386.

_____ (1975). Status origins, track positions, and delinquent involvement: A self report analysis. *Sociological Quarterly*, 16, 264-271.

_____ (1978). Track position, peer affiliation and youth crime. *Urban Education*, 13, 397-406.

_____, & Pink, W. T. (1973). School commitment, youth rebellion and delinquency. *Criminology*, 11, 473-485.

Keniston, K. (1960). *The uncommitted: Alienated youth in american society*. New York: Dell.

Keupp, L. (1982). Zur Problematik der weiblichen Delinquenz. *Monatsschrift für Kriminologie und Strafrechtsreform*, 65, 219-229.

Kidwell, J. (1983). Middle-born children. *Journal of Marriage and the Family*, 44.

Killias, M. (1981). Kriminelles Verhalten wird gelernt, aber wie? *Monatsschrift für Kriminologie und Strafrechtsreform*, 64, 329-342.

Kipnis, D. (1971). *Character structure and impulsiveness*. New York: Academic Press.

Kleck, G. (1982). On the use of self-report data to determine the class distribution of criminal and delinquent behavior. *American Sociological Review*, 47, 427-433.

Kleck, R. E., Richardson, S. A., & Ronald, L. (1974). Physical appearance cues and interpersonal attraction in children. *Child Development*, 45, 305-310.

Klein, D. C., Fencil-Morse, E., & Seligman, M. E. P. (1976). Learned helplessness, depression and the attribution of failure. *Journal of Personality and Social Psychology*, 33, 508-516.

Klein, M. W. (1984). Offense specialization and versatility among juveniles. *British Journal of Criminology*, 24, 185-194.

Klinkmann, N., Gewalt und Langeweile. *Kriminologisches Journal*, 14, 1982, 254-276.

Knight, B. J., & West, D. J. (1975). Temporary and continuing delinquency. *British Journal of Criminology*, 15, 43-50.

Knox, G. (1981). Differential integration and job retention among ex-offenders. *Criminology*, 18, 481-499.

Kohlberg, L. (1964). Development of moral character and moral ideology. In M. L. Hoffman and L. W. Hoffman (Eds.), *Review of child development research (Vol 1)*. New York: Russel Sage Foundation.

_____ (1976). Moral stages and moralization: The cognitive-developmental approach. In T. Lickona (Ed.), *Moral development and behavior*. New York: Holt, Rinehart & Winston.

Kohn, M. L. (1959). Social class and parental values. *American Journal of Sociology*, 64, 337-351.

Kohnstamm, R. (1987). *Kleine ontwikkelingspsychologie* (1. Het jonge kind, 2. De schoolleeftijd). Deventer: Van Loghum Slaterus.

Kok, E. H. (1983). Een (motte)ballentheorie over vrouwencriminaliteit. *Tijdschrift voor Criminologie*, 25, 90-96.

Kommer, M. M. (1985). Criminaliteitsindicatoren: Verbetering gewenst, misbruik dient gestraft. *Delict en Delinkwent*, 15, 509-519.

Konopka, G. (1966). *The adolescent girl in conflict*. Englewood Cliffs, NJ: Prentice-Hall.

_____ (1973). Requirements for healthy development of adolescent youth. *Journal of Marriage and the Family*, 35, 291-316.

Kouwer, B. J. (1963). *Het spel der persoonlijkheid*. Utrecht: Bijleveld.

Kranz, D. E., & Vercruysse, E. V. W. (1959). *De jeugd in het geding*. Amsterdam: De

Bezige Bij.

Kratcoski, P. C. (1985). School disruption and violence against teachers. *Corrective and Social Psychiatry*, 31, 88-96.

Kraus, J. (1977). Causes of delinquency as perceived by juveniles. *International Journal of Offender Therapy and Comparative Criminology*, 21, 79-86.

_____, & Bowmaker, B. (1982). How delinquent are delinquents? A study of self-reported offenders. *Australian and New Zealand Journal of Criminology*, 15, 163-169.

Krebs, D. L., & Miller, D. T. (1985). Altruism and aggression. In G. Linday and E. Aronson (Eds.), *Handbook of social psychology*, New York: Random House.

Kretschmer, E. (1955). *Körperbau und Charakter*. Berlin: Springer.

Kreuzer, A. (1972). An example of group juvenile delinquency: The "Rockers". *International Criminological Police Review*, 27, 2-8.

_____ (1983). Kinderdelinquenz und Jugendkriminalität. *Zeitschrift für Pädagogik*, 29, 49-70.

_____ (1985). Jugendkriminalität. In G. Kaiser, H. Kerner, F. Sack, and H. Schellhoss (Eds.), *Kleines Kriminologisches Wörterbuch*. Heidelberg: Müller.

Krisberg, B. (1974). Gang youth and hustling: The psychology of survival. *Issues in Criminology*, 9, 115-131.

Krohn, M., & Wellford, C. F. (1977). A static and dynamic analysis of crime and the primary dimensions of nations. *International Journal of Criminology and Penology*, 5, 1-16.

Krohn, M. D. (1974). An investigation of the effect of parental and peer association on marijuana use: An empirical test of differential association theory. In M. Rendel and T. P. Thornberry (Eds.), *Crime and delinquency: Dimensions of deviance*. New York: Preager.

_____, & Massey, J. (1980). Social control and delinquent behavior: An examination of the elements of the social bond. *Sociological Quarterly*, 21, 529-543.

_____, Akers, R. L., Radosevich, M. J., & Lanza-Kaduce, L. (1980). Social status and deviance: Class context of school, social status, and delinquent behavior. *Criminology*, 18, 303-318.

Kuiper, C. M., & Feij, J. A. (1983). Adolescentie: Persoonlijkheid en klachten, vrije tijdbesteding, rook- en drinkgewoonten. *Gedrag*, 11, 168-181.

Kulik, J. A., Stein, K. B., & Sarbin, T. R. (1968). Dimensions and patterns of adolescent antisocial behavior. *Journal of Consulting and Clinical Psychology*, 32, 375-382.

Kurdek, L.A., & Krile, D. (1982). A developmental analysis of the relation between peer acceptance and both interpersonal understanding and perceived social self competence. *Child Development*, 53, 1485-1491.

Kvalseth, T. O. (1977). A note on the effects of population density and unemployment in urban crime. *Criminology*, 15, 105-109.

Lab, S. P. (1984). Patterns in juvenile misbehavior. *Crime and Delinquency*, 30, 293-208.

Lafaille, R. (1978). *Afwijkend gedrag en sociale problemen*. Den Haag: Vuga.

LaGrange, R. L., & White, H. R. (1985). Age differences in delinquency: A test of theory. *Criminology*, 23, 19-43.

Lamb, M. (1979). Paternal influences and the father's role. *American Psychologist*, 34, 938-943.

Lambert, N. M., Hartsiugh, C. S., Sassone, D., & Sandoval, J. (1987). Persistence of hyperactivity symptoms from childhood to adolescence and associated outcomes. *American Journal of Orthopsychiatry*, 57, 22-32.

Landau, S. F. (1976). Delinquency, institutionalization, and time orientation. *Journal of Consulting and Clinical Psychology*, 44, 745-759.

_____ (1981). Juveniles and the police. *British Journal of Criminology*, 21, 27-46.

Landsbaum, J., & Willis, R. (1971). Conformity in early and late adolescence. *Developmental Psychology*, 4, 334-337.

Lane, D. A. (1987). Personality and antisocial behaviour: A long-term study. *Personality and Individual Differences*, 8, 799-806.

Lane, R. (1986). *Roots of violence in black Philadelphia, 1860-1900*. Cambridge, MA: Harvard Univ Press.

Lange, J. (1929). *Verbrechen als Schicksal. Studien an kriminellen Zwillingen*. Leipzig: Thieme.

Langeveld, M. J. (1979). *Mensen worden niet geboren*. Nijkerk: Intro.

Langeveld, W. (1975). *Vorming tot emancipatie*. Groningen: Tjeenk Willink.

Langlois, J. H., & Stephan, C. (1977). The effects of physical attractiveness and ethnicity on children's behavioral attributions and peer preference. *Child Behavior*, 48, 1694-1698.

La Pierre, R. T. (1934). Attitudes versus actions. *Social Forces*, 13, 230-237.

Lasseigne, M. W. (1975). A study of peer and adult influence on moral beliefs of adolescents. *Adolescence*, 10, 227-230.

Laub, J. H., & Sampson, R. J. (1988). Unravelling families and delinquency: A reanalysis of the Glueck's data. *Criminology*, 26, 355-380.

Lauer, R. H., & Handel, W. H. (1977). *Social psychology: The theory and application of symbolic interactionism*. Boston: Houghton Mifflin.

Laufer, W. S., Johnson, J. A., & Hogan, R. (1981). Ego control and criminal behavior. *Journal of Personality and Social Psychology*, 41, 179-184.

Lawrence, R. (1985). Schoolperformance, containment theory and delinquent behavior. *Youth and Society*, 17, 69-96.

Laybourn, A. (1986). Traditional working class parenting: An undervalued system. *British Journal of Social Work*, 16, 625-644.

Leeuw, F. L., Van der Hoeven, E., Nederhof, A. J., & Bak, P. D. (1987). *Sociale bindingen van jongeren, kleine criminaliteit en beleid*. Leiden: Leids Instituut voor Sociaal Beleidsonderzoek.

Lefkowitz, M. M. (1977). *Growing up to be violent*. New York: Pergamon Press.

Lemert, E. M. (1972). *Human deviance, social problems and social control*. Englewood Cliffs, NJ: Prentice-Hall.

Leonard, E. B. (1982). *Women, crime, and society. A critique of theoretical criminology*. London: Longman.

Lerner, R. M., & Lerner, J. V. (1977). Effects of age, sex and physical attractiveness on child-peer relations, academic performance, and elementary school adjustment. *Developmental Psychology*, 13, 585-590.

Lerner, S. E., & Linder, R. L. (1975). Birth order and polydrug abuse among heroin addicts. *Journal of Drug Education*, 5, 285-291.

Leventhal, G. (1977). Female criminality: Is Women's Lib' to blame? *Psychological Reports*, 41, 1179-1182.

Leventhal, G. S. (1970). Influence of brothers and sisters on sex-role behavior. *Journal of Personality and Social Psychology*, 16, 452-465.

Levy, L., & Herzog, A. (1974). Effects of population density and crowding on health and social adaptation in the Netherlands. *Journal of Health and Social Behavior*, 15, 228-240.

Lewin, K. (1935). *A dynamic theory of personality*. New York: McGraw-Hill.

_____ (1951). *Field theory in social science*. Chicago: Umiv. of Chicago Press.

Lewis, H. (1954). *Deprived Children*. London: Oxford Univ. Press.

Liazos, A. (1978). School, alienation and delinquency. *Crime and Delinquency*, 24, 355-371.

Liker, J. K. (1982). Wage and status effects of employment on effective well-being among ex-felons. *American Sociological Review*, 47, 264-283.

Linden, R. (1978). Myth of middle-class delinquency: A test of the generalizability of the social control theory. *Youth and Society*, 9, 407-432.

Liska, A. E. (1969). Interpreting the causal structure of differential association theory. *Social Problems*, 16, 485-492.

_____ (1971). Aspirations, expectations, and delinquency: Stress and additive models. *Sociological Quarterly*, 12, 99-107.

_____ (1975). Causal structures underlying the relationship between delinquent involvement and delinquent peers. *Sociology and Social Research*, 58, 23-36.

_____ (1978). Deviant involvement, associations and attitudes: Specifying the underlying causal structure. *Sociology and Social Research*, 63, 73-88.

_____ , & Reed, M. D. (1985). Ties to conventional institutions and delinquency: Estimating reciprocal effects. *American Sociological Review*, 50, 547-560.

_____ , & Tausig, M. (1979). Theoretical interpretations of social class and racial differences in legal decision-making for juveniles. *Sociology Quarterly*, 20, 197-207.

Lively, E., Dinitz, S., & Reckless, W. (1962). Self concept as a predictor of juvenile delinquency. *American Journal of Orthopsychiatry*, 32, 159-168.

Lobitz, G. K., & Johnson, S. M. (1976). Normal versus deviant children: A multimethod comparison. *Journal of Abnormal Child Psychology*, 3, 353-376.

Loeber, R. (1982). The stability of antisocial and delinquent child behavior: A review. *Child Development*, 53, 1431-1446.

_____ (1986). What policy makers and practitioners can learn from family studies of juvenile conduct problems and delinquency. In J. Q. Wilson and G. C. Loury (Eds.), *From children to citizens: Families, schools and delinquency prevention*. New York: Springer.

_____ , & Dishion, T. (1982). Early predictors of male delinquency: A review. *Psychological Bulletin*, 94, 68-99.

_____ , & Schmaling, K. B. (1985a). Empirical evidence for overt and covert patterns of antisocial conduct problems: A meta-analysis. *Journal of Abnormal Child Psychology*, 13, 337-353.

_____ , & Schmaling, K. B. (1985b). The utility of differentiating between mixed and pure forms of antisocial child behavior. *Journal of Abnormal Child Psychology*, 13, 315-335.

_____ , & Walter, D. (1988). Artifacts in delinquency socialization and generalisation studies. *British Journal of Criminology*, 28, 461-477.

_____ , Weisman, W., & Reid, J. B. (1983). Family interaction of assaultive adolescents, stealers and non-delinquents. *Journal of Abnormal Child Psychology*, 11, 1-14.

Loring, I. (1718). *Duty and interests of young persons*. Boston.

Lorr, M., & Jenkins, R. L. (1953). Patterns of maladjustment in children. *Journal of*

Clinical Psychology, 9, 16-19.

Lösel, F. (1975). *Handlungskontrolle und Jugenddelinquenz.* Stuttgart.

Lund, N. L., & Salary, H. M. (1980). Measured self-concept in adjudicated juvenile offenders. *Adolescence*, 15, 65-74.

Lundman, R. (1974). Routine police arrest practices. *Social Problems*, 22, 127-141.

Lykken, D. T. (1982). Fearlessness: Its carefree charm and deadly risks. *Psychology Today*, 9, 20-28.

Maccoby, E. E., & Jacklin, C. N. (1974). *The psychology of sex differences.* Stanford: Stanford Univ. Press.

_____, & Jacklin, C. N. (1980). Sex differences in aggression: A rejoinder and reprise. *Child Development*, 51, 964-980.

_____, & Martin, J. A. (1983). Socialization in the context of the family: Parent-child interaction. In P. Mussen (Ed.), *Handbook of Child Psychology*, 4, New York: John Wiley and Sons.

Mack, J. L. (1969). Behavior ratings of recidivists and nonrecidivist delinquent males. *Psychological Reports*, 25, 260.

Magnusson, D., Stattin, H., & Allen, V. L. (1985). Biological maturation and social development: A longitudinal study of some adjustment processes from mid-adolescence to adulthood. *Journal of Youth and Adolescence*, 14, 267-283.

Mann, D. W. (1981). Age and differential predictability of delinquent behavior. *Social Forces*, 60, 97-113.

Mannheim, H. (1965). *Comparative Criminology.* London: Routledge and Kegan Paul.

_____, & Steward, W. A. C. (1964). *An introduction to the sociology of education.* London: Routledge and Kegan Paul.

Manning, M. L. (1983). Three myths concerning adolescence. *Adolescence*, 18, 823-829.

Mansfield, R., Gould, L., & Zvi Namenwirth, J. (1974). A socioeconomic model for the prediction of societal rates of property theft. *Social Forces*, 52, 462-472.

Mapes, G. (1968). Campus shoplifting. *Security World*, 29-32.

Marash, M. (1986). Gender, peer group experience, and seriousness of delinquency. *Journal of Research in Crime and Delinquency*, 23, 43-67.

Marcia, J. E. (1966). Development and validation of ego-identity status. *Journal of Personality and Social Psychology*, 3, 551-558.

Marcus, B. (1961). A dimensional study of a prison population. *British Journal of Criminology*, 1, 130-153.

Marjoribanks, K. (1979). *Families and their learning environment.* London: Routledge and Kegan Paul.

Markus, H. (1977). Self-schemata and processing information about the self. *Journal of Personality and Social Psychology*, 35, 63-78.

Markus, G. B., & Zajonc, R. B. (1975). Birth order and intellectual development. *Psychological Review*, 82, 74-88.

Marmet, O., & Meyer, A. (1988). *Kleine sociale psychologie.* Nijkerk: Intro.

Marwijck Kooij-Von Baumhauer, L. (1984). *Scholen verschillen.* Groningen: Wolters-Noordhoff.

Matsueda, R. L. (1982). Testing control theory and differential association: A causal modelling approach. *American Sociological Review*, 47, 498-504.

_____, & Heimer, K. (1987). Race, family structure, and delinquency: A test of differential association and social control theories. *American Sociological Review*, 52, 826-840.

Matthijssen, M. A. J. M. (1986). *De ware aard van balen*. Groningen: Wolters Noordhoff.

Matza, D. (1961). Subterranean traditions of youth. *The Annals of the American Academy of Political and Social Science*, 338, 102-108.

_____ (1964). *Delinquency and drift*. New York: John Wiley and Sons.

_____ (1969). *Becoming deviant*. Englewood Cliffs, NJ: Prentice-Hall.

_____, & Sykes, G. M. (1961). Juvenile delinquency and subterranean values. *American Sociological Review*, 26, 712-719.

Maurer, A. (1974). Corporal punishment. *American Psychologist*, 29, 614-626.

Mawby, R. T. (1977). Truancy: Data from self-report study. *Durham and Newcastle Research Review*, 8, 21-34.

_____ (1980). Sex and crime: The results of self-report study. *British Journal of Sociology*, 31, 525-543.

Maxim, P. S. (1985). Cohort size and juvenile delinquency: A test of the Easterlin hypothesis. *Social Forces*, 63, 661-681.

Maxwell, G. (1966). Adolescent powerlessness and delinquent behaviour. *Social Problems*, 14, 35-47.

Mays, J. B. (1963). *Crime and the social structure*. London.

McClelland, A. M. (1982). Changing rates or changing roles: Adolescent female delinquency re-assessed. *Journal of Adolescence*, 5, 85-98.

McClintock, F. H. (1963). *Crimes of Violence*. London: MacMillan.

McCord, J. (1978). Comments on "self esteem and delinquency". *Journal of Youth and Adolescence*, 7, 291-293.

_____ (1979). Some child-rearing antecedents of criminal behavior in adult men. *Journal of Personality and Social Psychology*, 34, 1477-1486.

_____ (1982). A longitudinal view of the relationship between parental absence and crime. In J. Gunn and D. Farrington (Eds.), *Abnormal offenders, delinquency and the criminal justice system*. New York: John Wiley and Sons.

_____, & McCord, W. (1964). The effects of parental role model and criminality. In R. Calvin, *Readings in juvenile delinquency*. Philadelphia.

McCord, W., McCord, J., & Zola, I. K. (1959). *The origins of crime*. New York: Columbia Univ. Press.

McCrae, R.R., & Costa, P. I. (1985). Comparison of EPI and psychoticism scales with measures of the five factor model of personality. *Personality and Individual Differences*, 6, 587-597.

_____, & Costa, P. I. (1986). Clinical assessment can benefit from recent advances in personality psychology. *American Psychologist*, 41, 1001-1003.

McDermott, M.J. (1983). Crime in the school and in the community: Offenders, victims and fearful youth. *Crime and Delinquency*, 29, 270-282.

McDonald, L. (1969). *Social class and delinquency*. London: Faber and Faber.

McGuire J. M. (1973). Aggression and sociometric status with preschool children. *Sociometry*, 36, 542-549.

McGurk, B. J., Bolton, N., & Smith, M. (1978). Some psychological, educational and criminological variables related to recidivism in delinquent boys. *British Journal of Social and Clinical Psychology*, 17, 251-254.

McKissack, I. J. (1973). The peak age for property crimes. *British Journal of Criminology*, 13, 253-261.

_____ (1974). A less delinquent cohort. *British Journal of Criminology*, 14, 158-164.

McMichael, P. (1979). The hen or the egg, which comes first - antisocial emotional disorders or reading ability? *British Journal of Educational Psychology*, 49, 226-238.

Meddinus, C. (1965). Delinquents perceptions of their parents. *Journal of Consulting Psychology*, 29, 592-593.

Megargee, E. I., & Hokanson, J. E. (1970). *The dynamics of aggression*. New York: Harper and Row.

Menard, S., & Moore, B. J. (1984). A structuralist critique of the I.Q.-delinquency hypothesis: Theory and evidence. *American Journal of Sociology*, 89, 1347-1378.

Merrill, M. A. (1947). *Problems of child delinquency*. Boston: Houghton Mifflin.

Merry, S. E. (1981). *Urban danger: Life in a neighbourhood of strangers*. Philadelphia: Temple Univ. Press.

Merton, R. K. (1968). *Social theory and social structure*. New York: The Free Press.

_____, & Nisbet, R. A. (1961). *Contemporary social problems*. New York: Harcourt, Brace and World.

Meyer, J. P., & Pepper, S. (1977). Need compatibility and marital adjustment in young married couples. *Journal of Personality and Social Psychology*, 35, 331-342.

Middelton, R., & Putney, S. (1962). Religion, normative standards, and behavior. *Sociometry*, 25, 141-152.

Miller, J. Z., & Rose, R. J. (1982). Familial resemblance in locus of control: A twin-family study of the internal-external scale. *Journal of Personality and Social Psychology*, 42, 535-540.

Miller, M. (1965). The place of religion in the lives of juvenile offenders. *Federal Probation*, 29, 50-54.

Miller, M. O., & Gold, M. (1984). Iatrogenesis in the juvenile justice system. *Youth and Society*, 16, 83-111.

Miller, P. M. (1974). A note on sex-differences on the semantic differential. *British Journal of Social and Clinical Psychology*, 13, 33-36.

Miller, T. P. (1961). The child who refuses to attend school. *American Journal of Psychiatry*, 118, 398-404.

Miller, W. B. (1958). Lower class culture as a generating milieu of gang delinquency. *Journal of Social Issues*, 14, 5-19.

_____ (1973). Race, sex and gangs: The Molls. *Society*, 11, 32-35.

_____ (1983). Youth, gangs and groups. *Encyclopedia*, Vol. 4, 1671-1679.

Milliones, J. (1978). Relationship between perceived child temperament and maternal behavior. *Child Development*, 49, 1255-1257.

Minor, W. W. (1981). Techniques of neutralization: A reconceptualization and empirical examination. *Journal of Research in Crime and Delinquency*, 18, 295-318.

_____ (1984). Neutralization as a hardening process: Considerations in the modelling change. *Social Forces*, 62, 995-1019.

Mischel, W. (1961). Preference for delayed reinforcement and social responsibility. *Journal of Abnormal and Social Psychology*, 62, 1-7.

_____ (1976). *Introduction to Personality*. New York: Holt, Rinehart and Winston.

_____, & Galligan, C. (1964). Delay of gratification, motivation for the prohibited gratification, and responses to temptation. *Journal of Abnormal and Social Psychology*, 69, 411-417.

Mitchell, J., & Dodder, R. A. (1980). An examination of types of delinquency through path analysis. *Journal of Youth and Adolescence*, 9, 239-248.

_____, & Dodder, R. A. (1983). Types of neutralization and types of delinquency.

Journal of Youth and Adolescence, 12, 307-318.

Mitchell, S., & Rosa, P. (1981). Boyhood behavior problems as precursors of criminality: A fifteen year follow-up study. *Journal of Child Psychology and Psychiatry*, 22, 19-33.

Moffitt, T. E., & Silva, P. A. (1988). IQ and delinquency: A direct test of the differential detection hypothesis. *Journal of Abnormal Psychology*, 97, 320-333.

Monachesi, E. D., & Hathaway, S. R. (1969). The personality of delinquents. In J. N. Butcher (Ed.), *MMPI: Research development and clinical applications*. New York: McGraw-Hill.

Monahan, T. (1957). Family status and the delinquent child: A reappraisal and some new findings. *Social Forces*, 35, 251-258.

Money, J., & Ehrhardt, A. A. (1972). *Man and woman, boy and girl*. London: John Hopkins Univ. Press.

Mönks, F. J., & Heusinkveld, H. G. (1973). De mythe van de generatiekloof. In J. de Wit, H. Bolle, and J. Jesserun Cardozo-Van Hoorn (Eds.), *Psychologen over het kind*. Groningen: Tjeenk Willink.

Montagu, A. (1959). *Human heredity*. New York: World Publishing Company.

Montemayor, R., & Eisen, M. (1977). The development of self-conceptions from childhood to adolescence. *Developmental Psychology*, 13, 314-319.

Mooij, T. (1980). Schoolproblemen en uitval in het voortgezet onderwijs. *Pedagogische Studiën*, 57, 369-382.

_____ (1982). Onderwijsleersituatie en lesondergravend gedrag van lto-leerlingen. In E. Diekerhof (Ed.), *Leren, wat moet je ermee?* Muiderberg: Coutinho.

_____ (1984). Leerlingproblemen en leerlingverzet: Een diagnose van het onderwijs. In C. Van Calcar et al. (Eds.), *De school, een wissel tussen leven & werk*. Lisse: Swets en Zeitlinger.

Moore, D. R., Chamberlain, P., & Mukai, L. H. (1979). Children at risk for delinquency: A follow-up comparison of aggressive children and children who steal. *Journal of Abnormal Child Psychology*, 7, 345-355.

Morris, R. R. (1964). Female delinquency and relation problems, *Social Forces*, 43, 82-99.

_____ (1965). Attitudes toward delinquency by delinquents, non-delinquents and their friends. *British Journal of Criminology*, 5, 249-265.

Murstein, B. I., & Christy, P. (1976). Physical attractiveness and marriage adjustment in middle-aged couples. *Journal of Personality and Social Psychology*, 34, 537-542.

Mury, G., & De Gauléjac, V. (1974). Les jeunes de la rue. *Sauvegarde de l'Enfance*, 24, 560-583.

Mutsaers, M. (1987). Experiment criminaliteitspreventie binnen het LBO. *Justitiële Verkenningen*, 13, 85-112.

Neidhart, F. (1970). Bezugspunkte einer soziologischen Theorie der Jugend. In F. Neidhart et al., *Jugend im Spektrum der Wissenschaften*. München: Juventa Verlag.

Nettler, G. (1978). *Explaining crime*. New York: McGraw-Hill.

Neustrom, M., Jamieson, G., Manuel, D., & Gramling, B. (1988). Regional unemployment and crime trends: An empirical examination. *Journal of Criminal Justice*, 16, 395-402.

Newcomb, A. F., & Bukowski, W. M. (1983). Social impact and social preference as determinants of children's peer group status. *Developmental Psychology*, 19, 856-867.

Newman, P. R., & Newman, B. M. (1976). Early adolescence and its conflicts: Group identity versus alienation. *Adolescence*, 11, 261-274.

Newton, C. H., Sheldon, R. G., & Jenkins, S. (1975). The homogenization process within the juvenile justice process. *International Journal of Criminology and Penology*, 3, 213-227.

Nielsen, A., & Gerber, D. (1979). Psychosocial aspects of truancy in early adolescence. *Adolescence*, 14, 313-326.

Noblit, G. W. (1976). The adolescent experience and delinquency: School versus sub-cultural effects. *Youth and Society*, 8, 27-44.

Norman, W. T. (1963). Replicated factor structure in peer nomination personality ratings. *Journal of Abnormal and Social Psychology*, 66, 574-583.

Normandeau, A. (1971). Quelques faits sur le vol dans les grands magasins à Montréal. *Canadian Journal of Criminology and Corrections*, 13, 251-265.

Nye, F. I. (1958). *Family relationships and delinquent behavior*. New York: John Wiley and Sons.

_____, & Short, J. F. (1957). Scaling delinquent behavior. *American Sociological Review*, 22, 326-331.

_____, Short, J. F., & Olson, V. J. (1958). Socioeconomic status and delinquent behavior. *American Journal of Sociology*, 63, 381-389.

Oakley, A. (1972). *Sex, gender and society*. New York: Harper and Row.

O'Brien, R. M. (1989). Relative cohort size and age-specific crime rates: An age-period-relativity-cohort-size model. *Criminology*, 27, 57-78.

O'Donnell, W. J. (1979). Adolescent self-reported and peer-reported self esteem. *Adolescence*, 14, 465-470.

Offer, D., & Offer, J. (1978). *From teenage to young manhood*. New York: Basic Books.

Offord, D. R., Poushinsky, M. F., & Sullivan, K. (1978). School performance, IQ and delinquency. *British Journal of Criminology*, 18, 110-127.

Ogbu, J. (1974). *The next generation*. New York: Academic Press.

Ogburn, W. F. (1950). *Social change with respect to culture and original nature* (1922). New York: The Viking Press.

_____, & Nimkoff, M. F. (1946). *Sociology*. Boston: Houghton Mifflin.

O'Hagan, F. J. (1976). Gang characteristics: An empirical survey. *Journal of Child Psychology and Psychiatry*, 17, 305-314.

Olejnik, A. (1980). Adults' moral reasoning with children. *Child Development*, 51, 1285-1288.

Olweus, D. (1978). *Aggression in the schools: Bullies and whipping boys*. Washington: John Wiley and Sons.

_____ (1979). Stability of aggressive reactions in males: A review. *Psychological Bulletin*, 86, 852-857.

_____ (1980a). Familial and temperamental determinants of aggressive behavior in adolescents: A causal analysis. *Developmental Psychology*, 14, 644-660.

_____ (1980b). The consistency issue in personality psychology revisited - with special reference to aggression. *British Journal of Social and Clinical Psychology*, 19, 377-390.

_____ (1987). Schoolyard bullying - grounds for intervention. *School Safety*, 4, 4-11.

O'Malley, P. M., & Bachman, J. G. (1979). Self esteem and education: Sex and cohort comparisons among high school seniors. *Journal of Personality and Social Psychology*, 37, 1153-1159.

Ooyen-Houben, M. M. J., & Berben, E. G. M. J. (1988). Protectieve factoren. Een paradigmatische ommezwaai of nieuwe kleren van de keizer. *Justitiële Verkenningen*, 14, 90-117.

Orlebeke, J. F. (1972). *Aktivering, extraversie en sterkte van het zenuwstelsel*. Assen: Van Gorcum.

Orsagh, T., & Witte, A. D. (1981). Economic status and crime: Implications for offender rehabilitation. *Journal of Criminal Law and Criminology*, 72, 1055-1071.

Osborn, S. G., & West, D. J. (1978). The effectiveness of various predictors of criminal careers. *Journal of Adolescence*, 1, 101-117.

_____, & West, D. J. (1979). Conviction records of fathers and sons compared. *British Journal of Criminology*, 19, 120-133.

Osgood, D. W., Johnston, L., O'Malley, P. M., & Bachman, J. G. (1988). The generality of deviance in late adolescence and early adulthood. *American Sociological Review*, 53, 81-93.

Osofsky, J. D., & O'Connell, E. J. (1977). Patterning of newborn behavior in an urban population. *Child Development*, 48, 532-536.

Ouston, J. (1984). Delinquency, family backgrounds and educational attainment. *British Journal of Criminology*. 24, 2-26.

Owen, D. R., & Sines, J. O. (1970). Heredity of personality in children. *Behavior Genetics*, 1, 235-248.

Palmer, T. (1974). The California Youth Authority Treatment Project. *Federal Probation*, 38, 3-14.

Panella, D. H., Cooper, P. F., & Henggeler, S. W. (1982). Peer relations in adolescence. In S. W. Henggeler (Ed.), *Delinquency and adolescent psychopathology*. Boston: John Wright.

Parker, J. G., & Asher, S. R. (1987). Peer relations and later personal adjust-ment: Are low-accepted children at risk? *Psychological Bulletin*, 102, 357-389.

Parker, R. W., & Horwitz, A. V. (1986). Unemployment, crime and imprisonment: A panel approach. *Criminology*, 24, 751-774.

Parsons, T. (1951). *The social system*. Glencoe, Ill: The Free Press.

_____, & Bales, R. F. (1956). *Family, socialization and interaction process*. London: Routledge and Kegan Paul.

_____, & Shils, E. (1962). *Toward a general theory of action*. New York: Harper and Row.

Paternoster, R. (1989). Absolute and restrictive deterrence in a panel of youth. *Social Problems*, 36, 298-309.

_____, & Triplett, R. (1988). Disaggregating self-reported delinquency and its implications for theory. *Criminology*, 26, 591-625.

Patterson, G. R. (1980). Children who steal. In T. Hirschi and M. Gottfredson, *Understanding crime: Current theory and research*. Beverly Hills: Sage.

_____ (1986). Performance models for antisocial boys. *American Psychologist*, 41, 432-444.

_____, & Dishion, T. J. (1985). Contribution of families and peers to delinquency. *Criminology*, 23, 63-79.

_____, & Stouthamer-Loeber, M. (1984). The correlation of family management practices and delinquency. *Child Development*, 55, 1299-1307.

Pawlik, K. (1968). *Dimensionen des Verhaltens. Eine Einführung in Methodik und Ergebnisse faktoranalytischer psychologischer Forschung*. Bern: Hans Huber.

Peery, J. C. (1979). Popular, amiable, isolated, rejected: A reconceptualization of sociometric status in preschool children. *Child Development*, 50, 1231-1234.

Perry, D. G., Kusel, S. J., & Perry, L. C. (1988). Victims of peer aggression. *Developmental Psychology*, 24, 807-814.

Perry, J. D., Guidebaldi, J., & Kehle, T. J. (1979). Kindergarten competencies as predictors of third grade classroom behavior and achievement. *Journal of Educational Psychology*, 71, 443-450.

Peters, J. F. (1985). Adolescents as socialization agents to parents. *Adolescence*, 20, 15-27.

Peterson, D. R., & Becker, W. C. (1965). Family interactions in delinquency. In H. C. Quay, *Juvenile Delinquency*, New York: John Wiley and Sons.

_____, Quay, H. C., & Cameron, G. R. (1959). Personality and background factors in juvenile delinquency as inferred from questionnaire responses. *Journal of Consulting Psychology*, 23, 395-399.

Peterson, G. B., Hey, R. N., & Peterson, L. R. (1979). Intersection of family development and moral stage frameworks: Implications for theory and research. *Journal of Marriage and the Family*, 41, 229-235.

Peterson, V. W. (1969). Tipping the scales of justice. *Security World*, 6, 15, 17-18, 22, 125.

Philips, J. C., & Kelly, D. H. (1979). School failures and delinquency, which causes which? *Criminology*, 17, 194-207.

Piaget, J. (1965). *The moral judgment of the child*. New York: The Free Press.

Pickford, J. H., Signori, E. I., & Rempel, H. (1967). Husband-wife difference in personality traits as a factor in marital happiness. *Psychological Reports*, 20, 1087-1090.

Pierson, G. R., & Kelly, R. F. (1963). HSPQ norms on a state wide delinquent population. *Journal of Psychology*, 57, 243-249.

Piliavin, I. M., Vadum, A. C., & Hardijck, J. A. (1969). Delinquency, personal costs and parental treatment: A test of reward-cost model of juvenile criminality. *Journal of Criminal Law, Criminology and Police Science*, 60, 165-172.

Piliavin, I. M., Thornton, C., Gartner, R., & Matsueda, R. L. (1986). Crime, deterrence, and rational choice. *American Sociological Review*, 51, 101-119.

Pinatel, J. (1971). *La société criminogène*. Paris.

Pink, W. T. (1984). Schools, youth and justice. *Crime and Delinquency*, 30, 349-461.

Pirog-Good, M. A. (1986). Modelling employment and crime relationships. *Social Science Quarterly*, 67, 767-784.

Plomin, R. (1983). Developmental behavioral genetics. *Child Development*, 54, 253-259.

_____, & Rowe, D. C. (1977). A twin study of temperament in young children. *The Journal of Psychology*, 97, 107-113.

_____, & Rowe, D. C. (1979). Genetic and environmental etiology of social behavior in infancy. *Developmental Psychology*, 15, 62-72.

Polk, K. (1969). Class, strain and rebellion among adolescents. *Social Problems*, 17, 214-223.

_____ (1971). A reassessment of middle-class delinquency. *Youth and Society*, 2, 333-353.

_____ (1975). Schools and the delinquency experience. *Criminal Justice and Behavior*, 4, 315-338.

_____, & Pink, W. T. (1971). Youth culture and the schools: A replication. *British*

Journal of Sociology, 22, 160-171.

_____, & Schafer, W. E. (1972). *Schools and delinquency*. Englewood Cliffs, NJ: Prentice-Hall.

_____, Frease, D., & Richmond, F. L. (1974). Social class, school experience and delinquency. *Criminology*, 12, 1974, 84-96.

Pollak, O. (1950). *The criminality of women*. Philadelphia.

Poole, E. D., & Regoli, R. M. (1979). Parental support, delinquent friends and delinquency: A test of interaction effects. *Journal of Criminal Law and Criminology*, 70, 188-193.

Porter, B., & O'Leary, K. D. (1982). Marital discord and childhood behavior problems. *Journal of Abnormal Child Psychology*, 8, 287-296.

Porteus, M. A. (1985). Developmental aspects of adolescent problem disclosure in England and Ireland. *Journal of Child Psychology and Psychiatry* and Allied Disciplines, 26, 465-478.

Postma, H. (1931). *De oorzaken van antisociaal gedrag bij kinderen liggende in de samenstelling van het gezin.*

Prentice, N. M., & Kelly, F. J. (1963). Intelligence and delinquency: A reconsideration. *Journal of Social Psychology*, 60, 327-337.

Quay, H. C. (1964a). Personality dimensions in delinquent males as inferred from factor analysis of behavior ratings. *Journal of Research in Crime and Delinquency*, 1, 33-37.

_____ (1964b). Dimensions of personality in delinquent boys as inferred from the factor analysis of case history data. *Child Development*, 35, 479-484.

_____ (1965a). *Juvenile Delinquency*. New York: Van Nostrand Reinhold Company.

_____ (1965b). Psychopathic personality as pathological stimulation seeking. *American Journal of Psychiatry*, 122, 180-183.

_____ (1966). Personality patterns in preadolescent delinquent boys. *Educational and Psychological Measurement*, 16, 99-110.

_____ (1987a). *Handbook of juvenile delinquency*. New York: John Wiley and Sons.

_____ (1987b). Intelligence. In H. C. Quay, *Handbook of juvenile delinquency*. New York: John Wiley and Sons.

_____ (1987c). Patterns of delinquent behavior. In H. C Quay, *Handbook of juvenile delinquency*. New York: John Wiley and Sons.

_____, Peterson, D. R., & Consalvi, C. (1960). The interpretation of three personality factors in juvenile delinquency. *Journal of Consulting Psychology*, 24, 555.

Quensel, S. (1971). Delinquenzbelastung und soziale Schicht bei nichtbestraften männlichen Jugendlichen. *Monatsschrift für Kriminologie und Strafrechtsreform*, 54, 236-262.

Quinney, R. (1977). *Class, state and crime: On the theory and practice of criminal justice*. New York: McKay.

Rahav, G. (1980). Birth order and delinquency. *British Journal of Criminology*, 20, 385-395.

_____ (1982). Family size and delinquency. *Sociology and Social research*, 66, 43-51.

Randolph, M. H., Richardson, H., & Johnson, R. C. (1961). A comparison of social and solitary male delinquents. *Journal of Consulting Psychology*, 25, 293-295.

Rankin, J. H. (1977). Investigating the interrelations among social control variables and conformity. *Journal of Criminal Law and Criminology*, 67, 470-480.

_____ (1983). The family context of delinquency. *Social Problems*, 30, 446-479.

Reckless, W. C. (1961). Halttheorie. *Monatsschrift für Kriminologie und Strafrechtsre form*, 44, 1-14.

_____, & Dinitz, S. (1967). Pioneering with self-concept as a vulnerability factor on delinquency. *Journal of Criminal Law, Criminology and Police Science*, 58, 515-523.

_____, & Dinitz, S. (1972). *The prevention of juvenile delinquency*. Columbus, OH: Ohio State Univ. Press.

_____, & Shoham, S. (1963). Norm containment theory as applied to delinquency and crime. *Excerpta Criminologica*, 3, 637-644.

_____, Dinitz, S., & Murray, E. (1956a). Self-concept as an insulator against delinquency. *American Sociological Review*, 21, 744.

_____, Dinitz, S., & Murray, E. (1956b). The self component in potential delinquency and potential non-delinquency. *American Sociological Review*, 21, 744-746.

_____, Dinitz, S. & Murray, E. (1957). The "good boy" in a high delinquency area. *Journal of Criminal Law, Criminology and Police Science*, 48, 18-25.

Regoli, R. M., & Poole, E. D. (1978). The commitment of delinquents to their misdeeds: A re-examination. *Journal of Criminal Justice*, 6, 261-269.

Reinarman, C., & Fagan, J. (1988). Social organization and differential association: A research note from a longitudinal study of violent juvenile offenders. *Crime and Delinquency*, 34, 307-327.

Reinert, G. B., & Zinnecker, J. (1978). *Schüler im Schulbetrieb*. Hamburg: Rowohlt.

Reiss, A. J., & Rhodes, A. C. (1961). The distribution of juvenile delinquency in the social class structure. *American Sociological Review*, 26, 720-732.

Rest, J. R. (1983). Morality. In P. H. Mussen (Ed.), *Handbook of child psychology*. New York: John Wiley and Sons.

Reynolds, D. (1980). Schoolfactors and truancy. In L. Hersov and I. Berg (Eds.), *Out of school*. New York: John Wiley and Sons.

Rhodes, A. L., & Reiss, A. J. (1970). The religious factor and delinquent behavior. *Journal of Research in Crime and Delinquency*, 7, 83-98.

Ricks, M. H. (1985). The social transmission of parental behavior: Attachments across generations. In I. Bretherton and E. Waters (Eds.), Growing points of attachment theory and research. *Monograph of the Society for Research in Child development*, No 209, 50, Chicago: Umiv. of Chicago Press.

Riege, M. G. (1972). Parental affection and juvenile delinquency in girls. *British Journal of Delinquency*, 12, 55-73.

Rijksen, P. (1955). *Sociale en psychologische aspecten der gezinsonvolledigheid*. Assen: Van Gorcum.

Riley, D. (1987). Time and crime: The link between teenager lifestyle and delinquency. *Journal of Quantitative Criminology*, 3, 339-354.

_____, & Shaw, M. (1985). *Parental supervision and juvenile delinquency*. London: HMSO.

Riskin, J., & Faunce, E. E. (1970a). Family interaction scales I. Theoretical framework and method. *Archives of General Psychiatry*, 22, 504-512.

_____, & Faunce, E. E. (1970b). Family interaction scales III. Discussion and methodology and substantive findings. *Archives of General Psychiatry*, 22, 527-537.

Roback, A. A. (1927). *Bibliography of character and personality*. Cambridge.

Robert, C. N. (1973). Le vol des mineurs dans les grands magasins. *Revue de droit pénal et de criminologie*, 53, 473-496.

Robert, P., & Lascoumes, P. (1974). *Les bandes d'adolescents*. Paris: Les Editions

Ouvrières.

_____, Pasturaud, C., Krementchousky, A., & Lambert, T. (1970). Jeunes adultes délinquants. *Annales Internationales de Criminologie*, 9, 657-682.

Robins, L., & Hill, S. (1966). Assessing the contributions of family structure, class, and peer groups to delinquency. *Journal of Criminal Law, Criminology, and Police Science*, 57, 325-334.

_____, West, P. A., & Herjanic, B. L. (1975). Arrests and delinquency in two generations: A study of black urban families and their children. *Journal of Child Psychology and Psychiatry*, 16, 125-140.

Rodick, J. D., & Henggeler, S. W. (1982). Parent-adolescent interaction and adolescent emancipation. In S. W. Henggeler (Ed.), *Delinquency and adolescent psychopathology*. Boston: John Wright.

Roff, M. (1961). Childhood interaction and adult conduct. *Journal of Abnormal and Social Psychology*, 63, 333-337.

Roff, J. D., & Wirt, R. D. (1984). Childhood aggression and social adjustment as antecedents of delinquency. *Journal of Abnormal Child Psychology*, 12, 111-126.

_____, & Wirt, R. D. (1985). The specificity of childhood problem behavior for adolescent and young adult adjustment. *Journal of Clinical Psychology*, 41, 564-571.

Rojeck, D. G., & Erickson, M. L. (1982). Delinquent careers: A test of the career escalation model. *Criminology*, 20, 5-28.

Rollins, B. C., & Thomas, D. L. (1979). Parental support, power and control techniques in the socialization of children. In W. R. Burr, R. Hill, F. I. Nye, and I. L. Reis (Eds.), *Contemporary theories about the family, I*, London: The Free Press.

Rosen. L. (1970). The broken home and male delinquency. In M. Wolfgang, L. Savitz, and N. Johnston (Eds.), *The sociology of crime and delinquency*. New York: John Wiley and Sons.

_____ (1985). Family and delinquency: Structure or function. *Criminology*, 23, 553-573.

_____, & Nielson, K. (1982). Broken homes. In L. Savitz and N. Johnston, *Contemporary criminology*. New York: John Wiley and Sons.

Rosenberg F., & Rosenberg, M. (1978). Self-esteem and delinquency. *Journal of Youth and Adolescence*, 7, 279-291.

Rosenfeld, J., & Rosenstein, E. (1973). Toward a conceptual framework for the study of parent-absent families. *Journal of Marriage and the Family*, 35, 131-135.

Rosenthal, A. M. (1964). *Thirty-eight witnesses*. New York: McGraw-Hill.

Rossi, P., Waite, E., Bose, C. E., & Berk, R. E. (1974). The seriousness of crimes: Normative structure and individual differences. *American Sociological Review*, 39, 224-237.

Rotenberg, M., & Nachshon, I. (1979). Impulsiveness and aggression among Israeli delinquents. *British Journal of Social and Clinical Psychology*, 18, 59-63.

Rothstein, E. (1962). Attributes related to high social status: A comparison of the perception of delinquent and non-delinquent boys. *Social Problems*, 10, 75-83.

Rowe, D. C. (1983). Biometrical genetic models of self-reported delinquent behavior: A twin study. *Behavior Genetics*, 13, 473-489.

_____, & Osgood, D. W. (1984). Heredity and social theories of delinquency: A reconsideration. *American Sociological Review*, 49, 526-540.

_____, & Plomin, R. (1981). The importance of nonshared environmental (E1) influences in behavioral development. *Developmental Psychology*, 17, 517-531.

Royce, J. R. (1973). The conceptual framework for multi-factor theory of individuality. In J. R. Royce (Ed.), *Multivariate analysis and psychological theory*. London: Academic Press.

Rubel, J. (1978a). *HEW's Safe School study: What it says and what it means for teachers and administrators*. Maryland: Institute for Reduction of Crime.

_____ (1978b). Analysis and critique of HEW's Safe School report to the Congress. *Crime and Delinquency*, 24, 257-265.

Rubin, J. Z., Provenzano, F. J., & Luria, Z. (1974). The eye of the beholder: Parent's views on sex of newborns. *American Journal of Orthopsychiatry*, 44, 512-519.

Rubinstein, H. (1980). *The link between crime and the built environment: The current state of knowledge*. Washington DC: National Institute of Justice.

Ruma, E. H., & Mosher, D. L. (1967). Relationship between moral judgement and guilt in delinquent boys. *Journal of Abnormal Psychology*, 72, 122-127.

Rushton, J. P. (1987). Distal-proximal approaches to aggression: A reply to Campbell, Munce and Bibel. *British Journal of Social Psychology*, 26, 185-186.

_____, & Chrisjohn, R. D. (1981). Extraversion, neuroticism, psychoticism and self-reported delinquency: Evidence from eight separate samples. *Personality and Individual Differences*, 2, 11-20.

_____, & Erdle, S. (1987). Evidence for aggressive and delinquent personality. *British Journal of Social Psychology*, 26, 87-89.

_____, Russell, R. J., & Wells, P. A. (1985). Criminality and genetic similarity theory. *Journal of Social and Biological Structures*, 8, 63-86.

Rutenfrans, C. J. C. (1983). Opp en vrouwencriminaliteit. *Tijdschrift voor Criminologie*, 25, 82-89.

_____ (1989). *Criminaliteit en sexe*. Arnhem: Gouda Quint.

Rutter, M. (1971a). Normal psychosexual development. *Journal of Child Psychology and Psychiatry*, 11, 259-283.

_____ (1971b). Parent-child separation: Psychological effects on children. *Journal of Child Psychology and Psychiatry*, 12, 233-260.

_____ (1972). *Maternal deprivation reassessed*. London: Penguin.

_____ (1977). Brain damage syndromes in childhood: Concepts and findings. *Journal of Child Psychology and Psychiatry*, 18, 1-21.

_____ (1979a). Maternal deprivation, 1972-1978: New findings, new concepts, new approaches. *Child Development*, 50, 283-305.

_____ (1979b). *Changing youth in a changing society. Patterns of adolescent development and disorder*. London: Nuffield Provincial Hospital Trust.

_____ (1980). School influences on children behavior and development. *Pediatrics*, 65, 208-220.

_____, & Giller, H. (1983). *Juvenile delinquency: Trends and perspectives*. New York: Guilford.

_____, Graham, P., Chadwick, O. F. D., & Yule, W. (1976). Adolescent turmoil: Fact or fiction? *Journal of Child Psychology and Psychiatry*, 17, 35-36.

_____, Tizard, J., & Whitmore, K. (1970). *Education, health and behavior*. London: Longman.

_____, Maugham, B., Mortimer, P., & Ouston, J. (1979). *Fifteen thousand hours: Secondary schools and their effects on children*. London: Open Books.

Ryder, R. G. (1967). Birth to maturity revisited. *Journal of Personality and Social Psychology*, 7.

Saklofske, D. H., & Eysenck, S. B. G. (1983). Impulsiveness and venturesomeness in Canadian children. *Psychological Reports*, 52, 147-152.

Salas, L., & Surette, R. (1984). The historical roots and developments of criminological statistics. *Journal of Criminal Justice*, 12, 457-465.

Sampson, R. J. (1986). Effects of socioeconomic context on official reaction to juvenile delinquency. *American Sociological Review*, 51, 876-885.

_____, & Castellano, T. C. (1982). Economic inequality and personal victimisation: An areal perspective. *British Journal of Criminology*, 22, 363-385.

Santrock, J. W., & Tracy, R. (1978). Effects of children's family structure status on the development of stereotypes by teachers. *Journal of Educational Psychology*, 70, 754-757.

_____, & Warshak, R. A. (1979). Father custody and social development in boys and girls. *Journal of Social Issues*, 35, 112-125.

Satterfield, J. H., Hoppe, C. M., & Schell, A. M. (1982). A prospective study of delinquency in 110 adolescent boys with attention deficit disorder and 88 normal adolescent boys. *American Journal of Psychiatry*, 139, 795-798.

Savin-Williams, R. C. (1979). Dominance hierarchies in groups of early adolescents. *Child Development*, 50, 923-935.

_____, & Demo, D. H. (1984). Developmental change and stability in adolescent self-concept. *Developmental Psychology*, 20, 1100-1110.

Savitz, L. (1967). *Dilemmas in criminology*. New York: McGraw-Hill.

_____, Rosen, L., & Lalli, M. (1980). Delinquency and gang membership related to victimization. *Victimology*, 5, 152-160.

Scarpitti, F. R. (1965). Delinquent and non-delinquent perceptions of self. Values and opportunity. *Mental Hygiene*, 49, 399-404.

Scarr, S. (1965). The inheritance of sociability. *American Psychologist*, 20, 524.

_____ (1966). Genetic factors in activity motivation. *Child Development*, 37, 663-673.

_____ (1969). Social introversion-extraversion as a heritable response. *Child Development*, 40, 823-832.

_____, & McCartney, K. (1983). How people make their own environments. *Child Development*, 54, 424-435.

Schachter, F. F., Shore, E., Feldman-Rotman, S., Marquis, R. E., & Campbell, S. (1976). Sibling deidentification. *Developmental Psychology*, 12, 418-427.

Schaefer, E. S. (1965). Children's report of parental behavior: An inventory. *Child Development*, 36, 413-424.

Schafer, W., Olexa, C., & Polk, W. (1972). Programmed for social class. In W. Schafer and K. Polk (Eds.), *Schools and delinquency*. Englewood Cliffs.

Schaie, K. W., & Parham, I. A. (1976). Stability of personality traits: Fact or fable. *Journal of Personality and Social Psychology*, 34, 146-158.

Schaufeli, W. B. (1988). *Unemployment and psychological health: An investigation among Dutch professionals*. Groningen: Rijksuniversiteit.

Schelsky, H. (1957). *Die skeptische Generation*. Düsseldorf: Eugen Diederich Verlag.

Schneider, H. J. (1987). *Kriminologie*. Berlin-New York: Walter de Gruyter.

Schur, E. M. (1971). *Labelling deviant behavior*. New York: Harper.

Schuurman, M. I. M. (1984). *Scholieren over onderwijs*. Leiden: NIPG.

_____ (1985). Schoolorganisatie en functioneren van leerlingen. In B. P. M. Creemers, J. H. G. I. Giesbers et al. (Eds.), *Handboek schoolorganisatie en onderwijs management*. Alphen aan den Rijn: Samson.

Schwabe-Holein, M. (1984). Kinderdelinquenz. *Praxis der Kinderpsychologie und Kinderpsychiatrie*, 33, 301-308.

Schwartz, M., & Tangri, S. S. (1965). A note on self-concept as an insulator against delinquency. *American Sociological Review*, 30, 922-926.

Schwartz, R. D., & Orleans, S. (1967). On legal sanctions. Chicago: Umiv. of Chicago Press.

Schwendinger, H., & Schwendinger, J. R. (1976). Delinquency and the collective varieties of youth. *Crime and Social Justice*, 5, 7-25.

Scutt, J. A. (1978). Debunking the theory of the female "masked criminal". *Australian and New Zealand Journal of Criminology*, 11, 23-43.

Sears, R. R., Maccoby, E., & Levin, H. (1957). *Patterns of child rearing*. New York: Harper and Row.

Sebald, H. (1968). *Adolescence: A sociological analysis*. New York: Appleton Century Crafts.

Sehli, A. (1971). Le traitement judiciaire des groupes de mineurs. *Revue de Droit Pénal et de Criminologie*, 52, 193-206.

Sellin, T. (1968). La "Nationale Crime Commisssion" et la recherche criminologique. *Revue de Science Criminelle et de Droit Pénal Comparé*, 3, 565-583.

Sells, S. B., Demaree, R. G., & Wills, D. P. (1970). Dimensions of Personality I. Conjoint factor structure in Guilford and Cattell trait markers. *Multivariate Behavioral Research*, 5, 391-422.

Selman, R. (1971). The relation of role taking to the development of moral judgment in children. *Child Development*, 42, 79-91.

Shannon, K. A. L., & Kafer, N. F. (1984). Reciprocity, trust and vulnerability in neglected and rejected children. *Journal of Psychology*, 117, 65-70.

Shapiro, D. (1965). *Neurotic styles*. New York: Basic Books.

Shapland, J., Rushton, J. P. & Campbell, A. (1975). Crime and Personality: Further evidence. *Bulletin of the British Psychological Society*, 28, 66-88.

Shaw, G. K., & Hare, E. H. (1965). The Maudsley Personality Inventory. *British Journal of Psychiatry*, 111, 226-235.

Shaw, C. R., & McKay, H. D. (1969). *Juvenile delinquency in urban areas*. Chicago: Umiv. of Chicago Press.

Sheppard, M. A., Goodstadt, M. S., & Willett, M. M. (1987). Peers or parents: Who has the most influence on cannabis use. *Journal of Drug Education*, 17.

Sherman, L. W. (1980). Causes of police behavior: The current state of quantitative research. *Journal of Research in Crime and Delinquency*, 17, 69-100.

Shideler, E. H. (1981). Family disintegration and the delinquent boy in the United States. *Journal of Criminal Law and Criminology*, 72, 709-732.

Short J. F. (1957). Differential association and delinquency. *Social Problems*, 4, 233-239.

_____ (1958). Differential association with delinquent friends and delinquent behavior. *Pacific Sociological Review*, 1, 20-25.

_____, & Strodtbeck, F. L. (1965). *Group process and gang delinquency*. Chicago: Univ. of Chicago Press.

Shorter, E. (1976). *The making of the modern family*. New York: Basic Books.

Shulman, M. H. (1951). Intelligence and delinquency. *Journal of Criminal Law and Criminology*, 41, 763-781.

Siegal, M. (1984). Economic deprivation and the quality of parent-child relations: A trickle-down framework. *Journal of Applied Developmental Psychology*, 5, 127-144.

Siegel, L. J., Rathus, S. A., & Ruppert, C. A. (1973). Values and delinquent youth: An empirical re-examination of theories of delinquency. *British Journal of Criminology*, 13, 237-245.

Sigvardsson, S., Cloninger, C. R., Bohman, M., & Von Knorring, A. L. (1982). Predisposition to petty criminality in Swedish adoptees III. Sex differences and validation of the male typology. *Archives of General Psychiatry*, 39, 1248-1253.

Simcha-Fagan, O., & Schwartz, J. E. (1986). Neighbourhood and delinquency: An assessment of contextual effects. *Criminology*, 24, 667-703.

Simon, R. J. (1975). *Women and crime*. Lexington, MA: Heath.

Simon, W., & Gagnon, J. H. (1976). The anomie affluence: A post Mertonian concept. *American Journal of Sociology*, 82, 356-378.

Singer, J., Brush, C., & Lubin, S. (1965). Some aspect of deindividuation: Identification and conformity. *Journal of Experimental Social Psychology*, 1, 356-378.

Skogan, W. G. (1977). Dimensions of the dark figure of unreported crime. *Crime and Delinquency*, 23, 41-50.

Slavin, S. H. (1978). Information processing defects in delinquents. In L. J. Hippchen (Ed.), *Ecological-biochemical approaches to treatment of delinquents and criminals*. New York: Van Nostrand Reinhold Company.

Slocum, W. L., & Stone, C. L. (1963). Family structure patterns and delinquent type behavior. *Marriage and Family Living*, 25, 202-208.

Smart, C. (1976). *Women, crime, and criminology: A feminist critique*. London: Routledge and Kegan Paul.

Smith, D. A., & Visher, A. (1980). Sex and involvement in deviance/crime: A quantitative review of the empirical literature. *American Sociological Review*, 45, 691-701.

Smith, J. A. (1980). A survey of adolescents' interests: Concern and information. *Adolescence*, 15, 475-482.

Smith, R. M., & Walters, J. (1978). Delinquent and non-delinquent's perception of their fathers. *Adolescence*, 13, 21-28.

Smith, S. (1982). Victimization in the inner city. *British Journal of Criminology*, 22, 386-404.

Snow, M. E., Jackson, C. N., & Maccoby, E. E. (1981). Birth-order differences in peer sociability on thirty three months. *Child Development*, 52, 589-595.

Snyder, J. J. (1977). Reinforcement analysis of problem and nonproblem families. *Journal of Abnormal Psychology*, 86, 528-535.

_____, & Patterson, G. (1987). Family interaction and delinquent behavior. In H. C. Quay (Ed.), *Handbook of juvenile delinquency*. New York: John Wiley and Sons.

_____, Dishion, T., & Patterson, G. R. (1986). Determinants and consequences of associating with deviant peers during preadolescence and adolescence. *Journal of Early Adolescence*, 6, 29-43.

Social and Cultural Planning Bureau (1980). *Jeugdwerkloosheid: Achtergronden en mogelijke ontwikkelingen*. Rijswijk: SCP.

_____ (1985). *Jongeren in de jaren tachtig*. Rijswijk: SCP.

_____ (1986). *Sociaal en cultureel rapport*. The Hague: Staatsuitgeverij.

_____ (1988). *Sociaal en cultureel rapport*. The Hague: Staatsuitgeverij.

Soppe, H. (1975). De invloed van reflexiviteit/impulsiviteit op informatieverwerking in waarnemen en denken. *Nederlands Tijdschrift voor de Psychologie*, 30, 385-411.

Spivack, G., & Cianci, N. (1987). High-risk early behavior pattern and later delin quency. In J. D. Burchard and S. N. Burchard (Eds.), *Prevention of delinquent behavior*. Beverly Hills: Sage.

Sroufe, A. (1984). Attachment classification from the perspective of infant care-giver relationships and infant temperament. *Child Development*, 55, 576-585.

Stagner, R. (1974). *Psychology of personality*. New York: McGraw-Hill.

Stanfield, S. (1966). The interaction of family variables and gang variables in the aetiology of delinquency. *Social Problems*, 13, 411-417.

Stanton, M. (1974). The concept of conflict at adolescence. *Adolescence*, 9, 537-540.

Stark, R. (1979). Whose status counts? *American Sociological Review*, 44, 668-669.

_____ (1987). Deviant places: A theory of the ecology of crime. *Criminology*, 25, 893-910.

_____, Kent, L., & Doyle, D. P. (1982). Religion and delinquency: The ecology of a lost relationship. *Journal of Research in Crime and Delinquency*, 19, 4-24.

Starr, J. M. (1981). Adolescents and resistance to schooling: A dialectic. *Youth and Society*, 13, 189-227.

Steenstra, S. J., & Bogaards, C. (1978). *Achtergronden van zware geweldsmisdrijven. In Geweld in onze samenleving*. The Hague: Staatsuitgeverij.

Steffensmeier, D. (1980). Sex differences in patterns of adult crimes 1965-77: A review and assessment. *Social Forces*, 58, 1080-1108.

Stein, K. B., Sarbin, T. R., & Kulik, J. A. (1968). Future time perspective: Its relation to the socialization process and the delinquent role. *Journal of Consulting and Clinical Psychology*, 32, 257-264.

Steinberg, L. D., Catalano, L., & Dooley, D. (1981). Economic antecedents of child abuse and neglect. *Child Development*, 52, 975-985.

Sterne, R. S. (1964). *Delinquent conduct and broken homes*. New Haven: College and University Press.

Stevenson, H. W., Hale, G. A., Kennedy, T. H., & Moely, B. E. (1967). Determinants of children's preference for adults. *Child Development*, 38, 1-14.

Steward, R. A. (1977). Factor analysis and rotation of responses to the Junior Eysenck Personality Inventory. *Psychological Reports*, 40, 559-601.

Stinchcombe, A. I. (1964). *Rebellion in a high school*. Chicago: Quadrangle Books.

Stoddard, S. (1717). *Three sermons preached lately at Boston*. Boston.

Stott, D. H. (1950). *Delinquency and human nature*. London: Carnegie United Kingdom Trust.

Strelau, J. (1982). Biologically determined dimensions of personality or temperament. *Personality and Individual Differences*, 3, 355-360.

Strodtbeck, F., & Short, J. (1964). Aleatory risks versus short-run hedonism in explanation of gang action. *Social Problems*, 12, 127-140.

Sugerman, B. S. (1967). Involvement in youth culture, academic achievement and conformity in school. *British Journal of Sociology*, 18, 151-164.

Sutherland, E. H., & Cressey, D. R. (1978). *Principles of Criminology*. New York: Lippincott.

Sutton-Smith, B., & Rosenberg, B. G. (1970). *The siblings*. New York: Holt, Rinehart and Winston.

Sviridoff, M., & Thompson, J. (1983). Links between employment and crime. *Crime and Delinquency*, 29, 195-212.

Sykes, G. M., & Matza, D. (1957). Techniques of neutralization: A theory of delinquency. *American Sociological Review*, 22, 664-670.

_____, & Matza, D. (1961). Juvenile delinquency and subterranean values. *American Sociological Review*, 26, 98-106, 712-719.

Syrotuik, J. M. (1978). The relationship between birth order and parole outcome. *Canadian Journal of Criminology*, 20, 456-458.

Taft, D. R. (1950). *Criminology, a cultural interpretation*. New York: MacMillan.

_____, & England, R. W. (1964). *Criminology*, New York: MacMillan.

Tangri, S. S., & Schwarz, M. (1967). Delinquency research and the self-concept variable. *Journal of Criminal law, Criminology and Police Science*, 58, 182-190.

Tanner, J. M. (1962). *Growth at adolescence*. London: Blackwell.

Tennent, T. G. (1970). Truancy and stealing. *British Journal of Psychiatry*, 116, 587-592.

Thomas, A., & Chess, S. (1977). *Temperament and development*. New York: Brunner-Marzel.

Thomas, A., Chess, S., & Birch, H. G. (1968). *Temperament and behavior disorders in children*. New York: New York Univ. Press.

Thompson, W. E., & Dodder, R. A. (1983). Juvenile delinquency explained? A test of containment theory. *Youth and Society*, 15, 171-194.

Thornberry, T. P., & Christenson, R. L. (1984). Unemployment and criminal involvement: An investigation of reciprocal causal structures. *American Sociological Review*, 49, 398-411.

_____, & Farnworth, M. (1982). Social correlates of criminal involvement: Further evidence on the relationship between social status and criminal behavior. *American Sociological Review*, 47, 505-518.

_____, Moore, M., & Christenson, R. L. (1985). The effect of dropping out of high school on subsequent criminal behavior. *Criminology*, 23, 3-18.

Thrasher, F. M. (1927, 1963). *The gang: A study of 1.313 gangs in Chicago*. Chicago: Umiv. of Chicago Press.

Timmermans, J. M. (1987). *Samenhang in de zorg voor jeugdigen*. Rijswijk: Sociaal en Cultureel Planbureau.

Tismer, K. G. (1987). Psychological aspects of temporal dominance during adolescence. *Psychological Reports*, 16, 647-654.

Tittle, C. R. (1983). Social class and criminal behavior: A critique of the theoretical foundation. *Social Forces*, 62, 334-358.

_____, & Rowe, A. R. (1973). Moral appeal, sanction threat and deviance: An experimental test. *Social Problems*, 20, 487-498.

_____, & Welch, M. R. (1983). Religiosity and deviance: Toward a contingency theory of constraining effect. *Social Forces*, 61, 653-682.

_____, Villemez, W. J., & Smith, D. A (1978). The myth of social class and criminality: An empirical assessment of the empirical evidence. *American Sociological Review*, 43, 643-656.

Tobias, J. (1967). *Crime and industrial society in the nineteenth century*. New York: Schocken Books.

_____ (1970). The affluent suburban male delinquent. *Crime and Delinquency*, 16, 273-279.

Toby, J. (1957). The differential impact of family disorganization. *American Sociological Review*, 22, 505-512.

_____ (1960). Review of family relationships and delinquent behavior. *American Sociological Review*, 25, 282-283.

_____ (1982). Affluence and adolescent crime. In R. Giallilombardo (Ed.), *Juvenile delinquency: A book of readings*. New York: John Wiley and Sons.

_____ (1983). Violence in school. In M. Tonry and N. Morris (Eds.), *Crime and justice: An annual review of research, Vol. 4*. Chicago: Umiv. of Chicago Press.

Todor, N., & Marcia, J. (1973). Ego identity status and response to conformity pressure in college woman. *Journal of Personality and Social Psychology*, 26, 287-294.

Tomlinson-Keasy, C., & Keasy, C. B. (1974). The mediating role of cognitive development in moral judgment. *Child Development*, 45, 291-298.

Topping, R. (1941). Case studies of aggressive delinquents. *American Journal of Orthopsychiatry*, 11, 485-492.

Torsell, B. A., & Klemke, L. W. (1972). The labelling process, reinforcement and deterrent? *Law and Society Review*, 6, 393-403.

Trasler, G. B. (1979). Delinquency, recidivism and desistance. *British Journal of Criminology*, 19, 314-322.

_____ (1987). Biogenic factors. In H. C. Quay (Ed.), *Handbook of juvenile delinquency*. New York: John Wiley and Sons.

Turati, F. (1883). *Il delitto e la questione sociale*.

Tygart, C. E. (1988). Strain theory and public school vandalism: Academic tracking, school social status, and students' academic achievement. *Youth and Society*, 20, 106-118.

Vagg, P. R., & Hammond, S. B. (1976). The number and kind of invariant personality (Q) factors: A partial replication of Eysenck and Eysenck. *British Journal of Social and Clinical Psychology*, 15, 121-129.

Vandenberg, S. V. (1972). Assortative mating, or who marries who? *Behavior Genetics*, 2, 127-157.

Van der Kooij, R. (1987). Naar een expertmodel voor emotioneel en sociaal probleem gedrag. *Nederlands Tijdschrift voor Opvoeding, Vorming en Onderwijs*, 3, 288-299.

Van der Linden, F. J., & Roeders, P. J. B. (1983). *Schoolgaande jongeren, hun leefwereld en zelfbeleving*. Nijmegen: Hoogveld Instituut.

_____, & Stoop, W. (1977). *Jeugd in Roosendaal en Nispen*. Nijmegen: Hoogveld Instituut.

Van Doorn, J. A., & Lammers, C. J. (1967). *Moderne Sociologie*. Utrecht-Antwerpen: Het Spectrum.

Van Fulpen, H. (1985). *Volkshuisvesting in demografisch en economisch perspectief*. The Hague: Social and Cultural Planning Bureau.

Van Heck, G. L., Hettema, J., & Liedelmijer, K. C. (1990). Temperament, situatievoorkeuren en situatie-transformaties. *Nederlands Tijdschrift voor de Psychologie*, 45, 1-16.

Van Hessen, J. S. (1964). *Samen jong zijn*. Assen: Van Gorcum.

Van Hezewijk, R. W. J. V., & Bruinsma, G. J. N. (1979). Vrouwenkriminaliteit: De achilleshiel van de criminologie. *Tijdschrift voor Criminologie*, 21, 221-231.

Van Kampen, D. (1974). De Eysenck Personality Inventory. *Nederlands Tijdschrift voor de Psychologie*, 29, 125-135.

Van Kerckvoorde, J., Vettenburg, N., & Walgrave, L. (1984). Over de justitiële en maatschappelijke kwetsbaarheid van jonge werklozen. *Panopticon*, 5, 296-310.

Van Tulder, F. P. (1985). *Criminaliteit, pakkans en politie. Schattingen met een macromodel*. Rijswijk: Social and Cultural Planning Bureau.

Van Voorhis, P., Cullen, F. T., Mathers, R. A., & Garner, C. C. (1988). The impact of family structure and quality on delinquency: A comparative assessment of structural and functional factors. *Criminology*, 26, 235-261.

Vedder, C., & Somerville, D. (1970). *The delinquent girl.* Springfield: Charles D. Thomas.

Velarde, A. J. (1978). Do delinquents really drift? *British Journal of Criminology*, 18, 23-39.

Velema, W. (1983). Het huis uit. *Psychologie*, 2, 20-30.

Venezia, P. S. (1971). Delinquency prediction: A critique and suggestion. *Journal of Research in Crime and Delinquency*, 8, 108-117.

Von Mayr, G. (1877). *Die Gesetzmässigkeit im Gesellschaftsleben.*

Voorhees, J. (1981). Neuropsychological differences between juvenile delinquents and functional adolescents: A preliminary study. *Adolescence*, 16, 57-66.

Voss, H. L. (1964). Differential association and reported delinquent behavior: A replication. *Social Problems*, 12, 78-85.

Waas, G. A. (1988). Social attributional biases of peer-rejected and aggressive children. *Child Development*, 59, 969-975.

Wachs, E. (1988). *Crime-victim stories: New York City's urban folklore.* Indiana: Indiana Univ. Press.

Wadworth, M. (1979). *Roots of delinquency: Infancy, adolescence and crime.* Oxford: Martin Robertson.

Wagner, H. (1971). The increasing importance of the peer group during adolescence. *Adolescence*, 6, 53-58.

Wallach, M., Kogan, N., & Bem, D. (1962). Group influence on individual risk taking. *Journal of Abnormal and Social Psychology*, 65, 75-86.

_____, Kogan, N., & Bem, D. (1964). Diffusion of responsibility and level of risk taking in groups. *Journal of Abnormal and Social Psychology*, 68, 263-274.

Wallbank, J. (1985). Antisocial and prosocial behavior among contemporary Robin Hoods. *Personality and Individual Differences*, 6, 11-19.

Wallimann, I., & Zito, G. V. (1984). Cohort size and youthful protest. *Youth and Society*, 16, 67-81.

Walsh, A., & Berger, A. J. (1989). Violent crimes, sociopathy and love deprivation among adolescent delinquents. *Adolescence*, 22, 705-717.

Walsh, L. M., & Kurdek, L. A. (1984). Developmental trends and gender differences in the relation between understanding of friendship and sociability. *Journal of Youth and Adolescence*, 13, 65-71.

Walters, G. D., & White, T. W. (1989). Heredity and crime: Bad genes or bad research? *Criminology*, 27, 455-485.

Warner, C. A. (1982). A study of the self-reported crime of a group of male and female high school students. *Australian and New Zealand Journal of Criminology*, 15, 255-272.

Wasson, A. S. (1980). Stimulus seeking, perceived school environment and school misbehavior. *Adolescence*, 15, 603-608.

_____ (1981). Susceptibility to boredom and deviant behavior at school. *Psychological Reports*, 48, 901-902.

Wattenberg, W. W., & Balistrieri, J. J. (1950). Gang membership and juvenile misconduct. *American Sociological Review*, 15, 744-752.

_____, & Saunders, F. (1954). Sex differences among juvenile offenders. *Sociology and Social Research*, 39, 24-31.

Weiner, N., & Willie, C. V. (1971). Decisions by juvenile officers. *American Journal of Sociology*, 77, 199-210.

Weis, J. G. (1976). Liberation and crime: The invention of the new female criminal. *Crime and Social Justice*, 6, 17-27.

Weiss, W. W. (1980). Erziehung zur Selbständigkeit. *Zeitschrift für Pädagogik*, 1.

Wellford, C. F. (1975). Labelling theory and criminology: An assessment. *Social Problems*, 22, 332-345.

Wells, L. E., & Rankin, J. H. (1983). Self-concept as a mediating factor in delinquency. *Social Psychology Quarterly*, 46, 11-22.

_____, & Rankin, J. H. (1986). The broken homes model of delinquency: Analytic issues. *Journal of Research in Crime and Delinquency*, 23, 68-93.

Wells, R. S. (1976). Severe parental punishment and delinquency: A developmental theory. *Journal of Clinical Child Psychology*, 5, 17-21.

_____ (1978a). Teacher survival in the classroom. *Journal of Research and Development in Education*, 11, 64-73.

_____ (1978b). Delinquency, corporal punishment and the school. *Crime and Delinquency*, 24, 336-354.

Werner, E. E. (1987). Vulnerability and resiliency in children at risk for delinquency: A longitudinal study from birth to young adulthood. In J. D. Burchard and S. N. Burchard, *Prevention of delinquent behavior*. Beverly Hills: Sage.

Wesselingh, A. (1979). *School en ongelijkheid*. Nijmegen: Link.

West, D. J. (1969). *Present conduct and future delinquency*. London: Heinemann.

_____ (1982). *Delinquency: Its roots, careers and prospects*. London: Heinemann.

_____, & Farrington, D. P. (1973). *Who becomes delinquent?* London: Heinemann.

_____, & Farrington, D. P. (1977). *The delinquent way of life*. London: Heinemann.

Whitehill, M., De Myer-Gapin, S., & Scott, T. J. (1976). Stimulus seeking in antisocial preadolescent children. *Journal of Abnormal Psychology*, 85, 101-104.

Wiatrowski, M. D., & Anderson, K. L. (1987). The dimensionality of the social bond. *Journal of Quantitative Criminology*, 3, 65-81.

_____, Griswold, D. B., & Roberts, M. K. (1981). Social control theory and delinquency. *American Sociological Review*, 46, 525-541.

_____, Hansell, S., Massey, C. R., & Wilson, D. L. (1982). Curriculum tracking and delinquency. *American Sociological Review*, 47, 151-160.

Wicker, A. A. (1969). Attitudes versus actions: The reliability of verbal and overt behavioral responses to attitude object. *Journal of Social Issues*, 25, 41-78.

Wiegman, O., Baarda, B., & Seydel, E. R. (1982). *Agressie en criminaliteit*. Deventer: Van Loghum Slaterus.

Wilcock, K. D. (1964). Neurotic differences between individualized and socialized criminals. *Journal of Consulting Psychology*, 28, 141-145.

Wilde, G. J. S. (1962). *Neurotische labiliteit gemeten volgens de vragenlijst-methode*. Amsterdam: Van Rossum.

Wilkinson, K. (1980). The broken home and delinquent behavior: An alternative interpretation of contradictory findings. In T. Hirschi and M. Gottredson (Eds.), *Understanding crime: Current theory and research*. Beverly Hills: Sage.

_____, Stitt, B. G., & Erickson, M. L. (1982). Siblings and delinquent behavior: An exploratory study of a neglected family variable. *Criminology*, 20, 223-239.

Willems, E. (1967). Sense of obligations to highschool activities as related to school size and marginality of student. *Child Development*, 38, 1247-1268.

Williams, J. R., & Gold, M. (1972). From delinquent behavior to official delinquency. *Social Problems*, 20, 209-229.

Williamson, H. (1978). Choosing to be a delinquent. *New Society*, 46, 333-335.

Willis, P. (1977). *Learning to labour*. Westmead: Saxonhouse.

Wilson, E. O. (1978). *On human nature*. Cambridge, MA: Harvard Univ. Press.

Wilson, H. (1974). Parenting in poverty. *British Journal of Social Work*, 4, 241-254.

_____ (1975). Juvenile delinquency, parental criminality and social handicap. *British Journal of Criminology*, 15, 241-250.

_____ (1980a). Parental supervision: A neglected aspect of delinquency. *British Journal of Criminology*, 20, 203-235.

_____ (1980b). Parents can cut the crime rate. *New Society*, 54, 456-458.

_____ (1982). Parental responsibility and delinquency: Reflections on a white paper proposal. *The Howard Journal*, 21, 23-34.

_____ (1987). Parental supervision re-examined. *British Journal of Criminology*, 27, 275-301.

_____, & Herbert, G. W. (1978). *Parents and children in the inner city*. London: Routledge and Kegan Paul.

Wilson, J. Q. (1968). *Violence in the streets*. Chicago.

_____, & Herrnstein, R. J. (1985). *Crime and human nature*. New York: Simon and Schuster.

Winch, R. F. (1958). *Mate selection: A study of complementary needs*. New York: Harper.

Winder, C. L., & Rau, L. (1962). Parental attitudes associated with social deviance in preadolescent boys. *Journal of Abnormal and Social Psychology*, 64, 418-424.

Wise, J. (1983). Vandalisme, hoe met zachte hand te bestrijden? *Psychologie*, 2, 34-38.

Wolff, P. H., Waber, D., Bauermeister, M., Cohen, C., & Ferber, R. (1982). The neurophysiological status of adolescent delinquent boys. *Journal of Child Psychology and Psychiatry*, 23, 267-279.

Wolfgang, M. E. (1970). *Youth and violence*. Washington DC.

_____ (1983). Delinquency in two birth cohorts. *American Behavioral Scientist*, 27, 75-86.

_____, Figlio, R. M., & Sellin, T. R. (1972). *Delinquency in a birth cohort*. Chicago: Umiv. of Chicago Press.

Woodward, M. (1955). The role of low intelligence in delinquency. *British Journal of Delinquency*, 5, 281-303.

Wootton, B. (1959). *Social science and social pathology*. London: Allen and Unwin.

Wright, D. (1971). A sociological portrait: Sex differences. *New Society*, 18, 825-828.

_____ (1974). *Psychologie van het morele gedrag*. Utrecht-Antwerpen: Het Spectrum.

Yablonski, L. (1962). *The violent gang*. New York: MacMillan.

Yeudall, L. T., Fromm-Auch, D., & Davies, P. (1982). Neuropsychological impairment of persistent delinquency. *Journal of Nervous and Mental Disease*, 170, 257-265.

Yinger, J. M. (1960). Contraculture and subculture. *American Sociological Review*, 25, 625-635.

_____ (1965). *Toward a field theory of behavior: Personality and social structure*. New York: McGraw-Hill.

Zeldith, M. (1956). Role differentiation in the nuclear family: A comparative study. In T. Parsons and R. F. Bales (Eds.), *Family socialization and interaction process*. London: Routledge and Kegan Paul.

Zeleny, L. D. (1933). Feeble-mindedness and criminal conduct. *American Journal of Sociology*, 38, 564-578.

Zieman, G. L., & Benson, G. P. (1983). Delinquency: The role of self-esteem and social values. *Journal of Youth and Adolescence*, 12, 489-500.

Zimmerman, J., Rich,, W. D., Kellitz, I., & Broder, P. K. (1981). Some observations on the link between learning disabilities and juvenile delinquency. *Journal of Criminal Justice*, 9, 1-17.

Zimring, F. E. (1981). Kids, groups and crime: Some implications of a well-known secret. *Journal of Criminal Law and Criminology*, 72, 867-885.

Zinnecker, J. (1982). Porträt einer Generation. *In Jugend '81, Leverkussen*, 80-122.

Zuckerman, M. (1974). The sensation seeking motive. In B. A. Mahler (Ed.), *Progress in experimental personality research*, Vol 7. New York: Academic Press.

_____ (1979). *Dimensions of sensation seeking. Beyond the optimal level of arousal.* New York.

_____, & Link, K. (1968). Construct validity for the sensation-seeking scale. *Journal of Consulting and Clinical Psychology*, 32, 420-426.

_____, Buchsbaum, M. S., & Murphy, D. L. (1980). Sensation seeking and its biological correlates. *Psychological Bulletin*, 88, 187-214.

_____, Eysenck, S. B. G., & Eysenck, H. J. (1978). Sensation seeking in England and America: Cross cultural, age and sex comparisons. *Journal of Consulting and Clinical Psychology*, 46, 139-149.

_____, Kuhlman, D., & Camac, C. (1988). What lies beyond E en N? Factor analysis of scales believed to measure basic dimensions of personality. *Journal of Personality and Social Psychology*, 54, 96-107.

_____, Bone, R. N., Neary, R., Mangelsdorff, D., & Brustman, B. (1972). What is the sensation seeker? Personality trait and experience correlates of the Sensation-Seeking-Scales. *Journal of Consulting and Clinical Psychology*, 39, 308-321.

Zussman, J. U. (1980). Situational determinants of parental behavior: Effects of competing cognitive activity. *Child Development*, 51, 792-800.

INDEX